Computers and the Teaching of Writing in American Higher Education 1979–1994:
A History

Qualitative
Dissertation ideas:
P 174 — Social interaction among
(fiction) writers in building
courage to go to the dark
places where the talent leads.
— Jong

In preparation for
**New Directions in Computers
and Composition Studies,**
Gail E. Hawisher and Cynthia L. Selfe, Editors

Computers and the Teaching of Writing in American Higher Education, 1979–1994: A History

Gail E. Hawisher
Paul LeBlanc
Charles Moran
Cynthia L. Selfe
Authors

Sibylle Gruber
Margaret Faler Sweany
Associate Editors

 Ablex Publishing Corporation
Norwood, New Jersey

Printed in the United States of America

Library of Congress Cataloging-in-Publication Data

Computers and the teaching of writing in American higher education,
    1979–1994: a history/Gail E. Hawisher...[et al.], authors;
  Sibylle Gruber, Margaret Faler Sweany, associate editors.
      p.   cm.—(New directions in computers and composition
  studies)
      Includes bibliographical references (p.   ) and indexes.
      ISBN 1-56750-251-2.—ISBN 1-56750-252-0 (pbk.)
      1. English language—Rhetoric—study and teaching (Higher)—United
  States—History—20th century. 2. English language—Rhetoric—Study
  and teaching (Higher)—Data processing—History. 3. Computer-
  assisted instruction—United States—History—20th century.
  I. Hawisher, Gail E. II. Gruber, Sibylle. III. Sweany, Margaret Faler
  IV. Series.
  PE1405.U6C66 1996
  808', 042'0285—dc20   96–3769
                                                          CIP

Ablex Publishing Corporation
355 Chestnut Street
Norwood, New Jersey 07648

We dedicate this book to each other, in mutual friendship and admiration. Because the whole has become so much greater than the sum of our individual contributions, we ask that all future citations to this book acknowledge all four authors—Gail E. Hawisher, Paul LeBlanc, Charles Moran, and Cynthia L. Selfe.

We also dedicate this book, with affection and gratitude, to the computers and writing community and to our many helpful colleagues at Ablex. This rich and diverse collection of individuals and groups has supported all four authors of this volume in many generous ways and, for this, we thank them.

Contents

PREFACE

Lisa Gerrard
University of California at Los Angeles

At the CCCC in Boston, 1991, 10 computers and writing special-ists began a workshop on "A Decade of Change: New Directions in Computer and Composition Studies" by explaining, one by one, how we had come to computers and writing. This biographical moment turned out to be far more interesting than the standard self-intro-duction; each story was different, many were surprising, and each formed a piece of the history of our discipline. It was the first time I seriously thought about computers and composition as having a history.[1]

My story—the 3-minute version I told at the CCCC workshop—was how I sought computers and discovered computers and writing—not as an entrance to academia (though I was just starting my career), but as an exit from it. In the 1970s, prospects for academic em-ployment in the humanities were bleak, and I decided that when I finished my dissertation—a "feminist study of romantic women in nineteenth-century English, French, and Spanish fiction"—I would become a computer programmer. In 1980, a year past my PhD, I still saw myself both in and outside academia. I taught composition at UCLA while learning to program in COBOL and UCSD Pascal, con-tinued to research the female *bildungsroman*, jotting my references on blue note cards, and began investigating computers and writing, noting those references on yellow cards.

---

[1]The workshop was cosponsored by the CCCC Committee on Computers and Com-position and chaired by Gail Hawisher. The workshop leaders were Janet M. Eldred, Ron Fortune, Lisa Gerrard, Gail Hawisher, Andrea W. Herrmann, Paul LeBlanc, Cyn-thia L. Selfe, Chris Neuwirth, Fred Kemp, and Patricia Sullivan.

Fourteen years later, as I read the manuscript for the present text and looked over my old yellow note cards, it occurs to me that there are probably many histories of computers and composition, and not just personal ones. The cards and the text tell two overlapping, compatible, but still rather different stories. The central events narrated in the text begin in the 1970s, are influenced by the development of process-based writing, and focus chiefly on college composition. In contrast, the yellow cards suggest that computers and composition began not in the late 1970s, but in the 1960s—and not with writing as process, but with efforts to automate the teaching of mechanics and the evaluation of student compositions. Some of the earliest publications on computer-based writing are John Engstrom and James Whittaker's (1963) "Improving Students' Spelling through Automated Teaching"; Diagon's (1966) "Computer Grading and English Composition"; Jack Hiller's (1968) "Opinionation Vagueness, and Specificity Distinctiveness: Essay Traits Measured by Computer"; and Ellis Page and Paulus' (1968) "The Analysis of Essays by Computer." Much of this work was done by psychologists and linguists as well as English teachers, and much of it addressed K–12 rather than college-age writers. Throughout the 1960s and early 1970s, it was mostly the K–12—not the college level—publications that generated excitement about computers and writing: *English Journal, Educational Technology, English Education,* and *Elementary English.*

Before Burns' (1979) dissertation "Stimulating Invention in English Composition through Computer-Assisted Instruction," describing the invention programs he devised for student writers, there was A. N. Yerkey's (1976) dissertation, "The Retrieval of Rhetorical Topoi: A Computer-Assisted System for the Invention of Lines of Arguments and Associated Data." Before Ellen Nold's (1975) article on ways to use computers in a writing course, "Fear and Trembling: The Humanist Approaches the Computer," there was Howard G. Poteet's "The Computer and the Teacher of English." Yet it was Nold's and Burns' work that seemed closest to our enterprise, and so it is they to whom we look as the forerunners of computers and writing as we

---

[2]Burns' software INVENT consisted of three programs—TOPOI, BURKE, and TAGI— which helped students analyze their paper topics by prompting them with questions. His dissertation described the results of using this program in four experimental composition classes. Nold's article was unique in that it addressed pedagogical applications beyond drill and practice; it was aimed at college instructors and was published in a mainstream academic journal (*College Composition and Communication*) that did not typically offer articles on technology.

practice it. Their teaching circumstances, their philosophy, and their goals were closely compatible with ours.[2]

Computers and the Teaching of Writing in American Postsecondary Education, 1979–1994, however, is less concerned with recounting every historical moment in computers and writing—it would take an encyclopedia to do that—than with tracing the development of a particular community; namely, a group of composition instructors, primarily at the college level, unusually likeminded in their outlook, teaching philosophy, and intellectual goals—instructors whose pedagogy has evolved along with composition research as it has focused on writing processes, socially produced learning, the egalitarian classroom, and multiculturalism. They meet at CCCC, NCTE, and the Computers and Writing conference and on listservs such as MBU (Megabyte University), WPA (Writing Program Administrators), and WAC (Writing Across the Curriculum). For the most part they think of themselves as a community.

The history of computers and writing as presented here also recounts a particular trajectory of software development—from the earliest grammar tutorials to prewriting programs, style analyzers, integrated packages, hypertext, multimedia, and networks—focusing on the software that has most interested the computers and writing community. Although we have occasionally concerned ourselves with other technologies (e.g., using Kurzweil scanners to teach editing), the computers and writing practitioners described in this book have generally found little use for the many other kinds of software that also fall under the rubric "computers and writing," probably because their pedagogical applications have been less immediate to us: foreign language translation software; concordance programs; software for the specialized needs of poetry, newswriting, fiction writing, or script writing; textual collation software; or the advanced features (such as font smoothing) of desktop publishing and text-processing programs. These programs, the uses people have made of them, and the groups of users, technicians, and publishers who have grown up around them have their own stories to tell—ones probably quite different from ours.

When the 10 of us introduced ourselves at the Boston CCCC, we constructed a past. The Boston workshop was the first time our profession, however partially, had publicly acknowledged that it had a history. Three years later, the organizers of the 1994 Computers and Writing Conference celebrated the 10th anniversary of the conference by devoting three sessions to the history of computers and composition. This was an unusual move for a conference that has always looked forward rather than back, proud of its ability to connect new rhetorical or linguistic theories with cutting edge technology, and proud of its innovative teaching strategies. Such attention to the past suggests that computers and composition is becoming self-conscious as a profession, and that our enterprise is no longer simply a series of experiments within composition, but a coherent subdiscipline with its own identity.

The present book is the first full-scale effort to define computers and composition within its history. It charts the development of its classroom practices, research, journals, and conferences and poses them against the simultaneous histories that influenced this development: the evolution of the computer industry from the 1960s to the present, the growth of composition studies as a discipline, and the personal experiences of the earliest practitioners. It describes 15 years of developing a set of tools, a body of research, a library of journals and books devoted to our enterprise, a yearly national conference, and a recognizable and growing community of specialists. By recording this evolution, *Computers and the Teaching of Writing in American Postsecondary Education, 1979–1994* marks the maturity of computers and composition as a discipline.

INTRODUCTION: WRITING A HISTORY OF COMPUTERS AND COMPOSITION STUDIES

Miranda: *O brave new world. . . .*
Prospero: *Tis new to thee.*
　　　　—Shakespeare, *The Tempest*, Act V,
　　　　　　　　　　　　　　　scene i

This is a history composed of histories. It has a particular focus: the way in which computers entered and changed the field of composition studies, a field that defines itself both as a research community and as a community of teachers. In writing this sentence, however, we recognize its somewhat sinister suggestion that technology alone has agency. Thus we place beside this sentence a second: This history (made of histories) is not principally about computers but about people—teachers and scholars who have adapted the computer to their personal and professional purposes. From the perspective of the authors, each of these two sentences is equally true: Changes in technology drive changes in the ways we live and work, and we, agents to a degree in control of our own lives, use technology to achieve our human purposes. Ithiel De Sola Pool would call us "soft technological determinists" (1990, p. vii). We see tech-

A revolution in communications technology is taking place today, a revolution as profound as the invention of printing. Communication is becoming electronic. For untold millennia, man [sic], unlike any other animal on earth, could talk. Then, for about 4,000 years, [humankind] also devised ways to embody speech in a written form that could be kept over time and transported over space. Then, with Gutenberg, the third era began, and for the past five hundred years written texts could be disseminated in multiple copies. . . . We are now entering a fourth era ushered in by a revolution of comparable historical significance to that of print and the mass media. We have discovered how to use pulses of electromagnetic energy to embody and convey messages that up to now have been sent by voice, picture, and text. Just as writing made possible the preservation of an intellectual heritage over time and its diffusion over space, and as printing made possible its popularization, this new development is having profound effects of civilization. (Pool, 1990, pp. 7–8)

Teachers and researchers working within the field of computers and composition are also asking ... questions about how computers affect the social interactions among writers, the social and political structures of our writing classrooms, or the ways in which academic discourse communities change and endure. (Hawisher & Selfe, 1990, p. 6)

nology as agent, redefining writing, text, and therefore our work as writing teachers; and we see ourselves and our colleagues as agents too, using the emerging technology to further our own goals as teachers, scholars, and professionals in the field of English.

If it could be easily done, we would want to begin with a third sentence. This book is the story of how computers entered a field, and it is the story of how people in the field used computers. It is also, however, and perhaps at its deepest level, the story of the growth of a community. This community is loosely called "computers and composition," a community that sees itself as different from composition studies—which, of course, in its turn sees itself as different from English. As a number of sources have told us, this community has been close, warm and supportive, welcoming newcomers to its conferences and journals. Composed of people who have defined themselves by their connection to an emerging technology, the community has had the early energy characteristic of a group just formed around a set of issues.

The community has had an agenda: the need to develop a view of how computers could help writing teachers move toward better, more just, and more equitable writing classrooms and, by extension, to a better, more just, and more equitable system of education—and, insofar as education incubates culture—toward a better society. The community has understood from its beginnings that it needed to develop such a view because manufacturers, publishers, and educational administrators were developing their views, driven by motives that were often different from ours. If the community of teachers and scholars did not develop its own understanding of how computers should be integrated into the enterprise of teaching writing, it was certain that others would do so. At issue was, and still is, the character of literacy education and of American society.

WHO WE ARE

The authors of this book have been part of this community of teacher-scholars involved in computers and composition studies. As this community has evolved, so have we—from the writing process pedagogies of the early 1980s through the social and critical pedagogies of the 1990s. At the outset, we should remind readers that we are individuals with particular histories, values, and angles of vision. We speak from different perspectives of age, career path, and gender. Three of us teach at 4-year research universities; one of us teaches at a 4-year college and is now on leave, developing multimedia applications for a publishing firm. However, although there are four of us, an unusually broad authorship for a book that is not an anthology, the histories we tell are inevitably partial and selective. We are part of the community described earlier, but only a part. As historians, we have worked against the limits of our situation, incorporating others' voices and perspectives in interviews at the end of each chapter, in sidebar text, and in the MOO that concludes the book. We are still, however, only four, and the voices added to our history are not all possible voices, but our own selection of the available materials.

Of the four of us, none came to computers as programmers or as interface designers; we all came to computers as teachers, interested primarily in using computers to help writers. As a group, we share a primary concern for teaching—for pedagogy. Our concern for teaching is focused on the act of composing, the making of meaning, the production of dis-

Gail E. Hawisher, BA, English, MEd, English education (Augusta College), PhD, composition studies (University of Illinois, Urbana-Champaign), 2 children; interests: Center for Writing Studies, B.K.S. Iyengar Yoga, rhetoric & composition, running, gender studies, golf, CMC, German, computers & composition, traveling.

Paul J. LeBlanc, BA, English (Framingham State College), MA, English (Boston College), PhD, English (University of Massachusetts, Amherst), 2 daughters; interests: children and spouse, travel, sports, technology and education.

Charles Moran, BA, English, (Princeton University), PhD. English, (Brown University), 2 children; interests: Western Massachusetts Writing Project, running/biking/swimming, teaching with computers, singing with madrigal group, composition theory, sailing.

Cynthia L. Selfe, BS, Education (University of Wisconsin Madison); MEd and PhD, Curriculum & Instruction (The University of Texas, Austin); interests: cross-country skiing, composition studies, building rustic furniture, critical theory, reading trashy fiction, cultural studies, going to the movies, feminist theory, picking berries, computers and composition, living in Houghton, America.

The need to act and decide characterizes the participant role—to act and decide in response to the social demands of human co-existence. At the moment we have characterized the spectator role simply as a freedom from those demands, but we shall go on . . . to look at the way this freedom is used, what other characteristics develop. I have laboured the distinction between language in the role of participant and in the role of spectator because I believe it will prove important for a proper understanding of the manifold ways in which language works. (Britton, 1970, p. 105)

And, in the end, what we have to do for them is trust them. To begin to do which is to discover that some of the obvious things they say could have power if enough of a generation said them, and believed them, and refused to see their impracticability . . . and finally to admit that, among the injustices and extravagances of the young people's revolution, demands are being made that represent fragments of a world we have always wanted. (Britton, 1970, pp. 269–270)

course. Unlike many colleagues in English and in communication departments who focus their work on texts, we work with people as they compose texts. This history is also focused on the political and social environment that surrounds and in part determines our own acts of writing and students' acts of composing.

Like most teachers of composition, we have tried to obey the late James Britton's (1970) injunction that teachers should "trust" students (p. 269), which we interpret to mean that teachers should listen to what students are saying and take it, and them, seriously—students are writers, persons with valuable knowledge from whom others can learn. This pedagogical orientation also attracts us to computers because these machines can offer ways of helping students achieve their learning goals, and teachers their instructional goals. Electronic technology is not simply a medium for the mass-delivery of a managed curriculum.

As teacher-scholars, we have not written a history of technology. Included here in each chapter, however, is an overview of technological developments relevant to our subject during that time period. What this part of the history steadily shows is how late writing teachers have come to computers and their related technologies. ARPAnet was in place almost 30 years before computers and composition studies made significant use of its potential; computers were part of the fabric of the military, of business, and of the physical sciences decades before they were a significant presence in our world; journalists were composing and editing on networked computers years before teachers of writing became excited about the possibilities inherent in networked writing classrooms.

This should not be surprising to us, however, given the many factors influencing the integration of technology into English departments. Certainly the marginal status of composition studies in English departments and in the academy—itself an increasingly marginalized entity—helped ensure that writing scholars would not have early access to technology. In addition, the academic preparation of most English teachers during the 1950s, 1960s, and 1970s served to convince colleagues that libraries were needed, not number-crunching machines. Equipment budgets were therefore low and, given our history, when computers and composition specialists wanted equipment, it was not always easy to convince colleagues to expend departmental funds on equipment, training, and support staff. Further, just as computers became an important part of the enterprise of English Departments, the budgets of American institutions of postsecondary education came under tremendous pressure. As a result, few colleges and universities were able to give their teachers and students full access to the emerging technology.

The field did, in fact, seize the moment. When computers became useful to writers and to teachers of writing, writing professionals were there. So within the history(ies) presented here readers will hear the stories of writing teachers excited and energized by the prospect of integrating a new technology into their work. This task has not been easy, but it has always been exciting. Patricia Sullivan and Hugh Burns tell how difficult it was to persuade their dissertation committees that their work was "English" enough; James Collins, Elizabeth Sommers, and Peter Stillman tell of the struggles they and other teachers and writers had with early word-processing software; and Lisa Gerrard tells of her near-heroic struggle to adapt a mainframe line editor to her writing classes. These stories, and the collective story that this history represents, are part of the larger history of American education in the 1980s and 1990s—a time when the nation and

The writing teacher is indispensable as collaborator and audience, as facilitator and assignment-maker. Microcomputers alone cannot teach writers why revision is important, or how to bring a first draft to full meaning. (Sommers, 1985, p. 9)

My emerging technical skill was helping me to play instead of write, and I've learned this is something to watch out for. The hacker, a person intensely interested in computers and software, can get in the way of the writer. (Collins, 1985, p. 11)

its schools faced the need to function within radically new social, economic, and technological environments.

The debate on computers in schools comprises a new form of the old debate on what schools should be about and whose interests they should serve. From this perspective, the debate on computers in schools involves more than the technical issue of the computer's capacity; within this discourse is nested a struggle over the ideology and practice of the politics of literacy. (Olson, 1987, p. 182)

WHAT IS AT STAKE

The field of computers and composition is human and therefore political. This means that there is a great deal at stake. Will computers deliver managed curricula to teachers and students? Will computers replace teachers and drive us from face-to-face contact with students? Or will computers be ubiquitous in schools and classrooms, silently helping teachers and students achieve their purposes? If so, what will, and should, these purposes be? Many computers and composition specialists are beginning to recognize just how dramatically the values of democratic education will be played out during the next decade—especially within these new and still malleable electronic contexts. Because this is so, it is important at this time to pause and take the time to write a history (or, rather, a collection of histories) of where the field has been. The place of new technologies in English/writing classrooms is an important intellectual space for teachers, educators, and students to map.

Indeed, the electronic territory opened to teachers by this ideologically charged technology is one of the most important educational landscapes available for teachers of writing to explore. Within this territory teachers will face, for the next decade, the challenges associated with global literacy; the problems associated with the nature of education as a set of processes and the role of language within such processes; and the continuing unsolved challenge of students marginalized or silenced within schools due to race, gender, sexual preference, handicap, or age.

COMPUTERS, CHANGE, AND EDUCATIONAL REFORM

When teachers of composition talk about computers, they often talk about change—changing classrooms, changing curricula, changing educational systems—all for the better. Indeed the discourse surrounding computer use in composition classrooms, at least over the last decade and a half, has been characterized most often by a rhetoric of technology that stresses optimism and hope (Hawisher & Selfe, 1991), a rhetoric that reflects the enthusiasm and vision of teachers who want to make things better for students.

As authors, the history we present in these pages is shaped by the view that computers can serve as harbingers, emissaries, even agents of change. As a group, we believe that computers are changing the nature of the writing classroom in fundamental ways. Students writing on computers-turned-word-processors are finding themselves writing differently—not better, but differently—with this new writing instrument. The ability to revise easily and reprint rapidly has changed the look and feel of the academic paper: The final draft is only final because the writer, or the institution, has decreed that it be so. Indeed, the idea of a draft and the pedagogy that includes "drafting" is grounded in a pen-and-ink metaphor—much as the schools' summer vacation is grounded in an agrarian past. In addition, desktop publishing has made it possible for student writers to choose typefaces and formats, foregrounding the graphic design of a printed work and forcing many writing teachers to consider the academic paper as a graphic, as well as a word-filled, entity. Teachers and students with access to the Internet find themselves delighted, or overwhelmed, by the information available to them on the WorldWideWeb—an ability to connect with databases and people—

Must human beings submit to the harsh logic of machinery, or can technology be redesigned to better serve its creators? This is the question on which the future of industrial civilization depends. It is not primarily a technical question but concerns a fundamental issue in social philosophy: the neutrality of technology and the related theory of technological determinism. (Feenberg, 1991, p. v)

sources that have revolutionized the process leading to the research paper. Teachers and students with access to electronic mail find themselves able to draw on the expertise and knowledge of people in different situations, cultures, and geographical locations.

Further, computers have the potential to change institutions, the "school" and "college" alike. Student portfolios can be kept on a school's hard disk and can pass with the student from grade to grade. Students can work online together on collaborative projects—indeed this book is being created in online space that is in none of its authors' home towns: Urbana, Illinois; Amherst, Massachusetts; Springfield, Massachusetts; or Houghton, Michigan.

Although computer technology has altered reading- and writing-intensive classrooms in some dramatic ways and at many levels, however, it has not brought the deep, systemic changes in education for which many computer-using English teachers hope. Some theorists have suggested that far from bringing change, computer technology may have a complex and over-determined tendency to inhibit change. This vision of technology is associated with what Feenberg (1991) termed *instrumental* theories of technology, which assume that "technology is subservient to values established in other social spheres" (p. 5). From this perspective, computers are seen as tools that society uses in various ways to support existing cultural practices. Many reform-minded teachers, therefore, who look forward to an alliance that might help them address some of the problems that plague our educational system—the least of which is the continuing inequitable treatment of certain segments of our population because of race, class, handicap, or gender—will find that computers have arrived, but that familiar social and political problems remain unsolved.

Given this practical and disturbing observation, some computers and composition spe-

Instrumental theory offers the most widely accepted view of technology. It is based on the common sense idea that technologies are "tools" standing ready to serve the purposes of their users. Technology is deemed "neutral," without valuative content of its own. But what does the notion of neutrality of technology actually mean? (Feenberg, 1991, p. 5)

Schooling in the United States reflects inequitable practices of teaching and learning with computer technology. Curriculum and instruction remain differentiated by students' race, social class, language background, and gender. As the number of diverse learners grows, teachers and researchers are challenged to develop new

cialists have turned to related scholarly disciplines for insights. These individuals have often used critical theory, marxist theory, feminist studies, and cultural studies, for example, to explore the complex relationships among change, ideology, and technology—reading scholars such as Cheris Kramarae (1988), Henry Braverman (1974), Langdon Winner (1986), or Andrew Feenberg (1991). Through such readings, computers and composition specialists have learned how thoroughly ideology shapes many of the technological decisions that educators make; how it infuses processes of technology design, marketing, and use; and how it contributes an underlying stability to educational environments within which technology is employed. Indeed, these perspectives have helped computers and composition specialists see that technology can be an effective vehicle for ideology, a vital part of a larger social mechanism for reproducing particular ideologies, and even a perspective on our understanding of the world (Ellul, 1974; Heidegger, 1977) that blinds us to other ways of living and understanding.

pedagogies and practices to meet all learners' needs. How can schools, community centers, and other locations incorporate the best possible practices of teaching and learning for all participants regardless of their race, class, gender, or language background? How can we move beyond equality of opportunity to equity of opportunity to learn with and about computers? How can we broaden the focus of teaching and learning with technology from the individual student to encompass the family and the community? (Gomez, 1991, p. 318)

OUR HISTORY, OUR SOURCES

This history, or set of histories, is part of a larger project: the "writing" or "composing" or "construction" of the field of composition studies. In this project we follow the lead of such colleagues as James Berlin, Anne Ruggles Gere, David Russell, Winifred Bryan Horner, Robert Connors, Karyn Hollis, JoAnn Campbell, Gerald Nelms, Stephen North, and Robin Varnum. As historians writing in the mid 1990s, we recognize that the set of narratives presented here is not objective and that it cannot be the whole truth. Indeed, we recognize it as a hopeless task to even strive to make a narrative be, or seem, complete. Narrative, however, is powerful

In teaching writing we are providing students with guidance in seeing and structuring their experience, with a set of tacit rules about distinguishing truth from falsity, reality from illusion. A way of seeing, after all, is a way of not seeing, and as we instruct students in attending to particular orders of evidence—sense impression, for example, in the injunction to 'be concrete'—we are simultaneously discouraging them from seeing other orders of evidence—in the present example, the evidence of private vision or of social arrangement. (Berlin, 1987, p. 7)

As Karl Popper has argued in *The Open Society and Its Enemies*, in writing history "a point of view is inevitable; and the naive attempt to avoid it can only lead to self-deception, and to the uncritical application of an unconscious point of view" (247). Furthermore, there are lessons to be learned from Kenneth Burke's work—especially his discussion in *Language as Symbolic Action* of the ineluctability of "terministic screens"—the lessons of recent Marxist theory and of French and American poststructuralist cultural critics, the lessons from the contributions of American Neo-Pragmatists—particularly Richard Rorty—and, most important here, the lessons garnered from the poststructuralist historiography of Hayden White and Michel Foucault—all strongly arguing that it is impossible to perceive any object except through a terministic screen. It is thus incumbent upon the historian to make every effort to be aware of the nature of her point of view and its interpretive strategies, and to be candid about them with her reader. (Berlin, 1987a, p. 17)

and important, one of the ways in which humans make meaning for themselves and for others. This set of histories, or narratives, is written, therefore, with a sense of its value, trying to come as close as we can to what Gerald Nelms (1994) termed *human objectivity.* In his description of an experientialist historiography for composition studies, Nelms argued that historiographers in composition studies have dismissed the possibility of the objective account without describing an alternative. Nelms suggested an alternative, what he terms a *human objectivity,* a paradigm in which historians do everything possible to widen their own perspectives by accumulating and assimilating others'.

As historians, we have tried to widen our own perspectives, and to some extent, believe this has happened. However, we remain four situated individuals who have read ourselves into the lives and works of people whose histories are told here. Many of these peoples' voices have been brought directly into this history. Through the inclusion in our narrative of interviews and sidebar documents, we tried to make the history as multivocal as possible. James Berlin's (1987b) goal has served us well:

> Our only hope in not being able to know everything, in not knowing how to account for every concrete event and for all events completely, is to know as many versions of the whole as we can, as many conceptual systems in their concrete application as possible, thereby striving "by way of concept, to transcend concept." (p. 59)

A NOTE ON OUR SOURCES

In preparing to write this history, we tried to cast a wide net and thereby include as broad a range of sources as possible. We read through much of the printed literature of composition studies and computers and composition studies, looking for trends and developments. We have read through the programs of academic conferences in these fields, tracking the emergence and eventual assimilation of "computers" as a topic for conference presentations. We have assembled the history of *Computers and Composition*, the journal that is closest to the history's focus, and have written the history of "Computers and Writing," the academic conference that has served the community best. We have recorded, transcribed, and edited substantial interviews with a range of people in the field, including pioneers, experienced computer-using teachers, and teacher-scholars who are in or just emerging from PhD programs and are now beginning to shape the field. At national conferences we have told people about our project and urged them to contribute their stories to this history—they have responded so generously that we have not been able to do justice to the materials they have given us. Trent Batson, Ron Fortune, Lisa Gerrard, and Dawn Rodrigues have served as historical consultants for the text, and we are grateful for their suggestions, many of which are incorporated into the history.

And yet, of course, a great deal has been left out. Not fully told are the stories of part-time faculty, or of graduate students, who have been required to teach in computer-equipped classrooms. Not solicited are the stories of program administrators, deans, or provosts, many of whom have had important roles in the integration of computers and writing instruction. Nor is the field viewed from the perspective of the Fund for the Improvement of Post-Secondary Education (FIPSE) and other grant-giving entities. The history(ies) offered here represents our perspective: that of four teachers and scholars who have participated in the work of the field and who have been moved to write a

You covered a huge amount of territory, and yet it's all so clear and interesting. And you did a great job tying changes in the computer industry and in composition with computers and writing.
Your perspective is very similar to mine—reading the book was like reliving the last 15 years. . . . The corrections I noticed . . . have mostly to do with my personal experience. (Gerrard, email correspondence, August 18, 1994)

I think the way you've all collaborated on each chapter by providing different angles of vision to surround the computers and composition section is an effective way to present the hitory of the discipline. . . .I think that because you as co-authors are embracing radical theory, you may be overlooking some mainstream computers and composition realities. . . . I think that teachers and technology together could make a difference . . . if teacher training were improved. (Rodrigues, email correspondence, August 28, 1994)

Your history, to be blunt, seems more a history of publications about computers and writing than a history of what happened. . . . My own, admittedly biased and limted perspective, was that we had reached a dead end by 1986, that

CMC opened up new possibilities ... but that because it was a radical concept, needed lots of push. (Batson, email correspondence, September 9, 1994

1926: The era of talking motion pictures is introduced by *The Jazz Singer*, starring Al Jolson.

1927: Charles Lindbergh makes the first solo nonstop flight across the Atlantic Ocean.

1929: FM radio is introduced.

1930: More than 18 million radios are owned by 60 percent of U.S. households.

1930s: Music has shifted from the romantic style of Brahms and the early Mahler to the atonality of Schoenberg, art to the cubism and expressionism of Picasso, and poetry to the minimalism of Ezra Pound, T.S. Eliot, and William Carlos William.

1932: RCA demonstrates a television receiver with a cathode-ray picture tube. In 1933 Zworkin produces a cathode-ray tube called the iconoscope, that makes high-quality television almost a reality. (Kurzweil, 1990, p. 471)

history—not the history, but a history, of the field's emergence and early years.

A NOTE ON THE BOOK'S STRUCTURE

In planning this book, we decided on a chronological structure. We still think that this was a wise choice, at least for what will be the first extended historical project in the field of computers and composition studies. Geography could have been our metaphor, and the history one of sites, of places where computers and compositionists were particularly active. We could have written the history of "great" individuals who had a particular impact on our field. This alternative was so attractive that built into the otherwise-chronological narrative are interviews—short, autobiographical narratives at the ends of chapters 2–5. The history of places, and the history of people, remain to be written.

Having chosen a chronological structure, we faced a number of major problems. First, we were working in two fields—education and technology—having very different rates of change. Education changes slowly; technology during this period has changed rapidly. Despite our post-Kuhnian tendency to view the field in terms of a paradigm shift and radical, catastrophic change, change happens slowly in the field of composition studies, and in the field of education generally. Classrooms today, as one of us has noted elsewhere (Moran, 1992), are hardly distinguishable from the classrooms of the 1900s. Computer technology, on the other hand, is changing at a dizzying, almost exponential, rate of speed, and, in terms of its impact on American society, at a rate that approaches the catastrophic.

One result of the difference in the two fields'

rates of change is that teachers in the history will seem either overly resistant to the new technology or excessively-enthusiastic about its potential. Computer technology races ahead, and teachers scramble to keep up. Thus they complain—and rightly so—about the cost of technology, about teachers' and students' limited access, and about aspects of our professional situation: the lack of teacher education efforts available, or the need to learn about computers while trying to keep up in other areas—composition studies, linguistics, education. When teachers of writing do keep up, they find themselves sounding like techno-evangelists, almost annually reexcited about the pedagogical potential of some radically new-to-us technological development—first word-processing systems, then the networked classroom, then online class discussion, then multimedia, then the WorldWideWeb.

A second problem following from the choice of a chronological structure is the tendency to suggest too often that the field is a static, fixed entity moving through time. First, the field discovers word processing, then networks, then multimedia, then the Internet. The field is not a fixed entity, however. It is a framework, one whose atoms are always changing, as individual teacher-scholars enter and leave. Further, people come into the field with widely different connections to computer technology; thus an individual entering the field in 1994 may recapitulate the field's development in a single year, following the same developmental curve as someone who entered in 1980—first word processing, then the Internet—but faster, in compressed form. Conferences and journals find that they need to speak, therefore, to both seasoned teacher-scholars and to teachers who are discovering computers for the first time. The field also has its own generation gap: those who had to learn about computers in midcareer, and those who were, in a sense, al-

The historian . . . could thus be viewed as one who, like the modern artist and scientist, seeks to exploit a certain perspective on the world that does not pretend to exhaust description or analysis of all the data in the entire phenomenal field but rather offers itself as one way among many of disclosing certain aspects of the field. . . . [T]he methodological and stylistic cosmopolitanism which this conception of representation promotes would force historians to abandon the attempt to portray "one particular portion of life *right side up* and in *true* perspective," as one famous historian put it some years ago, and to recognize that there is no such thing as a *single* correct view of any object under study but that there are *many* correct views, each requiring its own style of representation. (White, 1978, pp. 46–47)

most "born to computers." Comprising the computers and composition community are veterans, people who programmed in Spitbol or in Apple Basic in the late 1970s and early 1980s, and young newcomers, often graduate students. The latter is a new generation, people who habitually net surf and who participate in, and create, our field's MOOs, MUDs, and MUSHes. For this generation, the technology seems almost transparent—not, as it was for the previous generation, something to be learned.

A third problem with the choice of chronology is that development occurs within institutions as well as within individuals or within this entity defined as our field. At the close of the 1994 Computers and Writing conference, Karl Schnapp posed this problem, one that is not solved here and that awaits the next history:

> Although I understand the necessity of writing a history of computers and writing, it seems to me that part of the "history" is actually an on-going "process." That is, some of the events and changes you'll consider "history" *still* haven't arrived at my campus. Trends evident elsewhere are only *now* being discussed by people in my department. (C&W, 1994)[1]

Karl Schnapp also speaks for the authors of this history who sometimes say this of their own colleges and universities.

However, the choice of a chronological structure has been made—at least for this volume. It begins in 1979, with the advent of the microcomputer, because this was the technologi-

1946: Television enters American life even more rapidly than radio did in the 1920s. The percentage of American homes having sets jumps from 0.02 percent in 1946 to 72 percent in 1956 and more than 90 percent by 1983.
1947: An airplane flies at supersonic speed for the first time, in the United States.

1948: Norbert Wiener publishes *Cybernetics,* a seminal book on information theory.

1949: George Orwell's novel *1984* envisions a chilling world in which very large bureaucracies employ computers to enslave the population.

1952: The CBS television network uses UNIVAC to correctly predict the election of Dwight D. Eisenhower as president of the United States.

1953: Two statements of major importance to modern existentialism appear: *Philosophical Investigations* by Ludwig Wittgenstein, and *Waiting for Godot* by Samuel Beckett. (Kurzweil, 1990, pp. 472–473)

[1]At the 1994 Computers and Writing Conference in Columbia, Missouri, the authors asked participants to write down any comment they would like to see included in the history. These comments were given to the authors or e-mailed to them. C&W, 1994 is used throughout the book to indicate passages we collected in this way.

cal development that put computing in the hands of individual teachers. It concludes in 1994 because the manuscript was due at the publishers in March of 1995. Like a final draft in a word-processing system, it comes to a somewhat arbitrary end: Deadlines are deadlines. Thus in February of 1995 we click on the "print" icon, and that is the end of the revising. Between the starting and ending dates, we divide the history of computers and composition studies into five time periods: 1979–1982, when the first personal computers came on the open market and English composition teachers first began to use these machines systematically to support composition studies; 1983–1985, when the profession's enthusiasm for computer technology was at its peak; 1986–1988, a period marking the emergence of computers and composition studies as its own discipline; 1989–1991, a period during which the field took a second, critical look at what was happening; and 1992–1994, a period when the field discovered the Internet and when multimedia became commercially viable—15 event-filled years in all.

Each chapter in this volume begins with a section headed "Considering Contexts," which describes the field of composition studies and the field of computer technology during this time period. "Considering Contexts" is followed by "Observing Trends," a section that sketches the patterns and themes evident within the field of computers and composition studies itself. The third section of each chapter, titled "Recognizing Challenges," traces the connections between the trends of computer use in composition classrooms and the institutional, professional, social, and political structures within our culture.

The final section of chapters 2–5, titled "Our Colleagues Remember," includes interviews with key figures in computers and composition studies. This section is designed to provide a holis-

1962: Thomas Kuhn publishes *The Structure of Scientific Revolutions* in which he theorizes about the nature of the growth of scientific knowledge.

1964: Marshall McLuhan's *Understanding Media* foresees electronic media, especially television, as creating a "global village" in which "the medium is the message."

1970: The floppy disc is introduced for storing data in computers.

1975: More than 5,000 microcomputers are sold in the U.S., and the first personal computer, with 256 bytes of memory, is introduced. (Kurzweil, 1990, pp. 474–478)

1976: Joseph Weizenbaum, who created the ELIZA program, which simulates a Rogerian psychotherapist, publishes *Computer Power and Human Reason*. He argues that even if we could build intelligent machines, it would be unethical to do so.

1977: Steven Jobs and Stephen Wozniak design and build the Apple Computer.
The Apple II, the first personal computer to be sold in assembled form, is successfully marketed. (Kurzweil, 1990, pp. 474–78)

tic sense of trends and patterns as they were and are perceived by colleagues teaching and studying within the field—in the words and voices of individuals who have shaped our thinking about technology. Among the voices in these interviews are those of the field's pioneers (Hugh Burns, Helen Schwartz, Lillian Bridwell-Bowles, Lisa Gerrard); researchers and scholars who have contributed to its growth (Patricia Sullivan, Michael Joyce, and Myron Tuman), and young teacher-scholars who are the present and the future of the field (Rebecca Rickley, Pamela Takayoshi, Locke Carter, Johndan Johnson-Eilola, Michael Day, and Eric Crump).

We hope in this book to tell a story—not *the* story, but one story nonetheless—of an emerging and maturing field of study. The story has important implications not only for computers and composition specialists but also for English educators faced with the task of preparing future teachers of English in teacher-education institutions, for practicing and potential teachers of English who want to develop a critical vision of technology and its relation to composition studies, for graduate students who want to enter and contribute to this exciting field, and for administrators who are responsible for understanding the ways in which technology connects with teaching, learning, and the structures of educational institutions. Because we believe in human agency—our own, the students', and that of other teachers and scholars—this history is fundamentally hopeful. Chronicled here is the development of a community, one that has come together around an emerging technology, a conference, and a journal. Heard in the interviews and in the MOO that concludes chapter 6 are the voices of people deeply engaged by what they are doing and confident of its positive human outcomes.

1

1979–1982: THE PROFESSION'S EARLY EXPERIENCE WITH MODERN TECHNOLOGY

The grand debate in English composition circles these days concerns the problem of whether or not we teachers of composition should be more concerned with the processes of composition or the products of composition—whether we should be helping the students understand how they can create a piece of sustained thought or whether we should teach the students how to evaluate their own written work. . . . Enter rhetorical invention. Enter creativity theory. Enter the computer.

—Burns, 1981, p. 31

THE CONTEXT OF COMPOSITION STUDIES: COMPUTERS AND AMERICA'S WRITING CRISIS

Computers arrived on the American scene in a substantial way in the 1960s. To most writing teachers practicing at this time, however, they remained a professionally invisible presence.

1960: About 6,000 computers are in operation in the United States.

17

1964: IBM solidifies its leadership of the computer industry with the introduction of its 360 series.

1967: The software business is born when IBM announces it will no longer sell software and hardware in a single unit. (Kurzweil, 1990, pp. 474–476)

Educational technology's gift to composition is the programmed or auto-instructional text, developed in World War II for use in training manuals, popularized in the 60s, and still used to enhance a variety of language skills. Typical of these is Joseph Blumenthal's *English 3200*, a fully programmed text that teaches traditional grammar and syntax in the course of 3,232 frames. (Woods, 1981, p. 402)

A letter to Johnny's mother, by Rudolf Flesch: The teaching of reading—all over the United States, in all the schools, in all the textbooks—is totally wrong and flies in the face of all logic and common sense. Johnny couldn't read until

Computers invisibly tracked stock transactions, bank balances, airline tickets and reservations; they "crunched numbers" for scientists and mathematicians. In what David Russell (1991) has called "The Age of Scan-Tron" (p. 241), the computer made the replacement of the essay examination by the multiple-choice exam possible, and in the 1960s and 1970s computers were first used in schools and colleges for administrative purposes such as payroll and scheduling. The computer as model inspired "programmed" textbooks such as Joseph Blumenthal's (1972) *English 3200* and James Brown's (1980) *Programmed Vocabulary*, textbooks that William F. Woods, in a 1981 review of composition textbooks published in *College English*, would call with heavy irony "educational technology's gift to composition" (p. 402). In the 1970s, programmers at IBM and Bell Labs had developed EPISTLE and WRITER'S WORKBENCH, both style-checking programs, and Computer-Assisted Instruction (CAI) programs had been developed at such institutions as Stanford, the University of Illinois, Brigham Young, and the University of Texas. Before 1980, however, computers were hardly visible in our field.

Wide-scale use of computers in American classrooms began in the early 1980s, driven by the advent of the microcomputer, what would later be called the "PC," or Personal Computer. The PC entered a preexisting context or "scene," to use a term from Burke's Pentad, a context that the computer altered by its presence, but that also determined the ways in which the computer would be used in educational settings.

THE POLITICAL AND ECONOMIC CONTEXT: THE WRITING CRISIS

We could responsibly date the beginnings of the "modern" era in our field from the cover story in the December 9, 1975 issue of

Newsweek titled "Why Johnny Can't Write." Ringing a change on Rudolph Flesch's (1955) *Why Johnny Can't Read*, this article both voiced and created an impression that America seemed ready to accept: that there was a "Writing Crisis" which threatened the nation's health, stability, and security. The *Newsweek* article was triggered by the NAEP report of 1974, which found that writing skills had declined since the previous assessment conducted in 1969. No matter that the 1979 assessment showed apparent gains (Russell, 1991); the "Writing Crisis" had by 1979 become an integral part of our view of young people. In 1979, Penguin published Thomas C. Wheeler's *The Great American Writing Block*, subtitled *Causes of the New Illiteracy*. In 1981, James Hill, the Chair of that year's Conference on College Composition and Communication (CCCC), spoke of the "growing crisis of literacy in our country" (CCCC Program, p. 3), and focused the convention on an attempt to understand what such a crisis would mean to the profession of English.

The ease with which this writing crisis entered our collective consciousness is the subject for a major cultural study, one that lies outside the scope of this volume. It is clear, however, that the rapid and widespread acceptance of the writing crisis was linked to demographic, political, and economic factors which were important players in the game that computers would enter in the early 1980s.

Chief among these is the passing of the post-World War II "Baby Boom" through the portals of American higher education. The 1960s had seen a tremendous increase in the number and capacity of American colleges and universities. During this period teachers' colleges and agricultural colleges had become full-fledged universities, and the two-year junior or community college had become a significant institution with its own journals and professional identity.

half a year ago for the simple reason that nobody ever showed him how. Johnny's only problem was that he was unfortunately exposed to an ordinary American school. (Flesch, 1955, p. 2)

"Why Johnny Can't Write"
If your children are attending college, the chances are that when they graduate they will be unable to write ordinary, expository English with any real degree of structure and lucidity. If they are in high school and planning to attend college, the chances are less than even that they will be able to write English at the minimal college level when they get there. If they are not planning to attend college, their skills in writing English may not even qualify them for secretarial or clerical work. And if they are attending elementary school, they are almost certainly not being given the kind of required reading material, much less writing instruction, that might make it possible for them eventually to write comprehensible English. Willy-nilly, the U.S. educational system is spawning a generation of semi-literates. ("Why Johnny Can't Write," 1975, p. 58)

The causes of the "literacy crisis" in the mid-70s are no clearer now than they were when the furor was at its peak. Whether television was responsible for the decline in standardized test scores, whether the scores were attributable to a broader population of students taking the test, or whether the scores were truly indicative of a general decline in verbal skills among young people are no longer crucial questions. The important fact in retrospect was that many people believed that high-school and college students didn't write as well as they used to. (Faigley & Miller, 1982, p. 557)

I gathered . . . two-thousand freshman themes, half of them written by my own students during the period 1973–1976, the rest written from 1950–1957. . . . I charted the themes for the revelatory kinds of mistakes. Such errors, it turned out, were astonishingly more pervasive in the themes written in the '70s. That fact seems to me to constitute strong presumptive evidence in favor of the popular impressionistic view that progressive acclimation to an oral culture is diminishing students' ability to write well. (Sloan, 1979, p. 156)

In response to the public's concern, colleges and universities began to reexamine their writing programs, which in some cases had been abolished a few years

The surge of baby boomers into the nation's colleges produced a national youth movement, as college students flexed their political muscle in an activism that would hasten, if not bring about, the end of the Vietnam War. In the early 1980s, however, the college-age "boom" was followed by the beginnings of the "baby bust"—the result of a precipitous decline in the national birth rate beginning in the early 1960s. The decline in America's college-age population would continue deep into the 1990s. During the 1980s, however, despite the decrease in the college-age group, college and university enrollments held remarkably steady (National Center of Educational Statistics, 1993), in part because institutions responded to the diminished applicant pool by extending their mission and recruiting populations previously excluded: a range of what were often termed "nontraditional" students, including working women, minorities, and the poor. It is this new constituency, diminished in number and changed in character, that was so easily considered illiterate—and by an electorate, its children now graduated from college, that had a less personal stake in public education.

In a letter to the editor written in response to *Newsweek*'s "Why Johnny Can't Write" (1975), Walker Gibson, past president of NCTE and then Director of the University of Massachusetts' Rhetoric Program, reflected on the double and conflicting messages sent by the article and the context in which it appeared. On the very pages carrying the article that deplored the illiteracy of the nation's youth, there were advertisements for television sets, television programs, and movies. Could *Newsweek*, Gibson wondered, be serious about a literacy crisis when it presented the crisis in the context of print commercials for visual communications media? What, he wondered, was going on? (*Newsweek* chose not to publish the letter.)

Looking back on this period from the present time, it is possible to see in this contradiction a distant early warning of the attacks on public secondary education that would follow in the mid- and late 1980s and in the 1990s would widen their focus and include postsecondary education. During this period we have experienced two conflicting trends: an increase in the calls for educational reform, and a decrease, in real dollars, of the funds allocated to education. It is not too much to say that "Why Johnny Can't Write," in which a problem was simultaneously described and exacerbated, was an early document in the vexed history of American public education in the late 20th century.

RESPONSE OF THE ACADEMY

Whether or not Johnny, and Jill, could write, the perception of widespread illiteracy took hold and became, for American schools and colleges, a political reality. Educational institutions practically fell over themselves trying to prove to the public that writing at their institutions was indeed being taken seriously. David Russell (1991), in his history of the writing across the curriculum movement, saw this response as in part a function of "the new academic executive" (p. 275), a career administrator who would be more responsive than an educator to the political realities of the world outside the academy. James Berlin (1987), citing studies by Thomas Wilcox (1973) and Ron Smith (1974), found that during the period of 1967–1973, first-year writing was on the decline. Post-1975, however, "English departments everywhere have responded to the call for more and better writing instruction" (p.

earlier on the stated grounds that high-school graduates no longer needed such training. One visible result of this reexamination is the emphasis in college courses on writing outside the university. (Faigley & Miller, 1982, p. 557)

The fact is, English teachers are doing awfully well, against enormous odds, in continuing to involve at least some young people in the joys and powers of reading and writing. You will note in the National Assessment's report—and you should have noted it in your article—that among 17-year-olds, "good writers are as good as they were, and there may be a few more of them than there were in 1969." Under the circumstances, that is a truly remarkable achievement. Meanwhile, if we want to feel the real force of the nonprint media on our culture, all we have to do is scan the pages of *Newsweek*. It's all there, large as life. (Gibson, 1975, p. 2)

Begun in 1974 by James Gray of the University of California-Berkeley and his friend and teacher Cap Lavin ... the Bay Area Writing Project (BAWP) ... relies on eleven assumptions concerning teachers, teaching, and writing:

1. Schools and universities must work as partners to solve the "writing problem." New, collegial, nonhierarchical relationships between university and school staffs must

be developed. The traditional top-down program dissemination for planning school change is no longer acceptable as a staff development model.

2. Although most teachers are not adequately trained as teachers of writing, effective teachers of writing are found at all levels of school instruction.

3. These teachers can be brought together in summer institutes and trained to teach other teachers of writing in workshops held throughout the school year.

4. The best teachers of teachers are other teachers.

5. Teachers of writing must write themselves.

6. Effective programs must involve teachers from all grade levels and content fields.

7. Writing is a skill developed over time and requires constant practice.

8. Writing is a powerful tool to facilitate thinking, learning, and understanding.

9. True change in classroom practices occurs over time.

10. Effective staff development programs are ongoing and systematic.

11. That which is known about the teaching of writing comes from both research and the practice of those who teach writing. (Gomez, 1990, pp. 68–69)

183). The responses have been legion and various, including the introduction of writing across the curriculum programs, the establishment of writing centers, the establishment and growth of the Bay Area Writing Project, which by 1982 was operating at 80 sites, and the professionalization of writing instruction through the establishment of graduate programs in rhetoric and composition.

Even the Modern Language Association of America, in its "Report of the Commission on the Future of the Profession," (1982) argued that it was fruitless to look to the recent past and mourn a "scholarly arcadia lost" (p. 941). The better course, the report argued, would be to join with the field of Composition Studies and make common cause: "Recent advantages in composition research and pedagogy suggest challenging prospects for new and more fruitful alliances throughout the profession. The creation of texts and the study of texts can only enhance each other" (p. 943). The report recommended that "institutions of higher learning recognize the teaching of writing as an essential activity" (p. 951). But, like the *Newsweek* article, the MLA report carried conflicting messages. The report makes it clear that the reason for its recommendation—that literature and writing sit down at the same table—was the disastrous job market for humanities scholars in the early 1980s and the hope that the "literacy crisis" would be a way out. The report opens with an "establishing shot" that contextualizes its recommendations: "Few of us have remained untouched by the serious difficulties afflicting our profession." It then lists the "serious difficulties": "Enrollments decline in many of the humanities, younger and older PhDs cannot make a living by teaching, and aging scholars of language and literature take 'retraining' courses to prepare for remedial teaching" (p. 941). In the report writers' eyes the teaching of writing is "remedial" and a little distasteful—it is not what PhDs in English should be doing, but it is the last, best hope.

THE PEDAGOGICAL AND THEORETICAL CONTEXT

Computers thus entered our scene at a moment when there was a loud and public call for the improvement of writing instruction, and at the beginning of what was to be a long and difficult period of retrenchment in American public education. If we shift our gaze from the political and economic to the theoretical and the pedagogical, however, we move into an arena of unrelieved excitement, change, and energetic, fruitful debate. In the field of Composition Studies, the "Writing Process" movement, what Richard Young (1978) and Maxine Hairston (1982) were to call a *paradigm shift*, was in full voice in 1979–1982. Instead of "product," we were to look at "process." The work of the London Schools Project was entering the American mainstream, and "learn to write" was being challenged by "write to learn." Through the work of Donald Graves and others, the strata of education were becoming permeable, as teaching methods from "elementary" education were now advocated at the secondary and postsecondary levels. Writing labs and centers increased in number during this period, becoming sites for research as well as for instruction.

THE WRITING PROCESS: IN THE ASCENDANT

During this early period, computers connected with this excitement most directly through the multifaceted and protean entity called "The

I should say that though the "slave market" (as recruitment at MLA meetings is called) is a frenzied and, lately, a cruel spectacle, I have never resented its existence. On the contrary, the function of low-cost employment agents seems to me one of the more honest, direct, and useful functions that the MLA performs, or did perform when openings still existed. But I deplore the values that are applied in the market... because of the "profession," which after all is the metaphysical force that makes the MLA what it is. (Ohmann, 1976, p. 41)

The attempt to focus curricula on serving the needs of the liberal corporate state which began in the sixties reached new extremes in the late seventies and under the Reagan administration in the eighties. Part of the success of this conservative turn was a national backlash engineered by the Nixon administration against what was portrayed as the political and personal excesses of the protest movements of the sixties and seventies. During this period, corporate models of profitability came to prevail in the organization of public institutions. Schools everywhere were charged with being "accountable" for the "products" they were producing. Students were now considered a commodity. (Berlin, 1990b, p. 212.)

In 1971, the Schools Council approved the establishment of a three-year development project—"Writing Across the

Curriculum"—under Nancy Martin's directorship, to investigate in collaboration with teachers in schools the practical application of our research. The research team . . . has continued to work in collaboration with the development project and we have thus had the benefit of the assistance of the two project officers, Peter Medway and Harold Smith, in preparing this report. (Britton, 1975, p. xi)

Hairston's (1982) 12 main features of the new paradigm for teaching writing:

1. It focuses on the writing process; instructors intervene in students' writing during the process.
2. It teaches strategies for invention and discovery; instructors help students to generate content and discover purpose.
3. It is rhetorically based; audience, purpose, and occasion figure prominently in the assignment of writing tasks.
4. Instructors evaluate the written product by how well it fulfills the writer's intention and meets the audience's needs.
5. It views writing as a recursive rather than a linear process; pre-writing, writing, and revision are activities that overlap and intertwine.
6. It is holistic, viewing writing as an activity that involves the intuitive and non-rational as well as the rational faculties.

Writing Process." It seems appropriate, therefore, to sketch a brief history of this movement.

In 1963, Richard Braddock, Richard Lloyd-Jones, and Lowell Schoer (1963), in their landmark study *Research in Written Composition*, included 24 research questions that together mapped what they termed "unexplored territory" (p. 52). The last of these questions, "Of what does skill in writing really consist?" (p. 53), can be seen as the question that produced the knowledge on which writing process pedagogy would be based. In 1978, Richard Young, drawing on the work of Daniel Fogarty (1959), described the "current-traditional paradigm," and, invoking Kuhn, spoke of a developing "crisis" in our discipline that suggested an impending paradigm shift (p. 30). In 1982, just 4 years later, Maxine Hairston (1982), in an article in *College Composition and Communication* titled "The Winds of Change: Thomas Kuhn and the Revolution in the Teaching of Writing," announced that the paradigm shift had taken place. The "emerging paradigm" (p. 85), as she termed it, "focuses on the writing process" (p. 86).

The Writing Process movement was political, theoretical, and practical. As a political movement, it drew, as James Marshall (1992) has argued on the rhetoric of other "movements" of the time, particularly that of the Civil Rights and the Anti-War movements. Adherents to the Writing Process movement saw themselves participating in a revolution, a struggle against an established "other," called "Current Traditional Rhetoric." For a body of theory, the movement drew on the work of cognitive psychologists and linguists, and on retrospective, autobiographical accounts of professional writers such as the *Paris Review* interview series, *Writers at Work*, published by Penguin in paperback, 1977–1981, in five series. As a body of practice, it drew on the work of such teachers and theorists as Janet Emig, Peter Elbow, and Donald Murray.

This entity called the Writing Process was generally understood to be a sequence—sometimes of "steps" undertaken sequentially, and sometimes of discrete "activities" undertaken in a sequence that was seen to be recursive. In its simplest, linear form, the process involved three stages/activities, often called prewriting, writing, and revising, as they were by Donald Murray in 1972, or rehearsing, drafting, and revising, as Murray later called them in 1980. Because this model of the three-stage process had such a powerful effect on the early uses of computers in our field, we want to look at ways in which these three elements were understood.

Prewriting

"Prewriting" was a term that first appeared in our literature in 1965, in Gordon Rohman's article in *College Composition and Communication* titled "Pre-Writing: The Stage of Discovery in the Writing Process." The term *prewriting* was often seen as being synonymous with "invention" generally—a term defined by Richard Young (1976) as "the rhetorical art concerned with discovering the subject matter of discourse" (p. 1). The concept of prewriting accompanied the reopening of the field of invention to the teaching of writing. In classical rhetoric, invention was the art of discovering the most powerful arguments and evidence to support your case. In current traditional textbooks, invention most often became an empty category, a species of magic related to the doctrine of inspiration. This magic happened, or it did not, in a realm not accessible to the teacher. Current traditional textbooks characteristically urged the student writer to begin with an outline—a think–write model that pre-

7. It emphasizes that writing is a way of learning and developing as well as a communication skill.
8. It includes a variety of writing modes, expressive as well as expository.
9. It is informed by other disciplines, especially cognitive psychology and linguistics.
10. It views writing as a disciplined creative activity that can be analyzed and described; its practitioners believe that writing can be taught.
11. It is based on linguistic research and research into the composing process.
12. It stresses the principle that writing teachers should be people who write. (p. 86)

WRITING IS A PROCESS

Writing is a craft before it is an art; writing may appear magic, but it is our responsibility to take our students backstage to watch the pigeons being tucked up the magician's sleeve. The process of writing can be studied and understood. We can re-create most of what a student or professional writer does to produce effective writing.

The process is not linear, but recursive. The writer passes through the process once or many times, emphasizing different stages during each passage.

There is not one process, but

many. The process varies with the personality or cognitive style of the writer, the experience of the writer, and the nature of the writing task. (Murray, 1980, p. 4)

It is no accident that interest in the process of composing emerged at the same time as the interets in invention. All arts of invention present either explicitly or implicitly a conception of the design of arts of invention and the teachers choice of which art, if any, to teach. (Young, 1976, p. 2)

Freewriting is the easiest way to get words on paper and the best all-around practice in writing that I know. To do a freewriting exercise, simply force yourself to write without stopping for ten minutes. Sometimes you will produce garbage, but that's not the goal either. You may stay on one topic, you may flip repeatedly from one to another: it doesn't matter. Sometimes you will produce a good record of your stream of consciousness, but often you can't keep up. Speed is not the goal, though sometimes the process revs you up. If you can't think of anything to write, write about how that feels or repeat over and over "I have nothing to write" or "Nonsense" or "No." If you get stuck in the middle of a sentence or thought, just repeat the last word or phrase till something comes along. The only point is to keep writing. (Elbow, 1981, p. 13)

sumed that the writer did not set pen to paper until the thought processes, invisible and inaccessible, were complete. Along with the acceptance of the concept of prewriting came the belief that *invention*, the arts of discovery, could be taught. At professional conferences, panels on invention increased in number through 1982, dropping back in the mid-1980s as the field became more involved with other facets of writing.

During this period there coexisted three different and related approaches to prewriting. What we'll term the *writerly* approach was presented by authors like Donald Murray (1968, 1985) and Peter Elbow (1981) who, drawing on their own rich, personal experience, provided in such books as *A Writer Teaches Writing* and *Writing With Power* a wide array of techniques, tricks of the trade, and ways of getting the writing under way. A second, "new-rhetorical" approach was presented by theorists such as Young and Ross Winterowd. The new rhetoricians sponsored the development of heuristic procedures, models of the processes of cognition, often based on epistemologies found in Aristotle's topoi, Burke's pentad, or the linguist's "tagmemic" matrix. The aim of these procedures was the discovery and generation of subject matter. A third approach to prewriting, one that drew on techniques belonging to the worlds of meditation and psychoanalysis, was "freewriting," a procedure advocated by Macrorie (1970) and Peter Elbow (1973).

All three of these conceptions of prewriting—the "writerly," the "new rhetorical," and "freewriting"—influenced writer's-aid software that would be written in the 1980s. The "writerly" approach produced programs like William Wresch's WRITER'S HELPER, which presented to the writer an array of "aids"—a toolkit—and left it up to the writer to choose the appropriate tool at the appropriate moment. The new rhetorical work on invention led to

Hugh Burns' creation of TOPOI and the subsequent creation of MINDWRITER, an invention program that gave its user the choice of three heuristics, one based on Aristotle's *Rhetoric*, one on Kenneth Burke's dramatism, and one based on tagmemics, presented most fully in Young, Becker, and Pike's (1970) textbook, *Rhetoric: Discovery and Change*. Freewriting would lead us in two directions: the incorporation of free-writing prompts into computer-assisted composition software such as Mimi Schwartz's PREWRITE and the work of Marcus and Blau (1983) with "invisible writing," in which writers write invisibly on darkened computer screens.

Prewriting [software] programs received most of my efforts. I know it is hard to get students to use prewriting activities outside of class, and even English teachers tend to go comatose when the subject comes up. But I've always felt the only way to avoid correctly spelled drivel was to prewrite and prewrite and prewrite some more. WRITER'S HELPER approaches prewriting through levels, options, and electronic gimmickry. (Wresch, 1984b, p. 144)

Writing and Revising

The second and third stages of the writing process, "writing" and "revision" or "rewriting," were not, as was prewriting, so seemingly new. Writing teachers had always known that writers wrote and that writers revised. Nor were these two stages as closely linked, as was prewriting, to the mother discipline, "rhetoric." Writing and revision could less easily, therefore, draw on preexisting bodies of theory, rhetorical and linguistic. They could draw instead on the tradition of "craft," of the accumulated wisdom about writing as a practice. They could also draw on the increasing body of research, undertaken by such scholars as Linda Flower and John Hayes, on the ways in which student writers managed their writing processes. These researchers, drawing on the techniques and assumptions of cognitive psychology, observed student writing behavior, using such techniques as the compose-aloud protocol or pause analysis, and from observed behavior constructed models of the mind as it was engaged in the processes of writing.

The move in the late 1970s from "product"

Flower, L. S. (1979). Writer-based prose: A cognitive basis for problems in writing. College English, 41, 19–37.

Flower, L. S. (1981). *Problem-solving strategies for writing*. New York: Harcourt Brace.

Flower, L. S., & Hayes, J. R. (1980). The cognition of discovery: Defining a rhetorical problem. *CCC, 31*, 21–32.

Flower, L. S., & Hayes, J. R. (1980). The dynamics of composing: Making plans and juggling constraints. In L. Gregg & E. Steinberg (Eds.), *Cognitive processes in writing: An interdiscipli-*

nary approach. (pp. 31–50). Hillsdale, NJ: Erlbaum.

Flower, L. S., & Hayes, J. R. (1981). A cognitive process theory of writing. *CCC, 32,* 365–87.

One point that is becoming clear is that writing is an act of discovery for both skilled and unskilled writers: most writers have only a partial notion of what they want to say when they begin to write, and their ideas develop in the process of writing. They develop their ideas intuitively, not methodically. Another truth is that usually the writing process is not linear, moving smoothly in one direction from start to finish. It is messy, recursive, convoluted, and uneven. Writers write, plan, revise, anticipate, and review throughout the writing process, moving back and forth among the different operations involved in writing without any apparent plan. (Hairston, 1982, p. 85)

to "process" transformed the ways in which writing and revising were understood and taught. For the current-traditional teacher, writing was home work, and both writing and revision were black-box activities that took place outside of class. For the current-traditional teacher, having students write in class was an admission of failure, a practice reserved for discipline or for the morning when the class plan was not in place. For the teacher focusing on the writing process, however, writing and revising left the black box and entered the classroom, where these activities could be seen, studied, and coached. For this teacher, a good class was one in which writers wrote and revised, and in which the teacher, and perhaps even students, acted as editors and coaches.

This new classroom, one in which not the teacher but the activity of writing was central, was often called a writing workshop, by analogy to the classroom format in creative writing and what in schools was called the "manual arts"; or a writing laboratory, by analogy to the classroom format often found in the sciences. The workshop or lab was often described in terms that suggested the journalist's newsroom, particularly by ex-journalists such as Donald Murray and Roger Garrison. In *A Writer Teaches Writing* Murray (1968) described the ideal writing classroom as having four characteristics. First, "Each student should have his own desk. The desks might face the wall so students can concentrate on their own work, or the desks might be separated by soundproofed partitions." Second, "The teacher should have an office with a degree of acoustical privacy and a view of the classroom. He should be able to withdraw with a student and go over his paper, giving him individual criticism without the class hearing that personal criticism. It should be a place where both the teacher and the student feel free to be candid.

It is important that the room be soundproofed" (p. 109). Then, in the subjunctive, "There may be an arrangement of tables in a hollow square or circle in the middle of the room" for discussion; and finally, "it should be possible to arrange the tables so that small groups of students can work on each other's papers" (p. 110). In this classroom, writers work chiefly alone, as autonomous units. The teacher becomes the Bureau Chief, the writer's helper.

The writing rooms described by Garrison and Murray, and the conference-centered or tutorial-based pedagogy, whose literature was assembled by Muriel Harris (1982) in *Tutoring Writing: A Sourcebook for Writing Labs*, foregrounded the student writer's writing and the teacher/editor's intervention. With the advent of the microcomputer in the 1980s, the already-established writing labs and writing workshops became computer-writing labs and classrooms, with teacher/editors conferring, one-to-one, with student writers.

Marc Fraschella

CURRENT TRADITIONAL APPROACHES: STILL ALIVE AND WELL

It would be a mistake, however, to see the paradigm shift that Hairston and Young announced in 1982 as a discrete and complete event. Kuhn drew on the sciences for his examples, citing the rapid and complete replacement of the "old" geology by plate tectonics. Composition Studies, however, is not a "science," as Stephen North (1987) has reminded us. It is a community composed largely of practitioners who transmit their knowledge to one another in school corridors and faculty-room encounters. North has called this knowledge "lore," (p. 23) and Louise Phelps (1991) has,

No doubt Composition can safely be termed a field, broadly defined as being concerned with the ways in which writing is done, taught, and learned. It may be, too, that those whose major academic interests lie within the loose boundaries of this field can be said to form a profession, although only its post-secondary members would seem able to declare full-fledged, full-time standing. And, as is true of teaching generally, it is a profession with relatively limited control over the training, licensing, and review of its members, at least by the standards of, say, the legal and medical professions. (North, 1987, p. 364)

more charitably, called it "practical knowing" (p. 870) and "procedural knowledge" (p. 869). The relationship between teachers' knowledge and published research is often distant. Further, as Kathleen Welch (1987) sadly noted, "Of the hundreds of pounds of freshman writing books produced each year, few are constructed with any overt indication that composition theory has ever existed" (p. 269). In our field, then, practice is not always informed by contemporary theory; it may be informed by earlier theory, embedded in "procedural knowledge" and transmitted from teacher to teacher, or embedded in textbooks which become the theoretical center of a given course. The paradigm shift may have occurred in the pages of our journals, but it had not occurred in many, and perhaps not in most, American writing classrooms. Emig (1983) writing in 1982, argued that the old ways, or what she termed *the magical thinking paradigm*, still lived on in classroom practice.

Those who defined the writing process in the 1970s and early 1980s rarely spoke of a fourth "step," proofreading or copyediting. In England, the members of the National Association for the Teaching of English urged teachers to mark students' papers selectively and helpfully (Gibbs, 1979); in America, Donald Graves (1983) asserted that the good teacher "helps children work with editing that is within their grasp" (p. 58). Indeed, early models of the writing process, such as those described by Gordon Rohman (1965) and Donald Murray (1972), do not mention the final proofreading or copyreading at all. Lisa Ede (1992) has noted that a given paradigm is really a terministic screen, one that makes it possible to see what was before invisible, but one that also renders us unable to see some other things. She noted that we don't pay much attention to dictation as a locus of composing, despite its widespread use, because dictation does not fit with our models of the composing process. That we don't foreground final copyreading is perhaps because through the paradigm of the writing process we see this activity as the enemy, the activity foregrounded in current-traditional approaches.

However, much early work in the field of computers and writing focused on the possibility that the computer, given its ability to count and to sort, could be taught to "read" and could do for spelling and grammar what the calculator had done for mathematics. It could help the writer produce a more finished, more error-free product. From the perspective of the Writing Process paradigm, this could seem a positive development, one that would take care of the now-become-trivial business of proofreading and editing, as the calculator had taken care of basic arithmetic skills. On the other hand, work on the computer as reader and style checker, by emphasizing product at the expense of "process," could be seen as a threat to the newly emerging paradigm. As recently as 1990, collections of essays on computers and writing have carried what amount to attacks on the use of computers as style checkers (e.g., Collins, 1989; Dobrin, 1990; Ross, 1985). The continuing interest in the computer as style checker, and the amount of research on the adaptation of Bell Lab's WRITER'S WORKBENCH to our purposes, suggests that the current-traditional paradigm, and its interest in "product," was, in 1979–1982, far from dead. It also suggests to us that the Writing Process paradigm shaped the ways in which style checkers would be viewed and used in our field. Thus the new paradigm—as well as older, more traditional ways of viewing and teaching writing—framed the ways in which the young field of computers and composition would understand and use the new technology.

The WRITEWELL Series by Deborah Holdstein: A series of programs (projected number—15 tutorials and text-entry programs) that helps writers brush up on punctuation, sentencing, word choice, etc., with other programs in invention, composing, paragraphing, etc. Machines: All written in BASIC. Run on Apple 2+ and 2e. Will be adapted to other machines/languages. (taken from *Computers & Composition*, 1983, p. 7)

I make a distinction between two kinds of computer programs: those meant to respond to the form of a text and those meant to respond to the meaning. I will argue that the latter are not and will not be useful in composition. This limitation exists because computers can respond only to the form of a text, not to its meaning, and thus any apparent response to the meaning . . . is inevitably inaccurate. This inaccuracy makes these programs useless. (Dobrin, 1990, p. 40)

[Usage checkers], programs that check your diction, style or grammar . . . are designed to respond to meaning . . . such programs encourage misuse and the kinds of misuse encouraged are . . . pernicious. (Dobrin, 1990, p. 45)

THE TECHNOLOGICAL CONTEXT: FROM MAINFRAMES TO MICROS, THE EARLY APPLICATIONS

The First Personal Computer was the Alto, completed in 1973 and later marked as the Xerox 850 dedicated word processor. Unlike kits, it was capable of graphics, had a full-page screen, a mouse, drives, and software. It is not until 1976 that the Apple I, and 1977 the Apple II, will bring general-purpose computing into the realms of the home and school. (Eklund, 1993, pp. 460–461).

In place of thinking of a nation or a society as a collection of communities, we need to think of it as a complex set of overlapping networks of actual or potential communication or exchange. Unlike a group, not all of the members of a network are directly in communication with, or even directly aware of, one another; but they are connected by communication and relationships through mutually known intermediaries, and thus, the *potential* for direct communication or exchange is there.

Computerized conferencing systems offer the possibility of conveniently and cheaply communicating with large numbers of people. It is our view that these systems allow a person meaningful, frequent, and regular communication with five to ten

Although new developments in theory and praxis were taking place in composition studies, these developments took place in a world far removed from the world of computer technology, where radical advances were announced daily in trade journals. English studies has never been quick to adopt new technologies, and computers did not change old habits. Indeed, many of the new technologies that are just now being introduced in writing classrooms have been in existence for decades. Douglas Engelbart, for example, invented the mouse in 1964 and had NLS (oNLineSystem) up and running by 1968. It would be 25 years before Michael Joyce and Jay David Bolter would begin development of STORYSPACE, the first hypertext system designed for composition classes. In 1970, Murray Turoff developed the first Computer-Mediated Communication (CMC) system, which allowed multiple users to work together online (Hiltz & Turoff, 1978). More than a decade later composition studies would discover ENFI (Electronic Networks for Interaction), develop the "virtual classroom," and build a variety of synchronous and asynchronous programs, including SEEN, COMMENT, and INTERCHANGE. Line editors, too, had long been the province of computer scientists and other colleagues in the sciences who had discovered in the 1950s their usefulness in writing documents (although such low-level use of scarce and expensive computing power was considered a bit decadent). These crude text editors were the progenitors of the relatively powerful word-processing programs that became commonplace in English in the early 1980s.

For technology to find a toehold in English

in the 1960s and 1970s, a number of political and economic forces had to converge. The post-Sputnik panic that resulted in new funding initiatives, curriculum reform, and uses of technology for education in math and the sciences led to the creation of computer-assisted instruction (CAI) programs that often included literacy modules. Those reading and writing CAI modules were the progenitors of later composition software. At the same time that Cold War educational initiatives played a key role in the growth of educational technology, service and information were becoming the cornerstones of the American economy. By 1950, 50% of all jobs were in service and information; by 1980 that percentage would climb to 75%. The service sector of the economy had two key characteristics: an extensive use of computers (which had, in large part, created the information sector), and the need for literate employees. As a result, computers seemed a natural and appropriate means for delivering both instruction and aid to those employees. At these same work sites in the 1970s the first grammar and style-checking programs emerged, programs like EPISTLE and WRITER'S WORKBENCH. Years later, and for a number of reasons including the cost and inconclusive results of using CAI, the movement away from product concerns in composition studies, and the limitations of viewing computers as mere delivery systems for instruction, the new field of computers and composition would come to hold both CAI and grammar/style checkers in low regard. However, during the 1970s these uses of computers in writing instruction represented the state of the art, uncharted territory for English professionals unaccustomed to using technology. It is little wonder that Ellen Nold (1975) would title the first published article on computers and writing "Fear and Trembling: The Humanist Approaches the Computer."

times more people than is possible with current communication options. (Hiltz & Turoff, 1978, p. xxviii)

A computer cannot substitute for a teacher, just as a book, film, or videotape cannot. Nothing can take the place of a good teacher. However, a good teacher can and does use available resources, and the computer—now perhaps consigned to bookkeeping or to drilling or to running regressions—is one such resource. (Nold, 1975, p. 273)

Although it might appear strange to suggest that impulses within public education are part of military agendas, the fact is that the U.S. military since at least World War I has had a substantial impact on school practice. Because of its enormous budget, protected in the name of national security, the military serves as a vanguard innovator in technological research and development. By seeding new research and shielding the products of this research from market and democratic forces (Smith, 1985), the military permits many esoteric technological enterprises to mature. . . . Educational technologies that have emerged from this military research include . . . teaching machines, computer-assisted and computer-managed instruction, and video-disc applications. Educational models and methods derived from this research include programmed instruction, instructional design, . . . individualized instructional packages, simulation software . . . and intelligent tutoring systems. (Noble, 1989, pp. 16–17)

COMPUTER-ASSISTED INSTRUCTION

In the 1960s and 70s much of the existing work in computers and education involved CAI. Computer industry giants like IBM, Control Data Corporation, and Mitre Corporation were rushing to explore the educational marketplace. Government agencies like the National Science Foundation (NSF), the U.S. Office of Education, and The Defense Advanced Research Projects Agency (DARPA) were seeking to reform and enlist American education in a response to Cold War politics (Thurston, 1994). Private foundations like the Carnegie Corporation and the Annenberg/CPB Project were funding new answers to old educational questions. These various entities provided the substantial funding necessary to create the large, complex, and expensive first-generation CAI systems. This was, from the perspective of the investors, an entirely reasonable investment in a technology that would "sweep the country and ultimately change the structure of education" (Chambers, 1988, p. 21).

Most CAI programs shared a common structure: drill and practice, or tutorials, or both—in a given content area. Not only could the programs repeat instructional exercises at various levels and with endless patience; they could record performance, chart student progress, and be used for record keeping, a process often called CMI, or Computer-Managed Instruction. Because they were designed for mainframe computers that would then serve hard-wired or modem-linked terminals, the programming was complex, time-consuming, and expensive. The programs were difficult to customize and tended not to share any common hardware platform. The best-known CAI systems were PLATO, TICCIT (together costing $60 million in development funds), and those created at Stanford by Patrick Suppes and Richard Atkinson, although there were many other CAI systems running by the mid-1970s (Thurston, 1994).

In 1960, with funding from the NSF and Control Data Corporation, Donald Bitzer and his colleagues at the University of Illinois, Urbana–Champaign, began work on PLATO (Programmed Logic for Automatic Teaching Operations). From the central system at the University, PLATO conveyed instructional programs to hundreds of sites around the world in subject areas ranging from reading to Chinese, from mathematics to biology—and for all grade levels, elementary through postsecondary education. PLATO's historical importance lies in its hardware and software innovations. It utilized plasma tube displays, the forerunners of modern cathode-ray display monitors; a touch control system, a forerunner of modern touch screens; animation and graphics capabilities; and an authoring language, TUTOR, that attempted to simplify and encourage the creation of faculty-developed instructional materials (Chambers, 1988).

At about the same time as PLATO's development, Suppes and Atkinson received Carnegie Corporation funding for the development of drill and practice CAI in math and language arts for elementary-school-age students. With further funding by the NSF and the Office of Education, the programs came to be used by thousands of students across the country and are still used today. Alhough most CAI has had mixed and inconclusive results, the Stanford materials have enjoyed positive results in one-year and longer longitudinal studies. The early work of Bitzer, Suppes, Atkinson, and their colleagues provided the foundation for TICCIT (Time-Shared Interactive Computer Controlled Information Television) Project, an NSF funded joint project of the Mitre Corporation, The University of Texas, and, later, Brigham Young University. Directed by Victor Bunderson, the pro-

A group of engineers and educators ... at the University of Illinois, Urbana, designed a computing system (PLATO) especially for effective and efficient teaching. It was a large system that provided instructional computing to about 1,000 simultaneous users throughout the university and also a number of other colleges and schools in Illinois. (Zinn, 1993, p. 261)

Getting electrons to move faster and in single file, or really fast in ranks of 256 electrons side by side, that was going to happen just with the science part of it. But the Human side of it— once you got that kind of speed, what can you use it for? How can design be changed so that everyone can benefit? ... In 1982, we were just at the beginning of this. (Burns, November 10, 1993, personal communication)

ject designed whole first-year college courses in mathematics and English. More important than the final product was the design approach, which not only implemented the latest technology (graphics, color), but drew on the expertise of teams of content experts, instructional design experts, and technical experts using new learning and instructional theory—a design model that would later be adopted for the creation of composition software at institutions like Carnegie Mellon and the University of North Carolina.

The important legacy of CAI is not the teaching that it accomplished but the advances it promoted in hardware and software design. By the late 1970s, funding for CAI had diminished greatly and its use was limited. CAI was in part a victim of its own early and enthusiastic claims, but it had also proven expensive and complicated to use (particularly in the view of Humanities faculty). It had become a victim of its own poor support materials, poor training for users and, finally, of its own ineffectiveness as an instrument for teaching and learning. The most powerful indictment of CAI came from students, who found the programs boring and even preferred lecture classes to the use of some systems.

Though the Delphi conference was designed for a specific limited purpose, the software provided a basic conferencing capability that could be modified to fit other conferencing situations. A group of dispersed persons was able to add items to a permanent, mutually accessible written transcript, which could be accessed, reviewed, and added to at any time by any of the participants. (Hiltz & Turoff, 1993, p. 51)

GRAMMAR AND STYLE CHECKERS

Besides the continued development of CAI, the 1970s also saw the emergence of grammar and style-checking programs. These programs, first developed by corporations, processed text for errors in usage, spelling, and punctuation and for stylistic features such as the number of "to be" verbs, the use of active and passive voice, word clusters deemed clichés, and abstract nouns. The programs could also give feedback on sentence length, word counts, and readabil-

TICCIT (Time-Shared Interactive Computer controlled Information Television,) was a "medium-sized computer system with video technology to obtain low-cost operation with about 100 simultaneous users. The hardware and software design was coordinated with the development of instruction materials carefully preity levels. Two of the earliest such programs were IBM's EPISTLE (later CRITIQUE) and Bell Laboratories' WRITER'S WORKBENCH, although they have been followed by a large number of similar programs including GRAMMATIK, EDIT!, EDITOR, RIGHT WRITER, and EDITORIAL ADVISOR. Grammar and style checkers were among the earliest available computer-based writing tools and were, in the 1970s, tremendously popular. They were popular with developers because they were the easiest writing tool to create, given that they were based on reasonably clear procedural rules and were popular with users because they reflected existing pedagogical theory and practice: attention to grammar, style, and the correction of a finished product. Discussions of a paradigm shift came later, at the end of the decade, and the then-current product-based treatment of writing valued the analysis of grammar and style as central concerns of the writing teacher.

The programs were popular with teachers because they promised to alleviate some of the teachers' dullest and most burdensome work—the careful marking of student compositions. They were also popular with writers, who found in the new tools help with rules that had been for many of them difficult and never fully understood. Moreover, because the current-traditional approach to writing blurred the boundary between correct writing and good writing, the programs' implicit promise was to create good writing.

Grammar and style checkers are widely used today in educational and professional settings. In the most powerful word-processing programs available in the 1990s, grammar and style checkers are available, along with spell checkers, online handbooks, and the thesaurus, as a menu choice. Although their parsing ability and functionality have improved to some extent, these programs differ very little from their forerunners of the 1960s and 1970s.

pared according to rules of effective instruction by instructional design teams at Brigham Young University in Utah, to provide basic remedial instruction in mathematical skills at small colleges. (Zinn, 1993, p. 261)

My intent was to create a grading program that would automate the explication of the myriad black-and-white grammatical errors that I encountered, yet leave me a "window through the program" to deal with complex or subtle errors. I did not ever plan to have the computer find the errors; let me be clear about that. The human presence is required. It was the repetitive drudgery that I wanted to eliminate. (Marling, 1984, p. 797)

MAKING CONNECTIONS: THE EARLY DEVELOPMENT OF COMPUTER-MEDIATED COMMUNICATION

Computer communications systems have been in existence since the early 1970s although their use would not filter into computer-based composition studies until the early 1980s (Wright, 1994). These CMC systems had their origins in Richard Nixon's 1971 wage and price freeze when, in a search for greater national efficiency, the Office of Economic Preparedness (OEC) identified a need for better communications and commissioned Murray Turoff to create a computerized conference system called EMISARI (Emergency Management Information System and Reference Index). A number of other similar systems were being developed at about the same time: At the University of Michigan, Robert Parnes developed CONFER; Harry Stevens, a colleague of Turoff's at the New Jersey Institute of Technology, and George Reinhart created PARTICIPATE; and The Institute for the Future, a California research group, developed PLANET.

In addition to the development of conferencing software, wide-area computer networks came into being during the late 1960s and early 1970s. In 1968 the government's Advanced Research Projects Agency (ARPA) created ARPANET, a kind of overarching network connecting thousands of other smaller networks. Other WAN's such as USENET and FIDONET followed, but perhaps the most important of all for the academic professional was BITNET (Because It's Time Network). Created in 1981 with mainframe connections between CUNY and Yale, it has grown into a large, worldwide network. Originally designed for researchers in the sciences, BITNET came to be widely used by scholars in the humanities as

The Delphi conference and its descendant, the EMISARI computerized conferencing system, represented a highly innovative technique for using a computer to structure human communication for information exchange and collective effort to solve a problem. (Hiltz & Turoff, 1993, p. 49)

By 1977, Arpanet had 111 host computers at various uniersities, corporate research centers and government agencies. By 1989, over 60,000 computers were connected to Internet (its progeny). (Roberts, 1993, p. 336)

At The City University of New York (CUNY), we decided to explore the feasibility of such exchanges on a large scale. Early in 1981 we surveyed more than 50 universities in the eastern United States and Canada in an effort to determine the

well. Today 80% of the more than 700 scholarly conferences on the Internet are in the social sciences and the humanities (Wright, 1994).

THE MICROCOMPUTER REVOLUTION

Despite the significant funds invested in academic computing during the 1960s and 1970s, by the middle of the latter the computer remained largely within the province of the sciences, especially in research settings, and of academic administration. This situation would almost instantly change with the development of the microcomputer. In 1972 Ted Hoff, an engineer at Intel Corporation working on calculators, suggested packing all the arithmetic and logic circuitry needed for computation onto one silicon chip, the Intel 4004. That first chip, tremendously limited by today's standards, led to the 1974 commercial release of the first 8-bit microprocessor chip, the Intel 8080, and the microcomputer was born. Later that same year Ed Roberts of MIT announced the release of the Altair 8800, a microcomputer kit selling for $397 (or $498 assembled), and promptly received 5,000 orders. By the end of the year, the Altair 8800 was featured on the cover of *Popular Electronics*. Other microcomputer chips soon followed the Intel and Altair including the Zilog Z-80 and the Motorola 6809 and a number of mail-order kits followed, including the Scelbi-8B, the Sphere I, the Jolt, and the Mike (Mandell, 1979). These early microcomputers were incredibly primitive by today's standards; most came with between 1 and 4K of memory and no software whatsoever and they were purchased almost exclusively by electronics experts or enthusiasts. However, they set the stage for the explosion of microcomputer technology that continues unabated today.

breadth and seriousness of interest in creating an easy, economical system for interuniversity communications. Response to the survey was overwhelmingly positive.... Encouraged by results of the CUNY survey, we proceeded to implement those plans as a first step toward realizing a network of university users. The link was established in May 1981, and the new network, which we dubbed BITNET, was born. Since then nineteen other institutions have joined the network, for a total of 65 nodes ... More than fifteen other universities have stated their intents to connect in the near future. (Fuchs, 1983, pp. 16–17)

During the early 1970s, Jobs worked for Nolan Bushness at Atari designing video games. By 1976 he had talked Wozniak into leaving H-P and forming Apple Computer. From the day it opened for business in 1977, Apple prospered and quickly grew into a multi-million dollar company. (Rogowski & Reilly, 1993, p. 519)

Beginning in 1979, Apple awarded hundreds of thousands of dollars in grants to schools and individuals for development of educational software. The large software library that ensued is a key reason that more than 60 percent of computers used in the U. S. primary and secondary schools are Apple Computers. (Fallon, 1993, p. 70)

The IBM PC set de facto standards that enabled the personal computer market place to grow as it has . . . they remain the largest manufacturer of personal computers. (Press, 1993, p. 644)

Stephen Wozniak and Stephen Jobs are to the microcomputer what Wyatt and Surrey were to the English sonnet or Lennon and Mc-Cartney were to rock-and-roll music: They took what others had invented, put it together in better ways, and marketed the product. In 1976, Wozniak used the MOS 6402 microprocessor chip to build the Apple I. He left his job at Hewlett-Packard, joined forces with Jobs, raised $1300, and released the Apple II, an immediate commercial success. Apple Computers not only established the viability and potential of the microcomputer market; they made educators across disciplines and grade levels believe in and desire computers. Although a number of competing microcomputers would soon be successfully released, including Commodore Corporation's VIC 20 and PET and Tandy Corporation's TRS-80 Model 1, it was Apple and its aggressive pursuit of the educational market that revolutionized educational computing. Indeed, in 1981, computer-based learning was being used in 50% of American educational institutions and was predominantly microcomputer-based (Chambers, 1988).

Five years after the release of the Apple II, IBM entered the microcomputer market with the release of its PC (Personal Computer). The release of the IBM PC was important for a number of reasons. In technological terms, it heralded the use of new 16-bit microprocessors (the Intel 8088 in 1981) which significantly increased the power of the microcomputer and prompted IBM's competitors to improve their systems (Mandell, 1979). From a market perspective, IBM's investment in microcomputers and its large base of users meant a more rapid spread of microcomputer technology, particularly in higher education (although Apple would maintain its hold over the K–12 market through aggressive marketing, grant programs, and support). From a consumer perspective,

IBM's decision to use a nonproprietary or "open" operating system (one that could be used on different brands of hardware) and equally "open" technology would lead to the development of lower priced IBM clones and compatibles. More than 150 companies would come to enter the volatile microcomputer market—many soon falling by the wayside—and price wars kept prices, and profit margins, low. From a product point of view, IBM's decision to make MS-DOS (developed by Microsoft Corporation in 1981), its only operating system, meant that many software companies would create software for the new computer. Indeed, within 12 months of the IBM PC's release, the company was supporting 12 new Microsoft products, and 30 other companies had announced the development of DOS-based software programs.

Although many writing teachers had discovered the uses of mainframe computers for their own writing, and some, like Lisa Gerrard at UCLA, used mainframes for their writing classes, it was the creation of the microcomputer that brought computers into writing classes in a major way. The microcomputer's relatively low cost put technology within the reach of writing programs and writing instructors. When the two came together, there was no looking back. Writing teachers discovered in the technology a delivery vehicle for the new process approaches that were taking hold in the field generally, and they were spurred on by the enthusiastic claims of those early pioneers who had been working with mainframes. So naturally did microcomputers and attendant word-processing software lend themselves to writing that this has come to be the primary use of microcomputers in most educational settings. By the end of this first period in the use of computers in composition, computer writing labs and classrooms were appearing around the country. With FIPSE funding, Lil-

What is preventing humanists from using the computer for humanitarian purposes is merely their belief that they cannot use the machine. It is ironic that a group known to undertake calmly and surely the study of Latin, Greek, Russian, Chinese, Swahili, or Gaelic often balks at the much simpler task of learning the more logical, far less capricious language of the machine. (Nold, 1975, p. 273)

Computer programs can call forth creativity because they provide a fertile environment: privacy of communication and time. When students use good computer programs well, the computer provides a patient and non-treatening, fluid and provocative backboard against which to bounce ideas. (Nold, 1975, p. 271)

The design and development of PROSE, a program designed to facilitate instructor feedback on student texts, followed a much more formal track than did PREWRITE. The original idea developed out of classroom practice, specifically the observation of instructor feedback on student texts and a desire to improve the quality of the feedback. (LeBlanc, 1993, p. 34)

Nancy Kaplan recalls how she started PROSE:
Part of my interest in the project, to begin with, was not so much how it was going to have an immediate impact on student's writing behavior or their sense of their own autonomy and authority over their texts, because I've always known that instructors are far too intrusive in their students'

lian Bridwell-Bowles and Donald Ross would create one of the first nationally known computer-writing facilities at the University of Minnesota. Many others would soon follow.

OBSERVING TRENDS: WRITING TEACHERS WRITING SOFTWARE

Many who knew computing in the late 1970s also knew programming, perhaps because computing was then largely within the domain of the sciences where programming was part of the field's research methodology. Certainly the earliest experimenters with computers and writing became involved in programming while designing and developing educational software. Many of these pioneers were self-taught programmers, whereas others acted as designers and content experts and worked with hired programmers. What they had in common was enthusiasm for the new technology and frustration with the absence of software that could address the needs they identified in their classrooms or that could realize the educational potential they saw in the computer. Although the efforts of these first faculty software developers often went unrecognized and unrewarded, they were responsible for some of the best software developed for the computer-based writing classroom.

The tradition of software development in our field begins with Hugh Burns. In 1977 Burns was a doctoral student at the University of Texas, working with James Kinneavy and George Culp. Enrolled in a programming course, Burns used BASIC on a mainframe to create drill-and-practice programs like "Five Usage Toughies," which explained the difference between words like "affect" and "effect" and "principle" and "principal." He also created a program that generated haikus. As he worked on these programs, Burns was struck by a key limitation of then-current English software: It was based on "closed" programming in which the computer always had the correct answer for the question posed to the student user. Burns was intrigued by the idea of "open-ended" programming, in which the computer would pose questions for which it did *not* have answers. With a summer's worth of reading in Aristotle under his belt, Burns turned to the *Rhetoric* and created the first version of his invention program, TOPOI, based loosely on Aristotle's topics. Similar to Joseph Weizenbaum's ELIZA, TOPOI feigned a dialogue with the user, prompting the user for information about a subject. Burns would later add sets of prompts based on Kenneth Burke's pentad and on the tagmemic matrix described by Young, Becker, and Pike (1970). The object of all three sets of questions was to help a writer explore a topic and generate material for an essay that would follow.

Most early composition software focused on invention and prewriting, even though ease of revision would later become one of the most celebrated characteristics of computer-based writing. Models for prewriting were drawn from the "writerly" pedagogies of Murray and Elbow, the new-rhetorical approaches of Winterowd and Kinneavy, and the freewriting of Macrorie and Elbow. These models of prewriting were made operational in James Strickland's 1981 FREE, a freewriting program based on Elbow's work; Mimi Schwartz's 1981 PREWRITE, which prompted students for responses to literary subjects; Ruth Von Blum, Michael Cohen, and Lisa Gerrard's 1982 WANDAH (Writer's AND Author's Helper), which included four prewriting activities (freewriting, invisible writing, nut-shelling, and planning); William Wresch's 1982 WRITER'S HELPER, with its numerous prewriting activities; and Helen Schwartz's 1982 SEEN, software that helped students create hypothe-

work and that students are far too docile in that process . . . In my particular position, you see all kinds of horrors when you mark student papers; and it [the program] seems like a way—a fairly nonthreatening way—of handing instructors a new mechanism for doing their work that will encourage them to think about that work in new and different ways. (LeBlanc, 1993, pp. 34–35)

Computer-assisted instruction in prewriting can help by modeling what good teachers do in writing conferences: direct creativity, suggest strategies, play audience, and dislodge writer's block. (Strickland, 1985, p. 69)

Bad CAI prewriting programs . . . focus on surface-level concerns before higher order concerns, work on a model of learning, rather than the whole writing, teach the strategies as content rather than techniques to be used in the writer's own work. (Strickland, 1985, p. 71)

[SEEN] is a supplement to traditional methods of instruction. It not only tutors students in developing ideas about a particular literary work, but it helps them to internalize almost effortlessly the procedures appropriate for arguing evidence in a discipline. Furthermore, students' work can become the basis for individually chosen paper topics without taking hours of the teacher's conference time. Finally, SEEN can aid researchers in tracing an individual's cognitive development in a manner more convenient, less intrusive, and less costly than otherwise possible. (Schwartz, 1984a, pp. 47–48)

As a junior college English teacher for two or three eternities, one of the things that has always bothered me about much of the student writing I see is a lack of organization and development. . . . There are of course a number of ways of dealing with this problem short of a career change. After taking several computer science courses, it oc-

ses about literary works. WRITER'S HELPER and SEEN would later go on to win NCRIPTAL/EDUCOM Software Awards, and Burns' program would evolve as part of the Deadalus Instructional System (now the Deadalus Integrated Writing Environment), winner of the 1990 NCRIPTAL/EDUCOM award.

There were many other writing/teaching programs under development in the early 1980s. Dawn and Raymond Rodrigues were developing CREATIVE PROBLEM SOLVING; Kathleen Kiefer and Charles Smith were working on an educational version of WRITER'S WORKBENCH for Bell Labs; Cynthia Selfe and Billie Wahlstrom were creating process-based CAI for composition with WORDSWORTH II; Stephen Marcus had completed COMPUPOEM, software that helped students write and study verse; and Michael Cohen and Richard Lanham had completed HOMER, a program based on the latter's work in stylistics and a model for the later GRAMMATIK. At Miami Dade Community College, instructors were using RSVP (Response System with Variable Prescriptions), a grading program and predecessor of instructor feedback programs like GRADER and PROSE. Work had also begun on Ross and Bridwell's ACCESS (A Computer Composing Educational Software System); BANK STREET WRITER, the first commercial word-processing program developed for children; and Christine Neuwirth's first draft programs at Carnegie Mellon University.

This burst of software development had a number of causes. Microcomputers had for the first time put technology into the hands of writing teachers, and programming languages that were increasingly easy to use were making software easier to develop (although learning to program remained a formidable obstacle to interested faculty). Funding was available from a variety of sources: hardware manufacturers eager for software to drive sales of their computers; corporations that wanted to improve writing within their organizations; textbook publishers enthusiastic about a new market and the power of software to sell accompanying texts, and government agencies like the National Science Foundation (NSF), the Fund for the Improvement of Postsecondary Education (FIPSE), and the Department of Education (DOE). It was, for example, an Apple Corporation grant that gave William Wresch a microcomputer on which to create WRITER'S HELPER (LeBlanc, 1993); a FIPSE grant that funded Bridwell and Ross's work; a grant from AT&T that supported Kiefer and Smith's adaptation of WRITER'S WORKBENCH; and support from Harcourt Brace Jovanovich that funded the commercial release of WANDAH as HBJ WRITER (LeBlanc, 1993.

There were, of course, forces that would deflect and absorb much of this creative energy. These included textbook publishers' poor handling of faculty-developed software (insufficient support, poor marketing, and a failure to keep programs technologically current), faculty developers' inability to bring their software from a "classroom" level of development to a "market" level of development (including the development of support materials, portability across platforms, and bug-free programs), and traditional English departments' lack of support for such software development (ranging from ambivalence to hostility). These forces would take their toll later in the history of faculty-based software development in composition. In the years 1979–1982, however. compositionists were helping to define the use of computers in writing instruction by creating the software that shaped the technology. As Burns would say of the period, "I think a real revolution is—this is going to sound a little strange because this is not so much a hardware answer—the recognition that people had to write programs in order to design and write instruction" (Interview, this volume, Chapter 1). The "real rev-

curred to me that the computer might provide one more means. . . . Writer's Helper is essentially three groups of programs. The first group contains nearly a dozen prewriting programs, the second is a specially designed wordprocessor, and the last group contains several programs to analyze student essays. (Wresch, 1984b, pp. 143–144)

I argue for the support of ["computer people"] whose appearance is recent, whose teaching is nontraditional, and whose research is often unfamiliar and perplexing. They are among those who can be victimized by the established categories and measures of evaluation in traditional English and humanities departments but who, I believe, have appeared at one of those "moments of intellectual opportunity" [which we should] seize, nurture, and bring to life in order to invigorate the larger body English that must survive for the sake of all of us. (McDaniel, 1990, p. 86)

olution," if we can call it that, involved people. If instructors had to learn to program, they also had to learn how to use the new programs in their classes.

RECOGNIZING CHALLENGES: LIMITS AND POTENTIAL IN THE EARLY YEARS

Making the "Copernican Turn"

Copernicus can be said to have written a critique of the Ptolemaic conception of the universe. But the idea that the earth goes around the sun is not an *improvement* of the idea that the sun goes around the earth. It is a shift in perspective that literally makes the ground move. (Johnson, quoted in Scholes, 1985, p. 99)

Our students were demanding that we become "computer literate," so, with a knowledge of mainframe computers and stylistic computing in our repertoires, we set out to discover what there was available to a writing program that wanted to survive into the twenty-first century. We found very little that satisfied us in our year-long search for appropriate software. (Bridwell & Ross, 1984, p. 107)

Before the computer could be seen as a writer's helper, computer users had to make what Bernhardt has called *the Copernican turn* (C&W, 1994) and come to see the computer not as a computational device or data processor, as it had been seen since its invention, but as a writing instrument. This redefinition was not quick or easy. It represented a paradigm shift as fundamental to computers and composition studies as the shift in composition studies from a product-oriented to a process-oriented paradigm. Many professionals in our emerging field remember using computers as data processors for research or in business/work settings, while at the same time they laboriously typed their dissertations on manual or electric typewriters. Lisa Gerrard remembers that while she was reading up on computers in the late 1970s, "[She] wrote [her] dissertation on a yellow pad and typed it every night—retyped stuff every single night—literally cut, pasted, and Scotch-taped hunks of it together" (Interview, this volume, chapter 2 page). Lillian Bridwell-Bowles described a similar experience:

I first started using computers for my research work as a graduate student in about '78 or so, and I was doing a statistical analysis of various things related to the composing process. I was counting revisions and analyzing whether or not they made any difference in writing quality, so I had lots of data and I used cards. I literally hand-punched my own data cards. . . . My dissertation was typed and retyped and retyped, and I still remember vividly when my advisor came back from Europe. I had already had my defense and he sat in his office and made little corrections and brought them out to me page by page and I corrected them with white-out. I remember thinking, "There's got to be a better way!"

Similarly, June Gilliam (1994) remembers her early exposure to computers as a writing teacher in 1979:

As a grad student and TA teaching composition in 1979, I had never heard of using computers for writing, much less for teaching writing. My own thesis was typewritten in 1983. However, I also worked (to eat) as a part-time secretary on campus and had to create a mailing list of alums as my computer "writing" project #1. At that time (1982) this was so complicated a task that one of the computer programmers on the CSUS campus mainframe was called in to help me! Later I learned to write letters, a much simpler task, on the mainframe computer. It never occurred to me that writing on a computer would become part of my teaching tool-kit, however. (C&W, 1994)

Getting to Know the "New Machine"

Once they had made the Copernican turn, those who wanted to learn computer hardware and software faced a near-vertical learning curve. Computers had, before 1980, been the property of disciplines such as Computer Sci-

Let me emphasize once again that no one expects that students will spend most of their school hours at consoles hooked up to computers. They will work at consoles no more than

20 to 30 percent of the time. All teachers everywhere recognize the help that books give them in teaching students. The day is coming when computers will receive the same recognition. Teachers will look on computers as a new and powerful tool for helping them to teach their students more effectively. (Suppes, 1980, p. 235)

ence, Engineering, and Physics. A few English professionals had worked with computers in style analysis or concordance building (Swaim, 1994); others had used computers to build bibliographies and other data structures (Donohue, 1994). Patricia Sullivan (Interview, chapter 3, page 166) encountered computers through her library, where the computer's potential for data storage and retrieval held the promise of efficiency.

For most English professionals, however, the computer was new and difficult territory. Bruce Leland's (1994) first encounter with the computer is typical of those of us who discovered the computer in the early 1980s:

> In 1982 computers were, for me, big machines that looked vaguely like furnaces, that filled entire rooms, that required keypunch operators to run and programmers to understand. The work they did, while no doubt useful to someone (those who gave machine-scorable tests, for instance), didn't seem relevant to me.
>
> In the spring of '83, my chair used some end-of-fiscal-year money to make an impetuous purchase a Commodore 64 computer. It sat in the department office, in a corner, for the entire summer. We looked at it, but we didn't touch it.
>
> That fall, when Faculty Development announced a 6-session class in Basic programming, the chair asked, well, insisted, actually that the grad. director and I attend. I learned that I could not break the machine, that I could have fun with it. I had started, and I have not stopped. (C&W, 1994)

Obtaining Access

A further challenge for those who wanted to use computers in their teaching was getting access to computers in the face of institutional cultures that saw writing as a trivial activity—relative to number crunching and data processing. Computer-center directors, and seasoned computer users in other disciplines, believed, based on history, that English had no business using computers and that, in particular, writers should not clutter up the machines with their writing. Doug Anderson (1994) remembered his struggle for access:

> In 1982, I had to finagle access to a computer at Texas A&I (Now Texas A&M-Kingsville). I ended up with permission to use the secretary's Displaywriter, with its huge floppies, in the Office of Institutional Advancement. I used it to typeset the student literary magazine. I was seen as a trouble-maker because I was teaching in the English Department. I wasn't allowed to use the computer lab—it was for computer faculty *only*. I had to explain to deans and vice presidents what in the world a writing teacher wanted to do with a computer terminal. When I explained that I also thought my writing *students* should have access, they knew I was a serious troublemaker! (C&W, 1994)

Adapting the Computer to our Pedagogical Goals

For those who had access to computers and who actually had them stationed in their classrooms, there was a deep pedagogical challenge: how best to use the new machines in the service of teachers' and students' goals for teaching and learning? Because there was no consensus among writing teachers about goals or strategies—has there ever been?—the computer was used in radically different ways. Robert Taylor (1980), in *The Computer in the School: The Tutor, Tool, and Tutee*, saw three

Extended use of the computer as tutee can shift the focus of education in the classroom from end product to process, from acquiring facts to manipulating and understanding them. (R. Taylor, 1980, p. 4)

different uses for the computer in classrooms. The computer could be a "tutor," used for CAI drill and practice or for the open-ended programming created by Weizenbaum and Burns, or the computer could be viewed as a "tool," the writer's instrument, to be used by the student writer in accomplishing a writer's work. Finally, the computer could also be seen as "tutee," an entity to be taught by the student.

Seymour Papert's (1980) *Mindstorms* cast the computer in the role of tutee, an entity to be programmed using the programming language LOGO. LOGO became an important instructional vehicle in elementary schools through 1985. Some (e.g., Brenner, 1982) even suggested parallels between composing an essay and programming a computer. However, the profession generally saw the computer in terms of its emerging process paradigm: as a tool the writer might use in composing, revising, and editing his or her work. This view of the computer was supported by rapid developments in word-processing programs written for microcomputers, programs that made revising much easier than it had been on the line-editors available on mainframe computers. In addition, Hugh Burns (1982), in "A Writer's Tool: Computing as a Mode of Invention," saw his invention program, which might have been seen to lie within the CAI/tutor category, as a writer's tool, one to be used in the early stages of the composing process.

The Challenge of Research

Researchers in the field faced two difficult challenges during this period. First, they had somehow to fit their research into the field of English—not always an easy task. Second, they felt pressed to discover whether computers made writing better or not—a research strand that has proved to be a dead end.

In his interview printed at the end of this

Increasingly, the computers of the very near future will be the private property of individuals, and this will gradually return to the individual the power to determine patterns of education. Education will become more' of a private act, and people with good ideas, different ideas, exciting ideas will no longer be faced with a dilemma where they either have to "sell" their ideas to a conservative bureaucracy or shelve them. They will be able to offer them in an open marketplace directly to consumers. There will be new opportunities for imagination and originality. There might be a renaissance of thinking about education. (Papert, 1980, p. 37)

The INVENT series of three programs helps writers prewrite by asking them questions about their topics. TOPOI is the program used for persuasive writing: its questions are based on Aristotle's 28 enthymeme topics. . . . BURKE is the program used for informative or journalistic writing; its questions are based on Burke's dramatisitic pentad. . . . TAGI is the program used for exploratory and informative writing; its questions are based on the tagmemic matrix of Young, Becker, and Pike. (Burns, 1984, p. 32)

chapter, Burns tells the story of how it became possible for him to write a computer-based dissertation within the world—not of English, but of English education. One factor was the curiosity, and broad-mindedness, of his dissertation advisor, James Kinneavy. Another was a visit to the UT campus by Patrick Suppes, a leader in CAI at Stanford. This visit generated a meeting with a campus administrator, who, with Kinneavy, provided the support that Burns needed. (Interview, this volume, chapter 1)

Patricia Sullivan, working in 1982 on interface design for the library at Carnegie Mellon, had a difficult time convincing her English department that what she was working on was English. The breakthrough, as she saw it, was Richard Young's suggestion that she retitle her dissertation, focusing on the process of research that was part of the writing of the research paper. "He suggested that I . . . focus both the first chapter and the background on writing research papers and the relevance that this had to writing research papers. That made my work less relevant to the librarian and more acceptable to the English Department" (Interview, this volume, chapter 3).

The second challenge faced by researchers was the extent to which research would be driven by a need to prove that computers indeed did improve student writing. Researchers in our field were not more culpable than those in composition studies generally, where there has been a steady search for our profession's philosopher's stone—that one discrete factor which would magically improve all students' writing. Could computers, however, be the real, the final, answer? Many had argued for the installation of computers in writing classrooms on the grounds that computers could, and perhaps would, improve students' writing. It was inevitable, therefore, that the research community should feel the need to supply some proof that computers were, indeed, of pedagogical value.

The prognosis for the use of word processors in college and university writing programs [is not] necessarily gloomy. . . . Although our understanding of the relationship between writing and word processing is right now, of course, rather rudimentary, the state of the art could, I submit, be improved. . . . Most word processors are far more complex and sophisticated than the typical writing student requires. Because they are intended for the modern office, these terminals include a great number of supervisory operations and format concerns which are largely irrelevant to writing and revising which may at the same time interfere with those activities. (Collier, 1983, p. 154)

Hugh Burns (1979), who was the first to complete a dissertation in the field, looked carefully at how students used the heuristics he developed. In reporting on this study with Culp (Burns & Culp, 1980), Burns concluded that the programs were of value to students in generating ideas, even if the computer couldn't "understand" students' responses. Kate Kiefer and Charles Smith (1983), who received a grant to modify the WRITER'S WORKBENCH programs for college students at Colorado State University, reported that students in the experimental sections using WRITER'S WORKBENCH could identify more errors than the control sections. Researchers such as John Gould (1981), Richard Collier (1982, 1983), and Robert Lawlor (1980) all examined and found some value for word processing as a writing tool with IBM programmers, nursing students, and a young child, respectively.

Despite challenges faced by the field during this time, or perhaps, to a degree, because of these challenges, those of us in our field who worked with computers during this early period remember it as a time of intense excitement and hope. The computer was becoming part of the nation's consciousness. Tracy Kidder's *Soul of a New Machine*, published in 1981, spent weeks atop the best-seller list. The computer was, to us, new and filled with promise—as it still seems in the 1990s, as we continue to explore its expanding universe.

OUR COLLEAGUES REMEMBER: INTERVIEWS WITH HUGH BURNS AND LISA GERRARD

In the following lightly edited transcripts of taped interviews, Hugh Burns and Lisa Gerrard remember their introduction to computers and their early work in the field. Hugh Burns, at the University of Texas and the Air Force Academy, and Lisa Gerrard, at UCLA, were pioneers—early settlers in a field that they were helping to create.

Hugh Burns: Looking Back

I think the story actually starts about 1972, '73, when I arrived at the Air Force Academy to join the faculty of English. I was a composition teacher and had just finished a Master's Degree in literature at the University of Southern California. I had the opportunity to be sponsored by the Air Force Academy to return to graduate school so, after a couple of years doing the operational work of the Air Force, I ended up at the University of Texas in January 1977.

I was interested in computers because I had been using computers for my own writing since long before I was teaching. I had the opportunity as a very young person working my way through school to use IBM magnetic tape electric typewriters that were available mostly in the business world. So word processing was a pretty common feature that I knew how to use. I also used line editors on mainframes when I could get my hands on one, usually in business settings. So I was already a user of computers, but not, in 1977, a programmer of computers.

In my first semester at the University of Texas, I was studying rhetoric with Jim Kinneavy. I was able to persuade him and my graduate committee to allow me to take computer programming so that I could become a better user of computers and perhaps even write a few programs.

I ended up moving with Jim Kinneavy over to English Education to continue my graduate work. Rhetoric was not a highly esteemed graduate program at Texas at that time. So, for those of us who wanted an interdisciplinary approach to rhetoric, Jim had a half time appointment in the College of Education. A number of us were the rhetoric people, as opposed to the English Education people, but we were often in the curriculum on the education side.

I wrote programs that first semester with my mentor there, working with Dr. George Culp in the Computer Science Department. His course was in programming, but writing programs in your own field. I wrote two kinds of programs. The first were drill and practice, of which there had been a number done through the late '60's and '70's in common use at our university. One program, for example, was called "Dialogue," the principal investigator was Susan Wittig. It was NSF funded and was basically 42 lessons in grammar and style based on the syntactic work of Noam Chomsky. It was pre-sentence combining kind of work; there were 42 lessons which ran on the mainframe DEC then at the University of Texas. I was fortunate enough to have located a couple of dumb terminals that had a mainline. I talked my way into having one of those terminals put into a little area I cordoned off in the writing laboratory. I was up and running, writing other kinds of "Dialogue" lessons, chiefly imitating the other kinds of software that were already there.

My first assignment for Culp was called "Five Usage Toughies." It was written in Basic [and was] a short little program that explained the difference between such choices as "affect" and "effect", "principle" and "principal"—that kind of software. That was my first project for Dr. Culp. After I'd finished that, he said, "What else can you do?" So, for my second project, I wrote some syntactic-structured stuff that generated poetry. We generated quite a lot of haiku based on the syntactic structure in different kinds of random choices from various word lists. That was fairly interesting. So, those were my first two projects.

In the summer, I took a conference course with George reading Aristotle. This made me ask, "What would a computer do if it could not answer the question?" For everything I had been doing in drill and practice, we had to program the computer to know the answer. And when students used that kind of program, they would often play around and not answer the question directly. So you wrote tricky little subroutines to get the computer to recognize a nonanswer and have it make a guess at the answer. It was really necessary for most users of computers to try to type in responses, but the computer is often not programmed to recognize these responses. So it became a little kind of a game. What would a computer do if it did not know the answer to a question? And that was the genesis of what became known as the invention programs, the prewriting programs we started to work on.

It was that first summer that I wrote my first version of a program called "Topoi," which combined an interest that Jim Kinneavy and I had in invention from Aristotle's *Rhetoric* and this notion of the computer not being able to answer the question, any question. So, we generated 10 questions. And the computer would just stay there and not have any response. We'd ask the question, "What are the good consequences of your topic?" And then you would type in your answer. Well, it turned out that students didn't always want to answer those questions. They wanted explanations and they wanted other kinds of information from the computers at that time. That sits for a little bit there in '77, just kind of a summer project.

Then after I finished my exams, I toyed with the ideas of two different dissertations. One was the complete development of such software and the other was to write a more theoretical dissertation on rhetorical invention.

Jim was very supportive early on, because I was studying Aristotle. He was my original chair, but as I drifted more often to computer science and the dissertation became more empirical and more applied software, Jim started to lose interest in it. However, I can take some glee in the fact that I am able, if not to convert people to the use of computers in such research, to at least get the idea across that they were useful tools. The moment I recall with Jim Kinneavy was actually, there were two moments. One was instructional. I had to vary a number of routines that would recognize gibberish in a student's answer, including some bad language. So, one of the students had typed a transcript and typed in a few off-color words and the machine caught it. "I can't pretend to answer such language," the computer typed out. And Jim thought that was just wonderful that there was enough smarts in the computer to catch that. The second thing that Kinneavy really enjoyed was when I was actually crunching the data from the experimental design. And I, in my experimental design, had three different groups and a control group. Back in the days of key punching your data stacks, I was basically looking for variables.

Prewriting transcripts were the most comprehensive. I worked with a number of questions: Which transcripts were the most factual? Which had the most surprise value? Those were some of the variables that Kinneavy writes about in *A Theory of Discourse*. I was able to run SPSS programs that would generate trends that would teach and inform about the difference between the heuristics. We actually had empirical data on how heuristics were used for different purposes and these data became an empirical validation of some of Jim's assumptions. He loved that! He also saw how quickly I was going through the data. One Sunday afternoon he came by the writing laboratory. I had the door open to my office there in the bottom of Parlan Hall at the University of Texas. He came in that Sunday as I was searching through the data, looking for different kinds of trends. He asked me three or four kinds of questions. "What if you co-vary the results and keep the students the same? Was there a difference between Tagi and Topoi?" And we would run that statistical model and I had to type my data entry question in code in the program to generate a new trend analysis, a multiple regression analysis of what the trend might be. He looked at me, and said, "You know, you are having too much fun. Dissertations are supposed to be harder than this." True story. The result of that was that Jim's secretary came back to me and asked me if the computer could alphabetize, if she could start using the line editor for Jim's own bibliography so that he could start his own database, because at that time he existed on 3x5 cards, carrying around these filing cabinets of notecards for all of his classes. So that was Jim's awakening. He probably thinks I'm still there as a student sometimes!

As I moved closer to writing my dissertation, we hit the dilemma of whether or not I should do the software or the theory. And a scholar named Patrick Suppes from Stanford University came to the University of Texas for a series of presentations. I had been imitating a variety of his programs—there was a lot of good CAI in philosophy during this time. And Suppes' work at Stanford was, to me, real cutting edge. He had done work in putting mainframes and terminals in peoples' homes. He had generated a lot of different kinds of programs that were really pretty neat in computer-assisted logic learning—symbolic logic learning. So here comes this computer assisted instruction guru to campus to speak, to give free lectures. I went to Suppes' lecture on linguistics. There were about 200 people there—I didn't have a chance to talk, but there was a reception held for Suppes and others and I went to that. Once there I had the opportunity to talk with him about my two dissertation proposals and ask him which one he would recommend I do: the theory of rhetorical invention, where I would be working more with Jim Kinneavy on Greek influences in invention, or the empirical software project. And he said, "If you can write the software, go ahead and do that and measure it and see if it has any effects. And if you do it in this open-ended model you have, that would be quite innovative."

He said that in front of my advisors and to the vice president, whose name was Susan Wittig. All of a sudden I had a topic. Susan came onto my committee at that point. That brought research funding to the project, so, they were able to say, "He will need additional support"—computer time, mainly. In those days, you had to buy your computer time. I did not take courses in instructional design along the way. I don't even know if there were many courses on instructional design during that time in the College of Education. You were linked to a mainframe over a modem during these days. Most of us who were even thinking about instructional design were all programming, either using BASIC or some very early version of LISP if we got into the languages. So we were all programmers. In those days, if you wanted to write instructional software, you wrote programs.

I was not alone. In the mid '70s the rhetoric programs were well thought of and sponsored by the NSF and Congress. I learned early on to write and ask for the latest the Senatorial hearings transcripts and reports. I started reading about tutors in the Senate hearings, in 1977, when John Seeley Brown was talking to the Senate about the evolution of intelligent systems in education. Then in 1980, there was a report by the Rockefeller Commission titled "The Humanities in American Life." It advocated "Intelligent, discriminating applications of electronic technologies in the classroom as their capabilities increased, and their costs decline." My originality, if that's what it was, was the idea that the prewriting application was useful. It could be stimulated by a variety of different heuristics, but those heuristics could also be computational. I wanted to be a better one-to-one tutor when students came by to talk to me about writing their papers.

When we later tried to transport those early programs back to the Air Force Academy, we had to learn new programming techniques in order to make these large programs run. And, lucky for a lot of us, this was when a thing called a microcomputer was starting to emerge, first a 45K Tandy and then a 64K machine. That's when I make my first computer buy, an Osborne, in 1982 a dual drive, 64K CPM with a four inch screen that would interface with a daisy wheel, letter-quality printer, the Smith-Corona TP1. I still have both of these machines—I'm certain they're going to be worth lots of money!

No one anticipated how fast the microcomputer revolution would come about. I kept on wanting to design bigger programs for the mainframe; it took others with a vision of how to make these programs available on microcomputer. I think the real revolution, though, is—this is going to sound a little strange, because it hasn't anything to do with hardware—the recognition that people had to write programs in order to design and write instruction. We started to write tools instead of writing tutors, lessons out of programs. Programmers started to write tools for designing and started to work with other aspects of programming, like the interface and the environment for doing different kinds of tasks.

And that's what really changed clever uses of interface. And this is work that was talked about in Xerox PARC, this is the work that would tantalize Steven Jobs at Apple when he saw the mouse as a point-and-click mechanism. So people could use computers and tools without having to be computer programmers. And that, I think, is the mind set that really radically changed for me. Getting electrons to move faster and in single file, or really fast in ranks of 256 electrons side by side, that was going to happen just with the science part of it. But the human side of it once you got that kind of speed, what can you use it for? How can design be changed so that everyone can benefit? And so, screen design, information environments, knowledge environments, transparent kinds of user interface designs were being thought of as a box. In 1982, we are just at the beginning of this!

Hugh Burns is an Associate Professor and Director of Educational Technology at Smith College. He is Chairman of the Daedalus Group. He is also President of Hugh Burns and Associates, a consulting firm working on new designs for schools.

Lisa Gerrard: Remembering Early Efforts

I became interested in computers and writing in a roundabout way. From 1970–1973, while a graduate student at Berkeley, I worked as a research assistant for a professor of Islamic history. I'd track down references, type up his notes on a typewriter, and then using a card reader, I'd punch data cards with the information from his research. After he'd written his book or article, I'd make stylistic revisions—by hand. This was the first time I experienced a computer as part of the writing process. Here we were using traditional technology a red pen and a typewriter and then the data card reader was stuck quite comfortably in the middle. I was getting my degree in comparative literature and didn't think critically about writing processes in those days, but I was intrigued to see a computer used in a writing project—and by a humanist, too.

By the mid-seventies, academic jobs for PhDs in comparative literature had pretty much disappeared, and I was watching my friends complete their degrees and then go into management training in a bank or off to the mountains to write poetry. I wanted to finish my degree, but I didn't really expect to use it. So while I was writing my dissertation, I began casting around for other ways to make a living. I took a series of tests at the career counseling center—the kind that match your skills and personality against those of people in different careers—and scored high as a computer programmer. I didn't even know what programmers did, but I went to the library and began to read about computers—basic stuff like input devices and binary arithmetic. I wasn't sure how any of this related to me.

I had a friend who had lost his community-college job in Philosophy and had found a job at the Bank of America as a programmer. He told me at the time that you couldn't get a degree in computer science—it didn't exist. Companies simply trained you to program. So with a Humanities background, he's working at the Bank of America as a programmer, and every person in his department had a graduate degree in music or in foreign languages. My background, in comp lit, is basically a foreign-language background.

For me, this was right up my alley. They apparently felt that people who were good in my field made good programmers. With my friend's encouragement, I started to read up about what computers were—what a central processing unit was. Most of the literature on the subject was very technical and dull, but I was still curious about what was going on there in the computer world. Meanwhile, I wrote my dissertation on a yellow pad and typed it every night. I retyped stuff every single night and literally cut, pasted, and Scotch-taped hunks of it together. I just missed the word processing generation, which probably would have shaved 2 years off the dissertation process.

I never did apply for a programming job. Instead, I left Berkeley to work in UCLA Writing Programs in 1980. Richard Lanham was just starting the program, and he was eager for the faculty to bring technology into composition; we had talked about this at the interview—for me the opportunity to work with computers was a major attraction of the job. The position had a 4-year limit, so I figured that when the job ended, I'd probably look for work in a computer field. Dick also hired Michael Cohen, who had been a graduate student in the English Department, and had left UCLA to work as a programmer at the Jet Propulsion Lab in Pasadena. Michael was interested in space projects, so when NASA began to put more money into military uses of technology and less into space exploration, he left JPL and returned to UCLA as Writing Programs' computer consultant.

When I arrived at UCLA in 1980, there was Michael, there was me, and one or two other people who were interested in computers. I took a couple of programming courses—first, a managerial computing course, later a course Michael gave in UCSD Pascal. I also used an IBM 3033, which was a mainframe computer that had been there for quite some time intended for programmers, not for writers. It had a text editor, Wylbur, that was designed for programmers—not really a word processor, but you could pretend.

So I learned to use Wylbur—my first computer experience. This was a revelation the most wonderful thing. The difference between working with Wylbur and typing on a typewriter was night and day, even though, in retrospect, it was clunky compared to what we have now. With the line editor you had to insert commands that were not in English—there'd be a dot and then some esoteric command to do something, like centering or double spacing. A lot of the formatting had to be done separately with a separate procedure once you were finished with the document. Everything about the set up was inconvenient! There were a couple of terminals in various spots on campus. The English department had a room with two terminals in it, so you could get a key and go up there. Your printout appeared in a bin in the engineering department. You'd go into this room, where anybody who used Wylbur anywhere on campus would have an address and a bin. Sometimes your printout disappeared, never made it into the bin. It was slow; it might be hours, and if it was busy, it might be a day, day and a half before you got your printout. In retrospect this was very, very cumbersome, But I thought it was the greatest thing.

I spent one quarter learning to use Wylbur. Then in the following quarter, I decided, "Okay, I'm going to see how my students do with this." I wrote a simple manual for us because, of course, the manual the computer center had written assumed you knew about computers already. The students were unbelievably good natured about this whole thing. I just told them that this is an experiment, that they were going to be typing their papers on this thing called Wylbur, and that they had to go to the Math/Sciences building to do their work. And they did it! And it was not a disaster. They actually thought it was a lot of fun.

I taught the class pretty much as a standard composition class where students had to write their assignments out of class. I encouraged them to try composing directly on the computer, but most of them accustomed to writing in longhand and then typing their papers used Wylbur as a typewriter. I created revision exercises for them to do on Wylbur, exercises in stylistic imitation, and prewriting activities. The students also used Homer, a style analyzer Michael Cohen wrote (based on Richard Lanham's *Revising Prose*) in 1979. Homer highlighted features such as "to be" verbs and prepositional phrases and created a bar graph showing sentence lengths. I was really experimenting. I wanted to see what would work.

That quarter there were three of us teaching with Wylbur. After that, it was just me. I was fairly isolated, except for Michael, who was terrific. We were very lucky to have him, in that he's someone who had tremendous technical knowledge, and what he didn't have, he could figure out.

Overall, I'd call our early work a success, and I think the students would agree. There were a lot of frustrations. My students were sneered at by the engineers sitting next to them who thought using a computer for writing was Mickey-mouse. The mainframe would crash, and students would lose a whole paper, a day's work, but they wouldn't be as upset about it as you would think. In their course evaluations, one or two people in each class said, "This is horrible! I suffered! This is a waste of time! I hate it!" But then there were 23 who said everything from "it was interesting, but sometimes it was a pain!" to "I really loved it!" For a brief period after Wylbur, I had my students use a minicomputer (an IBM 4143, I think) until we developed our own software, WANDAH. When WANDAH was ready to be tested, UCLA created its first computer lab for student writers, equipped with IBM PCs (double floppy drives, 256K), located in a corner of the library. We did that backwards: first we had the software; then we got the lab.

In 1980, I did all my writing on Wylbur. Then in 1981, Writing Programs installed a dedicated word processor in its administrative office an NBI (Nothing But Initials) with 8" floppy disks and faculty were allowed to use it after 5:00 p.m. and on weekends. We had to sign up for it in advance; everyone wanted to use it. It was fairly temperamental, as I recall, but it had a daisywheel printer, and the output was a whole lot crisper than the pale dot-matrix printouts that appeared in the Wylbur bins. By 1983, we had decided that WANDAH would run on the IBM PC, and to be able to do WANDAH work at home I bought my own PC. To get a sense of how my students would feel writing with WANDAH, I used WANDAH for all my writing. Eventually I moved to WORDSTAR and from there an assortment of other word processors. I still have the old PC, though.

In the early '80s, software was being used to teach writing in K–12, but there wasn't much going on at the college level. In 1980, it was mainly Ellen Nold's article and Hugh Burns' software. There were articles in *English Journal and Educational Technology* and other journals geared for K–12, but not much for college. Most of the work, whatever level it was for, was geared to sentence-level revision and grammatical correctness.

What influenced me more than this work was my reading in composition theory. Since I had not been trained in rhetoric and composition, I was learning about the composition theory that was coming down the pike and I was simultaneously changing the way I was teaching writing by using computers. I was therefore much more interested in revising process theory, generally. I became interested in prewriting things like the invisible writing which Steven Marcus was doing in Santa Barbara, and Linda Flower's ideas about writing—putting your ideas in a nutshell, for example.

So, the way WANDAH happened . . . WANDAH had a kind of serendipitous start. Ruth Von Blum, the project director, had a background in science education and computers and had built some of the first software for science teaching. Though her field was not composition, her interest in the relationship between science learning and cognitive psychology had led her to Linda Flower's work. While doing consulting at UCLA, she discovered Michael Cohen's Homer and shortly after, developed the idea for a program that would specifically address the writing process. Michael was the main programmer. All of us designed WANDAH. We worked as a team; we sat around a table and drew storyboards on giant poster paper. We poured all of our writing knowledge into that program. Michael's Homer made up a big chunk of the revising section. The prewriting routines and the peer editing came right out of my classroom activities—much of it tested in the Wylbur experiments of 1980–1982. The word processing functions came from our personal experiences as writers and what I had learned from teaching with Wylbur.

Because we wanted WANDAH to facilitate a recursive writing process, we designed the program so that students could easily move in and out of its three sections: prewriting, word processing, and revising. We designed our own word processor because we had learned from Wylbur how important it was that students spend as little time as possible learning the system. At that time, all the word processors on the market were really not designed for student writers or writers; they were designed for secretaries. WORDSTAR and some of the other programs assumed that you would be typing for hours and hours every day and would therefore remember those esoteric commands. But we wanted students to compose on the system; we wanted them to concentrate on their ideas, not on the computer. The decision to write our own word processor added a year to WANDAH's development.

Ruth picked the name WANDAH (Writing Aid And Author's Helper)—even though it was redundant because she thought it was time for a program with a woman's name. There was PLATO, Orville, Wylbur, Homer—but no woman.

When UCLA sold WANDAH to Harcourt Brace Jovanovich, I was concerned that instructors new to computers might not know what to do with the program. So I wrote an Instructor's Manual to be distributed with it (Harcourt renamed WANDAH HBJ WRITER). Later I wrote a textbook, a rhetoric, to go with the program. The program—and, of course, the book that went with it—sold poorly. Publishers worried a lot about piracy at that time, and some of them had already lost a lot of money on software; Harcourt was well aware that McGraw-Hill had lost a million dollars on software the year before. I think there was a lot of disagreement within Harcourt about how to market WANDAH, and some poor decisions were made. But WANDAH worked great at UCLA. Because we had a limited number of computers, we used it mostly in basic writing classes for high risk students—very few of them had ever touched a computer before. They really warmed up to "her"—that's how they referred to WANDAH. One of them even wrote her a poem.

Ruth did a good job publicizing WANDAH while we were working on it. So people from campuses around the country would come to UCLA to see what we were doing. That was my first inkling that there was a community out there interested in developing software. In 1984, I went to the computers and writing conference at the University of Minnesota. After being fairly isolated at UCLA, I was amazed to find myself in the company of a couple of hundred people all excited about computers and writing. People were experimenting like mad on mainframe, mini-, and microcomputers; nothing was standard, and nothing was taken for granted. It was a period of transition—both in writing pedagogy and in technology. Some people were taking current traditional approaches—hoping to turn grammar instruction over to computers; others were studying students' writing processes by recording their keystrokes. Whatever they were doing, chances are it worked only at their home campus, since the hardware was all different. But it didn't matter. I was so enthusiastic that I suggested to Lilly Bridwell—she and Don Ross had coordinated the conference—that we make this a yearly event. And she suggested that I organize the next one. So I did. By the time the conference took place, in 1985, computers and writing was a community with an identifiable body of work.

Lisa Gerrard is a Lecturer in the UCLA writing program and one of the original authors of WANDAH.

2

1983–1985:
GROWTH
AND ENTHUSIASM

*[Word processing] will become the norm
at colleges and universities, as it is now
the norm for professional writers. It will,
and should, become part of the writing
classroom.*
　　　　　—Charles Moran, 1983, p. 115

THE CONTEXT: THE FIELD
OF COMPOSITION STUDIES

During the period of 1983–1985, composition
studies absorbed the changes brought about by
the new emphasis upon process and began to
chart the course it would follow postprocess,
looking beyond the individual writer toward the
larger systems of which the writer was a part.
Although the field of composition studies was
changing, it was changing much more slowly
than computer technology, where change was
proceeding at an exponential (and, some felt,
catastrophic) rate. The Macintosh appeared in
1983, bringing the graphical user interface, or
GUI, to the PC; word-processing programs became more powerful; memory was becoming
cheap, and the Winchester hard disk arrived,

**How Macintosh can help
your students write better.
In 500 words or less.**
　　Red Smith, the dean of
American sportswriters, con-
tended writing was easy.
　　All you had to do was
"sit down at a typewriter
until tiny beads of blood
formed on your forehead."
　　Fortunately, things have
changed since Red's day.
　　Thanks to a remarkable
writing tool called the Macintosh personal computer.
　　Macintosh can't turn a
tome into the work of a Tol-
stoy. But it will help your
students express their
thoughts with far greater
speed and eloquence. And,
perhaps, even awaken a
love for language that
could last a lifetime.
　　Macintosh is a very
powerful computer. Yet, its
screen doesn't look like any
computer screen you've
ever seen. It looks like a

desktop. Full of objects writers are already familiar with.

Like the folders, a notepad, a clipboard, a ruler, pieces of paper. And, at the side, one of the most often used writing tools of all, a trash can. (Macintosh advertisement in CCC, 1986)

The *CCCC Bibliography of Composition and Rhetoric* provides approximately 2,500 annotated citations covering topics of concern to college-level teachers, researchers, and scholars in the broad disciplines of rhetoric and composition. Erika Lindemann created the *Longman Bibliography of Composition and Rhetoric, 1984–1985*. In 1988, CCCC in conjunction with SIU Press agreed to underwrite the publication. The CCCC Bibliography project has since published seven volumes detailing the scholarly work appearing in journals and presses. Since 1991, the project has been under the guidance of co-editors Gail E. Hawisher and Cynthia L. Selfe. Over 100 faculty and graduate students volunteer their time each year to create the book. (Preface, CCCC Bibliography, 1994, pp. ix–x)

I think the time has come to break those bonds—not necessarily physically, al-

capable of text storage in quantities that were then difficult to imagine. In 1985, an ordinary writer, or classroom teacher, could draw on computing power that 10 years earlier would have been available only to the highest echelons in the military or in finance.

Although it was not racing ahead in exponential leaps, as was computer technology, composition studies was clearly itself on the move. Signs of its growth and maturity are legion. The 1984 CCCC, held in New York, drew a record 2,495 registrants (NCTE data), and program chairs were able to be more selective in choosing presentations and panels. In 1984 the CCCC *Bibliography of Composition and Rhetoric* was undertaken; the 1984 volume was not to be published until 1987, but in 1984 the field had the impulse, and the energy, to begin to develop its own scholarly tools.

The field was also developing a sense of its own history. In 1984 Berlin published the first volume of his history of the field, *Writing Instruction in Nineteenth Century American Colleges*, a project he would continue with its companion volume, *Rhetoric and Reality: Writing Instruction in American Colleges 1900–1985*, to be published in 1987. The first edition of the *Bedford Bibliography for Teachers of Writing* (Gorrell, Bizzell, & Gerzberg) was published in 1984 as well, making available to the field in easily readable and annotated form a list of important works in the field. If we wanted to push the "coming of age" metaphor beyond the point of usefulness, we might say that Maxine Hairston's 1985 address to CCCC, "Breaking Our Bonds and Affirming Our Connections," was the moment when the field considered itself strong enough that it might entertain the possibility of leaving home. Hairston's address was her response to her own situation at The University of Texas, but it resonated with the experiences of thousands of her colleagues. It became a meaningful and important beacon for the profession as a whole.

RESEARCH AND PROFESSIONAL PUBLICATION

Research and publication in the field were, during this period, overwhelmingly concerned with the "writing process," writers' composing behaviors seen chiefly through the perspectives offered by cognitive psychology. The most frequently cited work in the field during the period of 1983–1987 was *Cognitive Processes in Writing*, edited by Gregg and Steinberg, which had been published in 1980 (Shanahan & Kamil, 1988). Its authors' research methodology differed from that used by Emig in her 1971 study, *The Composing Processes of Twelfth Graders*, in that students' reports of their own composing were treated like "data," coded and checked for internal reliability. The book's first chapter, written by Linda Flower and John Hayes, described the compose-aloud protocol, the data-collection instrument of choice for this group. In the chapter were the terms characteristically used in these studies: long- and short-term memory, task environment, retrieval chains, and information-processing load.

Running parallel to the studies of writers' composing behaviors were studies of the ways in which language contributed to students' learning. Rooted in the work of such educational psychologists as Vygotsky and Piaget, the work of Nancy Martin and James Britton had crossed the Atlantic and had begun to exert an influence on American research and teaching, particularly in the early work here on writing across the curriculum. The British strand, which came to be called "language and learning," or "language across the curriculum,"

though in some cases that may be a good idea—but emotionally and intellectually. I think that as rhetoricians and writing teachers we will come of age and become autonomous professionals with a discipline of our own only if we can make a psychological break with the literary critics who today dominate the profession of English studies. (Hairston, 1985, p. 273)

I think we need to be clear at the outset that a concern for Language across the Curriculum is not, in the final analysis, a concern for language—for the oracy and literacy of the students we teach—but a concern for the quality of learning in all subjects. This is politic—for how could teachers of the other subjects be persuaded that what the English teacher is paid to do must be shared around amongst all the members of staff? But it is far more than politic: It is no less than a challenge to all teachers to consider the processes of learning, both in their own subjects and in the whole curriculum. It is a challenge to them to make a much needed, little heeded distinction between rote learning and genuine learning—

little heeded because our policies for school organization and pupil evaluation tend to blur that distinction. What has to be realized is that learning is not a uni-directional process (what the teacher "gives off," the pupil absorbs) but an interactional one, essentially social in nature—teachers and students learning with each other and from each other. (Britton, 1983, p. 221)

The teacher who abandons the role of assessor, to become an advisor, begins to change the picture. And the writing changes too; it begins to take on the character of a conversation, one with reflections or questions. That is to say, the writer's own intentions begin to operate, and the teacher-audience is now seen as a real listener who may even be expected to reply, in conversation or writing. (Martin, 1983, p. 102)

NCTE Honors Heath for Research on Links between Language Differences, School Failure.
   Shirley Brice Heath, whose study of cultural differences in language and literacy learning has broad implications for education, received the 1985 David H. Russell Award for Distinguished Research in the Teaching of English. . . .
   Heath . . . spent ten years studying children's language development in two rural South Carolina blue-collar communities, one white, one black. Com-

came together with the writing across the curriculum movement in 1977 under the auspices of the English Composition Board at the University of Michigan (Freisinger, 1982, Stock, 1983) and in the landmark essay by Janet Emig, "Writing as a Mode of Learning," published in *College Composition and Communication* in 1977. In 1980, at the NCTE Annual Convention, Emig gave a two-day workshop titled "Language and Learning," bringing her own work, and that of Martin and Britton, into the American mainstream.

Connected to the "language and learning" strand—and indeed implicit in it—was a concern for the writer's context, a concern largely absent from the 1980–1985 work of the cognitive psychologists, whose work was principally a study of a writer working alone on a school-based writing task. Patricia Bizzell, writing in 1982, argued that the work of "inner-directed" theorists such as Flower and Hayes (p. 218) needed to be complemented by the "outer-directed" work of Vygotsky and of sociolinguists such as George Dillon (pp. 224–225). Part of the writer's context was other writers, other students. Developing its understanding of the social dimensions of writing, the field drew on the early work of James Moffett (1968), Kenneth Bruffee (1972), and Elbow (1973) on peer editing. During this period Bruffee (1984) himself moved more clearly in the direction of collaborative learning and writing.

Increasingly, researchers undertook to map the writer's context, moving beyond the act of composing and the role of the peer editor/responder, and beyond the concern for audience and purpose found in classical rhetoric—a move that Purves and Purves would call in 1986 a "cultural approach" to writing. To discover the context within which the writer and the writing proceeded, researchers drew on the methods of anthropology, and, in particular, Clifford Geertz's (1973) concept of the "thick description" of a situation or event. A landmark work in the field was Shirley Brice Heath's (1983) *Ways With Words*, a study of the ways in which language was used in two communities, "Trackton" and "Roadville." In 1984, Frederick Erickson, in an essay titled "School Literacy, Reasoning, and Civility: An Anthropologist's Perspective," called on us to take "a perspective on schools, teaching, and learning that places in the foreground the social organization and cultural patterning of people's work in everyday life" (p. 525). And in 1985, in a chapter in *Writing in Nonacademic Settings*, Lester Faigley argued that we take a "social perspective" (p. 235) on writers at work. In the same volume was a chapter by Lee Odell titled "Beyond the Text" and a chapter by Odell and Steven Doheny-Farina that outlined the assumptions and methodologies of ethnographic research in writing.

paring these children's language socialization with that of the mainstream townspeople who set the language patterns for school, she detected differences that reveal the roots of widespread school failure among the working-class children. (In *RTE*, 1986, p. 197)

CLASSROOM PRACTICE

What actually happened in classrooms during this period is extraordinarily difficult to pin down or characterize, as practice carried out by thousands of teachers always is. Robert Connors (1986) has suggested that textbooks are the best indicator of teachers' practice, whereas Thomas Kuhn (1970) has argued that textbooks generally lag behind practice and so are markers not of what teachers' practice *is*, but what it *was* in some real or imagined past. In our quest for a useful window on classroom practice we have reviewed conference programs at the annual conventions of composition studies' primary national organizations, NCTE and CCCC. The conferences are designed by conference chairs in collaboration with NCTE's professional staff; the conferences are shaped, at least in part, by the need to attract atten-

The implications of our view of culture, models of text, and the activity of writing for research are myriad, we believe, for although scholars have learned a great deal about writing as an activity in some cultures, they have learned little that one can truly generalize across cultures. Scholars should also be quite unsure about the precise ways by which a particular culture shapes an individual's knowledge, perceptions, and activities with respect to writing and text, and they should raise the question as to how great a role cultural variation plays in such shaping. We are convinced, however, that the field of study is broad and has profound implications for human understanding and cross-cultural communication as well as for educational planning. (Purves & Purves, 1986, p. 194)

The last twenty-five years have seen an unprecedented surge in the scholarship surrounding writing and the teaching of writing. We are in the midst of an information boom, and for those of us whose professional views have been developed and shaped by reading scholarly journals it is difficult to imagine things any other way. But today's discipline of composition studies is really a very new one. Before 1930, the teaching of rhetoric and writing in American colleges went forward with no important influence from journals at all. During the eighteenth, nineteenth, and early twentieth centuries, composition theory and pedagogy were overwhelmingly shaped by one great force: textbooks. (Connors, 1986, p. 178)

dees. To a degree, then, conference programs are driven by what teachers want to say and by what they want to know. We consider them, for these reasons, one useful, although indirect, indicator of teaching practice.

When we look at conference programs from 1983–1985, we see not an emerging debate between the cognitivists and those who adopted a more social, contextual view, but a field that is trying hard to escape the implications of the "basic skills" movement, a movement that was one of the inevitable outcomes of the "Why Johnny Can't Write" publicity of the mid-1970s. Ever on the search for the quick fix, American society was pressing its schools and colleges for easy ways to deal with this perceived problem. The chair of the 1982 CCCC, Donald Stewart, chose "Serving Our Students, Our Public, and Our Profession" as the conference theme. In his introduction to the conference program, Stewart noted that we were living in what he termed "a strange time": We, in the world of composition studies, were prospering, whereas our colleagues in literary studies were not. Yet what was the basis of this prosperity? Was it founded on assumptions we could accept? Stewart thought not, asking a rhetorical question: "Do those upon whom our prosperity depends have a true or a false perception of what literacy is and what we should be doing about the lack of it?" (1982, p. 3).

At the 1980 NCTE Annual Conference, hot topics, both in program sessions and pre/post-convention workshops, had been the relationship of television to English, holistic scoring and assessment, sentence combining, the Foxfire curriculum, advanced placement, and curriculum for the gifted and talented. In the 1983 NCTE program, however, the center moved away from this skills orientation and toward response to literature. The conference theme was

"Quality for All," and the epigraphs, from Shakespeare, Emily Dickinson, and St. Exupery, all pointed toward the power of the imagination to transform and create.

Both NCTE and CCCC conference programs of this period reveal, too, the dominance of the new, "process" paradigm, and of the language of cognitive psychology. Pre- and postconvention workshops during our period most often had in their titles phrases such as "peer editing," "prewriting," "thinking skills," and "problem solving." A typical workshop title was "The Process of Writing: From Rough Draft to Refinement," a workshop given at the 1984 NCTE annual convention. In the 1983 CCCC program, the most popular session category was "The Composing Process," with 40 sessions. In 1984, sessions in this category decreased in number to 20, but were still second most popular, behind "Approaches to Teaching" (numbering 30). In 1985, sessions on the composing process would again outnumber those in all other categories.

Given the field's continuing and developing interest in the composing processes of student writers, and given the continuing political pressure on the profession to produce better student writers, it is not at all surprising that computers came into the field of composition studies in two rather different ways. They came in as fancy typewriters, used by teachers in writing workshop classrooms (Sudol, 1985) that emulated the newsroom classroom described by Donald Murray (1968); and they came in as tools that would magically and mechanically improve students' writing through style- and grammar-checking programs, spell checkers, computer-assisted instruction packages, and programs that would have the ability to parse English prose, which then seemed just around the technological corner. That story, however, waits to be told later in this chapter.

I walked into the department head's office. "As you know . . . I'm designing and writing computer programs for the use of the department in writing classes. Will you consider my writing of computer software as publication?" Fortunately, we had talked enough about computers for him to know that the jargon "software" refers to the programs that tell the machine what to do. Nonetheless, he looked mildly surprised. "I don't know," he said. "I've never thought about it. We'll have to take it up with the Department Advisory Council. In the meantime, perhaps you should write some sort of justification since most of us know nothing about either the quantity or quality of the work involved." (Bourque, 1983, p. 67)

THE TECHNOLOGICAL CONTEXT

By 1983, microcomputers were sweeping the nation and companies raced to grab a share of the burgeoning market. Sales of micros climbed from 1.5 million in 1981 to over 4 million units in 1983, and in the 1983–1984 school year alone, 55% of schools without computers acquired at least one. Anyone considering the purchase of a microcomputer had a wide variety from which to choose and could do so at almost any price range, although the low-end machines like the Timex Sinclair 1000 and Texas Instruments TI-99 (priced at $99 and $299 respectively) were more electronic hobbyist toys. Although microcomputer manufacturers like IBM, Apple, Radio Shack, and Digital were prominent players in the market, a host of others presented viable and often less expensive alternatives. There was the Osborne 1, the Franklin ACE 1000, the Atari 800, the Commodore PET, the Zenith Z-100, the Onyx, the Morrow, the Xerox, the GridStar, and the Kaypro. One might pay as much as $3800 for the IBM PC or as little as $1400 for the Commodore 64. Companies like Lanier, A.B. Dick, Honeywell, and Wang produced dedicated word-processing microcomputers for office use—very sophisticated for their time—but these remained out of the financial reach of most teachers. The dedicated word processor was not attractive to teachers, and to consumers generally, because it was so narrowly specialized. The development of powerful word-processing software for less expensive, multipurpose machines eventually led to the demise of the dedicated word processor.

By 1983, the IBM PC had made 16-bit processing a standard for microcomputing, and memory requirements of more powerful application software increased the recommended amount of RAM for new systems. The 4K of

RAM in the original mail-order computer kits gave way to 16K and then to 64K. By 1983, experts were advising consumers to consider what then seemed the astronomical jump to 256K systems. The 5.25″ floppy disk was the standard storage medium, but others included the now-abandoned 8″ floppy, the audio tape— with the owner's home cassette-tape recorder acting as a drive—and, increasingly, the 3.5″ floppy. Many systems allowed the user to employ their television set as a monitor.

During the mid-1980s consumers could choose among a wide variety of printers to connect to their newly purchased microcomputer. Printers were a not-inconsiderable purchase, often more expensive than the microcomputers to which they would be attached. Daisywheel printers were essentially souped-up electric typewriters. They were loud, prone to breakdown, and produced what was then considered "letter quality" text at between 10 and 60 characters per second. Dot matrix printers represented a technological advance over the typewriter. They were fast and quieter than the daisywheel printers, but the text that they produced was sometimes a shock to teachers accustomed to typed student writing. Printer manufacturers included many of the microcomputer manufacturers like IBM, Apple, and Digital (although actual manufacture was often through a third party with the distributor's name added later) and others like Epson, Okidata, Diablo, Panasonic, NEC, Transtar, Qume, Smith-Corona, DaisyWriter, and Toshiba. Average price for a dot matrix printer was $600 to $800, whereas daisywheel printers often exceeded $2,000. Interestingly, although many microcomputer manufacturers of this period are now long gone from the market, the printer industry has proven to be much more stable, as many of the successful printer vendors of this period—such as Epson, Toshiba, and Panasonic—are still in business.

IBM Personal Computer Specifications
User Memory
16K-256K bytes
Microprocessor
16-bit, 8088
Auxiliary Memory
2 optional internal diskette drives, 5 1/4″, 160K bytes or 320K bytes per diskette
Keyboard
83 keys, 6 ft cord attaches to system unit
10 function keys
10-key numerical pad
Tactile feedback
Diagnostics
Power-on self testing
Parity checking
(Advertisement in *Classroom Computer News Directory*, 1983)

The most general use of computers in English departments is likely to be word processing. Most large campus computer installations support word processing, and Microcomputers with WORDSTAR or its equivalent have made word processing available to a growing number of potential users. At that level the computer is like the typewriter. Its use can be learned quickly and easily, and it seems likely that the increased efficiency it enables will make the computer terminal a standard fixture in academic offices, as the typewriter is today. The word processor can save much of the time spent in writing letters, creating syllabi, composing articles and books, keeping notes and bibliographies—in short most functions requiring written communication. Of course, someone will have to teach people how to use word processors. (Bourque, 1983, p. 68)

Suspicions Confirmed

The following fall (1988), as Assistant Director of the Writing Program at the University of Delaware, I assigned several instructors and TAs to teach over twenty-five computer sections of freshman composition; five were assigned to both IBM and Macintosh sections. Near the end of the semester, I decided to query the teachers who had taught groups using both types of microcomputers. In order not to influence their comments in any way, I merely

THE MACINTOSH ARRIVES AND SHAPES THE FUTURE

Apple Computers, the company that had ushered in the microcomputer age with the Apple I and II, unveiled the Macintosh computer in 1983. Apple marketed the small, combined CPU-and-monitor system as the "people's computer" and claimed that behind the system's design lay the assumption that it made more sense to teach computers about people than to teach people about computers. The validity of that claim aside, the new Mac, as it was quickly dubbed, broke new technological ground. Apple not only matched IBM's 16-bit processing but surpassed it, using Motorola's new 68000 16/32 bit chip. The chip moved data between storage and itself along 16 paths, but within the chip itself, processing took place 32 bits at a time. The 68000 chip handled more data, more quickly, than the competition. The Mac could run at 7.83 MHz (a clock speed of 7.83 million pulses per second), whereas the IBM PC ran at a much slower 4.77 MHz. The combination of processor and clock speed allowed the Macintosh to run at twice the speed of the IBM PC and at two thirds the cost (Mandell, 1979).

The Mac's processing capability and speed were necessary to support what would become the Macintosh's most important innovation: the use of a Graphic User Interface (GUI) running on a high-resolution display. Before the Macintosh, progress in microcomputer technology had not been in the direction of ease of use. To use the IBM PC, users needed to learn the esoteric line commands of DOS, and Apple II and II+ users struggled with Applesoft and Integer Basic. With the Macintosh and its mouse pointing device, however, users had an interface that dispensed with the command line and featured drop-down menus and click-on icons. On the Mac, when users wanted to delete a file, they simply dragged its file folder icon to the icon of a trash can and "dropped" it in. DOS users still needed to type lines such as "Del a: essayone.doc." Further, the Macintosh could display several windows on its screen, each running a different application. Although many PC users scoffed at the new GUI interface as being child-like and not serious, the success of the Macintosh and the power of GUI was irresistible. DOS itself, in the 1990s, would give way to Microsoft's WINDOWS and IBM's OS/2, GUIs for DOS-based microcomputers.

In addition to the GUI, the Macintosh had other advantages over the IBM PC. For storage, it used the new 3.5″ floppy diskette, more durable and smaller than its 5.25″ cousin. Some teachers also considered these smaller disks better for teaching applications—the relatively fragile 5.25 disks were likely to be crushed in students' backpacks. The Mac was also relatively light and small. Although it was not designed to be portable, the Mac weighed 9 pounds less than the most popular portable on the market at the time, Radio Shack's TRS-80 Model 100. Moreover, the Macintosh came with innovative software that took full advantage of the GUI interface and graphics capabilities of the system. These included MacWrite and Microsoft Word, which not only allowed users to point and click, but also allowed direct cutting and pasting of graphics, including those created with MacPaint, the Macintosh's graphics program, and unprecedented control over format and presentation, including multiple fonts and point sizes. Compared to the elaborate and counterintuitive command structures in leading word processing programs like WordStar and Applewriter, the Macintosh-based software was a quantum leap forward.

put a note in their mailboxes asking them only if they had noticed any differences in the writing of the IBM and Mac students in style, structure, and mechanics.

Quickly, four of the five instructors responded. Two showed up in my office saying, "Marcia, it just dawned on us that the sections we have been complaining about all semester because of the sloppy writing and the fluffiness of the topics are Macintosh sections. We don't have the same complaint about the IBM sections. Is that what you were thinking of?" Two instructors responded in writing, one saying: "Students write differently on the Mac—frankly, I think there writing is worse. . . . There is something about the large print and big margins on the Mac that seems to encourage a sentence structure and childish vocabulary." (Halio, 1990, p. 18)

Writers are burdened by physical and psychological constraints that the computer can help them overcome. The physical act of writing is slow and sometimes painful, and revising requires tedious recopying. . . . The computer text editor is a writing instrument that can lessen the effects of some physical and psychological constraints. The text editor enables writers to compose more quickly and freely because all changes they make in a text are automatically incorporated, thus eliminating the need to recopy. This takes some of the burden off short-term memory. In addition, the interactiveness of the text editor stimulates writers to take a reader's point of view and thus evaluate their writing and find their own mistakes. (Daiute, 1983, p. 134)

The Mac's big debut:
Apple's first Macintosh television commercial made its historic debut during the 1984 Super Bowl, right? Wrong. The famous "1984" ad, directed by film director Ridley Scott (*Alien, Blade Runner*), actually was run for the very first time by a local station in Twin Falls Idaho. It aired at 1:00 a.m. on December 15, 1983. Apple broadcast the ad in December so that it would qualify for the 1984 Clio Awards. (Pogue & Shor, 1994, p. 298)

Why Networking? A Class Full of Reasons.
The CLASSROOM MONITOR is a disk-sharing network. And more. It means the end of crowded demonstrations around a single APPLE. Now, you can run programs on one APPLE and let students watch your work on their individual monitors. Then, while your students are programming, you can display their work on your own monitor. (Advertisement in *Classroom Computer News Directory*, 1983)

By making microcomputers easy to use, the Macintosh ensured itself a place in the nation's classrooms.

MAKING CONNECTIONS: THE EMERGENCE OF NETWORK TECHNOLOGY

By 1983, network technology was no longer new. IBM and American Airlines had developed the SABRE reservations system in the late 1950s and early 1960s, and the next two decades saw the installation of countless high-end and expensive networks conveying data among physically distant sites and driven by powerful mainframe computers connected to minicomputers acting as message switchers and concentrators. Local Area Networks (LANs), linking computers in relatively close proximity (a few feet to a few miles apart), became more common in the late 1970s after the release of the first commercially available LAN, Datapoint Corporation's ARCNet. By 1980, most newspapers were composed on terminals connected to minicomputers, and by 1983, Xerox's breakthrough Ethernet LAN was already 10 years old.

It was the adoption of packet-switching technology for LANs in the early 1980s that made networks a viable and powerful alternative to large mainframe-driven networks and made a networked-writing classroom seem feasible, if not yet often affordable. Packet switching, which allows strings (or packets) of data to travel with their own routing information, allowed transmission channels to carry data traffic between multiple computers. Before this, circuit-switching technology created a machine-to-machine link that dedicated the transmission channel to just that connection, like a telephone call. With packet switching, LANs could move much more information at higher speeds. Ethernet, for example, could now transmit at 10 MBps, or 10 million bits of data per second. Other similar networks included the just-mentioned ARCNet, Wang Laboratories' Wangnet, Fox Research's 10Net, Sytek's Local-Net, Corvus System's Omninet, Ungermann-Bass' Net/One, and Amdax's CableNet. Apple introduced its Applenet in 1983, a low-speed LAN primarily designed for printer sharing but capable of linking up to 128 workstations.

During this period, Wide Area Networks (WANs) became much more powerful as well. Because WANs used telephone lines and networks as their data transmission channels, their function was improved by the new cellular telephone networks that were installed during 1983 and 1984. Even more important was Bell Laboratories' 1985 invention of the ballistic transistor. Replacing the original transistor invented in 1947, the ballistic transistor operated 1,000 times faster than its predecessor and thus enabled the simultaneous transmission of voice, data, and images.

These technological advances, taken together, made it possible for microcomputer users to communicate with one another, a capability that was not talked about much in the early instructional computing literature (e.g., Schwartz, 1982; R. Taylor, 1980). This communication took the form of electronic mail, bulletin boards, data exchanges, and, by 1983, the first real-time conferencing. BITNET enjoyed rapid growth and quickly became the primary network linking academicians in a wide range of disciplines. Other networks, often held together by hard-working sysops (system operators), became gathering places for a growing online community. Fidonet, started in 1983 by Tom Jennings, included over 16,000 bulletin boards internationally in 1993. The Fifth C, affectionately called PARTI by its members, was operated by Michael Spitzer at The New York

Welsch, Lawrence A. "Using Electronic Mail as a Teaching Tool." Communications of the ACM [Association of Computing Machinery], 25 (February, 1982), 105–108.
Shows how electronic mail allows responses from teacher to student to teacher, and between students. Discusses advantages and disadvantages for an engineering class, but the emphasis is on the process of writing. (Schwartz & Bridwell, 1984, p. 76)

[English Teachers had this to say about PARTI]:
Conferencing opens my world. In the middle of Iowa, one can become pretty provincial. "Fifth C" takes me out of the biases of one campus.

By discussing my work and concerns with other professionals in the area, I have learned about what other people are doing and gotten valuable criticism of my own work. In addition, it's a great morale booster to know that other people share your concerns and feel strongly about the work you do.

Done at my own convenience, with all "good"

time—not part of it being tired, etc. Able to respond at my leisure and not under pressure. I feel I know people better than from a paper at a conference. (Spitzer, 1989, p. 194)

Consider a future device for individual use, which is a sort of mechanized private file and library. It needs a name, and, to coin one at random, "memex" will do. A memex is a device in which an individual stores . . . books, records, and communications, and which is mechanized so that it may be consulted with exceeding speed and flexibility. It is an enlarged intimate supplement to his memory.

It consists of a desk, and while it can presumably be operated from a distance, it is primarily the piece of furniture on which he works. On the top are slanting translucent screens, on which material can be projected for convenient reading. There is a keyboard, and sets of buttons and levers. Otherwise it looks like an ordinary desk.

In one end is stored material. The matter of bulk is well taken care of by improved microfilm. Only a small part of the interior of the memex is devoted to storage, the rest to mechanism. Yet if the user inserted 5000 pages of material a day it would take . . .

Institute of Technology. It was the first online conference dedicated to computers and composition and the predecessor of Megabyte University (MBU), which is still going strong.

HYPERTEXT PEEKS OVER THE HORIZON

Hypertext theory, first articulated in Vannevar Bush's (1945) *Atlantic Monthly* article "As We May Think" was almost 40 years old by 1983. Douglas Engelbart designed and built the first actual hypertext system in 1968, his NLS (oN-Line System), and Ted Nelson coined the actual term "hypertext" and articulated a vision of intermingled and connected electronic texts (Joyce, 1994). By 1983 a number of hypertext systems were up and running on mainframe systems, mostly in research settings. These included the Hypertext Editing System (HES) at Brown University, which gave way to the File Retrieval and Editing System (FRESS) and led to the tremendously influential Intermedia hypertext system. Carnegie Mellon's ZOG led to the 1983 release of a commercial version called KMS. Peter Brown's GUIDE, developed at the University of Kent and released in 1985, was the first hypertext system for microcomputers. Perhaps most important was the work being done at the Xerox Palo Alto Research Center (PARC) by Frank Halacz, Thomas Moran, and Randall Trigg on a hypertext system called NOTECARDS. This program shaped the interface design of almost all subsequent hypertext systems and anticipated the most important microcomputer-based hypertext program, Bill Atkinson's 1987 HYPERCARD. HYPERCARD would popularize and extend the use of hypertext in English studies, but all the groundwork for our field's later enthusiasm for hypertext was in place by 1985.

Bush's Memex

OBSERVING TRENDS

As the enthusiasm for computer-supported writing environments grew, so did the discussions that surrounded such activity within the profession. The increased level of research, the availability of new computer tools, and the growing numbers of teachers interested in using the technology began to generate articles, conference presentations, and stories that begged to be shared. Although the profession of composition studies continued to make room for discussions of computers in professional journals like *College English and College Composition and Communication* and annual gatherings of NCTE and CCCC, the demand quickly outstripped available space. Between 1983 and 1985, therefore, scholars and teachers, increasingly identifying themselves as a specialized subgroup of composition studies and eager to validate their interests within the framework of professional recognition, established interest groups within existing national professional organizations; created their own journals (and, eventually, established a press and book series dedicated to the area of study); and started an annual conference to support the emerging discipline.

Conference Sessions on Computers and Composition

By 1983, both the annual NCTE convention and the CCCCs had experienced increasing numbers of session proposals dealing with computers and composition. Computer sessions at the NCTE had increased in number from 1 in 1981 to 7 in 1983; computers sessions at CCCC increased from 2 sessions in 1980 to 10 in 1983. Computer-related sessions

hundreds of years to fill the repository, so he can be profligate and enter material freely. (Bush, 1945, reprinted in 1991, p. 102.)

Obviously, the benefits of prewriting and revising are well recognized by composition teachers. Using the computer makes the process of composition more accessible to students. But if you want to develop programs or use exisiting ones, you need to recognize the dangers. The computer does not replace the teacher's guidance to the student in making informed decisions. How does the student know what details are appropriate in an essay, how to analyze the needs of her audience, or how to develop whatever cognitive processes are part of the course's objectives? You must still teach students these things. And if you have adequate computer facilities, you can use them for exercises to enhance the cognitive process, but you should not make students dependent on the computer. (Arms, 1983, p. 356).

Workshop
WORD PROCESSING IN THE CLASSROOM

(Sponsored by the CCCC Committee on Computers and Composition)
This workshop will meet at the Borough of Manhattan Community College, 199 Chambers Street, Room S-167. Round-trip bus transportation is provided: bus loads at 8:15 a.m., departs

at 8:30 a.m., from the 53rd Street entrance.

Chair: Audrey J. Roth, Miami–Dade Community College, Miami, Fla.

Associate Chairs: Hugh Burns, U.S. Air Force, Denver, Colo., Michael G. Southwell, York College, CUNY

Consultant: Joyce Armstrong Carroll, McMurry College, Abilene, Texas

The CCCC and the workshop leaders express their appreciation to Jim Brooks and Geoffrey Akst of the Borough of Manhattan Community College for their assistance in securing facilities for this workshop. (CCCC Program, 1984, p. 13)

Computer professionals . . . now have the power radically to turn the state of the world in directions conducive to life. In order to gain the necessary courage—not all of us are saints or heroes—we have to understand that for us as individuals, as well as for those we love, our present behavior is far more dangerous, even life threatening, than what healthy common sense now demands of us.

at the 1983 NCTE convention no longer were grouped under "Media and Technology," as they had been in 1981 and 1982, but under "Media and Computers," a signal that the computer was becoming something more to the field than television, film, and the overhead projector. Panels under the new "Media and Computers" rubric focused on teaching instructors about computers and on pedagogical applications of computer technology and included "So You want to Know More About Computers" (Bruce Appleby, Ron Evans, and Pamela Janello from Southern Illinois University), "The Computer and Technical Writing" (Cynthia L. Selfe, George Meese, and Billie J. Wahlstrom from Michigan Technological University), and "Word Processing for English Teachers: The Basics and Beyond" (Robert Caldwell of the University of Texas Health Science Center at Dallas, and Karen Piper of Texas Tech University). Pre- and postconvention workshops included Stephen Marcus's workshop on "Special Effects in Computer-Assisted Writing" and Sally Standiford (University of Illinois, Urbana–Champaign) and Anne Auten's (ERIC) "Using a Computer in Composition Instruction: Help or Hindrance?"

Also indicative of the NCTE membership's increasing interest in computers was its invitation of Joseph Weizenbaum, author of *Computer Power and Human Reason*, to address the General Session. During his talk, Weizenbaum encouraged teachers of English to use computers, but he also advised them to leave the programming and software development to professionals in computer science—advice that many of his listeners, already deeply committed to software development, were not prepared to follow.

Like the 1983 NCTE conference, the 1983 CCCC included sessions that were primarily pedagogical in nature and marked by enthusiasm for computer technology. Visible at this convention was the field's increasing coherence and professionalism, especially within the ranks of college and university faculty. This created a feedback loop: As the field of computers and composition assumed a more prominent role in professional conferences, scholars and teachers saw the possibility of focusing their academic work in an area that had, to this point, often seemed a nonacademic interest. The opportunity to present conference papers in refereed professional venues meant credit toward tenure, access to travel funds, and increased recognition within the profession. Individuals began to identify computers and composition as a primary target for their scholarly and professional work. Among the people whose work figured prominently during the 1983 CCCC were Helen Schwartz ("Computers as a Resource for Research Papers"), Lillian Bridwell ("Computers and Composing: Implications for Instruction for Studying Experienced Writers"), Chris Neuwirth ("From Process to Product: Integrating Computer-Assisted Instruction and Word Processing"), Mark Haselkorn ("The Computer in the English Department"), Hugh Burns ("Computer Literacy and the Composition Teachers"), Cynthia Selfe ("CAI and the Process of Composing"), and Raymond Rodrigues ("CAI invention and Revision Strategies").

One particular session at the 1983 CCCC, the meeting of the Special Interest Group called "The Fifth C: Computers," proved to be a landmark gathering. Led by Kathleen Kiefer of Colorado State University, where a field test of Bell Lab's WRITER'S WORKBENCH was then underway, this session attracted over 200 teachers from across the country. The enthusiasm displayed at this meeting, the growing evidence of interest in computers and composition as an area of pedagogical and empirical inquiry, and the recognition that teachers needed a way of sharing their interests and problems encour-

None of the weapons that today threaten every human being with murder, and whose design, manufacture and sale condemns countless people to starvation, could be developed without the earnest cooperation of computer professionals . . . . What does this say to us? (Weizenbaum, 1986, p. 10)

The computer can help beginning writers learn to revise their initial drafts with less emphasis on lexical substitution and grammatical correctness and with more emphasis on progressive reshaping of ideas through successive drafts. While the computer cannot cure directly students' psychological and cognitive blocks to revision, it can eliminate mechanical difficulties that hinder beginning writers, particularly the cramped illegibility of many students' handwritten drafts and their lack of time for extensive recopying. Once these difficulties are eliminated, students are better able to practice the composing processes used by experienced writers. (Bean, 1983b, p. 146)

Besides helping to individualize instruction in invention and to support or assist the recursive use of important activities in writing, computer-based invention may be more effective than traditional ways of teaching invention in still another way: it accommodates differences in student writing styles. Writers develop different writing strategies, and not all prewriting, invention, and heuristic processes work equally well for all writers, especially for inexperienced writers who have just been made conscious of their writing processes. And because students typically do not find or make time to practice several heuristic approaches, thereby finding one best suited to their individual writing styles and to the demands of their topics, they often dismiss invention strategies as useless gimmicks. A broadly-based

aged Kiefer to approach Cynthia Selfe and suggest the possibility of a jointly edited newsletter devoted to computers and composition as a field. The newsletter, *Computers and Composition*, published its first issue in November 1983.

Professional Journals and Computers and Composition Studies

As scholarship in the field of computers and composition was emerging as a focus at national conferences, it was simultaneously becoming a presence in professional journals. In May of 1983, for example, *College Composition and Communication* published three pieces focusing on word-processing applications in English classrooms: Colette Daiute's "The Computer as Stylus and Audience," John Bean's "Computerized Word Processing as an Aid to Revision" and Richard Collier's "The Word Processor and Revision Strategies." This same issue included a Staffroom Interchange piece on choosing a microcomputer system, authored by Joan Hocking and Cheryl Visniesky, and Bruce Appleby's review of *The Word Processing Book* by Peter A. Williams. In October 1983, CCC published three Staffroom Interchange pieces (Arms, 1983; Breininger & Portch, 1983; Kotler & Anandam, 1983) and a review (Bean, 1983a) focusing on computers and composition. The February 1984 issue offered an extensive bibliography on computers and composition (Schwartz & Bridwell, 1984), both a definition of the field and a guide to those who wanted to work in it. This same issue included a piece on computer-based invention (Rodrigues & Rodrigues, 1984) and a Staffroom Interchange contribution on evaluating computer-assisted instruction packages according to criteria from process-based composition instruction (Petersen, Selfe, Wahlstrom, 1984).

In October of 1985, the journal printed five feature articles on word processing (Case, 1985; Catano, 1985; Harris, 1985; Rodrigues, 1985; Sudol, 1985). As interest in the new field grew, additional articles soon appeared in three issues of *College English* authored by individuals who were rapidly assuming stature as leaders in the new field—William Wresch (December 1983), and Helen Schwartz (March 1984). *College English* also published one of the first articles on using computers to "grade" essays (Marling, 1984) and the first article in computers and composition to take a decidedly theoretical turn (Ohmann, 1985). In 1983, *Research in the Teaching of English* demonstrated an empirical interest in the field by featuring Kathleen Kiefers and Charles Smith's field test of Bell Lab's WRITER'S WORKBENCH software, then being used by writing students for the stylistic analysis of compositions.

Smaller journals also contributed to the discussion about computers and composition studies during this period. *The Writing Instructor*, a journal edited by graduate students at the University of Southern California, published a special issue on computer-assisted instruction for the teaching of composition in the summer of 1983. That issue contained seven articles, among them contributions by Stephen Marcus on computer-assisted instruction, Michael Southwell on the use of grammar tutorial programs for teaching basic writing students, and Cynthia Selfe and Billie Wahlstrom on using CAI to support a process-based approach to the teaching of composition.

Another special issue published in 1983, *Focus: Teaching English Language Arts*, a joint publication of the Southeastern Ohio Council of Teachers of English and the Ohio University Department of English Language and Literature, offered 26 short contributions on computers—a number of them by composition-studies colleagues who were newly enthu-

set of computer invention programs, however, could provide students with a set of procedures from which they could select the one(s) most likely to help them develop their ideas best. (Rodrigues & Rodrigues, 1984, p. 79)

I think we are in the midst of two arguments about the implications of computer-assisted instruction for the teaching of composition: one is false, one true.

The false argument arises as a dispute between scientists and humanists. When we conceived the "theme" of this special issue on computers in writing instruction . . . we expected to receive any number of submissions that breathlessly extolled the great promise of this new technology. We knew the science-oriented writers would assume, as Carolyn Kreiter-Kurylo does in her article, that teachers "must no longer ask whether computer-based education is relevant, but how computers can best be used to assist educators." We thought, however, that we must make ourselves vulnerable to the view that a substantial number of educators (read humanists) were opposed to the introduction of computer technology into their composition classrooms. . . .

What we did get . . . was no such thing. Yes, many writers did remain cautious about the ultimate place of computer technology in the composing process, but no one came forth with a condemning attack.

As to the true argument, it is obvious . . . that the position of computers in the classroom is in its most suggestive, creative and least conclusive stages. (Adams, 1983, p. i)

Writing & Computers is the first book, for both educators and concerned parents, to explore the potential of computers as an aid to writing. Discussing the benefits and problems of computer use and demystifying the writing process, Colette Daiute covers a broad range of writing-related computer applications—word-processing programs, electronic mail systems, language exercises, and linguistic games.

siastic about the connections between computers and the teaching of writing. This issue included pieces by Stephen Tchudi on computer-assisted invention, by Dwight Stevenson on the benefits and difficulties associated with integrating computers into the life of an English Department, and by Richard Gebhardt tracing the learning curve of an English teacher and writer new to computer technology.

Publishers and Computers and Composition Studies

Just as convention planners and journal editors were recognizing the increased interest in computers and composition studies, so were publishers—both in the popular and academic arenas. In 1983, Basic Books published Papert's *Mindstorms: Children, Computers, and Powerful Ideas*, and in 1984, the University of North Carolina Press published Jay David Bolter's *Turing's Man: Western Culture in the Computer Age*. These books, although not specifically dealing with issues in computers and composition studies from the perspectives identified with teachers of English, set the stage for more focused volumes to follow.

In 1984, NCTE published *The Computer in Composition Instruction: A Writer's Tool*, edited by William Wresch. Kent Williamson (personal communication, October 15, 1994) has described this book as "a breakthrough for NCTE–the first book on computers and writing that was received enthusiastically by members at all levels" (Williamson, personal communication, 1994). The book was the fifth-most-popular NCTE composition title during 1983–1985, and, according to NCTE's publication records, demand for this title remained strong for the next 4 years. The book featured the work of early software designers working on computer-assisted instruction for English composition classrooms. The focus in this collection—influenced by the larger profession's interest in writers' cognitive processes—was clearly on computer programs that allowed teachers of English composition to undertake effective process-based writing instruction. Despite the advice of Joseph Weizenbaum at the 1983 NCTE convention, many of the articles described computer programs designed and created by English teachers to meet the special needs of their composition students: SEEN by Helen Schwartz (1986); WANDAH by Von Blum, Cohen, and Gerrard (1986); WORDSWORTH II by Selfe and Wahlstrom (1983b); and TOPOI by Burns (1977c). Apparent in these chapters and these software efforts was a general dissatisfaction with commercially available software packages. Wresch's volume was soon followed by another collection, *Writing Online: Using Computers in the Teaching of Writing*, published by Boynton/Cook in 1985 and coedited by Collins and Sommers. This book sold well—some 8,000 copies between 1985 and 1994—and is still a minor presence on the Heinneman list (Stillman, personal communication, November 4, 1994). The focus of this book, the authors noted, was squarely on the teaching of writing, rather than on either hardware or software:

We have kept our priorities straight in *Writing Online* by making it more a composing book than a computing one. Throughout, the emphasis is on what's good for writers and teaching writing how computers should be used in composition classrooms. Integrating computers with our best teaching is better than changing our teaching to accommodate computers. (p. iv)

Particularly noteworthy in this volume was the emphasis on word processing rather than on style checkers, tutorial packages, or com-

She provides the reader with all the necessary tools for a better understanding of writing and computers. (Advertisement for Daiute, 1985)

English instructors [have] had a variety of sources from which to gain initial information about the educational uses of computers. What they didn't have, however, was a source that described these computer projects in detail and discussed how they were actually conceived and developed. The special journal issues usually had only four or five articles, most of them brief. And convention sessions typically had to observe a 20-minute time limit.

This book was created to solve these problems. First, because it is a book, it can describe more programs than journals and pamphlets and, in fact, this book examines 13 major projects under way in the United States. More importantly, each project is thoroughly described, including information on program operation, program development, and classroom use. (Wresch, 1984, p. 1)

mercial CAI packages. Other books, such as Colette Daiute's (1985) *Writing and Computers*, continued in this tradition.

Professional Groups Focusing on Computers and Composition

The success of the Fifth C at the 1983 Conference on College Composition and Communication (CCCC) convinced many teachers and scholars working in computers and composition studies that professional organizations could, and would, accommodate the growth of interest in computers within their existing framework of committees, commissions, assemblies, and special interest groups already in place. It seemed, further, that these organizations would be open to adding to their structures new, technology-based groups.

The National Council of Teachers of English, for example, had already established, in 1980, its Committee on Instructional Technology. This committee was chaired in 1983 by Robert Caldwell, an early supporter of computer use in English classrooms. The Council also sponsored a Commission on Media, which was first formed in 1980. However, the limited membership of these groups would not accommodate the numbers of Council members who wanted to be affiliated with a professional community focused on technology. As a result, at the 1984 annual NCTE convention, a group calling itself the NCTE Assembly for Computers in English (ACE) held its first organizational meeting. In 1985, the group was granted full status as a Council Assembly and, at the annual convention, sponsored a panel on software copyright issues.

In line with its effort to involve a number of Council members in conversations about computers, ACE published a widely distributed newsletter and sponsored a popular software

INSTRUCTIONAL TECHNOLOGY COMMMITTEE

Functions: to establish guidelines for the development of computer materials and other complex courseware in the English language arts; to develop guidelines for classroom use of new instructional technologies; to define those content areas and process objectives within the English curriculum which best lend themselves to delivery through new instructional technologies to suggest new uses of technology and needed areas of research in the use of interactive media (e.g., the composing process using word processors; use of computers in teacher training and in adaptive testing); to encourage the use of videodisc technology as a potential medium for instruction, information storage, and quality entertainment; to consider ways of gathering and disseminating teacher-made and/or teacher-tested

exhibit at the national conventions of NCTE. ACE proved to be so popular during the first year of its existence that Leni Cook (1985), the membership Chair, was able to write the following passage in the second issue of the *ACE Newsletter*:

> With members in such far-away places as Australia, Hong Kong, the Virgin Islands, Alaska, and Hawaii, the Assembly for Computers in English numbers over 700 elementary, secondary, and college instructors. Also joining are school districts, secondary English departments, government agencies, and publishers . . . . Forty-eight states are represented, only Delaware and Nevada have no members. (p. 1)

At the NCTE annual conference, the ACE software exhibit featured demonstrations by the growing numbers of English teacher/software developers who talked to interested conference participants about their own software packages and about other commercial software packages available for the teaching of English composition.

In CCCC, a similar movement was already underway—at times, involving many of the same pioneers. In 1982, CCCC had established its Committee on Computers in Composition, chaired by Audrey Roth and frequently referred to as "The Seven Cs" (CCCC plus CCC). Members of this committee included Hugh Burns (Air Force Academy), Michael Southwell (CUNY), David Dobrin (MIT and Lexicom), and Elray Pederson (Brigham Young University). Individuals in this group continue to support a software sampler at NCTE and CCCC annual conventions, as well as the now-annual Computers and Writing Conference. The purpose of both the SIG ("Fifth C") and the Seven Cs was to support the growing numbers of CCCC mem-

games, lessons and ideas on how to use computers; to make English teachers at all levels aware of how new technologies can be used to develop skills in language arts. (*NCTE Directory*, 1986, p. 36)

Guidelines for Review and Evaluation of English Language Arts Software
Prepared by the Committee on Instructional Technology, NCTE (Robert Caldwell, Chair)
Step 1: Familiarize yourself with the guidelines
Step 2: Use the software yourself
Step 3: Let your students use the software
Step 4: Use the guidelines to evaluate the software
Step 5: Complete the overall evaluation and write summary comments. (NCTE Guidelines, p. 37)

Writing Process Software and the Individual Writer.
Hot on the heels of researchers' findings regarding writing as a process is a conviction on the part of a number of educators that the microcomputer is an exemplary teaching tool for the process of writing. These people are trying to design software that best utilizes the new theories of writing process, and a large number of programs have been developed, predominantly by college and university teachers for elementary and postsecondary writers. A look at some of these in light of current theories may be useful to teachers cau-

tiously optimistic about the emerging technology's ability to improve their teaching and their students' writing. (Anderson, 1985, p. 11)

Research in Wordprocessing Newsletter. Dr. Bradford A. Morgan and Dr. James M. Schwartz, Editors.

In this issue . . .
Volume 3, Number 9, December 1985

The English Department Microlab: An Endangered Species? by Thomas T. Barker

Modern Language Association's 1985 Conference

Software for Text Analysis and Writing Instruction by Ellen McDaniel

Bibliography Update by Bradford A. Morgan

Software Review: Microsoft Word (Macintosh) by William Kemp

bers who saw the issues surrounding the use of technology as the primary focus of their teaching and scholarship.

Newsletters Focusing on Computers and Composition

In 1983–1985, a number of newsletters appeared to support the increased level of activity in computers and composition studies. Among the most widely circulated of these publications were the *ACE Newsletter*, sponsored by the NCTE Assembly on Computers in English; the *Research on Word Processing Newsletter*, edited by Bradford A. Morgan (South Dakota School of Mines and Technology) and James M. Schwartz (Wright State University); *The English Microlab Registry*, edited by Thomas Barker (Texas Tech University); and *Computers and Composition*, edited by Kathleen Kiefer (Colorado State University) and Cynthia L. Selfe (Michigan Technological University).

The English Microlab Registry (*EMR*), a listing and description of academic microcomputer labs within the United States, was begun in 1984 at Texas Tech University by Thomas Barker in an effort to share information about the growing numbers of computer-supported writing facilities sponsored by English Departments or composition programs. The registry, which started as a listing of approximately 41 facilities, was published until 1987 and recorded the registration of 17 to 24 new facilities each year (Barker, 1986). Its list of subscribers grew proportionately, beginning with approximately 30 in 1984 and swelling to 130 members in 1987 (Barker, personal communication, July 13, 1993). Each record in the registry contained the name of the school, a contact person, a list of the hardware and software that the lab used, and a 50-word statement describing the facility's pedagogical purpose. The records were updated twice a year on Barker's home computer, a 64 k DEC Rainbow.

Barker also regularly published various compilations of the data within the *English Microlab Registry*. A 1985 piece entitled "Microlab Facts," for example, noted 65 microlabs registered: 44% in universities, 23% in colleges, 16% in State Universities, 9% in community colleges, and 8% in Institutions/High Schools. At the time, the most common computers in these facilities, according to the *Registry*, were, in descending order, Apple IIs, IBMs, DEC personal computers, and the Macintosh. The most common uses of these machines, "compiled from a word use frequency analysis of Purpose statements in the *EMR*" were, again in descending order, "writing," "composition," "instruction," "business" and "technical," "research," "revising" and "editing," "remedial" and "basic," "reading," and "communications" (p. 2).

The *Research in Word Processing Newsletter* was first published in May of 1983 and continued as a monthly publication—except during summer months—until May of 1989. By 1989, the newsletter, funded by subscription, circulated to approximately 1200 subscribers, some of them—given the continuing interest in computers in the corporate sector—outside of academic institutions. The *Newsletter* provided readers with comprehensive bibliographic listings of new scholarship related to word processing, announcements of conferences, calls for papers, and short articles on topics involving the use of computer-supported writing software. The December 1985 issue of the newsletter, for example, contained an article on English microcomputer labs authored by Thomas T. Barker (1985), a description of the computer-related sessions at the Modern Language Association's 1985 conference by the editors, an article on software for text analysis for writing instruction by Ellen McDaniel (1985), a bibliographic update by Morgan

Manuscript Submissions Welcome [for the *Research in Word Processing Newsletter*] The Newsletter welcomes article submissions that pertain to word processing, text analysis, and research applications in professional writing situations. Also, hardware and software reviews are accepted. . . . Manuscripts either may be submitted as hard copy or on 5 and a quarter inch diskettes using WordStar, WordStar 2000, or standard ASCII code. If submitting disks, please make sure they are formatted either MS-DOS, PC-DOS, or a popular CP/M format (Kaypro, Zenith, etc.) ("Manuscript Submissions", 1985, p. 21)

(1985), and a software review of Microsoft WORD for the Macintosh by William Kemp (1985).

A third publication, *Computers and Composition*, eventually proved the most successful in terms both of longevity and continuing intellectual connections with the larger field of composition studies. *Computers and Composition* published its first issue in November 1983. The founding editors, Kathleen E. Kiefer (Colorado State University) and Cynthia L. Selfe (Michigan Technological University), outlined the journal's origins, focus, and function in the "Dear Readers" section of the first issue:

In March of 1983, we met at THE FIFTH C: COMPUTERS, a special interest group held at the Conference on College Composition and Communication in Detroit. There, we found over two hundred people, representing institutions of all sizes and teaching at all grade levels, interested in the very questions we had been wrestling with at Michigan Technological University and Colorado State University:

- Can the computer be put to work in helping us teach composition? If so, how and in what areas? What can computers do better than composition teachers? At what are they less adept?
- How can we integrate computers into our existing writing programs? How and where do they fit best? Do they fit at all?
- Can we use computers to solve some of the perennial problems associated with composition programs staffing, financial support, faculty workloads, class size, training for graduate students and paraprofessionals?
- How do our writing students react to computers? How do less skilled writ-

ers differ from skilled writers as they use computers for writing? How does using a computer change the composing process? How do our faculty react to computers? How do computers affect the writing or the teaching process?

- What software is now available that would help us teach composition skills or guide students through the composing process? If none is appropriate, how do we write our own?

- Will the spread of word processing encourage faculty outside of English departments to help their students become better writers? What will the role of the composition teacher be in helping colleagues teach writing?

- What steps are businesses and the computer industry taking that will affect our teaching of writing in the next ten to twenty years? Will research in artificial intelligence change the way we think about communicating with each other and with computers? (Selfe & Kiefer, 1983, p. 1)

Between 1983 and 1985, *Computers and Composition* published eight issues, each containing short pieces on topics of interest; announcements (e.g., about books, conferences, calls for papers, grant opportunities, software); and descriptions of software. The newsletter was short, averaging 3 pages per article and 13 pages per issue in the first year. In August of 1985 the newsletter became a small journal, moved its site of production from Colorado State University to Michigan Technological University, added a small editorial board of knowledgeable colleagues, and established a volunteer staff of technical communication students at Michigan Technological University.

With this printing, *Computers and Composition* marks the beginning of its third year. The first issue, published in November of 1983, was less than ten pages in length. The content came from friends and colleagues: Bill Wresch volunteered a review of his forthcoming book; Hugh Burns wrote a column on artificial intelligence research and its bearing on composition studies; Deborah Holdstein, Helen Schwartz, and Bill Marling, among others, provided reviews of software.

In contrast, the issue you are now reading contains over eighty pages of articles, theoretical perspectives, descriptions of research, tutorials, book reviews, and conference notices. We like to think that *Computers and Composition* is expanding for a reason, that it answers the needs of English teachers around the country and the world who want to use computers in their writing classrooms and programs. ("Letter from the Editors," 1985).

By 1985 *Computers and Composition* was publishing more substantial articles. The editorial statement of the journal in the first issue of the third volume spoke about "articles" rather than "announcements," as it had earlier, and it encouraged members of the newly formed community to begin thinking of themselves as authors as well as reader; as specialists who had something important to say about computer use in English classrooms:

> The message is simple. Read *Computers and Composition*. Pass it around. Encourage others to subscribe. And *write* about computers. Some ideas for submissions? We are seeking descriptions of computer-aided writing and reading instruction; articles about software development; surveys of computer use in writing programs at various levels; explorations of the various legal, moral, and ethical issues connected with using computers in writing programs; reports of on-going research programs and studies; discussions of how computers affect the form and content of written discourse, the processes by which such discourse is produced, and the impact of discourse on an audience. (Kiefer & Selfe, 1985, p. 5)

The growing sense of professionalism suggested by this editorial statement was not just the editors' construct. Teachers, scholars, and researchers began to submit articles to the journal in increasing numbers. Among the individuals who published in the first three volumes of *Computers and Composition* were those who would form the backbone of the emerging computers and composition community: Hugh Burns, Thomas Barker, James Collins, Robert Connors, Pamela Farrell, Lisa Gerrard, Craig Hansen, Deborah Holdstein, Glenda Hull, Jack Jobst, David Kaufer, Ellen

McDaniel, Charles Moran, Christine Neuwirth, Webster Newbold, Elray Pederson, Kenneth Risdon, Donald Ross, Helen Schwartz, John Smith, Catherine Smith, Elizabeth Sommers, John Theismeyer, Billie Wahlstrom, and William Wresch.

A Conference for Computers and Compositionists

The field's first professional conference took place in October 1982 at the University of Minnesota, under the guidance and leadership of Lillian Bridwell (now Bridwell-Bowles) and Donald Ross and under the aegis of the Fund for the Improvement of Postsecondary Education (FIPSE). In 1982, Bridwell and Ross had received a major 3-year grant from FIPSE for their project, which was titled "Integrating Computer Technology to Serve the Needs of Students and Teachers in Writing Courses." As Bridwell-Bowles now remembers the award, "It was for $250,000, which was enormous by English Department standards. We were in a way kind of shocked that we were that fortunate, but I think it was the beginning of something really important." (Interview, this chapter, page 114) The project focused on upper-division writing courses and was designed to provide juniors and seniors some access to computer-supported writing environments before they graduated from the university (Ross, personal communication, July 15, 1993). In October of 1982, as a part of this grant, Bridwell and Ross invited a small group of people who had been writing about computers and composition to the University of Minnesota to talk about technology use in English classrooms. Among the participants were Charles Smith and Kathleen Kiefer, who were working with WRITER'S WORK-BENCH at Colorado State University.

During April 12–14, 1984, still under the

Computers and Writing— Research and Applications April 12–April 14, 1984

The Effects of Computers on People and Texts

Computers and the Composing Process

Designing Software

Training and Assistance for Faculty

A Model for a Training Program

Writing and Computers: The St. Olaf Experience

Technical Considerations (Hardware, etc.)

Technical Writing and Advanced Composition

Basic Writers and Special Students

The Needs of Expert Writers

Text Analysis

Tools for Writing Teachers

A Comprehensive Computer-Aided Program in Writing

Political Impact on the Curriculum

Interactive Programs

Text Feedback: Uses and Abuses (Conference Program, 1984)

Alfred Bork, the keynote speaker, most assuredly was one of the stars of the conference. Attending each session and always on hand for advice and talk, he fit right into a group that had English educators at its heart. When asked how he did such a good job of assessing his role at the conference, he replied, "Everybody who comes to a conference has been to previous ones and has an idea as to what to do at a conference that is most productive. I also talked to Lilly and we discussed the possible roles I might have. In addition, I wanted to learn more about writing. I always learn at conferences: this one was no exception." (Hawisher, 1984a, p. 24)

UCLA Conference on Computers and Writing: New Directions in Teaching and Research
May 4–5, 1985

1. Pedagogy
Course and Lesson Design
"Algorithms and Arguments: A Programming Metaphor for Composition"—Diane Balestri

FIPSE grant, Bridwell and Ross put together a full-scale conference—160 participants—this time with a name: "Computers and Writing: Research and Applications." This conference offered sessions on word processing, computer-supported text analysis, various computer-assisted composition instructional packages, the effects of computer-assisted composition on student writers, text-to-voice systems, computer-based tutorial systems, and design issues in computer-assisted composition software. WANDAH, VOLKSWRITER, and RECOMP were among the software packages discussed in the sessions, and the panelists included names that continue to be familiar in computers and composition studies (Lisa Gerrard, Cynthia Selfe, Geoffrey Sirc, John Theismeyer, Christine Neuwirth) and those who have now carried their work into new fields (Ruth Berggren, Richard Collier, Ellen McDaniel, Sarah Liggett). In postconference interviews, participants seemed fully satisfied with the event. A few representative responses: "For only $45 we're getting a lot!" "I've seen first-hand programs I haven't seen before, and I've gotten wonderful ideas for research." "We should consider nonconcurrent sessions. The quality of papers is as good or higher than CCCC's in March." (Hawisher, 1984a, pp. 23–24). The participants noted what would become a steady tension at Computers and Writing conferences: the division between experts and novices. Some participants suggested somehow separating the two groups, advice that the community has chosen not to follow.

The conference proved popular among the growing number of computers and composition specialists: It gave teachers, scholars, and researchers a professional forum focused on their increasingly specialized interests in technology, and it gave them a place where they could continue to create a professional community. Bridwell-Bowles (Interview, this chapter) remembers these conferences as "your dream of what an academic conference ought to be like. People came and presented things, but more importantly there was a lot of free time, a lot of time for lunches and dinners and talking about where we all were. We didn't all agree and yet it was such a new community that factions hadn't developed. We could argue with each other very directly, and I think that all of us benefitted from that, from having to answer questions that people asked us very directly and in a personal way. I remember those years as a time of great hope and optimism." (p. 117)

After the first two meetings, the conference grew into a gathering that has become an established annual conference. In 1985, the Computers and Writing conference was held in Los Angeles, CA and coordinated by Lisa Gerrard, an author of WANDAH. That gathering attracted almost 300 participants and offered 74 different papers or presentations. The conference programs from 1983–1985 suggest that the field's work was proceeding in two distinct strands, the first highly practical and focused on classroom use of computers, and the second research-based and focused on the profession's curiosity about how computers might improve or change students' writing. Of the many papers presented at these conferences, only a few focused on theoretical issues associated with technology.

"Nibbles and Little Bytes: Some Techniques for Computer-Aided Instruction in Composition"—M. Kelly Lynch

2. Beyond Word Processing Extending the Audience
"Text-to-Voice Synthesis: What We Can Learn by Asking Writers to Proofread with Their Ears"—Elaine O. Lees
"Computer-Extended Audiences for Student-Writers"—Don Payne
"Computer Conferencing and Writing Style"—Michael Spitzer

3. Research & Theory
Computers and Writing at the College Level: Case Histories
"Expectations and Surprises: Three Years of Using the Computer in Writing Classes"—Valarie M. Arms
"Paperless Writing: A Preliminary Report"—Edward M. Jennings
"Computers and Writing at Yale: Implications for Pedagogy"—Stuart Moulthrop.)
("Directory," 1985)

TEACHERS SEARCHING FOR SOFTWARE

The rapid-fire growth of the microcomputer industry fueled a corresponding growth in the software industry, from 300 companies in 1970 to over 2,000 companies in 1983. Software sales skyrocketed from about $750 million in 1977 to

$475 *billion* in 1983. For writing teachers, the most important result of this growth was the development of increasingly powerful and user-friendly word-processing programs. Even during their first experiments with text editors on mainframes, writing teachers had believed that computers would be useful for the easy input and revising of text. To take advantage of this power, teachers had been willing to learn the complicated commands governing simple text editing. Many first-generation, microcomputer-based, word-processing packages were as difficult to use as the mainframe-based text editors had been—as users of the early WORDSTAR and APPLEWRITER and even BANK STREET WRITER remember. These early microcomputer-based, word-processing programs, however, laid the groundwork for the powerful programs of the next decade, as their developers created menu-driven interfaces, automated formatting commands, and auxiliary software programs like SPELLSTAR, WORDSTAR's optional error-correction program. Until the advent of these programs, it was not unusual for schools to develop their own word processing software, as William Marling and his associates did at Case Western Reserve University with their program WRITER.

After 1983, the variety and sophistication of available word processing programs like WORDSTAR, MACWRITE, VOLKSWRITER, BANK STREET WRITER, WORD JUGGLER, PC WRITE, PFS WRITE, and others brought an end to home-grown word-processing packages (although the Daedalus Group's 1989 QUICKSTART was a later exception). The introduction in 1983 of Apple's MACWRITE and Microsoft's WORD on the new Macintosh computer represented a radical transformation of word processing software. Indeed, most improvements in word-processing packages since 1983 have been refinements of the innovations introduced by these programs. In an essay on how one might choose among word-processing packages, Spitzer (1985) wrote:

Product Name:
WORDSTAR
Company: **MicroPro International**

General
Original Release Date: June 1979
Number of Revisions: Not available
Current Users: Not available
Minimum System: CP/M system or Apple (64K)
Documentation: 200-page tech manual, training guide, on-screen help.
Retail Price: CP/M–$495, Apple–$375. . .

When selecting a word processor, in other words, you will have to make tradeoffs. The easier the program is to learn and use, generally speaking, the less it will be able to do. . . .We hope that the MacWrite design strategy will be adopted by other software writers, so that the tradeoff noted here may soon become obsolete. (p. 31)

Spitzer's wish has been granted.

Although commercial software producers made great strides in the development of word-processing programs, they offered little else to writing teachers. Aside from word-processing packages, the two primary types of programs developed by commercial interests were spell checkers and style checkers: programs like WEBSTER, MACPROOF, and GRAMMATIK I. Spell checkers quickly became a staple of the computer writing classroom, first as optional add-on programs and then as integrated parts of more powerful word processing software. Style checkers received a mixed reception from the community of writing teachers. On the one hand, grammar checkers seemed to promise relief from the drudgery of marking students' mechanical errors; on the other hand, they simply did not do the job very well (Dobrin, 1990; Ross, 1985), and they renewed a focus on the student writer's finished product in the midst of the process paradigm shift. In the period from 1983–1985, these programs were still new and largely untested, but they became popular in business settings and found their way into many computer-based writing classrooms as well.

Teachers Writing Software

Whereas commercial software companies focused on word-processing, spell-checking, and style-checking programs, computer-using writ-

Summary
WORDSTAR is the most widely used word processing program in use today. Because it formats print according to the screen layout, and uses standard typing input, touch typists find it easy to learn and use. It also features a "horizontal scroll" for wide documents, and permits entire columns of text to be moved. ("WORD-STAR," 1983, p. 140)

Lifetree Software
Creators of
VOLKSWRITER
the most popular word processor for the IBM personal computer
introduces

- Horizontal scrolling
- True proportional spacing
- Extraordinary simplicity
- Live tutorials
- Textmerge
- dynamic pagination and proofing. ("VOLKS-WRITER," 1984, p. 38)

WORD PROOF:
Another program that stretches your word processing dollar is *Word Proof*, brought to you by none other than Big Blue. *Word Proof* gives you a spelling checker, thesaurus, mini-word processor and anagram solver—all for only $60. If IBM doesn't realize that *Word Proof* is worth a lot more than the cost of a DOS update, let's not tell them.

Overall Design. Although word proof includes a rudimentary word processor suitable for memos and letters, its real talent is as a spelling checker and online thesaurus. Faithful to its blue-blooded lineage, *Word Proof* works best with word programs and editors that sport the IBM logo: teach text, easywriter, the personal and professional editors, and Edlin. With a little prodding, however, it can handle DOS and near-DOS files created by other word processors. Wordstar users, of course, are out of luck. ("WORD PROOF," 1984, p. 58)

Two years ago, researchers at New York City's progressive Bank Street College of Education decided to find out how word processors might affect the writing of their students. They had a few hundred gradeschool children and a dozen microcomputers. But they lacked one necessary ingredient: a suitable writing program. Recalls President Richard Ruopp: "We tested the available word processors and found we couldn't use any of them." Result: the BANK STREET WRITER, a $69.95 computer program ($95 for the three-disc school package) that will turn an Apple, Atari or, by summer, Commodore computer into an uncomplicated word processor. Designed by Software Consultant Franklin Smith and a team of experts from Bank

ing teachers continued to design and develop their own software. Indeed, during the period of 1983–1985, developing software was a principal task of the community, as teacher/software developers began to find each other and share their software through newsletters and conferences. One of the first books published in the new field, William Wresch's (1984a) *The Computer in Composition Instruction*, was really dedicated to faculty software design. Further, many of the first published articles in the field were by composition specialists who were also creating software. Wresch's book includes Dawn and Ray Rodrigues discussing their creative problem-solving programs, Helen Schwartz writing about SEEN, Kate Kiefer and Charles Smith describing their adaptation of WRITER'S WORKBENCH, Michael Cohen and Richard Lanham describing HOMER, and Ruth Von Blum and Michael Cohen writing about WANDAH. The programs these teacher/programmers were creating addressed a wide variety of contemporary concerns in the field of composition studies generally: prewriting and invention, rhetorical modes, peer feedback, stylistics, organization, freewriting, writing about specific subject matter, revision, and grammar instruction.

Although many of those programs were innovative and went on to win awards for design and value, WANDAH (Writing-Aid AND Author's Helper) deserves special mention. Written in 1984 and supported by funding from the Exxon Foundation, the program was one of the most ambitious and comprehensive of the field's early attempts to provide the student writer with a full writing environment. Designed around its own then-powerful word processing program, WANDAH included prewriting aids (freewriting, nutshelling, planning, invisible writing) and review and revision aids (style, mechanics, organization). It also included its own style-, spell-, usage-, and punctuation checkers. Its "Commenting" function allowed others to insert comments directly into the writer's text. As the first attempt to create an integrated writing environment, WANDAH anticipated later programs like Wresch's WRITER'S HELPER II and the Daedalus Group's DAEDALUS INSTRUCTIONAL SYSTEM.

WANDAH's history post-1984, when it was purchased by Harcourt Brace Jovanovich, reflects the failure of the textbook industry's first foray into the software market. HBJ negotiated with UCLA's contract and grants administration an extravagant advance of $100,000 plus royalties for WANDAH, but the developers were largely ignored in the negotiations. As a result, HBJ succeeded in negotiating an elaborate copy-protection scheme that from their perspective protected their substantial investment, but that proved fatal to the product's success. HBJ also commissioned an accompanying text, geared to a college audience, and then proceeded to market HBJ WRITER to the secondary school market.

The development of WANDAH is a cautionary tale—one that was often repeated as teachers developed writing software. For many involved in software development during this period, the only hope of recompense for their time and hard work lay in the commercial sale of their programs. Their home departments, usually English, did not value their work (Bourque, 1983; LeBlanc, 1993). However, whereas English departments were generally indifferent—even hostile publishers were not. For the publishing industry, writing software was a marketable product. Faculty software developers and textbook publishers, therefore, sought one another out. Unfortunately for both parties, this was new and uncharted territory, and inexperience led to disaster. From the perspective of the faculty involved, publishers did not understand the complexity of software development and wanted to buy software for much less than its worth. Further, publishers adopted the practice of giving software away free with the

Street and Intentional Educations Inc., a software development firm in Watertown, Mass., the disc is not only changing the way some children hone their writing skills, it is also proving a commercial success. It is now the fourth fastest-selling word-processing program on the market, competing against such powerful best-sellers as WORDSTAR ($495), SCREENWRITER II ($129.95) and LETTER PERFECT ($149.95). (*Time*, 1983, p. 61)

What Writer's Workbench can do for teacher and student is simple: its programs raise questions about spelling, mechanics, diction, organization, and style—questions inexperienced writers often cannot ask themselves. As a result, the Workbench programs permit students to do more thorough correction and more purposeful revision before handing their papers in for marking. The Workbench programs do not, to be sure, directly address problems of logical and rhetorical effectiveness, but given their power to help students write more correctly and with greater sensitivity to diction and style, we think you'll find Bell's Writer's Workbench a valuable aid to your composition course. (Smith, C.R., Gingrich, P., & Kiefer, K., 1982, p. 2)

WANDAH

This is the latest . . . set of specifications for the word processor. As you will see, I have tried to make the system as simple and easy to use as possible, and I have tried to take into account as many criticisms as possible. Please note especially the revisions in the keyboard layout ... as well as changes in the copy routine. Before coding anything from the flowcharts, be sure you have the latest updates. (unpublished WANDAH document, Cohen, 1982, p. 1)

purchase of handbooks or textbooks, which made it seem to everyone involved that software had no value. Because of this practice, publishers did not record profits on the software they marketed, and they were therefore reluctant to fund revisions of the software. From the publishers' perspective, the market base for this new technology was still very small (microscopic compared to that for a best selling handbook, for example). From the program developer's perspective, of course, the market was—as it soon would become—practically infinite.

A much less gloomy story is told by software developers who turned to CONDUIT, the well-established, not-for-profit publisher of educational software. William Wresch, unhappy with the textbook publishers interested in his WRITER'S HELPER, turned to CONDUIT in 1983. Originally formed with NSF funding in 1972, CONDUIT understood the demands that classroom use placed on software. It therefore undertook a complete overhaul of Wresch's original code. It reduced the program's size, made it portable to more systems, increased its speed, and allowed for more user customization. The program had its commercial release in 1985 and has since gone on to become the best-selling, non-word-processing CAC software program in the field. Wresch and Helen Schwartz, whose program SEEN came to be handled by CONDUIT as well, believe that CONDUIT's treatment of teacher-developed software has been a model for others to follow.

The software development that we have so far described lay easily within both the current-traditional and writing-process paradigms then dominant. Whereas style- and spell-checker programs would help the writer achieve a carefully finished product, prewriting, writing, and revising software would help the writer compose. Two software projects undertaken at this time, however, lie outside the current paradigms: Michael Joyce and Jay Bolter's development of STORYSPACE, and Trent Batson's work with ENFI.

Bolter and Joyce began talking about a hypertext program for writing—although, as Joyce has said, they hadn't yet used the term HYPERTEXT—in 1982. In 1983–1984, when Joyce took his sabbatical from Jackson Community College and traveled to Yale, the two began serious work on the program. By the end of the 1985–1986 academic year, Joyce had a beta version of the program that he was using with students in a writing laboratory. Before the program could be brought to market, it would take years of debugging, but the project marks the beginnings of hypertext in composition instruction.

Just as Bolter and Joyce's work with hypertext would challenge the conventional view of text as linear, Batson's work with ENFI would challenge the view of the writer as autonomous author working on a stand-alone microcomputer. If the first vision of the computer as a writing tool was a "Copernican moment," as Bernhardt has suggested, so was the first view of networked computers as a site for the social construction of knowledge. Batson (email communication, July 18, 1994) described his experience as an epiphany:

> When LANs became available with microcomputers in the early 1980's, we in the Gallaudet English Department realized this technology might work where others had been too slow, too awkward, or too undistributed. Se we set about finding software to enable some kind of group interactive ability. In the spring of 1984, we discovered that the 1-Net LAN software included an optional group-chat function, called the "CB Utility." We asked a local vendor . . . to set up a network with that optional feature included.

ENFILOG

ENFI stands for "English Natural Form Instruction," a method of instruction developed at Gallaudet College. Using this method, all instruction is carried on through a local-area network of microcomputers, making it possible to use written English as the language of instruction with students who need extra help with reading or writing English.

Why do you receive this LOG? First, because, as we blunder along with this project we're always discovering new twists, new tricks, and old truths and we want you to know about them; second, because we want you to know we are alive and well and living in your future; and, third, because we hope that many of you will eventually find the means and the opportunity to try computer-mediated teaching. (Batson, 1986, p. 1)

It was wonderful. In the fall of 1984, we experimented with the new network and, in January 1985, received the first class of first-year students enrolled in a required composition course.

The experiment worked better than we had expected. The first group of students improved on our standardized tests more than any previous students on record.

Remember Alice in Wonderland and the mushrooms that made her too big or too small? It's a great introduction to being the first kid on your English Department block who is computer literate. You know how pitifully meager your knowledge of computers is; yet your colleagues consider you an expert. Moreover, you start attracting antisentiments from all sides, as a lightening rod attracts lightening.

The people who control the computers are friendly as long as you aren't in a position to shift allocations to your side of campus. And the folks back home start associating you with unemployment, killer robots, irremediable computer errors on their charge accounts, and the death of the humanities. (Schwartz, 1985b, p. 9)

In 1985, Batson established ENFILOG, a monthly newsletter. In addition, between 1985 and 1988 he gave, in his estimation, "about 45 conference presentations in those years, averaging two/month in the busy conference time, always about one aspect of ENFI or another" (email communication, August 9, 1994). Batson's insights would later find their way into the Daedalus workshop in Austin, TX, and emerge as INTERCHANGE—but that is a story that must wait for its proper chapter.

CHALLENGES, 1983–1985

Those working in the fledgling field of computers and composition studies faced a number of challenges during this period. As Helen Schwartz (1985b) noted, writing teachers had to learn to do many things they never had to do before. They had to learn to write grant proposals for the equipment itself, to find space for the computers in writing labs and classrooms, to design classroom spaces, and to write purchase orders for things they had never bought before: computer tables, office chairs, and static-resistant carpeting. They had, in effect, to become infrastructure mechanics, doing for themselves what other units, with a long history of labs and equipment, could delegate to departmental staff.

Learning About Computers

The greatest challenge, however, faced by writing teachers was their need to learn about computers themselves: to learn enough to be able to make intelligent choices in the purchase and establishment of writing classrooms and lab, and to be able to make intelligent choices about how these computers would be used in writing classrooms. There were dozens of manufacturers out there—Kaypro, Timex, Osborne, Wang, Digital, Apple, IBM—with different systems and software designed to run on those systems. Apples ran Apple DOS, IBM had launched Microsoft by adopting MS-DOS, Osborne and Kaypro used the CP/M operating system, and Digital used its own, proprietary operating system. In this marketplace that was just developing, what should a teacher, or a school, buy?

Journal articles often addressed this question, arguing for the particular virtues of a particular system. Yet this advice, because of the speed of technological change, was not good for long. Typical of the then-current advice was a long excerpt from *Word Choice*, by Roger C. Schlobin, published in the February 1984 issue of *Computers and Composition*. The subtitle of the *Word Choice* excerpt neatly described its purpose: "General Guidelines for Purchasing a Microcomputer with a Word-Processing Program." In this piece, Schlobin advised his readers to "Buy a computer that uses the 'CP/M' (Control Program for Microprocessors) operating system" (p. 7). Schlobin supported his advice with the observation that "the CP/M operating system is as close to an industry standard as there is." He made his argument despite the fact "that the CP/M approach eliminates the use of some popular computers (for example, the IBM-PC, Apple, TRS-80)." Digging himself deeper into what is, in hindsight, a pretty deep hole, Schlobin wrote, "For the most

Exhibitors:
A demonstration and exhibit area will be part of the conference activities where exhibits will emphasize and include examples of computer use in instruction. . . . In addition to providing for exhibits by vendors, non-commercial exhibits will be encouraged by universities or other developers of computer-based learning materials demonstrating the use of particular software. The demonstration area serves as a showcase for currently available materials . . . which illustrate exactly how computing can be used in instruction.

Exhibitors at the Conference will include the following:

Association for Computing Machinery
IEEE Computer Society
Computer Science Press
C&C Software
Mountain Computer
Apple Computer
Krell Software
Texas Instruments
Compress
Conduit
HRM Software
Acorn Computer Corporation
Science Research Associates
Computer Science Press
Acron Computers
National Computer Systems
Commodore Business Machines
Touch Technologies, Inc.
Scan-Tron Corporation

Telos Software Products
Micro Computer Distributors
Cicro Computer Corporation.
(NECC Program, 1984, p. 15)

The purchase of a micro-computer and a word-processing program or system will always be marked by personal needs, price, and local availability (although dealers can order programs they don't normally stock, and the programs frequently can be ordered directly from manufacturers). It's also difficult to go too far wrong with most selections. (Schlobin, 1984, p. 7)

part, these are mediocre computers anyway and are more the products of advertising than outstanding quality or ease of use" (p. 8). Schlobin went on to recommend that his readers choose a 8" disk drive and avoid the 5.25 format. In retrospect, this advice was desperately wrong, but its wrongness didn't really matter. Hardware was evolving so quickly that whatever hardware and software was purchased was obsolete in 3 or 4 years' time. Teachers needed good advice, and, because no one, given the rate of change, could predict the future of this new technology, this good advice was not to be found.

Even if teachers could somehow choose the right hardware, there was still the software to learn—both the operating system and the application. Teachers could avoid some of this additional work by settling for closed systems such as the dedicated word-processing office machines developed by such firms as Wang, Linear, or Digital; however, the dedicated word processors seemed not to be real computers. They seemed to belong to the world of dictation and the typing pool, not the world of composing original documents. And in the air, and in the field's new journals and newsletters, there was a great deal of talk and writing about computers and what they were capable of doing for writers—talk that Peter Stillman characterized in 1985 as "the hyper-excitations micro-computers have generated" (Collins & Sommers, 1985, p. iii). This excitement, whether "hyper" or not, had produced books in the popular press about writing on computers (e.g., McWilliams, 1982; Zinsser, 1983). Federal grant-giving organizations such as FIPSE and Title III were eager to fund projects that involved computers, and computer makers were glad to trade hardware for the time teachers might spend developing useful software on their machines. It seemed, therefore, that one really ought to know about computers.

Compared to text-editing programs available on mainframes, microcomputer-based word-processing programs such as APPLEWRITER I and BANK STREET WRITER, which seem tremendously limited by today's standards, were easy and powerful. However, they were not easy or friendly. To write on a microcomputer, one had to learn the word-processing software and the microcomputer's operating system, which had been designed by people who did not think, talk, or write in ways that teachers were accustomed to. For example, with a new Apple II+, it was wise to purchase *The Apple II User's Guide* (1981). In the third chapter of this helpful text, you discovered that you really needed to program the Apple if you were to do much with it at all. Thus a good second purchase was *Programming the Apple* (1981), which led one through the world of Applesoft and Integer Basic. Even when it was up and running, the Apple II+ equipped with APPLEWRITER I produced only upper-case script and did not line-wrap. To achieve a display of upper- and lower-case type, you had to buy a "Paymar Chip" and plug this in yourself. To accomplish moves like "saving" one had to type in a string of keystrokes that began with ESC ESC CTRL Q—not the most intuitive of routines. The IBM PC wasn't any easier to use: To make it go, one had to learn Microsoft DOS and a word-processing program that was remarkably difficult to learn—WORDSTAR. In his "Writing Teacher's Guide to Computerese," James Collins (1985) included a section of his journal in which he records his struggles with WORDSTAR commands. What is remarkable about this piece is that Collins is not complaining about the absolutely unintuitive command set; he's encouraging his readers to invest the time and mental energy required to learn this extremely difficult software.

Another WORDSTAR user was Stillman, who in 1985 described his learning process in his journal:

A Brief Introduction to WORDSTAR, by Doug Hesse: "WORDSTAR" is a computer program that allows you to process words, that is, to type them into the computer, move them around, add more words, take some words out, change the margins and spacing of your text, save your text to work on at some later time, and print your final result. (Hesse, 1986, P. 3)

More Advanced: Block Commands:

Moving Blocks. A block is simply a chunk of words. It can be of any length, from sentences to paragraphs to pages. WordStar will allow you easily to move blocks around your file. There are three steps for moving a block.

a) Mark the block. (This is a process of telling the computer where the block begins and ends.) Put the cursor at the start of the block and hit F7. . . . Then move the cursor to the end of the block and hit F8, "End of block." You'll note that everything you've marked will turn a lighter shade of green than the surrounding text.

b) Move the cursor to where you want the block to appear. Then hit ^KV. This will insert the block at that point. You'll notice that the block will still be marked (a lighter shade of green).

c) Hide the block. Basically, you're telling the computer that you no longer want it to pay attention to this chunk of words as a block. Hit ^KH. The chunk will return to its normal color. At this point you may need to reform paragraphs or adjust spacing. (Hesse, 1986, p. 7)

3/1 [on machine]: Am halfway through the User's Guide. Some of it makes clearest sense. Some of it doesn't. Furthermore, this 124-page book 'is not a substitute for the manuals that accompany software and the operating system.' (What's an 'operating system'?).

3/2 Already I'm tired of being pushed around. The *WordStar* manual tells me I must poke my way through a list of coded commands. Last key I punched resulted in a chaos of words, lines zinging around; scared me crapless. Just now recovered the righthand side of the page, which vanished five minutes ago. (p. 25)

3/6: Moved a block of type tonight, after reading how in Naiman's good little book [*WordStar*, Sybex, Inc. Berkeley, CA]. It was without a doubt the most exciting experience to date on this machine. Must've been 20 lines or so. KB at the beginning, KK at the end of the block, then a KV at its new destination (p. 26)

Further, with the IBM and most mainframes, one had to learn that when one failed to do something as the program required, there were only three routes one could take: Abort, Retry, or Fail. The language of computers was not our language; it was, as Selfe and Wahlstrom argued in 1985, the language of the military. In an entertaining and illuminating "protocol of our own initial session with a microcomputer" (p. 65), they chronicled their discomfort with the discourse they needed to enter:

The computer is a harsh teacher. It tells us we have made a FATAL ERROR and that our program is TERMINATED. Apparently, its programmers had chosen from a liberal bank of synonymous terms. Other computers in the room are ABORTing, KILLing, or BOMBing programs when they catch the scent of human error. Next to us, a pale young woman moans as her program CRASHES. She didn't have time to fire a single shot. (pp. 66–67)

Computers and Humanists

Why was this learning so hard? For two reasons: Writing teachers were busy, and writing teachers were, generally, humanists. To expand on the first, writing teachers were full-time employees charged with their own work, teaching writing to hundreds of students each year and doing research and scholarship in their own fields. Learning about computers was something that these professionals had to do in addition to what was already expected of them. In this, writing teachers were not unique; bankers and airlines and any organization that needed to process large amounts of data rapidly also had to incorporate computers into their operation or be left by the wayside. This learning process has been, for all concerned, expensive. Indeed, as Loveman (1990), Morrison and Berndt (1991), and Morrison (1991) have argued, computers initially, and perhaps still, consume a tremendous amount of time and energy and may, as a result, make institutions and individuals less, rather than more, productive.

Teachers were also humanists, and to humanists computers often seemed strange, foreign, alien. Bankers used them, physicists used them. But English teachers? As Nold had written in 1975, English teachers had to overcome their ignorance and fear of computers if they were to make appropriate use of computer technology. Most writing teachers fit into the category of "romantics" as defined by Robert Pirsig (1974) in *Zen and the Art of Motorcycle Maintenance*—humanists and therefore Luddites. Technology was often cast as the devil.

Clichés and stereotypes such as "beatnik" or "hippie" have been invented for the antitechnologists, the antisystem people, and will continue to be. But one does not convert individuals into mass people with the simple coining of a mass term. John and Sylvia are not mass people and neither are most of the others going their way. It is against being a mass person that they seem to be revolting. And they feel that technology has got a lot to do with the forces that are trying to turn them into mass people and they don't like it. (Pirsig, 1974, p. 17)

Indeed, many English teachers still see television as the enemy, threatening an age of illiteracy. In the early 1980s, for those in English Departments that emphasized the teaching of literature science and technology were permitted to exist only on the edges of our discipline: in science fiction, a genre seldom given serious scholarly attention, or technical writing, taught but not often valued except in institutions with technical or engineering emphases. The industrial landscape was beautiful for English teachers, as it had been for Wordsworth, only in the early morning, when it was asleep. As Hansen and Wilcox put it in 1984, "Between the green console and whirring disk drives of a microcomputer and your average humanities-educated writing teacher, the gap yawns perilously wide" (p. 3).

Because writing teachers were self-identified as technophobes, they found it hard to convince their colleagues that they really wanted and needed equipment, space, time, and the money required to provide computer support for their work. They did not often have data to manipulate, as did their colleagues in the social sciences, nor did they have numbers to crunch, as did their colleagues in mathematics and the sciences. They only had words, and, from the perspective of those who directed computer centers, words did not require computers. Many writing teachers, experimenting with campus mainframes, were told that they should keep word processing off these computers because it would interfere with the serious work of colleagues in the "hard" sciences and engineering. In high schools, computers were used first by mathematics, science, and business teachers; when English teachers began to understand their value to English, they had to beg and wrangle for time on computers that were already scheduled in other subjects.

Poetry and Word Processing: One or the Other, but Not Both

I won't be using a word processor tomorrow, or a hundred years from now. I'll still be listening for the voice of the absolute. Edmund Wilson, a writer of prose, said verse was a dying technique. But, in fact, it is not a technique, and we who write it are not dying as long as we believe in a reality that speaks in no uncertain terms. (Simpson, 1988, p. 12)

Computers and Writing Classrooms

Once teachers had learned about computers, they had to consider how to utilize the new machines in the service of pedagogical goals. Here the difference between the situation of the teacher and that of employees in the business world could not have been greater. In the world of business in the 1980s, hierarchy was a given. Someone ordered the equipment and set up the software; the employee used it as someone else had imagined she would. However, teachers run their own classes in many ways. They speak of "my" students and "my" classroom and often have a great deal of autonomy, which is a good thing. This autonomy carries with it, however, a price.

During the early 1980s, teachers were frequently asked to take the lead in deciding what equipment they wanted to ask for and how they want to use that equipment—not always an easy task for indivduals educated in humanist traditions. The depth of this challenge was suggested by the number of publications during this period which argued, explicitly or implicitly, for a particular hardware platform, software package, or pedagogical application. Often, to make technological decisions more accessible to teachers of writing, authors aligned computer-use with the three stages of the writing process: prewriting, writing/revising, and editing (e.g., Wresch, 1984a).

Underlying such representations, however, were fundamental disagreements about pedagogy: Should computers be used to free writers from some of the mechanical and trivial aspects of writing and help them compose? Or should technology be used for drill and practice, or to discover error—to help students write more correctly? This argument mirrored the debate that continued in the field of composition studies between "current traditional"

Microcomputers present a special challenge for English teachers and teacher educators. . . . We have . . . not one goal to accomplish but three: (1) to keep abreast of current developments in hardware and software applicable to writing; (2) to be informed of new issues in composition theory and pedagogy that might lend themselves to computer writing; (3) to design and implement innovative strategies for introducing teachers to trends in both composition and computers. (Hawisher, 1990, pp. 71–72)

Software Announcement by John Langan:
People teaching grammar and basic composition skills may be interested in a computer disk that has just been published to accompany *English Skills, Third Edition* (McGraw-Hill, 1985). There are 36 activities on the disk, providing students with supplementary work on topic sentences, unity, support, coherence, and a number of sentence skills. A unique feature of these activities is that explanations are provided for both correct and incorrect answers. The explanations reinforce learning when a student gives a correct answer, and they provide guidance when a student gives an incorrect answer. A disk is available for the Apple II series (Apple II, II+, IIe, and IIc); there is also a disk for the IBM PC. (Langan, 1985, p. 78)

Ellen McDaniel and Guy Bailey, both Assistant Professors in the English Department at Texas A&M University, have received two grants to support their research in human–computer communication. A grant from the Texas Engineering Experiment Station gives them 50% salary support, and an equipment grant from Texas Instruments has supplied them with computers to do their research. Drs. McDaniel and Bailey each have a TI Professional computer with 256K RAM, 10M Winchester hard disk, 3-plane color graphics, speech synthesis board, and a variety of software including word processing, spreadsheet calculation, database management, several languages, and speech recognition/command kit. (McDaniel & Bailey, 1984, p. 10–11)

Our initial assessment is that, despite some limitations, WRITERS WORKBENCH may indeed be a useful analytical tool available to teachers who are aware of both its merits and limitations. As a means of

and "new rhetorical" approaches to the teaching of writing. In the time from 1983–1985, articles in the new journal *Computers and Composition* were predominantly concerned with announcing, reviewing, or describing new software applications for the teaching of writing. In the four issues that constituted Volume 1 (November 1983 to August 1984), "Software" was the most frequent topic category, accounting for 8 of the 18 articles in the volume. "Writing Instruction" was a poor second, accounting for 2 of the 18.

However, implicit in every piece on software was a set of pedagogical goals and strategies. Articles on software were, really, articles on the teaching of writing in disguise. For instance, Elizabeth Sommers (1983), in the lead article in the second issue of *Computers and Composition*, argued for her own use of word-processing software in her classroom; a system, she argued, based on "sound pedagogical theory." Her sound theory was derived from Roger Garrison's work, which she had come to know through James Collins at SUNY-Buffalo. In this piece, Sommers described a classroom modeled on the Garrison/Murray newsroom workshop, where writers worked and the teacher was a roving, in-process editor. At this point in her career, for Sommers the computer was a writer's tool, a fancy typewriter to be brought into an existing format, the writing-process classroom.

In the same issue, teachers described uses for word-processing software that derived from the current-traditional, proscenium classroom. Harris and Cheek (1983), for example, described their situation at Purdue, where they adapted the Bell Labs software, WRITER'S WORKBENCH, to their writing program. They used the program as an add-on, a new feature of an existing course, one that gave students information about the surface features of their prose, one that, the authors saw, "allowed us to add into an already overloaded teaching schedule some writing assistance that we could not have offered otherwise" (p. 4). Jobst (1983), in an article titled "Computer-Assisted Grading of Essays and Reports," illustrated how a teacher, using word-processing software, could store and retrieve canned comments, attaching them to students' writing at appropriate places. "To produce the sense of a more personal response," Jobst wrote, "the lengthier commentaries either include the student's name (placed at different locations within the paragraphs) or a specific identification of the student's error" (p. 5).

In subsequent issues of *Computers and Composition* there would be published pieces that showed how the computer could be used for such activities related to writing as sentence combining exercises (McCann, 1984), prewriting heuristics (Parris, 1985), grading and marking papers (Lucking, 1985), and skills tutorials (Falk, 1985). As these articles show, the field was facing squarely the challenge of appropriate use, and individuals were all facing it in different ways, ways determined by their own histories and situation.

Keeping Current

The field's most difficult challenge during this period was the task of keeping current: to keep up with both the technology, which was rapidly changing, and the applications that colleagues in the field were creating. Working against this need to stay current was our professional isolation—one might even, in some cases, say *marginalization*. Sharon Rambo remembered that she purchased her first computer in 1983, "A Kaypro, of course—to aid in teaching writing, but not with any idea of stu-

analyzing surface-level problems in a student's text, it assists the teacher with some tedious editing and proofreading tasks, thereby giving the teacher more time to consider larger rhetorical questions of organization, structure, clarity, and so on. (Harris & Cheek, 1984, p. 3)

There are some clear benefits to using a sentence-combining computer program with free modifiers. As with other sentence-combining exercises, students are building a repertoire of ways to subordinate ideas. Moreover, students' syntactic abilities develop in a structured fashion. By using free modifiers, students will explore methods of combining ideas that they never thought of using before (e.g., appositives, absolute phrases). Finally, the use of free modifiers allows the computer programmer to write a sentence–combining exercise in which the user is constructing mature sentences. (McCann, 1984, pp. 1–2)

Lillian Bridwell and Donald Ross
University of Minnesota
Program in Composition and Communication
209 Lind Hall
207 Church Street, S.E.
Minneapolis, MN 55455

We are currently in our second year of a federally funded project designed to study the ways we can incorporate computers into our writing curriculum. We have surveyed a wide range of computer tools for writing and writing instruction, and offer our findings to you in two ways: 1) order our articles from us; they are listed with costs for mailing on the publications list we brought along; if you didn't get one, write to us to request it; 2) order our annotated bibliography of research on computers and writing from Greenwood Press, 88 Post Road, P.O. Box 5007, Westport, CT 06881—forthcoming in May. We would also be interested in any material you have that we haven't reviewed. (Bridwell & Ross, 1984, p. 10)

dents having them. I was a pioneer in my Big-10 writing department, with few people to talk with—and those few were almost exclusively male" (C&W, 1994). Many computer-using teachers read trade publications, but these were at the time either hacker-oriented or business-oriented and did not generally provide the information that teachers of writing needed. *Computers and Composition* began to give teachers what they needed. Irvin Peckham remembered the early issues of *Computers and Composition* in these terms: "I wish I could explain how important those early issues ... were for me. It was like being in a desert and hearing a voice from the sky" (C&W, 1994). Along with *Computers and Composition*, electronic conferences like PARTI emerged at this time and provided new forums for intellectual exchange. These early conferences would lead to Megabyte University, the annual Computers and Writing conferences, and a growing and increasingly connected professional community.

COLLEAGUES REMEMBER: INTERVIEW WITH LILLIAN BRIDWELL-BOWLES AND HELEN SCHWARTZ

In the following lightly edited transcripts of taped interviews, Lillian Bridwell-Bowles and Helen Schwartz remember their struggles in bringing computers to the attention of those working in composition studies. Like Hugh Burns and Lisa Gerrard, Lillian Bridwell-Bowles at the University of Minnesota, Minneapolis, and Helen Schwartz, then of Oakland College, were pioneers, forging connections among compositionists and those scholars and teachers doing research in instructional computing.

Lillian Bridwell-Bowles:
Remembering the Research

I first started using computers for my research work as a graduate student in about '78 or so, and I was doing a statistical analysis of various things related to the composing process. I was counting revisions and analyzing whether or not they made any difference in writing quality, so I had lots of data and I used cards. I literally hand-punched my own data cards and dropped them into a card reader and wrote programs to analyze the results. At that time, no one I knew was using computers for writing.

My dissertation was typed and retyped and retyped and I still remember vividly when my advisor came back from Europe. I had already had my defense and he sat in his office and made little corrections and brought them out to me page by page and I corrected them with "white-out." I remember thinking, "There's got to be a better way!"

Well, my dissertation was the last major thing that I wrote on a typewriter. I finished my degree and went to the University of Nebraska and there I was still working on revision. Then I analyzed things pretty much by hand because I didn't have the amount of data that I had for my dissertation research. So I used calculators and so on and didn't use computers at all for writing until I moved to the University of Minnesota and it was there in about '82 that we got a lab.

We happened to be housed in the building that was called "Old Main Engineering"; they renamed it Lind Hall years before I arrived, but the engineers have never given up the turf and periodically some tipsy engineering students will go out and spray paint "Old Main Engineering" over that. So we were surrounded by engineers. Don Ross, my colleague at Minnesota, was always hanging out with engineers and somehow he got connections with them and also I think this was related to his work at that time in Stylistics Analysis. He was analyzing literature using computer programs that he had designed. One was called "Eyeball." So he had access to the Teraks in some way, and I don't remember exactly how, but we got into the lab with the Terak computers in them. We also had terminals that gave us access to the mainframe.

At that time, everyone around us was using the Vax mainframe and so I started using a word-processing program on the mainframe called SCRIBE. Then I'd go to the Terak and do various little clean-up operations, but SCRIBE was mainly a program for people writing computer programs to write their documentation on it; it was not composing-process friendly. It was more than just a line editor—it had block moves and this, that and the other that you could do but it was very creaky.

At any rate, Don and I were both kind of fooling around with trying to write on the things and so I decided that there was an obvious connection between the research that I had been doing, looking at how people write, and this new technology. At first I thought just as a way to gather data, just a kind of an extension of my earlier work on revision, and so I wrote a grant in '81, right after I arrived at the University of Minnesota, to try to use the computers to gather the data about composing, particularly how people revised when they wrote. I could see it at it would be easy enough to capture keystrokes and so I did get that grant, an early University of Minnesota Graduate School grant. It was awarded in 1982. They gave me $5,000 to hire a programmer to try to figure out whether it would be possible to capture keystrokes and look at composing with an absolute record rather than just a paper trail. So that was how I got involved from the very beginning. It was a natural extension of my research into composing.

Then, as that evolved, Don and I began talking about using computers for students in classes. At that time in '81, nobody was doing much. We heard that various places were getting labs and so on, but it was really at the beginning of the whole movement to use computers. So it was then that we wrote the FIPSE grant. We got that award in '82. The grant went from 1982–1986 and it was for $250,000, which was enormous by English department standards. We were in a way kind of shocked that we were that fortunate, but I think that it was being at the beginning of something really important.

We proposed to do two things in our FIPSE grant. We first said that we would continue studying composing processes and that was my side of it, and then that we would develop curriculum and software for the teaching of writing and that was more Don's side of it. We collaborated on everything, but we did have that little separation of responsibilities. So I then continued the research that I had begun, trying to capture keystrokes and succeeded. I wrote two different programs, one to capture and then one to replay keystrokes and analyzed lots of different writers using computers for writing.

We got a whole bunch of Xerox 820s and those things were the first generation of microcomputers that were really practical, to fit on the desk and do anything, and they had huge computer disks that were eight inches, $8'' \times 8''$. They were floppy, really, that's where the term "Floppy disk" originated. They were really big and flimsy.

We used to have all these elaborate rituals for how to protect them and we would have fits with Don Ross because he would drink coffee constantly and we were so afraid that he would spill coffee on them. But he never did; he was very careful.

Don and I are polar opposites on life and we have entirely different ways of working. We were extremely complementary. I always thought that Don should work in a think tank somewhere because he has 5,000 ideas on any given topic and different ways of looking at things. I won't guess at the percentage that are hare brained, but then there those in the midst that are just brilliant. I always prided myself on being able to sort those out. Because we came from such different backgrounds and had mutual respect for each other, we were able to complement each other and support each other. The grad students who worked with us might have an entirely different view. Some might recall sitting around a table in the computer lab in '83 and '84, listening to Don and Lilly arguing with each other. I guess they were half glad that they were there and were half wishing they could be somewhere else. But I think a number of those students who went on to get their PhDs with us that thought that kind of debate was crucial in their graduate educations, to see that kind of intellectual debate going on and to be a part of it.

The Xerox 820s were mostly then for research, and we then wrote more grants and got IBM. So we put together a lab in about '83–'84, that academic year and put IBMs and some of the old Xerox 820s in the large lab, and it was at that point that we began to do classes there and we had to bring students in and introduce them to word processing and it was magic. You didn't have to do a whole lot more to motivate students other than to teach them about a 30-minute intro.

Students were quite eager for this technology. There was the sense that they were on the cutting edge too and we had lots of engineering students who were, of course, the first to get in line because they were so familiar with the computers in their classes. They had been introduced to them in the engineering classes, but I can't say that it was limited to the engineering students. We had all kinds of students who could immediately see why they would want to do this once you could show them how they could change a whole word or a phrase or move a sentence around.

I think that we had some sort of foresight that I'm very happy with, with the FIPSE project. We had the two points, one was research and the second was that the use of computers for writing was going to be inevitable. We just staked all of our energies on that. We really thought that that was going to be the case before it was self-evident to a lot of people that it would be the case. So we said that computers might be helpful in terms of improving students writing and they might not be, but whatever the case we felt that we simply had to provide instruction in the environment that we could foresee, so it was basically planning for the future in terms of the environment more than it was an argument that suddenly computers would magically solve all our problems.

I'm very proud of that. There are some things in your career that you go back and you say "Wow, I wish I could rewrite that or change that or erase it!", but I do not feel that way at all about that earliest work that we did. I thought that we were right at the time and I still think that I could stand behind everything that we wrote in that early proposal and it has turned out to be true I think that, as we can see now with hindsight, computers were not a panacea, but they were certainly something that none of us would give up!

Our first computers and writing conference here was in October of '82, at the Student Union here at the University of Minnesota and it was cheap, but good! We had a second conference in 1984. People came from all over the country and we were quite surprised. People were talking about all kinds of things. I remember there was a woman from IBM named Linda Misek-Falcoff and she was persuaded that the process of writing computer programs and documenting them was a direct analogy for the composing process. She had gone around within IBM and done all kinds of little workshops, because obviously they were ahead of us in terms of actually trying to use those old line editors and whatever they had to write with. So she had seen a direct parallel and that's an idea that has cropped up a number of times. In fact, the most recent incarnation of it is in a writing across the curriculum grant proposal that I just saw from a computer scientist who was arguing essentially the same thing. I don't happen to see that analogy as directly as they do, but that was typical.

Then there was a lot of work with the TJ Watson Research Center and that was Bell Labs' connection on how long it would take to write or correct things like the average business letter with or without computers. So they were doing time on task, efficiency studies of whether or not they should give these things to secretaries in a writing environment, in offices in particular. There were a lot of people who thought that this was really going to be the answer to students writing problems; they thought that it would eliminate the tedious part of writing and composing, especially error correction. So almost immediately there were all kinds of routines that were developed to go find this or that. The Bell Labs programs were immediately popular because people were looking for a way to shortcut to the paper grading problem and a lot of people did buy into that and think that this was going to end response to student writing problems. I remember Kate Kiefer and Charles Smith really went to work for Bell Labs and implemented their program, WRITER'S WORKBENCH, in a major way at Colorado State.

Lots of people were writing programs. Bill Wresch was typical of someone who cared about the teaching of writing and wanted to write programs to help speed up the process. His programs were very typical. People wrote little routines to go after things they particularly cared about and that the high-end style programs weren't finding. Helen Schwartz thought of SEEN very early on and she could see how to write programs to help students. Hugh Burns was a graduate student at Texas and had studied Burke and Aristotle and he had done a simple little program that queried students to get ideas for writing. All kinds of things that we had been doing for 2500 years were suddenly being seen in an electronic environment.

There was a lot of optimism that these things would make the mechanistic parts of teaching writing very simple and that would leave time for us to do more important things with students. The conferences were just your dream of what an academic conference ought to be like. People came and presented things, but more importantly there was a lot of free time, a lot of time for lunches and dinners and talking about where we all were. We didn't all agree and yet it was such a new community that factions hadn't developed. We could argue with each other very directly and I think that all of us benefited from that, from having to answer questions that people asked us very directly and in a personal way. I remember those years as a time of great hope and optimism.

Lillian Bridwell-Bowles is an Associate Professor of English at the University of Minnesota and Director of the Center for Interdisciplinary Studies in Writing.

Helen Schwartz: The Emergence of a Field

My work with computers began back in 1979 and there was lots of talk about computers and literacy requirements, but I didn't see much happening for literacy. I wanted to find out what that computer literacy was all about. I also happened to be dating someone who was a computer programmer at Ford Motor Company and I thought it would bring us together which of course it didn't. But it did get me started with computers.

By 1983 I had been working with readability programs, which were very popular in those early years. I learned to program. I had very little background in research methodology. Geez, I had little background in writing, except that I had been dragooned by the English Department at Oakland University to teach writing. But I did realize that my primary responsibility was to the humanity of my students and I wasn't going to use them as guinea pigs, especially when I realized there were real limits of the programs I was using in my business writing class, for example.

In 1980 I had a sabbatical and spent a half year at the University of Pittsburgh working with Tom Dwyer. He was in the Math and Computer Science Department and I would do reading in the field of composition and then I would do programming, in BASIC. I worked with Dwyer's idea of "Solo/Net/Works" and what he meant by that was people working alone but also working with others. I adapted that into SEEN. Of course, I was in Pittsburgh and if you did any reading you soon came across the name of Linda Flower and Dick Hayes, and they were there at Carnegie Mellon. So I walked down the hill and met them and soon started combining the theory with the solo/net/works approach and that became SEEN. SEEN was a place where you worked alone with a tutorial, but then you posted it on built-in bulletin boards before bulletin boards were even thought about.

The other important thing that happened before that 1983–1985 period was that I wrote "Monsters and Mentors" in 1982, which was published in *College English.* And I think that was only the third thing that had ever been published in the field. Before that it was Burns and Culp and Ellen Nold. So "Monsters and Mentors" led to a lot of consulting work for me and I also got a book contract to write *Interactive Writing* with Holt. Also in that year, Lillian Bridwell-Bowles (then Lillian Bridwell) had the first computers and writing conference and it was by invitation.

So by 1983, I felt that I was really engaged in the field. I got to have a lot more impact because people were making available places to meet and share experience. I think it was about that time that *Computers and Composition* was begun by Cindy Selfe and Kate Kiefer. I was on the editorial board. Before that, there were few places where people could "meet" in print. One of them was Computers in the Humanities and at that time they were very heavy into computational linguistics and stylistic analysis; the sort of thing that appealed to people who understood linguistics, stylistics, and computers, which was about seven people at the time. The other place was the *Journal of Computer-Based Instruction,* which was again very technical. They tended to have mostly training articles, things where you had to understand research literature to understand and find meaningful the articles.

What Kate and Cindy did, and then Cindy continued with Gail Hawisher, was create a place where people could meet in print and tell their experiences and talk about their successes and failures and talk about them in terms that people could understand. Because, although they publish research things, that was a time when much of the discussion in C&C was anecdotal. People could understand that and it provided a necessary sort of uncritical enthusiasm. The early stuff is often accused of being evangelical and it was, but in a sense that was very important for the time.

The other spaces that were coming into being came from professional organizations that were developing committees to work on technology. Audrey Ross, for example, started the computer committee of the 4-Cs and Hugh Burns was an early person on that, and Cindy and Dawn Rodrigues. I joined that in 1984 and there was also an NCTE Instructional Technology Committee that was going. MLA had a committee and I joined that in 1983. Those committees were important because they legitimized the field and that meant that it could get on the conference programs. The point is that those committees could start and influence the program and create access to further dissemination of knowledge.

Also important at that time in opening up spaces for people to meet was the start of the Fifth-C, which Michael Spitzer started at the New York Institute of Technology, and that was the first bulletin board where teachers of writing could meet and talk. Megabyte University later grew out of that. Bill Wresch's book was another important "place," even if as a book it was a one-way place. But it started getting knowledge out there. I mean I published the early research on SEEN in that book and a regular publisher wouldn't have published that. That book, which I still think is a very good one, said "Here are some important things that are happening."

In a sense, it was the emergence of a field and the end of the isolation in which many C&W people were working in before that. You could finally start making contact with other people and people would call you. Yet it was a time when the field was still small. When there was a conference, everyone who was doing anything in the field would be there and you could talk to them and ask them anything. We could share what we knew. People were very accessible. Things got easier and you didn't have to work as hard to be in a conversation. I remember the first time I got on the Fifth-C and how exciting it was to talk to people who shared your interest. It was like having a department full of people who were interested in the same things you were interested in. They were just like you and they thought computers were wonderful! For most of us, our departments, if you were *lucky,* as I was at Oakland University, would say "Oh, Helen's off on one of her crazys again and either she'll come to her senses or she'll come tell us about it." Lots of people were very marginalized in their departments. Oakland was really very supportive of my work at the time and I was really lucky.

In 1984, I entered into a commercial contract with CONDUIT to market SEEN. Before that I had been selling out of my house, sort of like a garage sale, making it and selling it out of the backyard. But I couldn't support it the way I wanted to. There were things that needed to be done better and then the chance to port it to the IBM, and I could see that the program was very sophisticated. Going to CONDUIT, I didn't really do it for the money (I think the only person who has made any money doing software was Bill Wresch). I went because they were going to reprogram it, they were going to support it, and I felt that they were a good company. Any money I got out of it would be a gift from heaven.

I have to say that it was important that I was tenured while I was doing that work. Anybody who was doing that work and was untenured at that time was in extreme danger. Many of them just left the Humanities. It's not unusual to find a director of computing who has a PhD in Medieval French. Because if they got into computers before they had tenure, they had to leave the field to get credit for their work. I had tenure and a supportive department. Those were fat times. Times were not real hard, and it was possible to get a sabbatical that wasn't to do a traditional book. Obviously things are changing now. So I was allowed to go off and explore computers and without a lot to go on. I don't know if I could do that today.

But so much came out of that. Because of "Monsters and Mentors," Holt approached me and I did what was the first freshman text to integrate word processing into writing instruction; that was *Interactive Writing* and that came out in 1984. Interestingly, the editor who signed the book left Holt and I was then assigned to the stenography group—you know business writing and how to teach stenography and that sort of thing—and I had to yell and scream. "I didn't belong there!" I really owed it to Charlyce Jones Owen, because she really fought to get the book back on the English list. It would have died and never reached anyone.

Here's the funny thing. They sent out a LOT of examination copies and the book then went on to sell poorly. I'm thinking I'm going to make thousands of dollars everyone talks about McCrimmons and of course I didn't. Holt paid for the dissemination of a useful book that they got very little return on. But I'm proud of that book, lots of people told me that it was an important book for them. It was good because I had wonderful reviewers. Hugh Burns was a reviewer and Valerie Arms, Lillian Bridwell, Ruth Gardner, Stephen Marcus, and Ruth von Blum. I mean, wow! They pushed me in certain ways and really improved the book. It was truly a collaborative project. It was really fun.

In 1984, Lilly and I did our first bibliography in 4-Cs. It was annotated and that was important because lots of people in this period were turning onto computers and wanted information. So when they said, "Tell me all you know." I could say, "Well, here's this bibliography." The thing that was so exciting about that time was that everything was taking off and almost everything you did was valuable and made a contribution. Lillian Bridwell had an outstanding record and she chose to go in a new direction and she brought all of her prestige and her knowledge to that. I had a very mediocre career before this and it was only after I started getting into computers that I started publishing, because then I had something I wanted to talk about. But the "communicators" made that possible: Cindy and Kate, Mike Spitzer, Bill Wresch. They provided the opportunity not only for the evangelical discussion, but also for the more critical examination that started in this period. It was the beginning of a movement. You were out there alone and suddenly you look around and all these people are saying, "Here we come too!"

Helen Schwartz is a Professor of English at Indiana University–Purdue University at Indianapolis.

3

1986–1988:
Emerging Research, Theory, and Professionalism

Learning is no longer a separate activity that occurs either before one enters the workplace or in remote classroom settings . . . . Learning is not something that requires time out from being engaged in productive activity; learning is the heart of productive activity.

—Shoshana Zuboff, *In the Age of the Smart Machine*, 1988, p. 395

THE CONTEXT: THE FIELD OF COMPOSITION STUDIES, 1986–1988

In the period 1986–1988, the field of composition studies had matured sufficiently so that it might reflect on itself and begin to attempt to understand what it was and what it was in the process of becoming. In 1987, James Berlin

Literary Theory and Composition, by Joseph J. Comprone

Studying Rhetoric and Literature, by Jim. W. Corder

Writing across the Curriculum, by James L. Kinneavy

Computers and Composition, by Hugh Burns

In general, one's axiological commitment and process theory will affect but need not determine large-scale classroom decisions. Certainly rhetorical axiology can be enacted in a collaborative pedagogy, but it *can* also be enacted through a models pedagogy, studying textual features of discourse accepted by a community, or through a presentational pedagogy carefully done. (Fulkerson, 1990, p. 419)

It is important to remember that the image the ecological model projects is again an ideal one. In reality, these systems are often resistant to change and not easily accessible. Whenever ideas are seen as commodities they are not shared; whenever individual and group purposes cannot be negotiated someone is shut out; differences in status, or power, or intimacy curtail interpersonal interactions; cultural institutions and attitudes discourage writing as often as they encourage it; textual forms are just as easily used as barriers to discourse as they are used as means of discourse. A further value of the ecological model is that it can be used to diagnose

published *Rhetoric and Reality*, bringing his history of the field to the year 1985 and providing composition studies with its first modern history. This same year saw the publication of Steven North's *The Making of Knowledge in Composition: Portrait of an Emerging Field*, Erika Lindeman's *Longman Bibliography of Composition and Rhetoric*, and Gary Tate's updated 1976 collection of bibliographical essays in the field. Memberships in NCTE, stable during 1983–1985, surged 26% in 1986–19888, while CCCC increased 5% (K. Williamson, personal communication, August 19, 1994). Attendance at the CCCC annual convention reached new highs every year (J. Joseph, personal communication, April 22, 1988).

This steady maturation was accompanied by a significant change: During the period from 1986–1988, the field of Composition Studies moved further in the directions earlier suggested and modeled by Lee Odell, Shirley Brice Heath, and Patricia Bizzell, gradually shifting its governing gaze from the isolated writer to the writer in context. Whereas most early visions of the writer at work foregrounded the writer and the text, in the mid-1980s the field began to foreground aspects of the writer's context: her situation in a complex called "culture." Richard Fulkerson (1990) has called this move from writer to context a newly-dominant "rhetorical axiology" (p. 414) that could serve to distinguish composition theory of the early 1980s from that of the late 1980s. It is tempting to connect this move with other, similar moves in other fields. In the life sciences, for example, ecology, or the study of the relations among living organisms, was becoming a defined subject of study. The individual organism was still in the picture, but less as an individual than as a part of a complex system of relations. In geology/geophysics, it was becoming natural to think about relations between convection currents in the earth's mantle as they might transfer heat to the oceans and thereby to the atmosphere, bringing earth, sea, and air together into a single system. In the teaching of literature, the profession began to feel the end of the "reader response" movement, as the transaction between reader and text became widely understood as itself located in a larger context, something that one might call *culture*. Works like Steve Mailloux's (1982) *Interpretive Conventions*, subtitled *The Reader in the Study of American Fiction*, led outward from the reader to cultural studies of the sort exemplified by Jane Tompkins's (1985) *Sensational Designs*, subtitled *The Cultural Work of American Fiction.*

We have no evidence to suggest cause and effect among the parallel changes that occurred in composition studies, the physical sciences, and literature. It is not at all clear that literature was following composition studies, or the reverse, or that developments in the physical sciences precipitated developments in our field. As historians, we must be content here to see the similar moves in disparate disciplines as most probably co-causal, each arising from the same complex of causes. We do believe, however, that advances in computer technology were a factor in this pan-disciplinary move from the study of the autonomous individual to the study of the individual in a complex called *culture* or *situation*. Certainly increased computing power facilitated the analysis and mathematical description of systems; calculations that before would not have been undertaken at all now became feasible. Systems could now be modeled and studied, and perhaps because they could be studied, they were. Further, the increasing use of electronic mail in business and in some areas of the academy began to be noticed in the field of composition studies. A few scholars began to use BITNET regularly, and, as they did so, their image of themselves as networked may have

and analyze such situations, and it encourages us to direct our corrective energies away from the characteristics of the individual writer and toward imbalances in social systems that prevent good writing. (Cooper, 1986, p. 373)

A defining technology develops links, metaphorical or otherwise, with a culture's science, philosophy, or literature; it is always available to serve as a metaphor, example, model, or symbol. A defining technology resembles a magnifying glass, which collects and focuses seemingly disparate ideas in a culture into one bright, sometimes piercing ray. Technology does not call forth major cultural changes by itself, but it does bring ideas into a new focus by explaining or exemplifying them in new ways to larger audiences. (Bolter, 1984, p. 11)

The subject for this prewriting dialogue was the rape and beating of a white woman in Central Park by a group of black youths, an event which had been widely reported by the news media:

Kremers: Antony—do you think the attack on the jogger was racially motivated?
Antony: I believe it was a racial attack. Those immoral beings were taken out their frustrations on that innocent woman.
Kremers: So you tie race and economics together,

Antony? They attacked her because she was a symbol of rich, white people?
Antony: Yes, they attacked her to make a statement, to feel power over someone. (Kremers, 1990, p. 37)

made them more receptive to the idea that knowledge was socially constructed. Further, unlike oral class discussion, online discussions generated archives and transcripts that could easily be printed out and studied. Teachers and scholars who had access to networked, computer-equipped classrooms could now read these transcripts and see their students in the process of constructing knowledge.

RESEARCH AND PROFESSIONAL PUBLICATION: COMPOSITION STUDIES

No matter what the academic field or other arenas of invention might be, we would be wise to examine not only the fact or result of a discovery, which has typically been credited to one person, but also the evolution of discovery in a social context. We will more fully comprehend the process of creating new ideas when we think of it as an act that is social even as it is individual, with the other always implicated in the invention of the I. (LeFevre, 1987, pp. 139–40)

In writing groups, people can become part of a community that takes aesthetic pleasure in a fine sentence, distinguishes between a convincing argument and one that fails to convince, and delights in clear and effective presentation of an idea. The product of writing groups, the polished prose, has importance, but even more significant is the process of the

In the closing pages of *Rhetoric and Reality*, James Berlin (1987a) noted that the schools of rhetoric he had defined—the objective, subjective, transactional, and epistemic—had become less well-defined as one moved toward 1985. The cause of this blurring of categories was, Berlin argued, "the tendency of certain rhetorics within the subjective and transactional categories to move in the direction of the epistemic, regarding rhetoric as principally a method of discovering and even creating knowledge, frequently within socially defined discourse communities" (p. 183).

A review of major publications in composition studies during this period confirms Berlin's judgment. LeFevre's (1987) *Invention as a Social Act* was an extended and powerful argument that we see authorship as a social process. In the same Southern Illinois Press series, Anne Gere's (1987) *Writing Groups* centered on the argument that "writing groups highlight the social dimension of writing." Writing groups, argued Gere, "provide tangible evidence that writing involves human interaction as well as solitary transcription" (p. 3). Nancie Atwell's *In The Middle*, also published in 1987, argued that the writing teacher's objective should be to create for her students a "literate environment," one that included writing groups, reading groups, and a great deal of social interaction focused on reading and writing. Rounding out this selection of major books published in 1987, Judith Langer and Arthur Applebee, in *How Writing Shapes Thinking*, took a contextualized view of the process of curricular change in a school setting.

Journal publication during this period also supports Berlin's and Fulkerson's taxonomies. "The Ecology of Writing" by Marilyn Cooper, appearing in *College English* in April 1986, argued that the revolution that had foregrounded the writing process had "dwindle[d] to dogma" (p. 364). A flat-out attack on the cognitivists' foregrounding of the apparently autonomous writer, Cooper drew on research in sociolinguistics and critical theory to propose "an ecological model of writing, whose fundamental tenet is that writing is an activity through which a person is continually engaged with a variety of socially constituted systems" (p. 367). Writing in the October 1986 issue of *College English*, James Reither laid out what he hoped would be a new definition of the writing process. Citing the earlier work of Gage, Bizzell, Odell, and Larson, Reither argued that "writing is not merely a process that occurs within contexts. That is, writing and what writers do during writing cannot be artificially separated from the social-rhetorical situations in which writing gets done . . . . Writing is not to context what a fried egg is to its pan. Writing is, in fact, one of those processes which, in its use, creates and constitutes its own contexts" (p. 622). Flynn, writing in the December 1988 issue of *College Composition and Communication*, brought the consideration of gender as part of the context of writing into the mainstream of composition studies. Drawing on the work of Chodorow, Belenky et al., and Gilligan, she found common ground between composi-

group, the means by which individuals experience and eventually become part of a literate community. (Gere, 1987, p. 123)

Feminist research and theory emphasize that males and females differ in their developmental processes and in their interactions with others. They emphasize, as well, that these differences are a result of an imbalance in the social order, of the dominance of men over women. They argue that men have chronicled our historical narratives and defined our fields of inquiry. Women's perspectives have been suppressed, silenced, marginalized, written out of what counts as authoritative knowledge. Difference is erased in a desire to universalize. Men become the standard against which women are judged. (Flynn, 1988, p. 425)

During the last several years, many colleges have supported interdisciplinary writing workshops to introduce colleagues across the curriculum to the *whys* and *hows* of teaching writing. Such workshops typically last from a few days to a few weeks and involve twenty to thirty faculty at a time. Those of us who conduct these workshops have developed a variety of strategies, exercises, and presentations to give our colleagues a better handle on how to use writing more often in their classes. Teachers commonly learn how to assign different kinds of writing to serve different purposes to a variety of audiences. A few teachers even alter their basic approach toward teaching as a result of the workshop pedagogy. (Young & Fulwiler, 1986, p. 3)

I found that I could not understand what constituted an appropriate text in any discipline without considering the social and intellectual activity which the text was part of. Too much of the texts directly invoked and acted against these contexts to treat the features of texts simply as isolated conventions. Moreover, the rhetorical gist of entire texts evoked the larger framework of meanings within the active disciplines. That is, I couldn't see what a text was doing without looking at the worlds in which these texts served as significant activity. (Bazerman, 1988, p. 4)

tion and feminist studies and sketched out an agenda for a feminist approach to composition studies.

The phenomenon known as "writing across the curriculum" is a special case of the field's increasing awareness of the contexts for writing. Increasingly, scholars studied academic discourse and the writing situation of students in academic settings. Among the important and characteristic publications in this area during this period were Charles Bazerman's (1988) *Shaping Written Knowledge*, a study of the composition of the experimental article in science, and David Jolliffe's (1988) *Writing in Academic Disciplines*, part of the Ablex "Writing Research" series. Indeed, writing across the curriculum, like computers and composition, was sufficiently established at this time to warrant a chapter in Tate's *Teaching Composition: 10 Bibliographical Essays* (Kinneavy, 1987). It is perhaps significant that, outside Burns' chapter entitled "Computers and Composition," computers are largely ignored in the other 11 essays in this collection. Indeed, the only indexed references to computers outside Burns' chapter are in the chapter called "Approaches to the Study of Style," where Edward P.J. Corbett (1987) wrote that the work of William Wresch and Richard Lanham suggest "the potential of the computer for the study of style" (p. 128).

CLASSROOM PRACTICE

These are the shadows cast by the peaks of the university over the entering undergraduate. Together they represent what the university has to say about man and his education, and they do not project a coherent image. The differences and

Although research in the field was broadening its view to include aspects of the writer/writing's context, there is convincing evidence that classroom practice was still substantially driven by two earlier paradigms: the current-traditional view of writing as knowledge to be imparted and the process view of the writer as individual engaged in a craft.

As evidence for the persistence of the current-traditional paradigm during this period, there is Sharon Hamilton-Wieler's (1988) "Empty Echoes of Dartmouth: Dissonance Between the Rhetoric and the Reality." Hamilton-Wieler had traveled to England and there led a 5-week graduate course for Canadian educators titled "Studies of British Education." There, in the words of one of her students, "In every classroom we visited we saw workbooks, worksheets, and spelling texts. The kids were interacting with paper, not with each other. You'd think in the country that inspired such views of language and learning as those of James Britton, Nancy Martin, John Dixon, and Harold Rosen that we would see these views in practice in the classroom" (p. 29). Drawing on her own experience of American and Canadian education, Hamilton-Wieler argued that what she and her students saw in British schools was the norm in American and Canadian schools as well. She notes that the existence of the current-traditional paradigm could be inferred from the rapid and wide acceptance of the arguments voiced by E.D. Hirsch (1987) in *Cultural Literacy* and by Alan Bloom (1987) in *The Closing of the American Mind.*

As evidence for the establishment of the process paradigm in classroom practice we draw on the MLA volume *New Methods in College Writing Programs* (Connolly & Vilardi, 1986). In the program descriptions, references to tutorials abound, as do references to remedial labs and writing centers, where one-to-one, teacher–student conferences seem to be the principal instructional format. Most program descriptions contain references to the "writing process" and mention both its stages (invention, writing, revising, editing) and their recursive nature. In their introduction to the book, the editors conclude that "the influence of James Britton, Janet Emig, Ann Berthoff, James Moffett, Donald Murray, Peter Elbow, and

the indifferences are too great. It is difficult to imagine that there is either the wherewithal or the energy within the university to constitute or reconstitute the idea of an educated human being and establish a liberal education again. (Bloom, 1987, p. 380)

Guidelines [for Cornell University's first-year writing program]
1. At least thirty pages of assigned writing.
2. At least eight (and at most fourteen) written assignments.
3. Opportunities for serious revision—not mere editing—of essays. (At least some of these revising assignments may satisfy numbers 1 above.)
4. Ample classroom time (between one-half and two-thirds) spent on work that is directly related to writing.

5. Reading assignments small enough (about a hundred pages per week, at most) to permit regular, concentrated work on writing
6. Individual conferences. (Bogel, 1986, p. 31)

This 76th Convention is the beginning of "What We Will Be." Here we can find new insights and reaffirm old ones. In both formal and informal settings we can discuss what we will be, should

other researchers and theorists . . . is having a practical impact on college writing programs" (p. 5). One contributor to this MLA volume, however, noted that his Britton-based pilot program existed in the context of a standard freshman writing program that was based on the *Harbrace College Handbook* and an anthology of essays (p. 150). This returns us to Hamilton-Wieler's (1980) argument that "the paradigm shift described in the rhetoric of [our] journals . . . [was] simply not a day-to-day reality in the majority of classrooms" (p. 31). In some college programs, even in 1986, the old process pedagogy was a radical departure from the norm.

This evidence of the distance between research increasingly concerned with writing as a social act, and practice, still driven by attention to product or process, is corroborated by a review of the programs and workshops given at the annual conferences of CCCC and NCTE. At the 1986 NCTE annual conference, sessions on aspects of the writing process lived side by side with sessions titled "A Social View of Literacy Learning" and "Literature as Cultural Expression." Even the "Promising Researcher" awards reflect a field in transition: In 1986, the awards were given to two ethnographic studies; in 1987 one of the winner's topics was "Cognitive and Linguistic Demands of Analytic Writing." At the CCCC annual conventions in 1986, "The Composing Process" was the largest category of sessions; in 1987 this same category was sixth largest; and in 1988 it had slipped to seventh, significantly less popular than "Social Contexts of Writing, Reading, and Speaking" and "Politics of Language Use—Gender, Race, Class, and Clan."

The 1987 CCCC Program Chair, David Bartholomae, noted the change in his "Greeting":

In the sessions and papers that make up the program, you will find the familiar themes and concerns of our profession: computers and writing, basic writing, business and technical writing, assessment, the history of rhetoric. You will also find a higher-than-usual concentration of sessions devoted to the social and political contexts of reading and writing, critical thinking, language and gender. (CCCC Program)

In 1987, the CCCC gave the first pre/post convention workshop specifically addressing issues of gender, titled "She/He Learns to Write: How to Integrate the Scholarship on Women into the Composition Classroom." The list of pre/post convention workshops also included two workshops on writing across the curriculum, further evidence of the emergence of a contextual perspective—but running concurrently with these relatively "modern" topics were sessions titled "Error, Correction, and Writing" and "Studying Cognitive Processes in the Classroom," attesting to the simultaneous existence of three paradigms: the current-traditional, the cognitive/process, and the social/epistemic. The profession's use of computers during this time would, not surprisingly, also reflect all three radically different sets of assumptions.

The Technological Context, 1986–1988: Faster, Cheaper, Better

The first half of the 1980s had been a time of great technological innovation: the advent of graphical interfaces, the emergence of more affordable networking technologies, and the development of new hypertext systems. The second half of the decade was a period of consolidation and distribution, a time when the computer revolution was won. The personal computer moved into the mainstream of Amer-

be, might be. To this convention program we have added the Rainbow Strand to further the dialogue about teaching the culturally and linguistically different student. We have provided coffeehouse sessions to explore the nature and future of the Council and the expectations of research. (McHugh, 1986, p. ix)

Preconvention Workshops
—Studying Cognitive Processes in the Classroom
—Teaching Writing as a Social Process
—Developing Writing across the Curriculum Programs
—Making the Best Better: Using Computers in the University or College Writing Center
—Constructing Text through Reading and Writing
—Technical Communication: Current Research, Theory, and Methods in Approaching the Writer-Reader Relationship
—Writing across the Curriculum Programs: The "Second Stage"
—Students and Teachers as Researchers: Ethnography, Observation, and Interpretation in Collaborative Learning
—Planning and Teaching Courses in Business Writing: What New Teachers Need to Know
—Tutoring in the Writing Center: Philosophy, Training, Survival. (Taken from the 1987 CCCC Convention Program, pp. 14–16)

ican life because the technology, developed earlier, was made less expensive, faster, and was increasingly standardized, and powerful new software programs made the computer a more powerful and more attractive tool in the hands of the business person, educator, and nonexpert user.

GUI Wins Out

Although the processing speed of next generation chips and the intricacies of new storage technologies may be impressive from a technical standpoint, software interfaces really define the way humans work and interact with computers. Thus, the emerging dominance of the Graphical User Interface (GUI) in the late 1980s may have been the single most important technological development of this period. Apple's Macintosh introduced the GUI to popular computing in 1983 and Apple—and Xerox PARC— certainly deserve credit for pioneering that new mode of human-computer interaction. It was the widespread adoption of Microsoft's WINDOWS operating system, however, that settled the new territory and spelled the end for the time-honored command-line interface of DOS.

Microsoft's founder and CEO Bill Gates championed his new operating system with a "WINDOWS everywhere!" motto and a strategy that aimed to make WINDOWS the world's dominant interface not only for personal computers but for hand-held systems, palmtop computers, and other computing devices that existed only on the drawing boards of research labs at the time of WINDOWS 1985 release. Despite Gates' ambition, WINDOWS started slowly. In 1985, it was bug-ridden, slow, and in the eyes of many, simply not as elegant or well-designed as the Macintosh operating systems it imitated (partly because it still worked through MS-DOS and was subject to DOS's limitations). Because a

GUI system runs in the computer's graphic mode, it requires tremendous processing power. Consider that a simple VGA monitor has 307,200 pixels on the screen that need to be redrawn over and over again with even a simple action like scrolling through a word processing document. WINDOWS performance on the then-state-of-the-art 80286-based computer was anemic (Seymour, 1989, p. 97).

In 1987, IBM released its new PS/2 line of personal computers, still built around the 80286 microprocessor, not the newer 80386 chip that WINDOWS really demanded, despite technical specifications that claimed a 286 system would be acceptable (Vose, 1987). This was a blow to Microsoft's attempts to have WINDOWS widely accepted. There was considerable feeling that consumers would not accept the mouse pointing device that a GUI system like WINDOWS demanded (and that Mac users had so enthusiastically embraced) and that software developers might not write their applications for the new interface. Yet Microsoft has always been patient with its new products and willing to allow their faults to be shaken out in the market and through subsequent versions. So when Microsoft released EXCEL, its spreadsheet imitation of Lotus 1-2-3, it did so only in a WINDOWS version, a signal that the world's largest software company was unwavering in its commitment to the GUI.

Microsoft's patience paid off when the 80386 chip reached the market and was then quickly followed a year later with the still-more-powerful 80486 microprocessor. Accompanied by other technologies like video accelerator boards, which speeded the screen redrawing earlier described, and more affordable memory, WINDOWS now had the hardware it required to run well. When WINDOWS version 2.1 was finally released in 1989, it addressed many of the flaws and bugs of the original version, and the operating system took off. Other graphic inter-

Still Waiting for Windows/386

Ready to run two, three, even ten applications at once on your 80386 system? MICROSOFT WINDOWS/386 can do the job, but speed-conscious users may find the company's prize heifer a white elephant.

Is Windows/386 truly "the soul of the new machines," the multitasking powerhouse that turns 80386-based computers into "sensitive, intuitive, highly visual" electronic tools? That's what Microsoft claims. Users may think otherwise. (Luhn, 1988, p. 116)

IBM Personal System/2 Model 60 (80286-based computer)

By far the most expandable of the three PS/2 models, the freestanding Model 60 opens seven free slots on its Micro Channel bus. It also has room for two full-height 5 1/4 inch devices and two half-height 3 1/2 inch drives. The Model 60's 44MB hard disk is about twice as fast as the Model 50's 20 MB counterpart, but with 80286 chips running at 10 MHz, the processing performance of the two machines is virtually identical. The Model 60's $5295 base price, however, is high compared with a similarly outfitted AT clone. (Brown, Knorr, & Bermant, 1987, p. 220)

Microsoft Mouse

Microsoft's mouse has been ergonomically redesigned for greater comfort and ease of use, and it now includes

a modular interface for compatibility with both IBM PC compatibles and PS/2s. Microsoft has repositioned the track ball of the mouse farther forward so that you can more easily move the mouse with only your fingertips and wrist rather than your whole arm. ("Update," 1987, p. 141)

Although developed in association with Microsoft, in many ways OS/2 is quintessential IBM software. Of course, no standard must be sold before, or after, its time, and here the Personal Systems picture grows murky. IBM has a reputation for superb timing, but with OS/2 still a year away, its hand was, to a degree, forced. The wait for this definitive operating system may yet try users' patience. (Bender, 1987, p. 185)

A new genre of composition textbooks is emerging, books which integrate instruction in word processing with instruction in writing and rhetoric. Every publisher, it seems, has been working to produce a textbook to capture the new market. Colette Daiute's *Writing & Computers* described using the word processor to teach writers of all ages, from children to adult, (Wesley, 1985), as did Linda Knapp's

faces for the huge IBM compatible market, systems like Digital Research's GEM/3 and Tandy's DESKMATE, were overwhelmed by the Microsoft juggernaut. (Seymour, 1989). By 1993, WINDOWS would become the standard interface for personal computers. It would sell more copies than all Macintosh computers combined and hold two-thirds of the market for operating systems (compared to a mere 13% market share for the Mac OS). IBM's OS/2, begun jointly by IBM and Microsoft, is a superior system in the eyes of many users, but it has posed no serious threat to WINDOWS' hold on the market. Chicago, the code-named version of WINDOWS that will not require DOS (thus making it a true operating system) and that will include many new features, is slated for release in 1995 and may come to fulfill Gates' vision of "WINDOWS everywhere."

OBSERVING TRENDS: GAINING CRITICAL MASS IN COMPUTERS AND COMPOSITION STUDIES

Seeming to echo the pace and character of the technology in which it was implicated, between 1986 and 1988 the field of computers and composition studies paused to consolidate what it had already accomplished—or, to change the metaphor, this was the end of a first generation and the beginning of a second. There were, during this period, fewer articles about computers in CCC and *College English*, and the Computers and Writing Conference, such an exciting event in 1982, 1984, and 1985, continued as an annual event through 1986 but was not held in either 1987 or 1988. The excitement of discovery was past and the funding agencies, once eager to support studies of the new technology, now turned to other, newer concerns. For the field, it was time to establish the position of individual faculty to convince colleagues that what computer specialists were doing was important, or—for most an impossible alternative—to return to business as usual and agree with the majority that the new technology was interesting but irrelevant to English studies.

The work that the field continued to do both reflected and influenced the character of its big sister, composition studies. In 1986, for most of us, the computer was still a stand-alone machine, one marvellous in its capability—and one used by a single writer, writing alone. Yet by 1988, many of us—not yet most of us—would see the computer as a means of connecting to a virtual space in which we might participate with others in the construction of knowledge. Rickly remembered that in 1984–1987 she was:

> deeply interested in evolving research on word-processing and writing as it related to evolving theories of writing process, revision, drafting, all seemed to be facilitated by the computer. Peter Elbow's "Closing My Eyes as I Speak: An Argument for Ignoring Audience" (1987) helped me see the computer as an extension of self—a creation, construction of self. (C&W, 1994)

She also remembers the semester when she came to see the computer as a site for the social construction of knowledge: "In 1988, I taught in the VAX lab using VAX e-mail, and began to recognize the incredible potential of construction and connectivity" (C&W, 1994). Rickly's narrative reflects the ways in which technology, teaching, and theory can interact. While Rickly was writing and teaching on stand-alone computers, she saw her students as autonomous writers. When she moved to a networked teaching environment—the VAX

The Word Processor and the Writing Teacher (Prentice Hall, 1986). Helen Schwartz's *Interactive Writing* (Holt Rinehart Winston, 1985) really zeroed in on huge market possibilities with a combined college rhetoric and introduction to word processing. (Appleby & Bernhardt, 1987, p. 478).

When we examine really good student or professional writing, we can often see that its goodness comes from the writer's having gotten sufficiently wrapped up in her meaning and her language as to forget all about audience needs: the writer manages to "break through". . . . It is characteristic of much truly good writing to be, as it were, on fire with its meaning. Consciousness of readers is burned away; involvement in subject determines all. (Elbow, 1987, p. 54)

My effort to outline a social view will be on the basis of one central assumption: human language (including writing) can be understood only from the perspective of a society rather than a single individual. Thus taking a social view requires a great deal more than simply paying more attention to the context surrounding a discourse. It rejects the assumption that writing is the act of a private consciousness and that everything else—readers, subjects, and texts—is "out there" in the world. The focus of a social view of writing, therefore, is not on how the social situation influences the individual, but on how the individual is a constituent of a culture. (Faigley, 1986, p. 534)

During the 1983–1984 academic year, I introduced the word processor into my high school writing class of eight students. I designed the course around it to permit the close observation of students, and I studied my class using ethnographic techniques: videotape, audiotape, teacher/ researcher journals, student journals, students' writing, and interviews. Ethnographic research encourages us to look at hypotheses—new lenses through which future learning situations can be viewed and may be more clearly understood. Observing the participants' patterns of behavior in their relationship to each other

lab–suddenly knowledge was being socially constructed in her class, in email transcripts that she could read and analyze. Through technology, practice had illuminated theory.

Butler remembered a more public occasion when technology and theory came together:

At the 1987 Conference of College Teachers of English, held in Corpus Christi, TX, I was on a panel with Nancy Peterson and Valerie Balester on social construction and collaborative learning. Fred Kemp, Paul Taylor, Locke Carter, and Hugh Burns had a panel on networked computers. Out of graduate-student courtesy, the Social Construction and Network Technology panel members attended one another's sessions. It was at this conference where theory and pedagogy collided with the technology. Shortly after, the UT computer lab became a collaborative learning/teaching facility. (C&W, 1994)

For Rickly and Butler, and for many others, networked computers fit nicely with what Lester Faigley (1986) termed *the social view*, a view that understands writing "as a social activity within a specific community" (p. 528). But how was this social activity to be studied? Quantitative studies involving pre- and posttesting, or case studies involving protocol analysis and keystroke capture, were not proving to be sufficiently useful tools. As a result, some research in computers and composition studies began to move toward qualitative research, using ethnographic methodology. The published research and teaching reports of this time, however, suggest that our field, like composition studies, was in transition: a few teachers and scholars were operating in the current-traditional paradigm, principally concerned with correctness and error; many, perhaps a majority, were operating in the writing process paradigm; and a few were beginning to adopt the social view. Further, the field was composed not only of cutting-edge researchers working with good equipment, but of teachers and scholars who were new to computers or who did not have access to the emerging technology. In journals, therefore, research reports on style checkers with their inherent emphasis on products existed side by side with early stories of the wonders of computer-mediated communication with its strong connections to social constructionism. Throughout the period of 1986–1988, these competing views of writing and writing instruction mark the discourses of both the traditional and the newly emerging professional forums.

The NCTE and CCCC Conventions

During 1986–1988, computers and composition established itself as a regular in the traditional forums of the profession. The number of computer sessions at NCTE conventions remained small—6 to 10. CCCC, on the other hand, gave computers and composition 20 sessions in 1987, about 9% of the concurrent sessions listed on the program. In addition to the concurrent sessions on computers, at NCTE the Assembly on Computers continued to sponsor software demonstrations and feature noted software developers who were members of the computers and composition community. CCCC in 1987 offered a parallel service, the "Software Sampler." Both conferences featured pre- and postconvention workshops on computers and writing. The 1986–1988 NCTE programs included two or three workshops at each convention, workshops with titles such as "Creating a Computer-Supported Writing Process" (1987) and "Conversing, Composing, Computing: Collaboration Around the World" (1988). The 1986–1988 CCCC programs also in-

and to the tasks at hand stimulates speculation about the nature of this behavior and about the effects of this social interaction on the learning process. (Herrmann, 1987, p. 79)

Special Event
Software Sampler
10:45 a.m.–5:00 p.m.
Atrium Room B, Lobby Level (South Tower)
Interested persons are invited to drop in and try a variety of text-processing software. Bring a blank disk for free copies of programs in the public domain.
Cochairs: Nancy Kaplan,, Cornell University, Ithaca, New York; Helen Schwartz, Carnegie-Mellon University, Pittsburgh, Pennsylvania.
Consultants: James A. Gifford, William Wresch, Peter Dow Adams, Theodore C. Humphrey, Lisa Gerrard, Elray L. Pedersen, Dawn Rodrigues. (CCCC Program, 1988, p. 26)

The COMP-LAB Writing Modules: Computer-Assisted Grammar Instruction, by Michael G. Southwell. I describe in this chapter an effort to exploit the potential of computers for providing instruction in grammar to students whose writing exhibits severe problems of correctness and clarity. These basic writing students are usually members of various ethnic minorites, and their writing problems are typically associated with some sort of nonstandard speech background. (Southwell, 1984, p. 91)

As co-director of the computer room at Bread Loaf and a teacher at Sewickley Academy outside of Pittsburgh, I've been able to investigate the use of electronic networks to create a real context for communication between student writers from different cultural backgrounds in the U.S. In the fall of 1986, students in two of my writing classes at Sewickley Academy exchanged writing on an electronic network with students from Wilsall High School in Montana and Little Wound High School on the Pine Ridge Sioux reservation in Kyle, South Dakota.

We used BreadNet, Bread Loaf's electronic network, to enhance real communication because of the computer's speed in transmitting written messages. Using a microcomputer, a modem, and an electronic mail service, I collaborated daily with the other two teachers two thousand miles away. (Schwartz, 1990, p. 17)

cluded two computers and writing workshops per year, with titles like "Evaluating Computer Software" (1986) led by Michael Southwell, well known at the time for the grammar modules he developed for basic writers, and "Computer Networks in the Writing Classroom" (1988), with Joy Kreeft Peyton and Trent Batson from Gallaudet University, Geoff Sirc and Terence Collins from the University of Minnesota, and Michael Spitzer from New York Institute of Technology.

The 1986–1988 computer-related sessions and workshops reflected diverse approaches to writing and pedagogy and a strong interest in research. The field was still interested in CAI, word processing, building computer-assisted writing facilities, and the efficacy of computers as writing and teaching tools. Sessions at NCTE in 1986 included "Invention Heuristic Computer Programs," "Developing and Implementing a High School Computer-Writing Program," and "Word Processing in Freshman Composition: A New Study." In 1988, session titles included "Computer Strategies for Teaching Revision," "Using BANK STREET WRITER and WRITER'S HELPER," and "Computers and Basic Writing: the University of Cincinnati's Controlled Study at the Beginning of Year 3."

The field was also becoming interested in the uses of networked computers. In both 1986 and 1987, the NCTE program included a session titled "Voices Across the Wires." These sessions featured teachers who were experimenting with BreadNet—a project of the Bread Loaf School of English—an electronic conference system coordinated by William Wright and aimed at linking teachers and students from different communities across the United States and eventually the world. Through BreadNet, students in suburban Pittsburgh, for example, could exchange email with their counterparts on an Indian reservation in South Dakota (Schwartz, 1990). Teachers' reports of BreadNet at these sessions acknowledged the value of talk in helping students create new knowledge with their peers.

Another important computer-related presentation at NCTE was Selfe's (1988a) "The Tie That Binds: Building Community and Fostering Dialogic Exchange through Computer-Based Conferences." In stressing the importance that a theoretical perspective brings to the profession's use of "computer conferencing," Selfe encouraged computers and compositionists to inform their teaching with poststructuralist theory. Her conference paper, which grew into a coauthored article (Cooper & Selfe, 1990), was to be in 1990 the first computer-related article *College English* had published since 1985.

Computers & Writing Conference

With 337 participants and 81 sessions, the *Fourth Computers and Writing Conference* (1986) was the largest to date. Coordinated by Glynda Hull, the conference was held at the University of Pittsburgh May 2–4. A look at the program of this conference, with its 81 computer-related papers, as contrasted with the CCCC and NCTE programs with their dozen or so sessions, gives a detailed view of the field at this time. This view is also captured in the introduction to *Critical Perspectives on Computers and Composition Instruction* ((Hawisher & Selfe, 1989), an anthology that had its beginnings at the Pittsburgh conference. The editors saw a change in the tenor of discourse about computers and composition in the work of the 1986 conference. Computers and compositionists were, they thought, beginning to lose their initial, uncritical enthusiasm for the technology and the promises it seemed to hold for writing instruction. In their introduction, Hawisher and Selfe characterized the field's pre-1986 professional discourse:

All discourse communities and the speech acts that serve as currency within those communities are essentially points of dynamism and change, as Bakhtin reminds us. Hence, members of discourse communities, even those existing within academic settings, continually re-adjust and red-define what discourse is normal or acceptable.... . Discourse communities change when the centripetal forces binding members together in discoursal agreement about conventions are overbalanced by the centrifugal forces indicating changing conventions are necessary or desirable—when, in other words, normative forces give way to revolutionary forces. Thus, we know that using discourse effectively as a social force involves understanding both the value of constancy, or convention, and the value of change, of resistance to convention. (Cooper & Selfe, 1990, p. 851)

Being wary of the gift-giver: Some questions about computers.
Chair: Cynthia Selfe
Gail Hawisher: Research in Word Processing: Facts and Fictions
Lance Wilcox: A Time for Every Medium under Heaven: Adapting the Writing Process to the Word Processor
John Thiesmeyer: Should We Do What We Can? (Conference Program for Computers and Writing, 1986, p. 15)

One theme that appears here and there at every [Computers and Writing] conference is fear and power. From 1984–1986, it centered on the individual; later it refers to larger social problems. In 1984 we worried both about students who feared computers and about the power the machines might hold over them: one presenter called it, "the lure of the cursor, the fear of the byte." We worried about our frightened, recalcitrant colleagues who saw no place for computers in English. We worried about controlling our own classes, and gave each other advice: "Tame that Tiger! How to Keep the English Instructor in Control" (1986). We wondered if style analyzers would take over students' revisions and if invention aids would contract rather than guide their imaginations. One presenter spoke of "Word Processing and Thought Control: the Fearful Side of Technology" (1984). Others cautioned against the inaccuracy of machine-assisted translation (1986) and the ill-effects of idea processors (1985). (Gerrard, in press)

BreadNet connects student writers across the country. . . . Much as you shared writing in your class, these writers shared their work with an interested audience that helped them to see their writing, culture, and ideas from a new perspective. Experiences normally taken for granted . . . had to be ex-

Until the mid-1980s, computer sessions at the annual meetings of the National Council of Teachers of English (NCTE) and the Conference on College Composition and Communication (CCCC) mainly involved enthusiastic English professionals sharing observational and anecdotal evidence that computers could serve us well. (p. x)

The presentations at the Pittsburgh conference, the editors went on to argue, provided not simply enthusiastic or anecdotal accounts of the marvels of computers, but rather thoughtful analyses of the role computers were now playing in the profession. They singled out as typical of this new discourse John Thiesmeyer's passionate critique of the inadequacies of computer-assisted writing software, William Van Pelt's charge that students were overwriting when they wrote with computers, and Gail Hawisher's analysis of the limitations of current research in computers and composition studies.

Of the 81 individual papers given at the Pittsburgh conference, 21 were principally reports of ongoing research—an increase both in number and ratio over the previous conference, where of the 64 papers and panels 12 had focused on research. At the Pittsburgh Conference, there were 12 sessions devoted to one specific research area: the effects of word-processing on writing and students' learning. A few presentations emphasized developing intelligent tutors for coaching writers (e.g., Shute, 1986; Wilensky, 1986), whereas others told us that computers would never sufficiently develop the capacity to understand natural language—that AI was of limited use for writers and writing instructors (e.g., Haugeland, 1986; Ross, 1986). The topic of CMC and its potential for writers and writing classes surfaced in Pittsburgh as well. Helen Schwartz, Valarie Arms, and Diane Balestri (1986) examined computer conferencing as "a medium for educators to exchange and develop ideas" (p. 9); Betsy Bowen and Jeffrey Schwartz, from the Bread Loaf School of English, reported their experiences using BreadNet with high school classes; and Trent Batson and Joy Peyton related the benefits of synchronous CMC and suggested that the use of CMC could benefit student writers.

The Pittsburgh Computers and Writing conference would be the last until 1989, when the conference would be reborn in Minnesota. The two-year hiatus indicates that the computers and composition community, still in 1994 a largely ad-hoc group depending on volunteer effort, was not from 1986–1988 able to muster the resources needed to run a major, annual conference. It serves as a reminder, too, of the extraordinary efforts of the directors of the first four conferences: Lillian Bridwell, Donald Ross, Lisa Gerrard, and Glynda Hull. To prevent future gaps in the conference, in 1988 the CCCCs Committee on Computers, with Helen Schwartz as its chair, made the C&W Conference a part of its charge. A subcommittee chaired by Gail Hawisher was formed to ensure that the conference would be an annual event—which it has indeed become.

Professional Print Publications: Books

The presentations at the Fourth Computers and Writing Conference emphasized new directions and reports of ongoing research, a characteristic of the academic conference. Books published in the field during this time, however, served to introduce teachers to computers and help them bring computers responsibily into their classrooms. We can regard Selfe's (1986) *Computer-Assisted Instruction: Create Your Own* as both the best and the last of our field's short love affair with CAI. The book is deeply practical: Selfe leads the reader through

plained to readers who had never witnessed those activities. Students found that while they were learning about life-styles in other parts of the country, they were also strengthening their writing skills and getting acquainted with the new technology of electronic communications. Other students in elementary and secondary schools across the country have shared their writing and interests through planned writing exchanges, impromptu teleconferences, and an electronic magazine established by Bread Loaf called *Voices of America.* (Elder, et al., 1989, pp. 160-161)

Computers and Writing Conference
The Committee on Computers for the Conference on College Composition and Communication (CCCC) invites colleges or other interested organizations to sponsor the Seventh Computers and Writing Conference. Commonly this three-day conference is held in April or May and attracts approximately 500 participants. For further information, please write Gail E. Hawisher, English De-

partment, Purdue University, W. Lafayette, IN47907. The CCCC Committee on Computers supports continuity in the annual Computers and Writing Conferences by coordinating the search for a sponsoring university and the transfer from site to site, providing advice and logistical support for the conference planner, and assisting in publicizing the conference. (Announcement, 1989, p. 327)

As you develop more experience teaching writing with the computer and as you acquire more sophisticated computer-writing tools, you will undoubtedly think of more yourself: skill files to keep track of student weaknesses and strengths, technological ways for your students to share their writing with students they might never meet face to face, electronic bulletin board applications, case study approaches to writing, context-based writing lessons, and so on. Sometimes you will devise new approaches that can only be accomplished with a computer, but often you will simply adapt the techniques of teachers who have taught writing without a computer. (Rodrigues & Rodrigues, 1986, p. 51)

What happens when writers don't use paper? In the spring of 1985 I conducted an advanced writing course using a central computer, time-sharing terminals, and an electronic bulletin board. Before we began, I imag-

"Getting Started on a CAI Project," to "Thinking About Screen Display," and finally to "Field Testing a CAI Lesson." However, the book is also theoretical: Selfe urges English teachers to consider pedagogical theory as they develop CAI. "If CAI is to be useful in a writing program," she wrote, "it must be informed by the same theoretical assumptions that underlie the teaching within [the] program" (p. 5).

Williamson (personal correspondence, August 19, 1994) noted that "by a generous margin," Dawn and Raymond Rodrigues' (1986) *Teaching Writing with a Word Processor, Grades 7–13* was NCTE's "most popular applied computer and writing title." It was the fourth-best-selling NCTE composition title in 1986–1988 and again during the period covered in chapter 5 of this volume, 1989–1991. These publication figures suggest that the book filled a real need. The authors encouraged teachers to abandon CAI and to use word processing as their "central software package" (p. 3) in the writing class. They provided teachers with a series of "Computer-Writing Lesson Files" that demonstrated how teachers' lessons on a particular aspect of composing could be created, stored, and then made available for students to call up on their own. Although in some respects these files were similar to the modules of some CAI programs, the Rodrigueses also showed how peer editing and collaborative writing could be facilitated in a word-processing classroom.

The computer as word processor was the focus of textbooks of this period as well. These books, like the Rodrigues' best-selling book described earlier, chiefly advised teachers on how their classes could be best served with word processing. Published in the same year were Gerrard's (1987b) *Writing With HBJ Writer*; Hult and Harris's (1987) *A Writer's Introduction to Word Processing*; B. Edwards' (1987) *Processing Words: Writing and Revising on a Mi-*

crocomputer; and Ronald Sudol's (1987) *Textfiles: A Rhetoric for Word Processing*. Word processing became the subject not just of professional books and textbooks, but of books aimed at the more general reader. The dust jacket of *Electric Language: A Philosophical Study of Word Processing* (Heim, 1987) stated enthusiastically that "the word processor has become a cultural phenomenon, the ubiquitous tool of the student and scholar, philosopher and poet, social scientist and historian."

In books published in 1987 there were also early signs of the profession's interest in the contexts of writing and instruction, and growing evidence that computer networks would become important to writing teachers. Although Gerrard's (1987a) *Writing at the Century's End: Essays on Computer-Assisted Composition* had little on word processing and less on CAI, it featured the first ethnographic study on the use of computers in an English class (e.g., Herrmann, 1987) as well as the first description of a paperless writing class in which all student and teacher contributions occurred over a network (e.g., Jennings, 1987). Although neither Herrmann nor Jennings pointed specifically to the social construction of knowledge in their chapters, both attest to the field's evolving interest in the social dimensions of writing.

Two books published in 1988 develop a contextual approach to computers and their use. In *Technology and Women's Voices*, Kramarae (1988) made issues of gender central to discussions of technology, arguing in the opening essay, "Gotta go Myrtle, Technology's at the Door," that technologies should be seen "not as machines, but as social relations." She argued further that one of the book's "contributions to discussions of *social relationships* is to consider them as organized and structured by technological systems which allow or encourage some kinds of interactions and pre-

ined all sorts of good things we might try to do. Along the way, the replacement of ink and paper with electronic dots produced some surprises. Looking back at what did happen in the paperless environment, I'm willing to declare that writing instruction, and the ways in which we evaluate its success, will change even faster and more radically than we have expected. (Jennings, 1987, p. 11)

All technological developments can usefully be studied with a focus on women's social interactions, even those developments which would initially seem to have little to do with women's lives. For example: girls' and women's uses of bicycles. I have been fascinated by nineteenth century feminists' accounts of the bicycle as a mechanical device which changed women's movement through their communities. Early feminists told stories of the ways women were discouraged (bottles and insults thrown their way) from riding bicycles. In some families bicycles and motor bikes are still considered more suited to boys' than girls' lives—and boys are often allowed more freedom at when and where they ride. (Kramarae, 1988, p. x)

There is a world to be lost and a world to be gained. Choices that appear to be merely technical will redefine our lives together at work. This means more than simply contemplating the implications or consequences of a new technology. It means that a powerful new technology, such as that represented by the computer, fundamentally reorganizes the infrastructure of our material world. It eliminates former alternatives. It creates new possibilities. It necessitates fresh choices. (Zuboff, 1988, p. 5)

vent or discourage other kinds" (p. 2). Shoshana Zuboff (1988), in *In the Age of the Smart Machine*, illustrated how lives of workers change in environments where daily work has been radically transformed through new information technologies. In her preface, Zuboff explained that her research began as a study of workers and the industrial revolution. She sought to understand changes in the "everyday life" of workers, changes that touched on "feelings, sensibilities, and expectations; the intimate details of eating, drinking, and socializing; the things that make us cry or laugh; and the things that make us mad" (p. xi). As her research progressed, however, she realized that society was again in the midst of an historical revolution and that workers at one point in time might well have "very different social constructions of reality" (p. xi) than those 10 years hence. She adjusted her study to foreground the social changes introduced by computers. Her methods, like Kramarae's and Herrmann's, were qualitative and ethnographic. This research methodology was one well suited to the study of complex systems and to the discovery that, as Andrea Herrmann (1987) put it, "the computer's presence in our classrooms appears unlikely to negate the powerful influence of the differential socialization of students by social class and its effects on their success or failure in school" (p. 86).

Professional Journals and Computers and Composition Studies

Both *College English* and *College Composition and Communication* in the period from 1986–1988 featured fewer articles on computers and writing than each had in the period from 1983–1985. Indeed, between 1985 and 1990 *College English* published no articles on computers. Clearly one element of the profession—the editors of these mainstream journals and the authors who would write for them—had determined that computers were not of primary interest to the fields of English and composition studies. After the first burst of enthusiasm, computers, at least from the perspectives of these two journals, seemed to disappear from sight—perhaps now considered part of the furniture, but more likely considered not the real business of English.

However, in a curious split, advertisements in these same journal pages show that publishers were targeting postsecondary English teachers as a market for computer books, software, and hardware. These advertisements also suggest that CAI software was still very much with us. In the January 1986 issue of *College English* was an advertisement for "Gorilla Software's Writing Lab" (1986, p. 3). For $349, the software would teach grammar, give posttests, and provide a record-keeping disk. It included a "Spice Lesson" intended to help students eliminate prepositional phrases and "redundant modifiers." In the corner of the ad, a gorilla sat in front of a range of mountains, pointing to a computer. In this same issue was an ad for a Zenith Dual Drive Z-148 PC for $998. Other issues of *College English* would carry advertisements for Sudol's *TextFiles: A Rhetoric for Word Processing* and the Rodrigues' *Teaching Writing With a Word Processor, Grades 7–13*.

College Composition and Communication, reflecting the interests not of English generally but of composition studies in particular, seemed to take the field more seriously during this period. Although it did not, as it had in 1983–1985, feature the computer in thematically organized issues, it did publish a number of articles on computers and writing. After a year's hiatus in 1986, CCC published five articles on computers in 1987, including Joyce Kinkead's "Computer Conversations: Email and

Writing Instruction," which was consigned to the small-type pages of the Staffroom Interchange. To our knowledge, this article on email or computer-mediated communication is the first article on this subject to appear in a mainstream composition journal. And although articles on computers and composition studies did not appear in Richard Larson's 1987 "Selected Bibliography of Scholarship," in 1988 he added a section at the end titled "Computers and Writing," where he listed Burns' (1987) chapter on computers in *Teaching Composition: Twelve Bibliographical Essays*, Lutz's (1987) study of professional and experienced writers, and Hawisher's (1987) research on the revision of college students. In 1987, CCC published Schwartz and Bridwell-Bowles' "A Selected Bibliography on Computers and Composition: An Update." As had its 1984 predecessor, this bibliography served to give the field definition, presenting it to its readership as a coherent world that might be studied and mastered.

During 1986–1988, *Research in the Teaching of English* (RTE) published six articles focusing on the "effects of word processing" (e.g., Daiute, 1986; Dickinson, 1986; Haas & Hayes, 1986; Hawisher, 1987; Lutz, 1987; McAllister & Louth, 1988). These articles differ both in their research methodology and in the target groups of writers examined. Although most of the studies were experimental, David Dickinson broke new ground in conducting an ethnographic study of a first and second-grade class using a computer. His conclusion—that the use of word processing created "a new social organization" for the class—was in keeping with the new emphasis on context emerging in composition studies. The *RTE* studies during this period covered the full spectrum of writing classes, from first grade classrooms to postgraduate classrooms. Dickinson took as his subjects first- and second-grade student writers; Haas and Hayes studied faculty and gradu-

NCTE Promising Researcher Award
1988 Finalist
Christina Haas, Carnegie Mellon University, Pittsburgh, PA.
How the Writing Medium Shapes the Writing Process: Effects of Word Processing on Planning.

ate students at Carnegie Mellon; Daiute studied junior high students; Hawisher studied advanced, first-year college students; Lutz studied professional writers and graduate students; and McAllister and Louth studied basic writers. *RTE*'s focus on the effects of word processing was characteristic of the field as a whole. Durst and Marshall's (1986a, 1986b, 1987a, 1987b, 1988a, 1988b) annotated bibliographies of studies on the teaching of English reported 25 studies of word processing in 1987 alone, and 50 studies of word processing from May 1986 through December 1988.

These studies—many of them dissertations—were, unlike the dissertations of Lillian Bridwell-Bowles and Lisa Gerrard written a decade earlier, typed into a computer turned word processor. As a sign of the quality of this work, Jane Z. Flinn was named a finalist in the 1986 NCTE Promising Research Award Competition for her work on "The Role of Instruction in Revision with Computers: Forming a Construct for Good Writing," the first dissertation on computers and composition to be so recognized. Her positive results—that students received higher scores on papers written with word processing—were, of course, what many had hoped for when we first discovered word processing, but Flinn's results were something of an anomaly in the research generally. Most studies failed to discover important differences between students writing on- and offline.

Computers and Composition

During this period, *Computers and Composition* began to look more like an established professional journal. Through 1986 and 1987, the journal's pages had the look and feel of the typewritten page. With the August 1987 issue, however, which marked the end of the journal's fourth year, the editors moved to PAGEMAKER 2.0

NCTE Promising Research Award
1986 Finalist:
Jane Z. Flinn, University of Missouri. The Role of Instruction in Revision with Computers: Forming a Construct for "Good Writing."

What did I just say? Reading problems in writing with the machine.
Abstract: Sixteen computer writers were informally interviewed about how they use the computer for writing tasks. While the writers felt that the computer was useful for some writing tasks, they also indicated that

writing with the computer had disadvantages. They reported reading problems such as difficulty in locating information, difficulty in detecting errors, and difficulty in reading their texts critically. Three experimental studies were conducted to compare the performance of college students reading texts displayed on a computer terminal screen and on a printed hard copy. Findings indicate that visual/spatial factors influence locational recall, information retrieval, and appropriate reordering of text. (Haas & Hayes, 1986, p. 22)

Letter from the Editors
Dear Readers
As we begin our fourth full year of publication, we have new features to unveil. . . . We're especially proud of our new logo and two-color format. It feels almost as if we've gone high tech. Our special thanks to Edith Greene, our graphic artist at Michigan Tech. We are most pleased by the quality of the articles we can share with you in this issue and the issues of the coming year. (Kiefer & Selfe, 1986, p. 4)

A Comparative Study of the First-Generation Invention Software
English departments have been slow to come to instructional computing partly because of the logistical, financial, and time-

and printed the pages on a laser printer. The contrast between the new and the old is visually striking. The August 1986 issue looks rather like a newsletter written for a small group or club. The August 1987 issue looks much like the issues of *Computers and the Humanities*, *CCC*, or *The Journal of Basic Writing* from this period. It is physically smaller than these journals—8¼ × 5½ vs. 9 × 6—but in typeface and page format, it was now in the major leagues.

Computers and Composition was also moving into the big leagues in content, as its authors and editors began to summarize and reflect upon the work they were doing. Hawisher's (1986) "Studies in Word Processing" reviewed 24 studies and concluded that without a more "systematic and reflective" approach to research, the profession would be left with "a confusing array of results [from studies in word processing] . . . often misinterpreted" (p. 25). In her 1988 update of this review, Hawisher included 16 new studies, drawing from them that we could now feel safe in knowing that writers "like" to write with computers and often produce longer products with fewer mechanical errors when they do so. However, she also wondered whether the computer itself was the only cause of this effect. Might it not be the collaborative and cooperative classroom atmosphere that was often characteristic of computer-equipped classrooms and writing labs? If this were true, she noted that the profession would need to develop a pedagogy that would suit the newly collaborative and cooperative writing environments.

Between 1986 and 1988 *Computers and Composition* also featured articles on familiar topics of continuing interest: how writing programs might integrate computers with their curricula (e.g., "Integrating Computers into the Writing Classroom: Some Guidelines," Dinan, Gagnon, & Taylor, 1986) and what sorts of software packages can best serve writing classes (e.g., "Matching Software and Curriculum: A Description of Four Text-Analysis Programs," Kinkead, 1986; "A Comparative Study of the First-Generation Invention Software," McDaniel, 1986). The journal also published articles that suggested new directions the field would take (e.g., "Interactive Networking: Creating Bridges Between Speech, Writing, and Composition," Thompson, 1988). Schwartz and Bridwell-Bowles (1987) included two articles from *Computers and Composition* in their special *CCC* bibliography, McDaniel (1986) and Hawisher (1986), marking both with an asterisk and noting them as a good place for "novice computer users [to] start" (p. 463). The bibliography also included articles from *Computers and the Humanities* by Glynda Hull (1987), the chair of the 1986 Computers and Writing conference, and Hugh Burns (1984), the developer of TOPOI; and Elaine Kerr's 1986 article from the *IEEE Transactions on Professional Communication*, "Electronic Leadership: A Guide to Moderating Online Conferences."

consuming problems of finding, evaluating, and using software. The result is a Catch-22 situation: Writing researchers and instructors know little about the software available or being designed; therefore they do not use it and as a result cannot contribute to its improvement in the usual cycle of implementation, analysis, and evaluation. This impasse also keeps us from overcoming our profession's technological naiveté and inexperience. (McDaniel, 1986, p. 20)

EMERGING TRENDS IN COMPUTERS AND COMPOSITION STUDIES

During 1986–1988, the profession was simultaneously consolidating its past work and absorbing the impact of new technological developments. Just as specialists in computers and composition were becoming more critical of the claims made for the value of word processing, computer-mediated communication (CMC), the most tangibly social of all writing media, made its way into the profession. With its ability to create electronic forums where writers could meet and exchange ideas online, it seemed an ideal technology for the writing classroom conceived now as a site for social

The 1988 EDUCOM/NCRIPTAL Competition
Best Curriculum Innovation, Writing
Title: ELECTRONIC DIALECTICAL NOTEBOOK
Authors: Susan Kirschner, John Miller, and Dan Revel
Equipment: Macintosh Plus
Publisher: Unpublished
Cost: (Not applicable)
The ELECTRONIC DIALECTICAL NOTEBOOK was developed to teach critical thinking and writing skills in a core course in Basic Inquiry at Lewis & Clark College. . .

Just as exchanges of written notebooks between peers encourage fresh perspectives, the ELECTRONIC DIALECTICAL NOTEBOOK challenges students to conceive of reading, writing, and thinking as social acts. (Johnston & Kozma, 1988, p. 32)

Conferencing is a print medium in the sense that it deals with written text that appears on the reader's screen. As with other forms of print, the writer is absent. . . .Participants in computer conferencing have to adapt to an environment exactly opposite to the world of the mime. They must use language as if they were having conversation, yet their messages must be written. (Spitzer, 1986, p. 19)

interaction. In journals and conferences, CMC, like word processing before it, was hailed as remarkable for its ability to transform writing classes into active social sites of intellectual exchange. Writing in 1988, Batson argued that classroom use of synchronous CMC "blurs social distinctions in the class, making the teacher less the center of most ideas and energy. Instead of staying above the fray as a disinterested expert, the teacher joins the class as a fellow writer" (p. 33). In the same article, he argued that "some of the current theories about how to teach writing [seemed to be] developed specifically with networks in mind" (p. 32). Thus the view of writing as social process, already beginning to inform teachers' ways of viewing word processing classrooms, found a more-than-comfortable fit with the communal cyberspace of computer networks.

   However, CMC entered more than writing classes during this time—it also became a part of faculty members' professional lives. The multivoiced conversation on PARTI, a national electronic discussion group founded by Michael Spitzer at New York Institute of Technology, provides evidence of this trend. Between December 1984 and August 1987 approximately 100 people joined the conference, which was supported by a $35,000 grant from Exxon. According to Spitzer (email correspondence, September 28, 1993), "Discussion topics on PARTI ranged from inquiries and responses regarding specific software packages to practical advice on setting up computer classrooms, to teaching strategies for use in classrooms with one computer or twenty computers, to a scholarly discussion of artificial intelligence and its impact on writing instruction and software." More important than the content of the discussions, however, was the fact that these conversations were taking place online, with writing instructors from one end of the country to another. Spitzer's online conference served to prepare many writing professionals for the arrival of the email lists, which made their presence felt to many with Fred Kemp's founding of Megabyte University in 1989.

We have noted in this chapter the increasingly professional appearance of *Computers and Composition*, the field's representation as bibliography in *CCC*, and the emergence of the field as a site for research in the six articles published during this period in *RTE*. All of this suggests the emergence of a field of study, which would lead to graduate courses in our specialty. Indeed, these graduate courses began to emerge. In the spring of 1986, Colette Daiute offered such a course at Harvard University. Ilana Snyder, an Australian scholar and educator, described this course in the following email communication. She provided a picture of the field in 1986 that squares with the picture sketched in this chapter: a mix of hands-on experience, theory, and research:

> I spent 6 months in Boston with my husband and two sons. Ray who's an Oncologist studied Biostatistics at Harvard, and I took Colette's course. I knew nothing about computers but intuitively felt that they could be useful for writing and the classroom.
>
> The course comprised 3 hours a week: 2 hours lecture and one hour in the Harvard lab: very well endowed with computers and support people . . . .
>
> Colette began the course with an overview of writing theory and research—the emphasis was on the shift from product to process and the more recent insight that context was important. She gave the 20 students about 15 articles—all on writing theory. When she'd established a strong theoretical rationale for an approach to the introduction of computers, she started talking about their possibili-

Harvard Graduate School of Education (Catalogue 1985–86)
Computers and Writing
P-425
Colette Daiute
The purpose of this course is to review computer writing tools and explore their effects on writers. We discuss the cognitive, social, and physical effects of computer tools such as word processors, electronic mail systems, and automatic text analysis programs on beginning and advanced writers. For example, we study the cognitive effects of using a keyboard and a writing instrument that responds to the writer. We also critique the argument that children readily can develop writing skills from their conversational abilities when they use computer networks, because these networks highlight the communicative functions of writing. In addition, we examine the role of interactive writing tools in changing the relationship between thinking, talking, reading, and writing. Topics include the story of writing tools and their impact on literacy, review of interactive writing hardware and software, developmental and psycholinguistic theories of language production, review and critique of recent research on interactive writing, access problems, privacy, and authorship issues. (Daiute, 1985–86)

Autobiog

ties. She presented the research from 1978 till 1985. She also used a Datashow to demonstrate different kinds of software: word processing, adventure games. We had a number of assignments. The first was an autobiography examining our writing history. The second was an evaluation of a word processing package looking at its features and how it achieved each feature. She encouraged us to look at as many packages as possible—I used both Apple 11es and IBMs. I compared Bank Street Writer and WordStar (!!!). The major assignment was a piece of resarch: we had to design a study, implement it and then write the whole thing up.

I did a controlled study at my kids' school (the Peabody Elementary School) with Year 7 students which compared students using an invention program (can't remember the name) for writing and a group using the same invention strategies without the computer. For me it was an invaluable assignment: I learned heaps about research processes and how to write it up. She gave all students a lot of her time in supporting these learning processes. But I do remember that she preferred to communicate via email (Yes—she had us all using email to communicate with her and each other). (email correspondence, August 21, 1994)

Since 1983, the *MLA Job Information List* has shown a marked increase in advertisements for people with computer training or experience, mostly for those who can bring that experience to technical writing and rhetoric and composition programs. Previously, most

RECOGNIZING CHALLENGES: DEFINING A SPECIALTY

By the middle of the 1980s, the field faced a number of complex challenges as it developed its own body of theory, research, and practice. Computers and composition was a relatively young and unfamiliar specialty within the larger arena of English composition—and within the even broader field of English studies. It thus had yet to identify—for itself or for other scholars—a recognizable set of intellectual tasks that would give it credence as a disciplined area of study. Computers and composition specialists were faced not only with the need to carve out an increasingly productive role for themselves within their home departments and programs, but also with the need to define the relationship between their emerging area of specialization and the larger profession of composition studies, and with the need to support an increasing sense of rigor in their scholarship and research.

of the people eligible to apply for such positions would have acquired their experience after receiving their degrees, and so would be coming from postgraduate positions or jobs. Today, graduate programs in rhetoric, composition, and technical writing around the country are beginning to produce writing specialists with heightened computer awareness and appreciation and more and more experience in applying computers in teaching and research. (McDaniel, 1990, p. 87)

Computer Specialists in English Departments: Wearing the White Coat

First among the concerns associated with disciplinary identity—at least in terms of immediacy to most computers and composition specialists—was the difficulty of defining what scholars and teachers within this growing field should be doing, and how they should be treated, at their home institutions. Certainly computers and composition specialists themselves were uncertain about the various career paths they could pursue within their special field of interest. Without a history or a tradition, the young field was wide open and exciting but could not offer its young scholars clear direction and purpose.

Some computers and composition specialists considered themselves primarily software designers charged with the project of creating computer-assisted instructional packages informed by the values of composition specialists and designed for use by English composition teachers (cf. Costanzo, 1986; Madden, 1987; Selfe, 1987). During this period, as LeBlanc (1993) noted in his historical overview of soft-

Annual EDUCOM/NCRIP-TAL Higher Education Software Competition
New Product Awards
Liberal Arts
Engineering
Accounting
Law
Innovative Computer Use Awards

ware design projects in composition studies, many ambitious and successful projects began or were completed. Among many examples were Mimi Schwartz's development of PREWRITE at Stockton State College (eventually to be published by MindScape); Nancy Kaplan, Stuart Davis, and Joseph Martin's development of PROSE at Cornell University (which won the 1987 NCRIPTAL/EDUCOM Award for Outstanding Software and was published by McGraw-Hill); The Daedalus Group's development of an instructional system at The University of Texas (which was to win the 1990 NCRIPTAL/EDUCOM Award for Outstanding Software); Christine Neuwirth's and David Kaufer's development of NOTES at Carnegie Mellon; John Smith's development of the WRITING ENVIRONMENT (WE) at the University of North Carolina at Chapel Hill; William Wresch's development of WRITER'S HELPER (which won the 1988 NCRIPTAL/EDUCOM Award for Outstanding Software) and WRITER'S HELPER II at the University of Wisconsin Stevens Point (published by CONDUIT); and Helen Schwartz's development of SEEN (published by CONDUIT) and ORGANIZE (published by Wadsworth) at Oakland University.

These efforts, however, were not undertaken without a great deal of difficulty. English Departments were not particularly receptive to software designers' efforts, often seeing the task of software design to be a distraction from the scholarly and pedagogical pursuits faculty were supposed to be attending to, often mistrusting and misunderstanding designers' efforts to market their software, and seldom providing the needed resources to support these efforts. As Paul LeBlanc (1993) pointed out:

Because program designers are writing teachers first, and program designers second, the development of a program, despite its rigors, must take place after the demands of a full teaching schedule. Indeed, 60 percent of the faculty program developers responding to EDUCOM's Academic Software Development Survey cite the lack of release time as the greatest barrier to program development (Keane & Gaither, 1988, p. 56). Mirroring [Nancy] Kaplan's experience, Keane and Gaither report that "faculty members expending considerable effort were not sure that administrators appreciated the importance of their work in software development" (p. 56). (p. 41)

This lack of support became more evident on a national scale as a generation of software developers began to approach tenure decisions in their home departments. By 1988, the field of computers and composition was growing, and some specialists had based a large proportion of their six years of pretenure work on the design and development of software for English composition classrooms. In 1987, Deborah Holdstein described the case of one software developer who faced the tenure-decision year:

Colleagues in more traditional disciplines denounce the work. Perhaps they're merely unfamiliar with software development. Perhaps they're threatened by the new technology. Perhaps they're genuinely concerned that technological pursuits violate the purer purposes of an English or humanities department. Whatever the reasons, by traditional standards, software compares rather badly with another tenure hopeful's book on prosody or another's on deconstruction, no matter how theory-based the software, no matter how many years of concentrated effort it demanded . . . . Come tenure time, he [the software developer] is trapped in a debilitating double bind. Whereas the obvious signals

"The Computer and the Inexperienced Writer," by Christine A. Hult
"Team Planning a Computerized Technical Writing Course," by Chris Madigan and Scott P. Sanders
"The Effects of a Full-Service Computer Room on Student Writing," by Richard Stracke
"Word Processing in the Business and Technical Writing Classroom," by Timothy Weiss
Computers and Controversy
"Grandfather and Computers," by Alan Peterson
Printout
"Printout: Textbooks for Writing with Computers," by Ken Autrey
Book Review
"Computer-Assisted Composition: Create Your Own," by Barbara L. Cambridge
Software Review
"A FAIR Response to Student Writing," by Stephen Hopkins and Earl Youngs.
Announcements

read, "Tenure will be given for this work," the more subtle signals require more scholarly semantic decoding: "This may be good for us, and we'll be eternally grateful, but it won't necessarily be good for you." (p. 123)

Other computers and compositionists saw themselves not as software designers, but rather as researchers charged with carrying out studies and agenda that would identify the effects computers were having on the composing processes and products of student writers. In *Computers and Composition* during this period, for example, 25%–50% of the feature articles in every issue were devoted to the reporting the results of research projects. In the pieces published during this period, scholars examined how individual programs such as WRITER'S WORKBENCH (e.g., Reid and Findlay, 1986), QUEST, and FREE (e.g., Strickland, 1987) seemed to affect the writing that students did; they investigated the effects of word-processing packages on students' writing processes, confidence as writers, and attitudes toward writing (e.g., Maik & Maik, 1987); conducted studies of revision patterns in computer-supported writing environments (e.g. Flinn, 1987); and tried to assess how the use of computers affected the quality of technical writing students' written products (e.g., T. Weiss, 1988).

At many institutions, the role of researcher proved a productive one for computers and compositionists to assume—although not entirely unproblematic, as we shall later note. The larger field of composition studies—influenced by the methods of cognitive psychology and educational case-study investigations—had already established, to some extent, the validity of empirical research as a scholarly pursuit for compositionists (North, 1987). As a result, many departments of English were familiar with such efforts and supported scholars who undertook them, providing release time, tenure and promotion, and merit raises to investigators who were able to publish research findings in recognized refereed journals such as *Research in the Teaching of English*, *Computers and Composition*, and *Written Communication*.

Researchers and the studies they conducted on computer use also gained some respectability in English departments because they were one of the first focuses for critical, reflective examinations within the emerging field. In a survey of research studies largely conducted during this period, for example, Hawisher (1989a) identified 42 studies that focused on writing in word-processing environments. Hawisher not only described and compared the findings of these studies, but, importantly, offered astute observations about the strengths and weaknesses of the results of various kinds of research. She noted that the ethnographic studies:

> in elucidating the subtle influences of computers in social interactions among students and teachers, suggest the importance of the cultural context in shaping writers' work . . . [that the] success or failure of students' encounters with word processing and writing might well depend on the context into which computers are introduced. (p. 56)

She also called for and recommended a rigorous and systematic approach to research on computers and writing that, if followed, would keep researchers busy for many years to come.

The road for computers and compositionists who focused on research, however, was not entirely free of obstacles. As we have noted earlier, *College English* published no articles on computers during this time, and *College Composition and Communication* featured fewer articles than in the period of 1983–1985. Smaller,

Flinn (1985)
Harris (1985)
Lutz (1983, 1987)
Nichols (1986)
Schipke (1986)
Selfe (1985)
(See Hawisher, 1989a, pp. 48–50)

Ethnographies
Curtiss (1984)
Dickinson (1986)
Herrmann (1985, 1987)
Reid (1985)
(Hawisher, 1989a, p. 51)

Those of us who write and teach with computers realize we are dealing with a tool that is at once more formidable than a typewriter, even in its most advanced form. If we are to make progress in our research so that studies into written composition and word processing are more than temporary explorations, we must continue to examine the effects of computers. But our research must be systematic and reflective, evaluating what we have learned in the past as we move toward the future. Without such an assessment, we have a confusing array of results that are often misinterpreted. (Hawisher, 1986, p. 25)

Our study suggests several generalizations that might help teachers adapt instruction as they move from a traditional to a computer classroom:

—Teaching in a microcomputer classroom creates serious time pressures, resulting in the need to streamline activities and to find efficient instructional strategies. Our teachers found it important to plan carefully, to prepare instructional handouts, and, in general, to structure classes more thoroughly than they did for traditional classes.

—Teachers appreciate a lab assistant, especially in the first few weeks of the term. Student workers or graduate students can be an effective part of teaching composition in a lab setting. A single graduate assistant—without the demands of planning and grading—can cover multiple sections.

—Teachers are more likely to adapt instruction to teaching in a microcomputer classroom if they are not simultaneously teaching regular sections of the same composition course. (Bernhardt, Wojahn, & Edwards, 1990, pp. 370–371)

more specialized journals accepted a larger proportion of research on computers and composition but attracted limited readerships and offered less prestige or visibility. *Computers and Composition*, for example, had only 500 to 550 subscribers a year during this period, whereas approximately 8,500 subscribers received *College Composition and Communication*. This situation, as McDaniel (1990) noted, resulted—among colleagues within the larger profession of English composition studies in a "double ignorance" about computers and composition research itself and about the publications that published such work. As a result, the work of researchers in the new field was "vulnerable to misinterpretation and prejudice" (p. 90).

Because work in computers and composition seemed not a sure route to tenure and promotion, some computers and composition specialists felt that they had to maintain two active programs of work in order to succeed: one designed to achieve recognition in more conventional areas of scholarship or research, and one in computer studies. Ellen Barton, for example, in addition to her work with computers, maintained an active research program in linguistics; John Slatin maintained an active record in literary studies; and Billie Wahlstrom kept publishing in communication theory. Despite these very real challenges, however, other computers and compositionists who focused their efforts on conducting investigations and publishing accounts of their research on technology were generally able to establish acceptable and sometimes comfortable levels of departmental support for their efforts.

If scholars who were conducting research on computers and composition topics were enjoying some level of acceptance through their association with the general endeavor of composition research, specialists who identified their contribution as curricular were encountering more difficulty. In general, these individuals saw their mission as helping teachers integrate technology successfully within specific classroom settings. Among the challenges that these colleagues identified were adequate access to reliable computer equipment, a sufficient number of technicians who could provide support for this equipment, the availability of flexible scheduling options that could accommodate new pedagogical approaches, a need for expert consultants who could answer the questions that both teachers and students had about individual applications and who were willing to dedicate the time necessary to do so, the myriad problems surrounding funding and logistics; and the time to plan carefully and innovatively for the integration of technology in specific classes (cf. Holdstein, 1987; Madigan & Sanders, 1988; McDaniel, 1990; Stracke, 1988).

McDaniel (1990) described the task these colleagues undertook and the challenges they faced:

> This is an enormous job, complicated by many logistical, administrative, political, financial, and pedagogical issues. Getting students to the computers or the computers to them involves a litany of responsibilities and concerns: justification, access, scheduling, monitoring, assistance, security, repair, maintenance, and so on. Also, instructional materials have to be changed, reshaped, or created anew to accompany the technology. Such effort is necessary and important and should be credited as such, but it often goes unnoticed. (p. 91)

Certainly, English department chairs across the country were having an increasingly difficult time providing the resources that these specialists were asking for in connection with their work: whole classrooms outfitted with

I even smile to myself—as an English professor (a Miltonist) and department chair now turned chief academic officer—at the memory of the absolute incredulity of one of our computer science majors that *English* should have its own dedicated laboratory of IBM PCs. What was very much an emergent field several years ago now has not just literature but bibliographies and journals. (Sadler, 1987, p. 32)

It should surprise no one by now that the introduction of the computer to the English department writing curriculum has been met with new variations on this old theme of resistance. And if there is as yet no systematic "theory" on appropriate training of college instructors for computers and writing (or much theory on computers and writing), there is even less practice. Where it exists at all, training in computers and writing is often haphazard (particularly when we compare college efforts with those at the secondary level), often foiled by the myriad components of hardware, computer-center time, and interdepartmental cooperation. (Holdstein, 1989, p. 128)

computers, elaborate personal workstations with costly printing capabilities, programming and technical assistants, travel funds for attending technology conferences, released time for undertaking software development, and curricular integration efforts.

Complicating this situation was the fact that many of the projects these faculty seemed bent on pursuing—designing and setting up computer-supported writing classrooms, creating computer-supported instructional materials for writing courses, teaching other faculty how to integrate computers into their literature courses—seldom fit neatly within the framework of traditional reward structures of tenure, promotion, or merit adjustments, which were oriented along the lines of conventional teaching, research, and publication criteria (cf. Gerrard, 1991; Holdstein, 1987; McDaniel, 1990). As Ellen McDaniel (1990) noted:

the computer person has the unenviable task of taking care of everything that has to do with computers in the department, from writing technical specifications on purchase orders and keeping inventory, to responding to surveys about educational technology that the department head receives. Such activities can easily fulfill the individual's faculty service obligation, but how that contribution is perceived varies from department to department. Some departments value the work; many do not. (p. 91)

This situation was exacerbated, further, by the fact that few departments, during this period, saw the need to have more than one faculty member concentrating on computer use. Computers and composition faculty often found themselves isolated from their immediate colleagues by an interest in technology.

Computer Specialists in Composition Studies: Defining Professional Relationships

A second, and related, challenge characterizing the period from 1986 to 1988 involved the increasingly obvious need to define the relationship between the nascent specialty of computer studies and the broader, more established field of English composition studies. If English departments had difficulty understanding and relating to the work of computers and composition specialists, the profession of composition studies seemed equally uncertain.

Although the major annual conferences in composition studies (the annual *Conference on College Composition and Communication* and the *Convention of the National Council of Teachers of English*) provided some room for computer sessions at their gatherings, both the time granted to the new field and the influence of the small field were limited—by necessity and by interest. At these gatherings, it became increasingly clear that conducting serious research in computers and composition, or even remaining up to date on the research that had been conducted, demanded more time and attention than many compositionists were able to devote to the task. As a result, panels focusing on computers and composition were increasingly populated by computer specialists who had designed computer software, who had received major grants to study computer-supported writing, or who had worked in large universities with already established computer-supported writing classrooms. These sessions were often characterized by specialized concerns about technology (e.g., software copyright policies, software piracy, computer networks, telecommunications), highly technical vocabulary (e.g., macros, microlabs, interactive fiction, minicomputers), and references to a rapidly growing body of research and re-

1986 CCCC

Panel: **Expanding Views of Computer Conferencing**
Regency Ballroom H, 3rd Floor
Chair: Stephen Marcus
Associate Chair: F. Michler Bishop, Jr.
Speakers:
Valarie M. Arms, "Structuring a Computer Conference: Models and Protocols."
Helen J. Schwartz, " The Affect and Effect of Computer Conferencing."
Diane Balestri, "Planning for Successful Outcomes of a Computer Conference."
Respondent: Charles Moran
Recorder: Barry M. Maid
(CCCC Program, 1986, p. 58)

Visual and Verbal Thinking: Drawing and Word-Processing Software in Writing Instruction
The advantage to cultivating visual and verbal thinking in a writing course through the use of drawing and word-processing software should be apparent. Some instructors, however, will argue that their students need as much work with language as possible and that spending time to develop students' visual as well as verbal abilities detracts from the development of the latter. Such an argument misses the point. But developing visual abilities more efficiently and more effectively is possible if we restrict writing instruction to verbal expression alone. It is ultimately a question of helping students learn to take full advantage of all of the cognitive resources they have available to them. Failure to do this amounts to handicapping students in their efforts to learn to think and to write. (Fortune, 1989, p. 160)

searchers that was accessible only in specialized journals (e.g., *Computers and Composition*, *Computers in the Humanities*, *Collegiate Microcomputer*). Such panels, as they became more specialized, were easily ignored by leaders in the profession who had established interests in other areas of scholarship and research. Given that the field of computers and composition studies did not fit easily within any of the major categories of English studies—writing program administration, writing centers, research on writing, literary studies, rhetoric, or teacher education—it was often considered overly narrow and technical even by most composition specialists.

Evidence of the field's marginalization was apparent both in the relative silence and the uncertainty with which the National Council of Teachers of English and the Conference on College Composition and Communication approached computers and composition studies during this period. During the mid 1980s, for example, computers received only minimal recognition by program chairs of the NCTE and the CCCC—both in their oral addresses to their respective conventions and in their written program notes—even though the rapid spread of such technologies had touched most schools around the country in important ways. In addition, although a steady number of sessions were devoted to computers and composition topics at these conferences, neither gathering knew exactly how to identify the work within the convention programs. In 1986 through 1988, for example, the NCTE program listed "media" as the category within which computer sessions were identified, along with television and film studies. The CCCC, during this same period, listed computers under a different topic area each year: "Language and Computers" (1986), "Computers and Writing" (1987), and "Computers and Instruction" (1988).

Faced with some sense of isolation within

the profession, increasing numbers of computers and composition specialists recognized the need to connect—in increasingly precise ways—the practical work in computers and composition to the rich veins of composition theory and research. Evidence of this realization existed not only in the papers that computers and compositionists presented at conferences, but also in the publications produced by these same individuals. In a collection of papers that grew out of the *Fourth Computers and Writing Conference* in Pittsburgh—edited by Hawisher and Selfe (1989) and published by Teachers College Press as *Critical Perspectives on Computers and Composition Instruction*—were pieces focusing on literacy concerns (e.g., Selfe, 1989a), reading problems (e.g., Haas, 1989b), basic writers (e.g., Gerrard, 1989), visual and verbal thinking (e.g., Fortune, 1989), and social theories (e.g., Eldred, 1989).

At the same time that some computers and composition scholars were working to combat the effects of specialization and disciplinary isolation, others were beginning to feel the need for increasing rigor and intellectual order within the new area of specialization (e.g., Eldred, 1989; Daiute, 1986; Haas & Hayes, 1986). In part, these scholars were influenced by the ongoing work of colleagues in the broader field of composition studies, which itself was becoming increasingly sophisticated in terms of social theories (e.g., Berlin, 1987; Faigley, 1986; LeFevre, 1987), scholarly and research methods (e.g., Lauer & Asher, 1988; North, 1987), and interdisciplinary connections (e.g., Cooper, 1986; Gere, 1987; Tompkins, 1985). In part, they also recognized that the sophisticated scholarship and research of these colleagues yielded both increased recognition and rewards at their home institutions and at national conventions. These individuals undertook efforts to connect their computer use or their research on computers to current themes

Connectivity—in writing theory or in microcomputer innovations—stresses that knowledge does not emerge from a vacuum. It helps to establish a collaborative environment. All these networking devices link not just terminal with terminal, but individual with individual or groups, mind with minds. With increased storage and particularly with networking, the "P" in PC comes to mean public as well as personal. (Eldred, 1989, p. 216)

1986: Using image processing and pattern recognition, Lilian Schwartz comes up with an answer to a 500-year-old question: Who was the Mona Lisa? Her conclusion: Leonardo da Vinci himself.

1987: Computerized trading helps push NYSE stocks to their greatest single-day loss.

1987: Current speech systems can provide any *one* of the following: a large vocabulary, continuous speech recognition, or speaker independence.

1988: Computer memory today costs 1/8 of what it did in 1950.

1988:   In   the   U.S. 4,700,000 microcomputers, 120,000   minicomputers, and 11,500 mainframes are sold in this year. (Kurzweil, 1990, pp. 481–482)

1986: The first edition of the CCCC *Longman Bibliography* (I was associate editor) was typed in· on PCs, uploaded to a mainframe—where it was organized, formatted in WYLBUR, SCRIPT, and something else and then transferred to the university printer for page marking,   etc.   (Randy Woodland, University of Michigan   at   Dearborn) (C&W, 1994)

1986: In early 1986, although I had published with Heinemann, *Every Child Is A Writer*, 1985, (utilizing technology extensively), I was still resistant to get/use a PC. I was thrilled with my IBM selectric typewriter. In late 1986, a colleague pointed out to me that PCs save *time*! This was   the   catalyst   that worked for me, so I came back to the states (I was living in Germany at the time) and spent a month researching and buying my first   computer.   (Joan Tornow,   University   of Texas, Austin) (C&W, 1994)

in composition studies. At yet another level, computers and composition specialists were also reacting against what McDaniel (1990) later termed the *white coat* syndrome—the expectation of both colleagues and administrators   that   computers   and   compositionists should occupy themselves with copying disks, installing   software,   troubleshooting   printer problems, and attending to cables.

However, they were also beginning to recognize the challenges associated with a scholarly project that drew on at least two very different fields. The mid-1980s marked a period of explosive growth in computer technology. By 1990, Raymond Kurzweil noted that computer technology was changing so rapidly that the power per unit was doubling—at the same cost—every 18–24 months (p. 8). Indeed, computer scientists and technology critics were hard pressed to keep up with changing technology and the increasing realization of how this technology was related to cultural and social issues. It was during the mid 1980s, for example, that the first commercial hypertext programs, GUIDE and HYPERCARD, were marketed; that local area computer networks (LANs) became viable options for English composition classrooms; and that synchronous communication   systems   like   REAL-TIME   WRITER   and Daedalus' INTERCHANGE were developed to support real-time conversational exchanges. It was also during this period that technology critics like Langdon Winner (1986), Joseph Weizenbaum (1986), Cheris Kramarae (1988b), and Shoshana Zuboff (1988), and C. Paul Olson (1987) published key works that tied technological issues to cultural and social formations.

Given this period of rapid expansion and growth in technology studies, computers and composition scholars found themselves hard pressed to keep up as technology experts. And, at the same time technology was expanding and changing, composition studies—as a professional field—was maturing and supporting increasingly sophisticated reflections on historical, social, and theoretical themes. Many computers and composition specialists, caught between the two worlds, felt an obligation to remain current both in their knowledge of technology and in their understanding of composition studies. Indeed, their sense of obligation was often heightened by departments that required an active record of nationally recognized publication in well-known composition journals and an active record of institutional service in computer-supported curricula and computer labs.

This complex set of forces threatened the very identity of computers and composition as a field. Rather than pursuing undiluted interests in technology and technological innovations, specialists in the field found ample reasons to concentrate on the *composition* part of computers and composition studies—to constitute their concerns as bound closely to composition studies. Given the complex forces involved—at scholars' home institutions, at professional conferences, in publication venues—this challenge would continue to shape the field of computers and composition for the next several years.

1986: I began work on my PhD in English with an emphasis in rhetoric/composition at Arizona State University (same year as David Schwalm came there to direct first-year comp) and was, *for the first time, required* to produce all written class work on a computer with word processing. This requirement was operationalized through the mandatory Introduction to Research in the English first semester weed-em-out course that all new grad students took. This was my first exposure and initiation into computers and writing—enacted on/with my brand-new Compaq outfitted with WordPerfect 4.1. (Martha Townsend, University of Missouri at Columbia) (C&W, 1994)

1987: By 1987, I had purchased my own IBM clone and WordPerfect software and had enrolled in Purdue's Creative Writing Master's program, where almost everyone used a computer on a wordprocessor. (Bonnie Charter, North Central Missouri College) (C&W, 1994)

COLLEAGUES REMEMBER: PATRICIA SULLIVAN

I was graduate student at Carnegie-Mellon beginning in 1980 and I left there in January of 1985, finishing my degree in Rhetoric in 1986. I primarily worked with Richard Young, although Linda Flower ended up directing my dissertation. When I went to Carnegie-Mellon, I was very interested in technology because of my previous training. I had been a student of

Walter Ong's in the '70s and he never used computers, yet he made a few choice predictions about how they impacted on the way we write. So, I was interested in trying to explore some of those ideas and see what kinds of impacts computers had on writing. It was one of my goals when I went to Carnegie-Mellon and one of the reasons that I chose Carnegie-Mellon, because it had so many computers and I thought I would have ample opportunity to study these questions.

When I came to Carnegie-Mellon I experimented on myself, writing online all the time to see what kind of impact that had on my writing style and practices. In '82, though, I got interested in library research when I was offered a part-time job in the library. They were starting a new project called the Electronic Library. I spent a lot of time in the library doing research, so I knew a lot of the librarians and they asked me to come over and take a part time job helping them with their online card catalog.

In '82, OCLC, which is the biggest library services company for online materials, had brought a company called Avatar, which had a very promising online catalog but a terrible front-end interface. The interface was three screens long and the language in it was totally technical. OCLC developed various interfaces for library patrons and had them user tested. Carnegie-Mellon was one of those test sites and I became the person who tested the interface.

They decided what they were going to put in the interface, cutting down the number of searches and changing the order of the searches, for example. I would then do things like sit by the terminals and talk to people as they tried to use the new interface and find out what they were trying to do and what they thought each of these searches meant and gather information. At that time most of the library and information science research was focused on librarians, particularly in the online area, because all of the online services until the early '80s were performed by librarians. So they were focused on trying to get librarians and patrons to learn how to do Boolean searches.

This was a big jump and they didn't have the research methods to use to go after the patrons; they didn't have the right language. There were all sorts of problems that librarians were facing as they tried to put their catalogs online, which they had decided they needed to do for economic and other reasons and because they just believed it was a better way to do it. Librarians are well-intentioned people and their main motivation was that they thought that patrons would ultimately be better served by online card catalogs.

Changes were being made in the MARC record, which is that absolute online record that books have in the OCLC system. Changes were made in the way you could search those records, based on what people really needed to find out. Let's take the key word *search*. There are many different ways that you could set up a key word search; you could say the key word is going to look at the title field or the author field. It could look at the book description; it could look at the Library of Congress Subject Heading. There are all these various fields that a key word could search for, but key word to a librarian meant the Library of Congress Subject Heading.

So originally they were setting up key word searches often to search that field and key word doesn't mean that to the rest of us. We might get very confusing results if we put in a key word and we got stuff back from the Library of Congress Subject Heading. So what happened is that as they did research with patrons they made adjustments not just to the front end, but with the back end as well and to what fields would be searched when various terms were used. Different companies made these decisions different ways. So you'll find there are a number of online card catalogs that you can purchase for your library, and they don't always search the databases in the same ways; it's not standardized.

The patrons' reaction to this technology . . . well, people were dazzled. It didn't matter that they were at Carnegie-Mellon and they were used to a lot of computers. They were dazzled that they could come into the library and put a term in and get 60 hits and they were also intimidated by that because as they started to look at those hits they may not have been what they were looking for. That's the nature of the card catalog; it's a gross kind of searching mechanism and to really be very precise about getting what you want you have to use Boolean searches.

The patron that walks in off the street is not going to know how to use Boolean searching. So there was a big debate inside library science whether patrons should be taught Boolean searching. There was anxiety that they weren't finding all of the sources that they could have found. That anxiety that the librarians had was not the same as the patrons' responses. The patrons were overwhelmed by the number, but it didn't bother them if they didn't get all the sources.

The bulk of the people that walk up to the card catalog are undergraduates. And all they want is a reference; they are most likely doing a paper and their teacher told them they needed references and so they're not invested in it the way the scholar would be invested in finding every resource.

So my dissertation became about search strategies and trying to compare expert and novice search strategies in order to understand better how the patrons search. I was not interested in the experts, but I had to use the experts because almost all of the research done was done on the experts. So, I needed to study expert searching in order to make sense of the project to the librarians and to fit it in to the literature that they had. I was really interested in the regular patrons. The other thing that I was doing was I was trying to develop a methodology for doing patron research. The librarians had used interviews and surveys as their main way of getting information about patrons and how they thought about things. And Information Science had used keystroke capture records, but you really needed process information at that point because they just didn't have any idea of how people went about using these catalogs, so it was difficult to see what changes they needed to implement.

So I worked on a method to try to put together interviews with protocols and keystroke capture records to get an integrated picture of how the people were going about this process of looking for resources that they needed. And instead of developing and using the canned questions that they used, I developed the questions by going through those initial sitting by the catalog sessions and then talking to people. So I used the actual questions that people brought to the library as the questions in my study.

At the time, my work was not well received in English. I was very well received by the librarians. They got my dissertation supported by a grant and they gave me any kind of help that I needed. They got me publishing in the library journals; they were so enthusiastic they changed the interface according to what I found out. It really was very gratifying work in that sense.

The English department originally didn't accept my proposal for my dissertation because they couldn't see how it was rhetoric. That was my fault. It seemed so obvious to me that I was studying how people who eventually would write with sources were doing the early work and actually finding the sources and thinking through their projects. When you have to look for things you have to label what your project is, you have to come up with "What am I looking for," "What am I after?" and in a sense you are doing some of the important categorizations of the work that you ultimately write about. In typical graduate student form, I just assumed that everyone would know that. It was interesting to have to convince them that what I was doing was rhetoric.

What I did was I had a long meeting with Richard Young and he suggested a different title for my dissertation. It ended up as "Rhetoric and the search for externally stored knowledge: Toward a computer age art of research." The other thing he suggested that I do was focus both the first chapter and the background on writing research papers and the relevance that this had to writing research papers. That made my work less relevant to the librarian and more acceptable to the English department.

But it has had a very frustrating effect because I finished my dissertation in '86 and talked about it at AERA that year and got very positive feedback. But because I had conceptualized it the way I did, I had trouble getting it accepted at CHI (Computer–Human Interactions) because it sounded too English. They don't have that much traffic with information science anyway. They're more the interface people. So I had trouble with CHI and I had trouble with some of the information science conferences because they didn't think it was information science, and my work was never accepted to be presented at 4Cs, even though I submitted it several years running.

I think that was my learning experience—being interdisciplinary. You have to learn all the languages of the groups that you're dealing with. You have to constantly reframe your project into the questions and interests that each of these groups have. I wasn't very good at doing that when I first started, and I think that my dissertation didn't get out to as big as a community because I didn't quite know how to be interdisciplinary—I was learning how to be interdisciplinary. I don't have that problem as much now. I will typically go to engineering conferences, to computer conferences, to English conferences; I don't have problems focusing. I think it's because I learned through the experiences of my dissertation work.

Pat Sullivan is an Associate Professor of English and Director of Technical Writing at Purdue University.

4

1989–1991: Coming of Age—The Rise of Cross-Disciplinary Perspectives and a Consideration of Difference

Modern technology is no more neutral than medieval cathedrals or the Great Wall of China; it embodies the values of a particular industrial civilization, especially those of elites that rest their claims to hegemony on technical mastery. We must articulate and judge these values in a cultural critique of technology.

—Andrew Feenberg, *Critical Theory of Technology*, 1991, p. v.

THE CONTEXT: THE FIELD OF COMPOSITION STUDIES, 1989–1991

In the period of 1989–1991, the field of composition studies continued to grow and define itself. Among the signs of continuing self-defini-

Composition studies distinguishes itself from other disciplines, whose focus is invariably on a body of knowledge or a set of texts, by its central concern with an *activity*, the act of writing. The major concern of most composition specialists is teaching writing well. To do this work effectively, they also attempt to answer broader questions about literacy by studying composing from historical, social, psychological, political, and academic perspectives, often borrowing useful concepts and methods from other disciplines. As members of an emerging discipline, composition specialists also encounter problems. They must learn new ways of thinking about their field, wrestle with terminology, develop better methods of teaching and research, create adequate bibliographical and research sources, and build support for their work among people who may be hostile, sympathetic, or indifferent toward it. (Lindemann & Tate, 1991, p. v)

With WAC, the old battles between access and exclusion, excellence and equity, scientific and humanist world views, liberal and professional education, all come down to very specific questions of responsibility for curriculum and teaching. WAC ultimately asks: in what ways will graduates of our institutions use language, and how shall we teach them to use it in those ways? And behind this two-part question lies a deeper one: what discourse communities—and ultimately, what social class—will students be equipped to enter? That is an extremely complex question in our heterogeneous society. It is a question that Americans have consistently begged because it forces us to face painful issues of opportunity, of equality, of democracy in education. (Russell, 1991, p. 307)

The research that led to this book began when we caught a glimpse of a purloined letter in our own field: the pervasive com-

tion were the publication of a free-standing volume titled *An Introduction to Composition Studies* (1991), edited by Erika Lindemann, the originator of the *CCCC Bibliography of Composition and Rhetoric*, and Gary Tate, the editor of the 1976 and 1986 volumes of bibliographical essays titled *Teaching Composition*. In addition, the MLA initiated its *Research and Composition Series*, held two literacy conferences, and increased the number of sessions devoted to the field of composition studies in its annual convention. Attendance at the CCCC annual convention continued to grow, reaching a record high at the 1990 convention, held in Chicago, with 3607 registrants—a record that stood through 1994 (Harvey, 1994).

Characteristic publications of this period include David Russell's (1991) history of the writing-across-the-curriculum movement in America, an important addition to the emerging history of the field; Patricia Bizzell and Bruce Herzberg's (1990) *The Rhetorical Tradition*, an anthology that made important texts readily available; Andrea Lunsford and Lisa Ede's (1990) *Singular Text/Plural Authors*, a substantial and wide-ranging study of collaborative writing; Gregory Clark's (1990) *Dialogue, Dialectic, and Conversation: A Social Perspective on the Function of Writing*, and Mike Rose's (1989) *Lives on the Boundary*, winner of the MLA's Shaughnessy Prize in that year. Characteristic journal articles of this period include Linda Brodkey's (1989) "On the Subjects of Class and Gender in 'The Literacy Letters'," published in *College English*; Mary Kupiec Cayton's (1990) "What Happens When Things Go Wrong: Women and Writing Blocks," published in the *Journal of Advanced Composition*; Peter Elbow's (1991) "Reflections on Academic Discourse: How It Relates to Freshmen and Colleagues," published in *College English*; Tom Fox's (1990) "Basic Writing as Cultural Conflict," published in the *Journal of Education*; and "Remediation as Social Construct: Perspectives from an Analysis of Classroom Discourse," authored by Glynda Hull, Mike Rose, Kay Losey Fraser, and Marisa Castellano (1991), and published in *College Composition and Communication*.

As the titles and subjects of these works suggest, the field's development during this period was characterized by the further expansion of its ongoing inquiry into the contexts of writing and teaching, focusing more steadily and thoroughly than before on issues of gender, race, and class. Implicit in much of this work was a critique of the writing-process movement—a movement that had been at least midwife to the birth of composition studies itself. The process movement of the late 1970s and early-to-mid-1980s began to be seen as inappropriately centered on the individual, autonomous writer, thus obscuring the social aspects of composing; and as inappropriately assuming a monolithic "student writer," thus obscuring the complex assortment of differences among writers. As in any dynastic or paradigmatic change, defining the new entailed defining the old, and pioneers in the writing-process movement were treated roughly in this period, in much the same way that current traditional rhetoric became the evil other against which Moffett, Emig, Murray, Elbow, and others had defined themselves in the late 1960s and early 1970s.

During this period we can discern a number of forces at work: feminist criticism, cultural criticism, critical pedagogy, and a reemergence of the assumption that part of the teacher's mission was to accustom students to the ways of academic writing. None of these forces was new to the field, yet during this period they gained strength and voice, as they moved their concerns to the center of professional discourse about composition studies.

monsense assumption that writing is inherently and necessarily a solitary, individual act. What caused us, six years ago, to look not through this assumption but at it, to see the purloined letter. . . . The answer to our mystery is simple and even perhaps predictable: our own experience as coauthors. Most succinctly, our interest in collaborative writing grew out of the dissonance generated by the difference between our personal experience as coauthors and the responses of many of our friends and colleagues. (Lunsford & Ede, 1990, p. 5)

This is an essay about the ways discourses construct our teaching. In postmodern theories of subjectivity:

1) all subjects are the joint creations of language and discourse;
2) all subjects produced are ideological;
3) all subject positions are vulnerable to the extent that individuals do not or will not identify themselves as the subjects (i.e., the effects) of a discourse.

Those who occupy the best subject positions a discourse has to offer would have a vested interest in maintaining the illusion of speaking rather than being spoken by discourse. (Brodkey, 1989, p. 126)

In this paper, we examine remediation as a social construct, as the product of perceptions and beliefs about literacy and learning, and we illustrate some ways in which inaccurate and limiting notions of learners as being somehow cognitively defective and in need of "remedy" can be created and played out in the classroom. We will look closely at one student in one lesson and detail the interactional processes that contribute to her being defined as remedial—this specific case, however, is also representative of common kinds of classroom practices and widespread cultural assumptions, ones we've seen at work in our other studies. (Hull & Rose, 1989, pp. 139–154)

In 1986 *Research in the Teaching of English* (RTE) completed its 20th year of publication. This essay takes the completion of these first two decades as the occasion for an historical reflection on one portion of the broad range of language arts research it includes: studies of writing related to teaching and learning. Such a reflection seems particularly timely because this 20-year anniversary coincides with the publication of George Hillocks' *Research on Written Composition: New Directions for Teaching* (1986), a companion volume to Braddock, Lloyd-Jones, and Schoer's 1963 book *Research in Written Composition*. Together these books serve as bookends for the first 20 years of RTE and for the period when a research community in composition studies was consti-

Research and Professional Publications

In 1989, in the field's principal research journal, *Research in the Teaching of English* (*RTE*), Anne Herrington (1989) called for increased tolerance of ethnographic and qualitative research in the pages of *RTE* and in the research community generally. She argued that the research community, in general, and Hillocks (1986) in particular, "privileges quantitative, experimental research" (p. 132). Qualitative, ethnographic research, she noted, was well suited to the gathering of data about the interactions within functioning, complex systems. It was, for composition studies, an approach well suited to the study of the relationships among, and differences between, individual writers. Further, it was an approach well suited to the study of the ways in which individuals used literacy within communities—the classroom-as-community, the family, the home, the neighborhood, the culture.

Given the field's move toward the study of systems, and given its broader understanding of writing as one aspect of a person's and community's literacy practices, it was not accidental that research methodology during this period became increasingly qualitative. Linda Flower and the researchers at Carnegie Mellon, who had heretofore used the methods of cognitive psychology, moved away from the consideration of the single, autonomous writer and toward what they termed a sociocognitive approach, changing the site of their research from the college classroom to schools and literacy centers and including in the focus of their research writers' social interaction (e.g., Flower, Wallace, Norris, & Burnett, 1994; Flower, Stein, et al., 1990). And, although techniques such as think-aloud protocols and questionnaires still tended to be the instruments of choice in studies reported in *RTE* (e.g., Earthman, 1992; Protherough & Atkinson, 1992), more researchers were turning to qualitative methodologies (e.g., Cleary, 1991; Scharer, 1992).

As *RTE* editors Langer and Applebee noted in their final "Musings" column in the December 1991 issue of the journal, during their tenure as editors the:

> accepted methodologies within the field have broadened considerably, and the war between qualitative and quantitative methodologies has abated if not ended. Qualitative research has become an accepted part of our tradition of inquiry and appears regularly in *RTE*; the obligatory defense of the researcher's decision not to "count" has also disappeared from most other journals and even from many dissertations. (p. 388)

In addition, as the researcher came increasingly to be understood as implicated in the complex activity that the profession called "research," the researcher herself moved into the foreground. Researchers and writers celebrated more individuality, working against the tradition of seeming-objectivity that was part of quantitative research and an aspect of an empirical paradigm. Sommers, as an example, began her article in the February 1992 issue of *CCC* in this way: "I cannot think of my childhood without hearing voices, deep, heavily accented, instructive German voices" (p. 23). She went on to review an article she published in CCC in 1987, and rejected the writer that she was then: "I have been the bloodless academic creating taxonomies, creating a hierarchy of student writers and experienced writers, and never asking myself how I was being displaced from my own work" (pp. 26–27). Belanoff (1990) began her article in *PreText*, "The Generalized Other and Me: Working Women's Language and the Academy," in the voice characteristic of

tuting itself. (Herrington, 1989, p. 117)

In many ways this study is the story of students' success. It is a study of writers in the act of entering a university-level academic discourse, who come with an impressive range of abilities that are fundamental to academic writing: the ability to summarize, to get the gist, to see key points and connections, and not least, to execute moves that make an essay seem coherent and on topic. The interviews and protocols show students who are also working and struggling with this assignment, wanting to appear smart, trying to say something "interesting," wanting this paper to show what they can do. Yet, despite their effort, these typical freshmen papers still fall short of the critical and creative thought we expect in academic writing. These students, like most freshmen, are in an important transition; there is another river to cross. The problem is how to characterize this transition. (Flower, et al., 1990, p. 221)

academic discourse, but then after a single paragraph of academic writing shifted to this voice:

> Hmmmmm. That's the beginning of a paper I trashed; well, no, I didn't trash the paper; I just trashed that version of the paper. Why? Two things ate at me while driving down the Northern State Parkway after finishing the paper. Notice the distancing and impersonal style: after reading these paragraphs, would you know that I came from a working-class background? But I knew it while I was writing them and that awareness floated in and out of my consciousness, gnawing. (p. 61)

Belanoff went on to finish the piece in this highly-personal, non-academic style. Both Belanoff and Sommers brought personal narrative and personal voice to the academic journal and contributed to what Susan Jarratt (1991) has termed a *discourse of difference*.

Classroom Practice

Change continued to be uneven, however. Lynn, in the December 1987 issue of *College English*, testified to the dominance of the process paradigm in American writing classrooms: "There may be teachers resistant to 'teach process, not product,' but they will soon be outnumbered by members of the Flat Earth Society" (p. 902). And Jensen and Tiberio (1989), in *Personality and the Teaching of Composition*, opened their chapter "Individual Writing Processes" by noting that "writing as a process . . . [is] a doctrine that has rarely, if ever, been seriously challenged" (p. 33).

Yet there was gathering evidence that teachers felt that the process paradigm, by itself, was not enough. Lynn noted that in the work

An eloquent and powerful example of how, even among women, voices differ, Hooks speaks directly to the issue of conflict in the title of her recent collection of essays, *Talking Back.* While the stereotype of women's speech under patriarchy is that it is silenced, Hooks remembers women's voices as strong and angry in her experience as a child in a southern black family and community. (Jarratt, 1991, p. 119)

It is our contention that the positions which students take in relation to authority—the ways in which they insert themselves into the

of Knoblauch and Brannon, and of Berthoff, the writing process was understood to be so organic, or recursive, that it was essentially unteachable. In many cases, this left the teacher in the position of one who was not teaching, at least in the active sense of the word: In some schools, the curriculum was so student-centered, there was little that the teacher could claim as her own. In retrospect, it seems as if this aspect of the writing-process movement— the fact that the teacher was reduced, in Donald Murray's (1979) phrase, to a "listening eye"—created both the impetus and space for change. Not everyone, after all, was a professional writer; not everyone could do what Murray did. As Myron Tuman (1988), drawing on Basil Bernstein, had argued in *CCC*, perhaps the pedagogy of self-discovery was not suited to all students—nor, as others extended this thought, was the straight process curriculum the best curriculum for all students.

In 1977, Mina Shaughnessy, a linguist by training, saw techniques such as error-analysis as the best hope for bringing what she termed *basic writers* into the academy. In the 1990s, given the period's focus on culture—on academic discourse communities and individuals' relation to these communities—the basic writer's difficulty was seen to be one of cultural difference: the writer, outside the academy, needed to learn the ways—the culture—of the academy without losing her own. This concept was an extension of the argument laid out in the *Students' Right to Their Own Language* (1974): that students entering college have a right to their own culture, and they have a need to enter the culture of the academy. As Bartholomae and Petrosky (1986) put it in their influential textbook *Facts, Actifacts, and Counterfacts*:

we are presenting reading and writing as a struggle within and against the languages

discourse of the discipline— determine in crucial ways their academic success or failure. Yet, knowledge of the status relations surrounding discourse production is kept out of the classroom and away from students, who are left to "remember" it for themselves. Such a pedagogy pretends that this crucial knowledge is located "inside," in a student's native intelligence or powers of logic or intuition. In actuality, however, this knowledge is socially constructed; it is itself cultural coinage, simultaneously minted and won through elaborate and ongoing culture wars in which various groups struggle for the power to define knowledge and set standards of language and behavior. (Ball, Dice, & Bartholomae, 1990, p. 340)

of academic life. A classroom performance represents a moment in which, by speaking and writing, a student must enter a closed community, with its secrets, codes, and rituals. The student has to appropriate or be appropriated by a specialized discourse, and he has to do it as though he were easily and comfortably one with his audience, as though he were a member of the academy. (p. 8)

The move toward the consideration of context led not only to a consideration of the writer's academic situation, but to a consideration of other differences, as well—of gender, race, class, and sexual preference—among writers, students, and teachers. These differences, argued such theorists as Jarratt, Vitanza, and Sullivan, are minimized or obscured by a pedagogy that takes students as a homogeneous "other" and stresses not our differences but our common, shared experience. Patricia A. Sullivan (1992) noted that "many composition scholars and teachers served as advocates for all students' rights to literacy regardless of a student's age, race, gender, socioeconomic background, or national origin." She continued, "It is composition's humane disregard for difference under an egalitarian ethic . . . that now renders it pervious to feminist inquiry and critique" (p. 39). As Victor Vitanza (1991) put it, existing pedagogies can be seen as a "reactionary devaluing of heterogeneity through the homogenization of heterogeneity (as mass society). While they allow, they simultaneously disallow and disenable" (p. 141). Similarly, Jarratt (1991), specifically targeting Murray and Elbow, wrote, "We need a theory and a practice more adequately attuned than expressivism is to the social complexities of our classrooms and the political exigencies of our country in this historical moment" (p. 111).

As they foregrounded difference, composi-

The Coalition Conference grew from seeds planted by representatives of eight professional associations concerned with teaching English in the United States. The officers and staff members of six of these organizations—the Association of Departments of English (ADE), the College English Association (CEA), the College Language Association (CLA), the Conference on College Composition and Communication (CCCC), the Modern Language Association (MLA) and the National Council of Teachers of English (NCTE)—met for the first time at the 1982 MLA convention to discuss subjects of general interest. Although the associations represented different constituencies within the field and were not, for the most part, accustomed to talking with one another, so urgent were their common concerns that they agreed to continue meeting after their annual conventions. (Lloyd-Jones & Lunsford, 1989, p. xvii)

relationships among writers
in Community Dialogue

tionists paid increasing attention to different cultures, races, classes, genders and sexual orientations represented in their classrooms—a situation that the participants in the English Coalition Conference of 1987 saw not as a problem but as a tremendous opportunity. America was undertaking an extraordinary experiment, attempting to become not only a political but a cultural democracy. The English classroom could, in the eyes of these conference participants, become a training ground and forum for this emerging cultural democracy.

The two reports of the English Coalition Conference (Elbow, 1990; Lloyd-Jones & Lunsford, 1990), foregrounded the image of an active classroom, with students writing and very much as James Moffett (1968), Murray (1968), and, later, Nancie Atwell (1987) described in their work, yet fundamentally different, too: The English classroom envisioned by the Coalition participants was seen not as a collection of individual writers, but as a complex system of relationships. Into the foreground moved social action, human interaction: complex negotiations across lines of difference. Moffett and Atwell foregrounded the individual writer; the Coalition foregrounded the interaction among members of a classroom group. Diversity was, in the eyes of the Coalition, a resource to be valued and exploited. Given difference among students, dialogue could be rich. As Elbow (1990) noted, the Coalition Conference, with its vision of a cultural democracy, was in part a local reaction to the voices of William Bennett and E. D. Hirsch, both of whom hoped for a common culture, chiefly Western European, and in particular a common canon of literature-as-information to be taught in the schools. Yet the Coalition and its reports were more than this—they serve as evidence that teachers' understanding of the English classroom, and therefore the writing classroom, had shifted dramatically. No longer

I've been nervous about this book from the beginning—a long time ago. I accepted the invitation of the MLA Executive Council to write a book about the 1987 English Coalition Conference, but only when it was made clear to me that I was being invited to write exploratory and subjective reflections rather than a full or official reporting. What I have written, then, is a series of professional and personal ruminations on the conference and in doing so, sometimes on the profession of English itself. (Elbow, 1990, p. v)

Sub Rpt ☆

were compositionists just writers teaching writing. Composition classrooms were now places in which writers worked with language, theirs and others, toward two related ends: the construction within the classroom of a cultural democracy, and the preparation of young people who would help to bring into being the cultural democracy that we hoped America might become.

The Technological Context, 1989–1991: From Personal to Interpersonal

The microcomputer had come to be known as the *personal* computer in the 1980s, but the period 1989 to 1991 saw the evolution of the personal computer into the *interpersonal* computer, connected to other computers through networks and/or modems. By 1989, the "war of the wires" was over, and 90% of networks ran Token Ring, Ethernet, or ARCnet networking technology. These networking technologies had grown to become mature, easy to install, reliable, fast, and affordable. Most importantly, these networks had evolved from printer-sharing systems to powerful communication systems. Although there remained a large number of networking protocols (the technical communication conventions that allow computers to "talk" to each other over networks), programs called protocol gateways were developed to address the lack of standardization—a problem that persists today. These gateway programs allowed one's existing protocol to look like whatever protocol other computers needed in order to connect. In addition, new telecommunication technologies accommodated the growth of wide area networks and set the stage for the later and explosive growth of the Internet. ARPAnet, the progenitor of Internet, was dismantled in 1989, and private companies like MCI took over the supply and maintenance of

When the microcomputer was first introduced, it was touted as a personal tool. But a major benefit of a computer is its capacity to locate and access public information more quickly and easily than traditional methods. Highlighting these benefits, most of the literature focuses now on communications features, on how to make these personal tools more social. Networks (local area and broader), modems, electronic bulletin boards, public domain powerhouses: these are the topics that fill the columns of *PC Week*, *PC Magazine*, *Byte* and the like. (Eldred, 1989, p. 209)

NeXT Mail makes publishing a truly collaborative process. Unlike ordinary e-mail, it lets you send and receive messages that include text, graphics, voice, even entire documents. Never has there been a more effective way to locate information, receive comments and get approvals. (Advertisement in *Academic Computing*, 1990)

the trunk lines that formed the foundation of the Internet (Wright, 1994).

Networking technology matured and standardized at the same time that new business management models based on teamwork, collaboration, and organizational productivity (instead of personal productivity) began to take hold in the workplace. Again, it is impossible to sort out the relationship between parallel developments in different fields—in this case, the fields of computer technology and of management theory. Yet the potential demand that the world of business represented certainly served as the primary factor in developing technology. Almost all microcomputer technology—during this period and others—was initially developed to meet the needs of the business world. The new generation of software applications dubbed *groupware* emerged to help networking technology serve emerging management philosophies. Groupware became a large category that included four overlapping kinds of applications based on network technology: electronic mail (email), information sharing, document management, and office automation.

Electronic mail represented—and continues to represent—the most commonly used and best known form of groupware. On the Internet, email is by far the most used of these applications, despite the press that other Internet services like Web servers and news readers receive. During this period, information sharing grew to include not only person-to-person messaging but also bulletin boards (of which there are more than 100,000 in use today), listservs (such as the Megabyte University listserv for the computers and writing community), and conferencing. Document management programs permit users to create shared databases of documents with search and retrieval systems that allow users within an organization to search for information in a variety of ways (by author, subject line, or string of key words, de-

The various terms applied to electronic conferences are interesting in that many suggest notions of people working and talking together over networks, sometimes in an attempt to create something new in ways that suggest activities appropriate for students. Even the word "networks" reflects the web of connections with which students and other participants can use the technology to communicate with people from all over the world. "Interactive written discourse," "computerized conferencing," "groupware," and "computer conversation" also suggest a dynamic relationship among network participants. (Hawisher & LeBlanc, 1992, p. 78)

Scientific American, September 1991, Special Issue:

"Communications, Computers and Networks," by M.L. Dertouzos.
The transformation of civilization through the fusion of computing and communications technologies has been predicted for at least 50 years. Now the revolution has truly begun. The impact will be as profound as was the shift from an agrarian to an industrial society.

"Computers, Networks and Work," by Sproull & Kiesler (1991)
"Does anybody know . . .?"
Such public vulnerability on corporate electronic bulletin

boards indicates how radically networks are changing the nature of work. Employees grow more open as well as less hierarchical and status conscious. Can management adapt to a more flexible and dynamic environment? (p.4)

Scientific American, September 1991, Special Issue:

"Computers, Networks and Public Policy."
Policy inevitably lags behind technology. For the benefits of the information age to be fully realized, legislators, the courts and technical experts must forge new rules of the road for data highways that include strong protection of personal freedom.

"Infrastructure for the Global Village," by A. Gore

"Common Law for the Electronic Frontier," by A. W. Branscomb.

"Civil Liberties in Cyberspace," by Mitchell Kapor.

The computer is the greatest "piano" ever invented, for it is the master carrier of representations of every kind. Now there is a rush to have people, especially schoolchildren, "take computer." Computers can amplify yearnings in ways even more profound than can musical instruments. But if teachers do not nourish the romance of learning and expressing, any external mandate for a new "literacy" becomes as much a

pending on the power of the system). Office automation systems allows group scheduling and can be used as part of a decision-support program (a database designed to present a user, who was confronted with a problem or question, with context-sensitive information). Lotus Corporation's NOTES is an ambitious software program that tries to combine the features of all four categories in a powerful and comprehensive way (Goulde, 1991). Although there have been complaints about the program's complexity and limitations, complaints that sound very much like those which followed the release of WINDOWS 1.0, the program has been a tremendous success in business settings. In academic settings, PACERFORUM, a collaborative software for the Macintosh, has been used extensively for instruction at such institutions as Syracuse University and the University of Illinois.

It was also during this period that the first generation of commercial online services like GEnie, CompuServe, and BIX were growing. These were command-line, host-based services; that is, users entered text commands much as they would in the DOS operating system, although the commands were simpler and often aided by text menus, and almost all of the computing or processing was done on the host server to which one connected. By 1992, second generation online services like Prodigy and America Online came into being, introducing GUI interfaces and moving towards a client/server model that presumed more processing power on the user end of the connection. During this period, there was also a steady rise in Internet use and the corresponding discovery of new electronic forums and methods of communication, including Usenet (a distributed bulletin board system linking around 6,000 newsgroups and covering almost any subject one might imagine), Internet Relay Chat (real-time conversation channels devoted to whatever topic their users desire and that disapper when the last user signs off), and FTP (File Transfer Protocol) access to large databases of information. These technologies had been developed long before (Usenet in the 1970s and IRC in the early 1980s) (A. Weiss, 1994), but as universities and colleges rushed to connect to the Internet, most faculty were just now getting their first look at these new communication tools. The excitement that users felt entering these virtual spaces and the opportunities that the new connectivity offered for communication and collaboration would continue to build until the Internet burst into the popular imagination in 1993, during what many call the "Year of the Internet" (D. Baron, personal communication, September 5, 1994).

crushing burden as being forced to perform Beethoven's sonatas while having no sense of their beauty. Instant access to the world's information will probably have an effect opposite to what is hoped: students will become numb instead of enlightened. (Kay, 1991, p. 138)

Multimedia: The Coming Wave

Multimedia computing has emerged so rapidly, and is now so widespread, that it is easy to forget how recent a development it has been in personal computing. Although the desktop publishing programs and presentation programs of the mid-1980s represent a kind of multimedia, 1991 was the year that multimedia as we think of it today—a medium in which text, graphics, sound, and video are linked and integrated—became a significant part of the computing scene. By 1991, the technology to support multimedia had evolved to a point where it was reliable enough and affordable enough to begin reaching desktops in serious numbers. NEC released the first double-speed CD-ROM drives, Kodak released the Photo-CD, Phillips created the first CD-R systems (allowing individual users to create their own CDs), and sound cards began to standardize around the SoundBlaster card specifications. In addition, the 80486 chip had become a standard on the market and provided the kind of processing

In March 1991, *Computers and the Human Conversation* was an Apple sponsored conference at Lewis and Clark College in Portland, Oregon. Susan Kirschner demonstrated her dialogue software, and Michael Joyce gave great multimedia demonstrations of his interactive fiction, AFTERNOON (C&W, 1994)

speed that audio, video, and graphics files demanded. These developments coalesced in a way that resulted in Microsoft's October 1991 announcement of the first standards for multimedia computing, called MPC1. The standards set minimum hardware and software requirements for multimedia computing in DOS-based computing—really Windows-based computing, because WINDOWS 3.1 was the software required by MPC1 (Yager, 1992, p. 217).

MPC1 meant that software developers finally had a reliable and agreed on platform for which they could develop titles (Hypercard developers might argue that the Macintosh had long provided such a stable platform, but Apple's share of the computing market continued to decline as very inexpensive PCs flooded the retail and direct mail markets). It would be another two years before multimedia computing gathered steam and resulted in the explosion of new companies and titles (3,000 new CD-ROM based titles were released for Christmas 1994, for example). However, 1989 to 1991 was the critical period: the birth of a new industry within computing.

Critical teaching aims to transform. That ambition is both subversive and entirely common, akin, that is, to the aim of any teaching. Schools, after all, accept the burden of assisting the nation's young people to become responsible and productive citizens. Hence, teaching is always a transformative act: students aren't expected to leave their classrooms thinking, knowing .... Critical teachers develop an informed reflectiveness about the conditions both within and outside schools that impinge on their

OBSERVING TRENDS

During the period of 1989 to 1991, many specialists in computers and composition studies were assimilating, and contributing to, composition studies' move toward social and critical pedagogies. Some also found themselves assimilating what might be termed the second Copernican turn (C&W, 1994), the first having been the shift from computer-as-data-processor to the computer-as-word-processor, and the second the shift from the computer as word-processor to the computer as global communication device. These two developments—the rise of social and critical pedagogies and the expansion of what is generally called computer-mediated communication (CMC)—were mutually reinforcing. CMC made available virtual spaces, virtual classrooms or online parlors where composition teachers could meet with colleagues and students and enact the social construction of knowledge. Further, these virtual spaces were supremely literate spaces. Every discussion could be reproduced as print and analyzed, in the spirit of critical pedagogy, for issues of power, inclusion/exclusion, and the play of race, gender, and class in these new social spaces.

Some computers and composition specialists also found themselves assimilating too, though less smoothly, to a second technological advance: what the industry was calling *multimedia* but that English teachers, with such close ties to printed texts, continued to call hypertext and hypermedia. The interest of English teachers in hypertext and hypermedia also represented some renewal of interest in the stand-alone computer. Both hypertext and hypermedia were based on connection, as was the theory and pedagogy of CMC. In hypertext and hypermedia, however, it was bits of text—or bits of text, sound, and video—that were being connected, usually by a single author, and usually with the single reader or user in mind. The important theoretical treatments of hypertext/media were generally attempts to fit the new media into the old: a demonstration that *Ulysses*, or *Tristram Shandy*, were hypertextual (Bolter, 1991); or a new way of presenting the text of *Joseph Andrews* and related literary materials (Delany & Gilbert, 1991). Hypertext and hypermedia presented themselves to compositionists chiefly as new instructional delivery systems or as new sites for composing (Joyce, 1988). Certainly, the nature of text was changed, and dramatically so; yet the implications of this change were not at all clear. In comparison, the implications of CMC seemed

quality of life and that of their students. (Knoblauch & Brannon, 1993, pp. 5–7)

Hypertext has only recently become a discipline in computer science. The term "hypertext" was coined two decades ago by Ted Nelson. Working with mainframe computers in the 1960s, Nelson had come to realize the machine's capacity to create and manage textual networks for all kinds of writing. (Bolter, 1991, p. 23)

Association is not really prior to writing, as the term "prewriting" suggests. Association is always present in any text: one word echoes another, one sentence or paragraph recalls others earlier in the text and looks forward to still others. A writer cannot help but write associatively: even if he or she begins with and remains faithful to an outline, the result is always a network of verbal elements. The hierarchy (in the form of paragraphs, sections, and chapters) is an attempt to impose order on verbal ideas that are always prone to subvert that order. The associative relationships define alternative organizations that lie beneath the order of pages and chapters that a printed text presents to the world. These alternatives constitute subversive texts-behind-the-text. (Bolter, 1991, p. 22)

NEW HYPERTEXTS!

—KING OF SPACE: Sarah Smith
A strange and dark fable of betrayal, lust, and terror. Did you know you can conquer space?

—WOE AND IZME PASS
Special hypertext issue of noted literary journal, *Writing on the Edge*, featuring STORYSPACE hypertexts by Michael Joyce, Carolyn Guyer and Martha Petry. Guest editor Stuart Moulthrop gathers eight striking new studies of hypertext by leading critics and theoreticians.

—WRITING SPACE: J. David Bolter
STORYSPACE edition of landmark study on computers and the history of writing. Indispensable.

—THE PERFECT COUPLE: C. Humphrey
Sarnille and Charlie are joined in a Perfect Love. (Mailing by Eastgate Systems, Inc., Cambridge, MA)

A vision came together for me that morning . . . .I realized that the people I had been interviewing [about their work with computers] were on the edge of a historical transformation of immense proportions, as important as that which had been experienced by the eighteenth- and nineteenth-century workers about whom I had read so

more immediately identifiable to many writing teachers.

During this period, CMC was a focus for research, yet it also became a hot topic in the popular press, as journalists and writers discovered for themselves the resources available to them on the Internet. The September 1991 issue of *The Scientific American* was titled "*Communications, Computers and Networks: How to Work, Play and Thrive in Cyberspace*," and the computer columns in the *New York Times* increasingly began to feature the Internet. Also, during this period, hypertext/hypermedia received from many quarters of the computers and composition community the same kind of enthusiastic response that the PC-as-writing-instrument had received in the early 1980s. Hypertexts/hypermedia became the object of research and development at many universities (Nielsen, 1990) and drew the attention of publishers and corporations as a medium for education and training.

The Conferences

Between 1989 and 1991, at NCTE and CCCC, the numbers of papers specifically titled "computers and . . ." declined. Beginning with this period, however, the authors of this history find it more difficult to use the titles of conference presentations as indicators of interest in the field of computers and composition. Certainly by this time most conference papers were being written and prepared on computers, and just as certainly computers were the writing instrument of choice for the students taught by the teachers who came to the conference. The gradual decline in the numbers of conference presentations specifically titled "Computers and . . ." seems to indicate that computers were becoming everyone's business—a seemingly transparent technology. As in the early CCCC programs, there were few presentations on writing instruments and media. Perhaps, as Zuboff (1988) had discovered in industrial sites, after an initial period of transition and discomfort, the new ways of working had become naturalized and transparent.

The computer-related papers that were given at NCTE and CCCC reflected the field's strong interest in CMC and hypertext/hypermedia. As was the case when the PC and word processing were new technologies, the conferences served during this period to bring news of CMC and hypertext/media to teachers and scholars in the field of composition studies. At NCTE, Stephen Marcus's (1989) "A HyperCard Project for English Teachers" brought writing teachers news of one new medium. Cynthia Selfe's (1989b) "English Teachers and Computers in the Classroom: Technology as A Catalyst for Social, Political, and Educational Reform," and an entire session on interchange, a program that facilitated synchronous online discussion in classroom settings, brought writing teachers news of CMC. Another paper, a retrospective account by Gail Hawisher of the relation between instructional software and pedagogical theory, reminded composition teachers, in their enthusiasm for the new media, to remember that they were teachers, as well as early adapters.

The presentations on CMC at CCCC focused on the new technologies as they intersected with social, political, and pedagogical issues. In greeting participants at the 1990 CCCC in Chicago, Don McQuade, Program Chair, announced that the conference included "the largest number of sessions in [the] organization's history devoted to social, racial, and ideological issues related to writing as well as to gender issues" (1990 CCCC convention program, p. 3). The 1990 sessions on CMC certainly fit McQuade's description, including

much . . . .I had long fantasized about what it would have been like to take a tape recorder into the workshops and factories of Britain in 1789 or 1848 and had considered the questions I would have asked in order to elicit the kind of insight I hungered for. (Zuboff, 1988, p. xiii)

NCTE Conference Session, 1990:
HYPERCARD, Multimedia, and the Teaching of English Cosponsored by the Assembly on Computers in English; open to all (Hilton/Clayton Room).
New technologies allow words, graphics, video, film, animation, and sound to be created and combined in wonderful ways. This session provides an introduction to these multimedia and "hypermedia" resources, demonstrating current and future applications to the teaching of English and the language arts. This session is cosponsored by the NCTE Commission on Media, with support from Apple Computer, Inc., and Scholastic, Inc.
Chair: Br. Kevin Cawley
Speaker: Stephen Marcus, "HyperCard, Multimedia, and the Teaching of English."
Local Host: Lucas L. Moore (1990 NCTE convention program, p. 128)

CCCC Conference Session, 1991:
Panel:
Computer and Composition: Political and Cultural Issues.

Dean Barclay's (1990) "Mail, Female, ENFI, and E-Mail: How Computerized Conversations Strengthen Community through Diversity," Cynthia Selfe's (1990a) "Technology and the Changing Nature of Literacy Education: Political Implications of Computer Use," and Janet Eldred's (1990) "Debugging Computer Pedagogy: Electronic Networks and the Illusion of Equality."

The CCCC sessions on hypertext/media, on the other hand, were relatively apolitical, more intent on introducing the new technology to the rest of the profession. Included in the program were Stuart Moulthrop's (1990a) "A Rhetoric of Response to Hypertext," Johndan Johnson-Eilola's (1990) "Shifting Perspectives: Evaluating Hypertext for Composition Instruction," John McDaid's (1990b) "The Shape of Texts to Come: Response and the Ecology of Hypertext," and Ron Fortune's (1990) "Hyper-Card in the Classroom: Literature, Writing, and Manuscript Studies." At the 1991 CCCC there began to be signs that the field was beginning to take a critical perspective on hypertext/media. The title of session E:18 can mark the turn: "(A) Freedom, (B) Repression, (C) Anarchy, (D) All of the Above: Hypertext and Ideology."

To these conferences came not only scholars and researchers in the field, but also teachers of composition for whom hypertext/media and CMC were new territory. Judith Kirkpatrick describes her experience at the 1991 Boston CCCC both as a transformation and as an invitation to join a community. She had attended the pre-conference workshop sponsored by the Seven Cs and had then moved to the exhibit hall. At the Seven Cs workshop, Kirkpatrick recalled:

From table to table I gained a sense of a convergence of ideas about an effective use of computers in instruction. At one table, for instance, participants talked to each other about ways to "take over" the un- or underutilized facilities on campus. Others spoke of the Daedalus system, whatever that was! I went down to the exhibition room for computers and found Daedalus waiting for exploration on a Macintosh. I explored the program for about two hours, uninterrupted, and from those two hours I'd say my most significant, radical professional transformation occurred. (C&W, 1994)

The structure created by the computers and composition community—including the Seven Cs workshop and the user-friendly exhibits in the Exhibition Hall—served in 1991, as it had in earlier conferences, to introduce newcomers not only to technology but also to the community of teachers and scholars who were identified with that technology.

Computers and Writing Conference

The Computers and Writing Conference provides a tightly focused view of the field in 1989–1991, one largely congruent with the wider view provided by the annual conferences of NCTE and CCCC. As we noted in chapter 4, the Computers and Writing Conference was not held in 1987 and 1988, but it returned to life— and new energy—with the Fifth "C&W" in Minneapolis, with just under 200 participants; the sixth in Austin, Texas, in 1990, with 304 participants; and the Seventh, in Biloxi, Mississippi, with 162 participants. (The numbers given here were provided by the organizers of each of the conferences: Geoff Sirc, Fifth Computers and Writing Conference at the University of Minnesota, 1989; Wayne Butler and Fred Kemp, Sixth Computers and Writing Conference, 1990; and Rae Schipke, Seventh Comput-

Technology."
Johndan   Johnson-Eilola, "Click Here . . . No, Here . . . Maybe Here: Hypertext and Anarchy." 1991 CCCC convention program, p. 72)

During the Renaissance the "entire world" began to condense into a real and compact whole. The earth became firmly rounded out, and it occupied a particular position in the real space of the universe. And the earth itself began to acquire a geographical definition (still far from complete) and a historical interpretation (even less complete). In Rabelais and Cervantes we see a fundamental condensation of reality that is no longer bled by otherworldly rounding out; but this reality rises up against the still very unstable and nebulous background of the entire world and human history. (Bakhtin, 1986, pp. 43–44)

If there is one central theme to this book, it is the belief that CMC will ultimately emerge as a new educational paradigm, taking its place alongside both face-to-face and distance education; at the same time, it will change the nature of "traditional" multimedia distance education. Online education has unique attributes, even though it shares some of the features of place-based education (notably group interactivity) and of distance education (notably the freedom from time and place constraints). CMC

ers and Writing Conference sponsored by Southern Mississippi University, 1991.)

Like NCTE and CCCC, sessions at the C&Ws during these years featured presentations on CMC and on hypertext/media. The number of sessions on each of these topics increased during the 3-year period. The focus of these papers turned increasingly—although certainly not exclusively—toward social issues involving race, gender, and class. In 1989 2 of the 17 sessions devoted to CMC focused on gender issues: Nancy Peterson's (1989) "Sounds of Silence: Listening for Difference in the Computer-Networked Collaborative Writing Classroom" and Lauri George's (1989) "Female Authority in the Computerized Classroom." In 1990, five of the 22 papers on CMC focused on issues of gender, sexual preference, and class; among them Rebecca Rickly's (1990) "The Electronic Voice: Empowering Women in the Writing Classroom," Louie Crew's (1990) "Discourse Analysis of GayNet," and Lester Faigley's (1990b) "The Postmodern Condition of the Networked Classroom," which became part of his award-winning book on composition studies, *Fragments of Rationality* (1992).

Although the 1989–1991 conference papers dealing with hypertext/media were largely of a technology-driven, how-to sort, there were also glimpses of an emerging theoretical orientation. At the 1990 C&W, for example, Stuart Moulthrop, Terence Harpold, and John McDaid explored the electronic social space created through hypertexts. Moulthrop (1990b) asked "what kind of idea is hypertext?" and went on to demonstrate how hypertext can privilege student readers by allowing them to modify the "literary object." Harpold (1990) used Bakhtin's treatment of Rabelais and the idea of carnival to suggest the democratizing influence of hypertext spaces which, Harpold argued, instantiated "heteroglossia," allowing multiple discourses to converge electronically. McDaid

(1990a) argued that hypermedia discourse with its "interactive fictions" and "simulated realities" historically will take its place as a medium alongside spoken language and print. All three implicitly connected CMC to hypertext/media, encouraging the audience to imagine textual and social worlds few had experienced, and, although uncritical enthusiasm or what Hocks (1993) would later call "the technotropes of liberation" tended to infuse the whole of the session, those attending sensed its significance. Richard Gebhardt (May 19, 1990, personal communication), then editor of *CCCs*, remarked that although he might not have understood everything that was said at this session, he knew that he had glimpsed the future. Many of the papers presented at the C&W conferences from 1989–1991 later appeared in journals or essay collections and helped define the issues that would constitute computers and composition as a field (e.g., Cooper & Selfe, 1990; Hawisher & Selfe, 1991a; McDaid, 1991, Moulthrop, 1991a).

has the potential to provide a means for the weaving together of ideas and information from many peoples' minds, regardless of when and from where they contribute. (Kaye, 1989, p.3)

Publishers, Professional Journals, and Computers and Composition Studies

During the period from 1989–1991, computers and composition studies began to integrate into its work more deeply than before the perspectives and methods of other fields. To the extent that many specialists in this field were also writing teachers and scholars of composition studies, individuals had always looked to other disciplines for perspectives on computers and technology—for example, to works such as Papert's (1980) *Mindstorms: Children, Computers, and Powerful Ideas*, Heim's (1987) *Electric Language: A Philosophical Study of Word Processing*, and Kramarae's (1988b) *Technology and Women's Voices: Keeping in Touch*. In this period, however, computers and compo-

Predicting the potential consequences of any new technology is an extremely complex problem. Simply forecasting the direct costs of new technology can be hard, and that is the easiest step. Understanding how the technology will interact with ongoing routine practices and policies is even more difficult. Imagining how that technology will lead to long-term changes in how people work, treat one another, and structure their organizations is harder still. A two-level perspective on technology change can help in anticipating potential consequences. A two level perspective emphasizes that technologies can have both efficiency effects and social system effects. (Sproull & Kiesler, 1991, p. 1)

The introduction of the telephone did more than enable people to communicate over long distances: it threatened existing class relations by extending the boundary of who may speak to whom; it also altered modes of courtship and possibilities of romance. Similarly the introduction of the electric light bulb seriously changed mass leisure and culture: for instance, night-time spectator sports, with their deep impact on mass culture, we became creatures of the light bulb. Clearly, then electronic communication opens major social questions. (Poster, 1990, p. 5)

So long as the text was married to a physical media, readers and writers took for granted three crucial attributes: that the text was *linear*, *bounded*, and *fixed*. Generations of scholars and authors internal-

sitionists were increasingly active in borrowing critical theories and research perspectives from such diverse disciplines as literary studies, social psychology, and distance education. Contributing to this trend was the exciting work on hypertext/media that built on the work of literary scholars. Similarly, the work done on CMC drew on an extensive body of preexisting literature in the fields of communications and of distance learning. In part, too, computers and composition specialists had left behind a concern for quantitative empirical research that would measure the effects of computers and had taken up in its place more speculative or theoretical work—much of which was based on theory borrowed from disciplines bordering on composition studies.

Several important books and special issues of journals had a particular impact on the field during this period. All might be considered to lie outside the field of composition studies, yet the boundaries of that field itself were shifting and becoming increasingly permeable—Geertz's "blurred genres" yet again. Mason and Kaye's (1989) *Mindweave: Communication, Computers and Distance Education*, Sproull and Kiesler's (1991) *Connections: New Ways of Working in the Networked Organization*, and Poster's (1990) *The Mode of Information: Post-structuralism and the Social Context* are typical of the cross-disciplinary texts that many computers and compositionists found important for their scholarship on computer-mediated communication. Distance education scholars in *Mindweave*, for example, demonstrated how CMC could be used and studied in educational settings and began to develop theoretical perspectives on the interactions that took place in virtual spaces. Sproull and Kiesler brought much of their research on organizational networked communication together in *Connections*, illustrating the advantages and disadvantages of CMC in the workplace. Other scholars from across the disciplines, such as Mark Poster, a historian, demonstrated how critical theory might shed light on the relationship of computers and power in institutional settings and society at large. Hypertext/media also received attention in book-length texts with Bolter's (1991) *Writing Space: The Computer, Hypertext, and the History of Writing*, Edward Barrett's (1989) collection titled *The Society of Text: Hypertext, Hypermedia, and the Social Construction of Information*, and Delaney and Landow's (1990) edited collection titled *Hypermedia and Literary Studies*.

The fall 1990 issue of *Signs*, titled *From Hard Drive to Software: Gender, Computers, and Difference*, brought together the work of feminist scholars focused on the emerging technologies, in particular Turkle and Papert's (1990) "Epistemological Pluralism: Styles and Voices Within the Computer Culture" and P.N. Edwards' (1990) "The Army of the Microworld: Computers and the Politics of Gender Identity." Both articles argued that computers were not a neutral technology—that girls and women would not have equal opportunities unless reform-minded educators, men and women alike, took action to ensure that they do. The work of the feminist project continued in 1991, as Cheris Kramarae and Jeanie Taylor formed WITS (Women, Information Technology, and Scholarhip), a special interdisciplinary group of women faculty, academic professionals, and students at the University of Illinois, Urbana–Champaign. The WITS agenda was to ensure that "new communications technologies will be structured and used in ways beneficial and equitable for all." (Taylor, Kramarae, & Ebben, 1993, p. 7).

The January 1991 issue of *Written Communication* focused on CMC, bringing together four articles by authors from such diverse fields as linguistics, psychology, technical communication, computer sci-

ized these qualities as the rules of thought, and they had pervasive social consequences. We can define HYPERTEXT as the use of the computer to transcend the linear, bounded and fixed qualities of the traditional written text. (Landow & Delany, 1991, p. 3)

This volume is an introduction to the Women, Information Technology, and Scholarship (WITS) working colloquium held at the Center for Advanced Study, University of Illinois at Urbana-Champaign. WITS grew from an idea conceived in April 1991 to an energetic collaboration of women that continues to grow. . . .

In our literature searches, we had difficulty finding publications that deal directly with the ways gender, race, and class hierarchies are made part of the circuitry in the new information technologies as they are used on campuses. Individually, we knew some of the problems, but we did not see our knowledge reflected in campus policies or in communication research. For example, we see many academic publications dealing with computers, knowledge, and intelligence, but few dealing with sexual harassment or with sexual division of labor in designing, using, and evaluating computer systems. (Taylor, Kramarae, & Ebben, 1993, p. 3)

ence, business administration, and rhetoric and composition. The authors of all four articles tried to identify the characteristics of CMC, examining how participants respond to it, and then, for those working in educational settings, exploring its potential for teaching and learning. In April of the same year, *Written Communication* included Selfe and Meyer's (1991) "Testing Claims for Online Conferences," in which the two authors focused on power and gender relationships in the discourse of Megabyte University, a computers and writing listserv started by Fred Kemp in 1989. The two researchers found that men and high-profile participants of the online forum tended to dominate the discussion.

As we were extending our perspectives and widening our field, we were also moving to consolidate what we had accomplished in the past decade (e.g., Handa, 1990a; Hawisher & Selfe, 1989; Holdstein & Selfe, 1990; Montague, 1990; Selfe, Rodrigues & Oates, 1989). Editors of new anthologies represented themselves as computer-using teachers charting new territory in elementary, secondary, and postsecondary education (e.g., Montague, 1990; Selfe, Rodrigues, & Oates, 1989) and as a second generation of teacher-scholars, embracing a new maturity in the field (e.g., Handa, 1990a; Hawisher & Selfe, 1989; Holdstein & Selfe, 1990). The Handa collection, *Computers and Community: Teaching Composition in the Twenty-First Century*, more than the others perhaps, began to incorporate many of the topics and issues that emerged in conference sessions during this period. Within its covers are chapters on synchronous computer-mediated communication (Langston & Batson, 1990), a postmodern pedagogy (e.g., Barker & Kemp, 1990), politics and ideology (e.g., Handa, 1990b), and feminist issues surrounding computers (e.g., Flores, 1990; Selfe, 1990c).

The field of computers and composition was slow to begin its own work on hypertext/media environments. It wasn't until 1991 that a book

Megabyte University is a computer-based conference that was created by Fred Kemp of Texas Tech University after the Fifth Annual Computers and Writing Conference held in Minneapolis, Minnesota in May 1989. Kemp wanted to provide the 210 paticipants from 36 states, 4 Canadian provinces, and one Far Eastern location (Malaysia) with a way of continuing discussions begun at the conference while transcending the temporal and geographic limitations of such a short-term gathering. As Kemp noted in an early exploratory note on Megabyte, the network was "intended not as a chat net or a technical exchange, but as a continuing discussion regarding important aspects of an emerging field, Computers and English." (Selfe & Meyer, 1991, p. 171)

With this volume, we seek to identify some of the important questions that schol-

written by members of the community featured hypermedia. Because Hawisher and Selfe's (1991a) *Evolving Perspectives on Computers and Composition Studies: Questions for the 1990s* intended to set an agenda for the future, it included significant mention of hypertext/hypermedia. Typical headings from three different chapters include "Definition of Hypertext," "What is Hypermedia?" and "Hypertext as It Is, and What It Lacks." Each of these sections begins by trying to give readers a feel for the technology and an overview of the rapidly changing intellectual landscape—suggesting that the field was still trying to catch up with evolving issues of technology. Many of these contributions acknowledged a continuing sense of enthusiasm about technology while raising some critical issues, bringing to the profession perspectives informed by cultural studies and critical pedagogy. For example, Kaplan's (1991) opening chapter "Ideology, Technology, and the Future of Writing Instruction" urged the profession to confront the political inequities that accompany educational uses of computers and Jessup's (1991) final chapter "Feminism and Computers in Composition Instruction" demanded that teachers and students alike examine the consequences of the "gender gap" in computer use.

The field's exposure in mainstream composition journals was spotty during these years. As noted in chapter Four, *College English* had not published an article on computers since 1985. In the December 1990 issue, *College English* ended its 5-year silence, publishing Cooper and Selfe's (1990) "Computer Conferences and Learning: Authority, Resistance, and Internally Persuasive Discourse," Slatin's (1990) "Reading Hypertext: Order and Coherence in a New Medium," and Nydahl's (1990) "Teaching Word Processors to be CAI Programs." These three pieces, together, provided a snapshot of the field. As their title suggests, Cooper and Selfe

ars, teachers, and researchers in the field of computers and composition must address to develop new perspectives on technology and advance confidently into the twenty-first century. The competition for the manuscripts that appear in this book of questions for the 1990s was held in the spring of 1989. From over fifty proposals, eight editors ... carefully selected the twenty or so that we thought best represented important issues shaping the profession and invited the authors to submit full manuscripts. From those manuscripts, we then chose only those that we agreed might lead to significant new contributions in the field. The final collection is comprised of fifteen chapters, each identifying and defining a particular area of exploration that needs to be undertaken by scholars and researchers. (Hawisher & Selfe, 1991a, p. 1)

Feminist research in other disciplines suggests that because we live in a patriarchal society, men and women tend to develop different epistemological frameworks that shape the way they think about the world as well as the way they learn. These frameworks will inevitably influence the way men and women conceptualize computers. (Jessup, 1991, p. 341)

Reading, in hypertext, is understood as discontinuous or nonlinear process which, like thinking, is associative in nature, as opposed to the sequential process envisioned by conventional text . . . .Reading in this sense has little to do with traditional notions of beginning at the beginning and going through to the end. Instead, the reader begins at a point of his or her own choosing—a point chosen from a potentially very large number of possible starting points. The reader proceeds from there by following a series of links connecting documents to one another, exiting not at a point defined by the author as "The End" but rather when he or she has had enough. Accordingly, the most common metaphors in discussions of hypertext equate reading the navigation or traversal of large, open (and usually poorly charted) spaces. (Slatin, 1990, pp. 874–875)

As off-the-shelf word-processing programs become more and more sophisticated, it's becoming possible to achieve many of the operations characteristic of elaborate CAI software or mainframe computers on ordinary PCs. In other words, although a word processor *is* "just a tool," it's a tool whose full instructional capabilities most writing teachers haven't discovered. (Nydahl, 1990, p. 904)

Abstract: This article presents a study examining the effects on planning processes of using pen and paper and word processing

brought critical theory and the work of Bakhtin to their research on CMC. Slatin introduced the *College English* audience to hypertext as a revolutionary new writing technology. Both of these articles spoke to the promise of the new technologies for transforming writing classes (Cooper and Selfe) and writing processes (Slatin). Nydahl's article, on the other hand, was less forward-looking and, indeed, spoke to the work that many, if not most, writing teachers were actually doing in their classes. Nydahl understood the computer not as a site for hypertextual composition, nor as a global communication device, but as a powerful writing instrument, harking back to the field's publications in the early 1980s. Using the macro function that was a part of most word-processing programs, Nydahl illustrated how it was possible for teachers and students to do style analysis using only a word-processing program: bold facing all passive constructions, for example, or all topic sentences. Nydahl's article reminded the profession that many teachers were not, indeed could not afford to be, on the cutting edge.

From 1989 through 1991, both *Research in the Teaching of English* and *College Composition and Communication* featured fewer articles on computers. Exceptions were Haas's (1989a) important study on word processing's possible effects on writers' planning processes in *RTE* and Hawisher and Selfe's article (1991b) on "The Rhetoric of Technology and the Electronic Writing Class"—the only piece that *CCC* published on computers in this timeframe outside its Staffroom InterChange pages.

These two articles indicated first an emphasis on isolated writers using word processing and, then, a move to the "connected" writer communicating and interacting with other writers over networked computers. Both pieces also manifested a critical perspective aimed at writers' use of word processing (i.e., Haas, 1989, found that writers planned less frequently and extensively with computers) and at teachers' use of computer-mediated communication (i.e., Hawisher and Selfe, 1991b, speculated that teachers might unwittingly use electronic conferences to control students and their discourse).

Computers and Composition

Although mainstream composition journals only occasionally turned their attention to the new technologies, *Computers and Composition* held a steady course during this period, drawing on the perspectives of cultural criticism and critical pedagogy and focusing on hypertext/hypermedia and CMC. The April 1990 issue of *Computers and Composition* featured articles growing out of the 1989 *Computers and Writing Conference*, articles that explored issues of inclusion/exclusion arising from attempts to bring CMC into classroom settings. In an online environment, who gets to "speak"? Who is silent? Who is silenced? Other important articles to appear in the journal from 1989–1991 included Douglas' (1989) "Wandering Through the Labyrinth: Encountering Interactive Fiction," the first article on hypertext to appear in a composition journal; LeBlanc's (1990) "Competing Ideologies in Software Design for Computer-Aided Composition" and DiMatteo's (1991) "Communication, Writing, Learning: Anti-Instrumentalist View of Network Writing."

From its beginnings in 1983, *Computers and Composition* had been instrumental in forming the community of teachers and scholars whose history we are writing. At this point in time, its editors felt that the field was powerful and broad enough to support awards for

for composing. The study employed a 2-by-3 factorial design and a think-aloud methodology. Experienced writers and student writers composed texts with pen and paper, with word processing, and with both media. Amount and kinds of planning were analyzed. Results showed significant differences between the pen and paper and the word processing alone conditions: when writers were using word processing alone, there was significantly less planning, significantly less planning before beginning to write, significantly less conceptual or high-level planning, and significantly more local or sequential planning than when they were using pen and paper. (Haas, 1989a, p. 181)

The first time I clapped eyes on a hypertext, I immediately thought of Roland Barthes' essay, "The Death of the Author." In the age of interactive fiction, the author is not simply dead, I decided, s/he's been quicklimed. I was not alone. (Douglas, 1989, p. 93)

1991 Computers and Composition Awards:
At the Eighth Computers and Writing Conference in Indianapolis, Indiana, the editors of *Computers and Composition*, on behalf of the Editorial Board, awarded the 1991 prizes for outstanding scholarship in

the field of computers and composition studies. Each of the awards highlights a dissertation and published article of exceptional merit.

For Best Dissertation in Computers and Composition Studies: The Hugh Burns Award:
Sarah Sloane, "Interactive Fiction, Virtual Realities, and the Reading-Writing Relationship."

For Best Article in Computers and Composition Studies: The Ellen Nold Award:
Nancy Kaplan, & Stuart Moulthrop, "Something to Imagine: Literature, Composition, and Interactive Fiction." (Announcement, *C&C*, 1992)

We would like to begin with an anecdote. Last fall, a conscientious graduate student walked into the new computer classroom at Colorado State, thinking it was just another computer lab. He sat down at the only available computer (which happened to be connected to the only available printer) and began working on a project. The teacher, who did not appreciate his rude entry into the middle of her composition class, immediately walked over to him and quietly explained that a class was in session. "It won't bother me," he said. Realizing that he needed to be addressed more directly, the teacher continued, "You'll have to leave the room." Incredulous, the student dutifully complied. Later that day, he

research and writing. In 1990, therefore, Hawisher and Selfe established two annual awards. The first, the Hugh Burns Dissertation Award, was designed to highlight important dissertation research projects. Because Hugh Burns was the first scholar in the field to complete a dissertation that explored how computers might complement the teaching of writing, it seemed appropriate to name the award for him. The second, the Ellen Nold Award for the best article in the field, recognized Nold as the author of the first article to appear on computers and writing in a journal focusing on composition studies, "Fear and Trembling: A Humanist Approaches the Computer," published in 1975 in *College Composition and Communication*. The awards were given to research on computer-mediated communication (e.g., Mabrito, 1989), software development issues (e.g., Houlette, 1991; LeBlanc, 1990), various topics related to hypertext environments or interactive fiction (e.g., Kaplan & Moulthrop, 1991; Neuwirth & Kaufer, 1990; Sloane, 1991), and review of word processing and human factors research (Sullivan, 1989). The editors of the journal also founded the Computers and Composition Press in 1989. The first two books emanating from this press were Selfe's (1989a) *Creating A Computer-Supported Writing Facility* and Hawisher and Selfe's (1991a) *Evolving Perspectives on Computers and Composition Studies*. The Press would operate jointly with NCTE from 1990 to 1995 and during this time publish LeBlanc's (1993) *Writing Teachers Writing Software* and Sullivan and Dautermann's (in press) *Electronic Literacies in the Workplace: The Technologies of Writing*. In 1994 the editors also established another series, New Directions in Computers and Composition Studies, with Ablex Publishing Corporation.

CHALLENGES

Although some scholars in computers and composition were relatively quick to embrace the progressive spirit of the interdisciplinary social theories informing composition studies during this period, the challenges of the social action and change associated with such theories proved to be more difficult. In fact, the more practical experience compositionists gained in dealing with integrating technology into English composition programs, the more they wrestled with the problems faced in the application of theory to practice and with the difficulties attending any attempt at using the technology to speed social change. Informing these struggles was the growing recognition that social action—whether or not it involved computers—was constrained by convention and situated in complex and overdetermined formations of social, political, and ideological forces.

Dealing with the Implications of Change in Classrooms and School Districts

The writing classroom was one of the principal sites for these struggles. As Hawisher (1988) had noted, computers had physically arrived in writing classrooms, but teachers and students had yet to adjust their accustomed strategies for teaching and learning to these now-new spaces: "The real challenge of working in this context [a computer-supported writing classroom], then, is to devise a pedagogy that capitalizes on ... computers ... yet goes beyond what we have previously contrived (p. 18).

Nor was this situation changing dramatically. Dawn and Raymond Rodrigues concurred with Hawisher's analysis in a 1989 *Computers and Composition* article entitled "How Word Pro-

complained to the lab director about the rude treatment he had been forced to endure. When the lab director reminded him that he had interrupted a teacher's class, he responded, "But the teacher wasn't teaching." The lab director asked how he knew that no teaching was taking place. The student replied, "All the students were doing was typing." (Rodrigues & Rodrigues, 1989, p. 13)

If we plan carefully and examine our integration of technology critically, computers have the potential for helping us shift traditional authority structures inherent in American education. We can, if we work at it, become learners within a community of other learners, our students. But the change will not happen automatically in the electronic classroom anymore than in a traditional classroom. We have to labor diligently to bring it about. (Hawisher & Selfe, 1991a, p. 64)

cessing is Changing Our Teaching." They compared the early idealism of the field with the realities that computer-using teachers were then faced with in making changes within the context of large educational systems. Among the problems the Rodrigueses identified were the economic barriers to fully realized technology integration: Buying computers, repairing and maintaining them, upgrading them, and educating teachers in their use had proved to be a project too expensive for many schools. As the authors noted, "We first envisioned the computerized classroom as the ideal context for teaching writing, but economics have not allowed that to materialize for many English Departments" (p. 20). At this time, the Rodrigues' (1986) *Teaching Writing with a Word Processor, Grades 7–13* was the fourth-best-selling title on NCTE's composition list (K. Williamson, personal correspondence, August 19, 1994), a statistic that suggests that many, if not most, teachers still needed an introduction to the pedagogical uses of computers in the language arts.

In another article in the same issue of *Computers and Composition*, H. Schwartz (1989) identified additional problems related to the integration of technology in the classroom focusing on the need for improved teacher education. She noted that the "widespread use of computers" (p. 60) in a school setting necessitated ongoing support for teachers as well as students, and that such support should include reduced teaching loads or other compensation for the quite-considerable learning involved in understanding how computer-applications might fit student needs and curricular goals. She wrote that "unless teachers are comfortable with the medium and able to adapt computer applications to their purposes, time required for teaching the mechanics of computer use can take time away from pedagogical concepts and practice" (p. 60).

Although great claims have been made for computers as agents of productive, democratic change, and although some research has been conducted, little evidence has been generated to support the notion that computers can—or will—serve as catalysts for the broader kinds of political reforms that would prove meaningful within our educational system. As a result, during the same period that some English professionals have looked to computers as possible allies in supporting fundamental pedagogical and political changes within literacy and composition programs, the daily

These teachers and others in the computers and composition community had begun to locate the complex relations that situated technology use not within an unproblematic field of radical potential, but within a realistic field of social and ideological formations that resisted change and reform. Their growing realizations indicated that electronic writing classes—now with access to the dynamic power of word-processing software, the far-reaching connectivity of networks, the transformative contexts of desktop publishing, and other exciting instructional media—supported only a limited potential for change.

Such a realization was not easy for computers and compositionists, nor did it happen overnight. By 1992, Elizabeth Klem and Charles Moran were still trying to make sense of the dynamic relationship between tradition and change as it was played out in computer-supported classrooms. They identified several ways in which the forces of tradition, represented in part by teachers who invested in— and were comfortable with—the existing system, and the forces of change, represented in part by the disruptive potential inherent in technology, came into opposition:

What we had not anticipated was that we'd see in these new classrooms a persistent and deep-rooted conflict between the teachers' own goals and those built into the new facility. It is generally thought that computers carry with them new pedagogies and that teachers will, in some undefined way, go along. Indeed, computers are often hailed as "The Catalyst for Broad Curricular Change" (Gilbert & Balestri, 1988). Our computer classrooms were designed, as noted above, to complement and reinforce the Writing Program's model of "good teaching." The room layout, with its notably absent teacher-place, privileged

instructional uses of computers in classrooms around the country have often belied the potential benefits of this alliance. (Hawisher & Selfe, 1994, p. 156)

Computer-supported writing labs/classrooms, however, are not guaranteed to provide the professional "elbow room" necessary for constructing our profession's new vision of computers and their role in writing programs. Their success depends on inventive faculty who take a unique, language-oriented approach to the design and operation of a computer facility, and the instructional activities conducted therein. (Selfe, 1989a, p. xx)

a workshop model of a writing class and aimed to cast the teacher as a fellow writer and editor albeit the most experienced writer in the room rather than as the center-of-the-class authority. Moreover, the network configuration sought to foster a class model in which much of the learning and writing happened as students collaborated on the in-process drafts.

What we saw in our teachers' classes, however, was a fair amount of dissonance: a genuine clash between the kind of writing class envisioned by the teacher and the kind of writing class privileged by the computer-equipped classroom and its architecture. Because we were not attempting to measure student learning, we can not relate what we saw to what progress students made. We have to admit, though, that the tug-of-war between the teachers and their classroom was on-going and sometimes quite striking. The teachers' behavior did not change significantly as the semester progressed, nor did the teachers noticeably adapt their teaching styles to the new environment. (pp. 22–23)

The growing realization that computers themselves would not drive change was connected to an increased professional sensitivity to social and political issues in educational settings. Computers and composition specialists noted that departments of English in colleges and high schools frequently introduced computers into their programs without the careful research and planning demanded for the use of new technology, and without thinking carefully about the design and implementation of instruction in computer-supported writing facilities. Such efforts, it became clear, the fundamental changes that proponents of technology saw to be possible: student-centered rather than teacher-centered classes, increased participation of marginalized students, expanded and increasingly democratic access to systems of publication and distribution, and the democratization of information.

Dealing with the Implications of Change in Teacher-Education Programs

As some experts noted, during this period and soon thereafter, despite the climate for change that the use of computers would seem to create, teachers educated within the current educational system often resisted any fundamental alteration of their instructional approaches and students' approaches to learning in computer-supported settings. Such teachers often continued to favor more traditional approaches supplemented by lectures, assignments, and classroom strategies. Given the traditional education of teachers and the inherent conservatism of the American educational system, needed changes never seemed to occur and, indeed, some needs within the system had become exacerbated.

Among the many problems—evidenced in English composition classrooms at least as frequently as they were in any other learning spaces during this time—were the continued marginalization of individuals due to race, gender, age, sexual preference, or handicap; the silencing, intentional or unintentional, of certain segments of our population, such as the very poor; and the unequal distribution of power within economic and social groups represented in our classrooms. These problems persisted, it became clear, because they were systemic and politically determined, not only within the framework of the educational system, but also within that of the culture and its economy. As liberatory and critical educators sketched the problem, "Schooling is a device through which a corporate society reproduces its class-based order . . . recreates a stratified society by socializing each new generation into its place in the established order" (Shor, 1987, p. 2). To address such problems in major ways, computers and composition specialists, as Mary Louise Gomez (1991) and Emily Jessup (1991) were beginning to tell the field, the very foundations of the culture would need to undergo fundamental reform (cf. Freire, 1990; Shor, 1987).

Such radical changes, of course, were unlikely; they faced stiff and continuing resistance from a wide range of educators, politicians, administrators, and taxpayers who had vested power in the current cultural situation. Indeed, the potential of fundamental change associated with technology was extraordinarily

The democratization of social relations in the classroom will not be automatic. Regression to authority will be continual. In the subgroups, students may set up a replica of their old schooling. The most advanced student in the team can dominate the others, become the new teacher-authority, and sabotage the collective process through anti-dialogue. (Shor, 1980, p. 111)

Although classrooms will be increasingly populated by diverse learners, their growing numbers alone do not make the case for changing teaching practices. Rather, it is this growth combined with concerns for equity that has spurred teachers and researchers to action. Educators now frankly acknowledge the critical necessity of addressing in this decade the distribution of opportunity. (Gomez, 1991, p. 320)

Today, more than a decade after personal computers first entered the English curriculum in force, few teachers feel prepared to carry out effective instruction in a virtual classroom, and even fewer English education programs can claim they adequately prepare teachers for assuming productive instructional roles in such classrooms. This state of affairs, while disturbing now, is bound to become increasingly problematic during the next decade as the pace of technological change accelerates. Our profession is not preparing teachers to deal with technology in its current forms and we are certainly not preparing them to deal with technology as it changes in the future. (Selfe, 1992, p. 24)

Joseph Weizenbaum (1976) has argued that computers often serve to "entrench and stabilize social and political structures" that might otherwise be reformed or radically altered (p. 31). Programs like GRAMMATIK II and CRITIQUE can be seen as serving such a function, reinforcing a still widespread understanding of literacy that Giroux (1976) ties to state needs, as illus-

dangerous to the existing systemic values within schools and, thus, to people who depended on the continued existence of the educational system for a livelihood. However, it was this very potential for change that attracted radical pedagogists' attention to technology—computers, during this period continued to be seen as having the potential to help teachers restructure human language activities (Heim, 1987; Selfe, 1989a), create a global community (Spitzer, 1989), explode traditional classroom boundaries and constraints (Hiltz, 1986), change the traditional teacher–student hegemony (Cooper & Selfe, 1990), and alter the very fabric of social and psychological interaction (Kiesler, Siegel, & McGuire, 1984).

Computers and compositionists were faced with the increasingly realistic understanding that efforts to initiate change would work, in the best of situations, only partially, locally, and temporarily. The conservative trend in instructional strategies during this period was also reinforced by teacher education programs. Many teacher-education programs devoted little or no time to emerging technologies, and few examined technology from critical perspectives. Few teachers, moreover, had access to any postservice education that helped them think critically about the use of computers within instructional settings (Selfe, Rodrigues, & Oates, 1989).

Without such pre- and in-service education—and faced with administrators who demanded a speedy and cost-effective integration of computers into English programs—English composition teachers often resorted to the readily available computer-assisted software packages prepared by commercial vendors. The packages were frequently authored by software developers who had little experience in the teaching of English. Moreover, as LeBlanc (1990) pointed out, software packages—such as style checkers—often served a highly conservative function themselves in that they reinforced the back-to-basics movement that supported (and continues to support) traditional authority structures within educational settings. Thus, teachers came to adopt computers, but nevertheless continued to resist meaningful change by using computers to reinforce older and often conventional ways of thinking about learning.

Dealing with the Implications of Change in Hypertext Applications

In addition to the conservatism that continued to inform the development and educational uses of style checkers and spelling checkers, teacher/scholars became increasingly aware of the challenges associated with hypertext and online conferences. By the end of the decade, experts were beginning to wonder how realistic early claims about hypertext's radical potential really were. Homemade HyperCard stacks were proliferating and large scale development projects were being featured at every conference, but no one seemed to be able to address in systematic ways the difficulties that readers had identified when trying to navigate hypertexts or that writers had identified when authering hypertexts for educational use.

Michael Joyce, in a landmark article published in 1988 ("Siren Shapes: Exploratory and Constructive Hypertexts") voiced this concern in 1988:

It is likely that the potential benefits [of hypertext] outweigh nearly all the short run perils save perhaps the most crucial one. The peril of overpromising threatens not just to sap the resilience of educators who must wade through the dross and justify the costs. It also threatens the credibility and creativity of innovators who find themselves having to disaffiliate and differentiate before they can discover. (p. 11)

trated in his examination of UNESCO literacy programs in developing nations. (LeBlanc, 1990, p. 11)

Common claims for hypertext include the possibility for promoting associative thinking, collaborative learning, synthesis in writing from sources, distributing traditional authority in texts and classrooms, and facilitating deconstructive reading and writing. (Johnson-Eilola, 1992, p. 97)

When we first set about designing a hypertext application for use in the composition class, we were eager to see examples of what other writing teachers were doing with nonlinear text—a desire that gradually gave way, as reality seeped in, to the discomfiting sense that we were entering largely uncharted territory. While we encountered a great deal of enthusiastic speculation (and not a little visionary zeal), it wasn't long before we grasped that hypertext's alleged power to transform composition instruction—whether by supporting familiar goals in fresh ways or by suggesting a whole new approach to reading and writing—remains for the most part unexplored. (DiPardo & DiPardo, 1990, p. 7)

Hypertext is emerging as a new medium for thinking, reading, and writing in many disciplines, including composition. It promises to become a redefining technology, a tool that reshapes not only practices but also abstract understanding of the thinking, reading, and writing activities it supports. Before that happens, even as we welcome its happening, we benefit by critically reviewing the conceptions of hypertext that are now driving design and development. (Smith, 1991, p. 224)

To address some of the challenges associated with hypertext, Joyce suggested undertaking a more critical analysis of hypertext projects and making a distinction between two kinds of hypertexts: "constructive" and "exploratory." Constructive hypertexts, Joyce noted, were those designed primarily for use by writers to "develop a body of information which they map according to their needs and interests, and the transformations they discover as they invent, gather, and act on that information." Exploratory hypertexts, in contrast, were designed primarily for readers. These texts encouraged readers to "create, change, and recover particular encounters with the body of knowledge, maintaining these encounters as versions of the material (i.e., trails, paths, webs, notebooks, etc.)" (p. 11).

However, the understanding of hypertext as a medium for reading and writing did not bring with it an understanding of how its radical potential was to be realized in the writing classroom. It was hard to ignore, even at this point in time, the fact that many of the large hypertext projects being touted by enthusiasts focused on conventional and canonical figures—Dickens, Fielding, and Shakespeare, for example. Early hypertext advocates, moreover, were tempering their initial enthusiasm with more serious and critical questions. John McDaid (1991), in "Toward an Ecology of Hypermedia," followed his analysis of hypermedia with these pointed questions:

- Does working with hypermedia in fact facilitate the teaching of composition? Or are we just wasting our time?
- Are the predicted social and cognitive impacts of digitality borne out in actual practice?
- If hypermedia seems to be having effects, how do we decide if they are good or bad?

- How can inequalities of access, particularly thorny with expensive hypermedia workstations, be addressed? What forms of activism are appropriate and necessary? What do we want? Who gets it? Who controls it? Who pays and how? (p. 219–220)

Additional complications with hypertext were also pointed out by Slatin (1990) in his *College English* article "Reading Hypertext: Order and Coherence in a New Medium." In this piece, talking about the difficulties that both readers and writers had reported experiencing when navigating hypertexts, Slatin acknowledged:

We regard a conventional text as coherent to the extent that all the material it contains strikes us as being related in an appropriately direct way to the subject and to the author's thesis and arranged in the appropriate sequence. The perception of coherence in hypertext seems to me much more problematic, however, though I don't have time to do more than suggest what might be involved. Nor do I know enough to do more than that. (p. 881)

As one solution to the challenges associated with coherence, Slatin suggested "a visual map of some kind" at the "metatextual level" (p. 881). However, he continued, such maps themselves remained "problematic" within a "fluid system of multiple participants" because they were inherently interested representations from a particular perspective.

Although these scholars came at the challenges associated with hypertext from various angles, they all suggested the many complications inherent in instantiating the radical potential of the medium in educational systems that were themselves situated within a web of established social forces and formations. Ex-

In the next ten years, we will probably have to confront serious challenges to our reception and conception of text. The resulting changes could drastically alter the institutional status of writing teachers, though, of course, this is hardly the first time a new educational technology has given rise to predictions of sweeping change. Hypertext and hypermedia give us a real opportunity for change. The most important questions before our profession, then, may be practical and political rather than theoretical. (Moulthrop, 1991a, p. 255)

When we create space for students, we allow them to discover that meaning is not fixed but socially reconstituted each time language is used. The skills-and-drills curriculum and standardized testing of language abilities is possible only in authoritarian discourse that assumes meaning is fixed and there can only be one right answer. The play of language in INTERCHANGE subverts authoritarian discourse by showing human discourse is composed of many voices. A student in another INTERCHANGE said it better: "When I first came to this class, it seemed abnormal to participate all the time. Now it seems abnormal to sit still and listen to a lecture for an hour and a half." (Faigleya, 1990, p. 310)

Online computer conferences have been of increasing interest to teachers of composition who hope to provide alternative forums for student-centered, collaborative writing that involve all members of their classes in active learning. Some expect them to provide sites for discourse that are more egalitarian and less constrained by power differentials based on gender and status than are face-to-face discussions. These expectations, however, are largely unsupported by systematic research. (Selfe & Meyer, 1991, p. 163)

Online, don't we often find, neither discussions nor conversations, but, a set of asocial monologues? People linked, yes, by a network; but each writing energetically, all writing simultaneously, and no one reading and responding very much— not *listening* as much as they would in a face-to-face, spo-

ploring the theoretical potential of hypertext was one thing; making it work with real readers and writers, in real classrooms taught by real teachers, was another.

Dealing with the Implications of Change within Online Forums

A third site in which computers and composition specialists wrestled with the challenges of tradition and change was in the field of CMC, and particularly in their attempts to bring online discussions into the writing class. By 1991, a great many claims had been made for the virtues of written "disussion" in online spaces. Computer-using teachers—after consulting the early work of scholars on the social and psychological aspects of computer mediated communication (e.g., Kiesler, Siegel, & McGuire, 1984; Sproull & Kiesler, 1991)—had expressed the hope that electronic discussions would provide forums within which writers and readers could create, exchange, and comment on texts (cf., Batson, 1988; Eldred, 1989; Flores, 1990). These spaces, it seemed, had the potential for supporting student-centered learning and discursive practices that could be different from, and—some claimed—more engaging and democratic than those occurring within traditional classroom settings (cf., Barker & Kemp, 1990; Cooper & Selfe, 1990; Eldred, 1989; Handa, 1990; Spitzer, 1989).

By 1991, these claims were beginning to be questioned and tested by computers and composition specialists—and, increasingly, were found to lack empirical support. One of the early articles to undertake this task was written by Cynthia Selfe and Paul Meyer (1991). Published in *Written Communication*, this piece set out to test the claim that online conferences were characterized by egalitarian patterns of involvement among participants, the democratic exercise of discursive power, and conversational patterns that avoided the traditional dominance of male participants. The study focused on 40 days of online conversation on Megabyte University—20 days of regular conversation and 20 days of conversation in which participants used pseudonyms. The online discussion involved at the time of the study approximately 210 computer-using teachers of English composition.

Among the findings from this study, Selfe and Meyers (1991) noted:

> It seems that Megabyte University offered fairly equal access to participants but at the same time tended to be dominated by men and higher-status members of the academic community . . . . The present study provides little support for the notion that pseudonym use on electronic conferences automatically results in more egalitarian participation. (p. 187)

This observation that electronic conferences, although they could be designed to provide an equal opportunity for participants to engage in discussion, did not necessarily result in such egalitarian patterns of discourse, attested to the complex nature of these forums and to the increasingly sophisticated research needed to understand the discourse that went on within them. Subsequent observations of online conferences added additional texture to descriptions of these electronic discursive communities. The November 1991 issue of *Computers and Composition*, for example, featured an article by Joseph Janangelo that traced two incidents of computer-based discourse: one that resulted in the humiliation of a student and one that involved surveillance of a faculty member. Other, similar studies identified related phenomena that suggested the complexity of online discourse forums and the need to

ken encounter? Divergent monologue, rather than convergent conversation? If participation in online conversation amounts to speaking to no auditor or writing for no reader, then we have not brought in any voices from the margin; we have created a context that isolates the individual participant, masking the essentially social nature of human discourse. (Moran, 1991, p. 51)

Gail E. Hawisher and Cynthia L. Selfe charge that our research on college writing and computer conferences constitutes "uncritical enthusiasm." We confess to the "enthusiasm" but plead not guilty to the "uncritical." (Schriner & Rice, 1991, p. 501)

We want to stress—and we thought we had in the article—that we were not so much singling out particular scholars and their work as we were reporting on the widespread and uncritical enthusiasm that seems to characterize the whole of computers and composition studies. Without a doubt, this same brand of enthusiasm has, at times been characteristic of our own work as well. Indeed, our identification of the rhetoric of technology grew directly out of an increasingly critical self-examination of earlier work we had contributed to the field. We are teachers, optimists at heart; we share with Schriner and Rice and many other colleagues a sense of hope that brings us back to the classroom each day with great expectations and the desire to initiate productive changes in writing classes, in students, and in our own work. (Hawisher and Selfe's (1991c) response to Schriner and Rice, 1991, 502)

We face a new world when we teach. There is no news here, for it has been ever so. Despite what we have thought of ourselves or our students, they remake us as we remake them, in reciprocal relation: no student who is not a teacher, no teacher not a student, no morning not new, at least to someone. (Joyce, 1992, p. 7)

study these electronic conversations in situated research projects.

If these scholarly projects shared a single theme, it was one of increasing caution. By 1991, in an article published by *College Composition and Communication*, Hawisher and Selfe expressed their concern about the "rhetoric of technology," a utopian discourse that masked many of the problems associated with technology and that minimized the barriers to integrating such technology productively in classrooms and the educational system. The claims made about computers and their value as catalysts for change, Hawisher and Selfe noted, were belied by evidence that computer-supported composition classrooms exhibited many of the same problems as traditional classrooms and that school districts which had purchased computer equipment were still experiencing many of the same problems that had plagued them before technology had arrived.

Over the next 4 years, computers and composition specialists would continue to record the disturbing encounters among the new technology, the traditions of American education, and the clearly felt need for institutional change. If computers really could support positive educational change—and some computer-using teachers persisted in believing that this was essentially true—what was the nature of such change? And where would it take place? Was change limited to those classrooms or teachers that already supported a critical or reformist vision of education? Did the claims about the potential of computers grow more from the continued enthusiasm of individuals and groups than it did from any real evidence of productive change? To what extent was the radical potential of technology ultimately constrained within existing social structures and ideological formations? Was technological change limited to local venues—individual classrooms, electronic conferences, single assignments? Was it possible, as some scholars were still ready to suggest, that technology could provide the basis for fundamental and far-reaching social reform?

INTERVIEW: MICHAEL JOYCE

The first I heard of writing technology in classrooms was a teaching writing fellow at Iowa. And some of what must have been quite precocious students asked if they could do their papers on text editors. I had very little idea of what all that was. I'm really a newcomer, compared to lots of people in this. I didn't get involved. I remember, in 1980 or so, a colleague in the department at Jackson talking about word processing and my being fairly cynical about it. I remember scoffing to people, and saying "What's he doing making hollandaise out of sentences?"

At any rate, I didn't start until 1982, when I got an Apple II. And I got it largely because as a novelist, a word processor seemed a donation from heaven, because novelists are always trying to move things from very deep in a manuscript to very early and vice versa. And almost instantly, when I got the word processor, the Apple, I realized that because something showed up on pg. 250 of a novel that "belonged" on pg. 15, it could probably just as well appear in the story on 250 or 15. And it seemed to me that it ought to be possible to write a story that changed everytime you read it. So, I really came into all this through fiction, through my own interest. I'm willing to credit myself with vision, in retrospect. At that time it was just a stupid belief that computers, once I got to them, could do everything. And I started calling around trying to find software that did this, and of course began my initiation in what was involved in hypertext.

I started working with the Applewriter in 1982 and wrote a novel on it. I started making calls around and writing people and asking them for software that would allow you to write a story that would change. Everybody told me there was no such thing, wouldn't be for 20 years, etc. Until, finally, I reached one particular person, Natalie Dehn, who was then at an Artificial Intelligence Lab and who had appeared in a computer magazine. She was teaching computers to write stories. She was actually doing the reading comprehension program, AI based, and I wrote to her blindly and she wrote or called back. First of all, she argued with my premises and said that she believed that the kinds of constraints that led writers to have to

choose one particular version of a story over others were fundamental. She took a highly informed and very provocative stance toward the compositional issues or the creative issues.

However, in the course of engaging me about it, she allowed that
there was somebody else equally crazy who had visited the AI lab
the previous year. That was Jay Bolter, and she put me in contact
with him. That led to the first contact I had with Jay. I wrote to him
and said "I want to do this thing. I want to write a novel that will
change every time you read it." He had an interest, as a classicist
and computer scientist, in trying to create a way for the computer
to tell stories, much in the way that Homer did. And so he and I
began in '83, and then quite seriously when I took my sabbatical at
Yale in '84 and '85, to work on the development of *Storyspace*. We
ended up with a working version of *Storyspace* before either one of
us had heard the word "hypertext."

I mean there was lots of literature there; you know, it dated back
to 1945. One of the problems is that it was so interdisciplinary, you
couldn't get a fix on it. There were people in Comp Sci, there were
people in AI, there were people indeed. Ted Nelson taught at Vassar
in psychology or something. The publications crossed disciplinary
boundaries and therefore didn't show up in the usual places. What
happened, finally, is we had a version of *Storyspace*, as I say, and
somebody put me onto *Literary Machines*. And I said, "Geez, that's
what we just did, this!" That's what we wanted to do. And this is, by
the way, not at all an isolated phenomenon. I'm constantly running
into people who invented hypertext—people invented hypertext on
their own, independently, and found one another.

I began teaching using *Storyspace* with basic writers. We didn't
have a classroom then; we used it with groups in a lab setting. As
we started to get a drop-in lab in January of '86 with a beta version
of *Storyspace*, or an alpha; a really clunky thing that wouldn't last
more than a few minutes. But I instantly started working with basic
writers long before I worked with my creative writers.

My collaboration with Jay was largely through telephone and mail
in the beginning. In fact, it has remained so because it was set that
way. It's something I always love to tell people; I really considered
Jay Bolter my major intellectual collaborator and also more and
more my best friend. In the time we have worked together since '83,
onward 10 years, I'm certain we have spent no more than two weeks
physically in each other's company! Jay wrote nearly every bit of
code through this period. We contracted out for some of the code to
contract programmers, but Jay has written nearly every single line

of *Storyspace*. This will be a genuine historical note: the very first *Storyspace* we had almost instantly done in Pascal on an IBM PC. It was a command line interface.

I'm the person who decided we ought to move to the Macintosh; Macintosh was very young then. But I believed that the kind of visual interface, the windows and what have you, were necessary. So we wrote it in Pascal, and at that time you couldn't write on a Macintosh. You had to write it under Lisa Pascal and then move it to MPW Pascal.

A major factor in the early days is just the fact that we both were scholars, writers, and thinkers in a postmodern age and a strong influence from the early stages was our mutual understanding of the intellectual history of the 20th century—of the decentering of text, of multiplicity, of multiple voices. We began early on writing and talking to each other about James Joyce, about Tristan Shandy, and about Umberto Eco. And, we were very clearly engaging ourselves in issues of the multiplicity of text, marginality, Derridian marginality, and all that. So, there was classroom practice, there was our own theoretical grounding, there was our need. It was driven by need, by a desire to write such things.

Hypertext, '87 was a real watershed for us. We had a working version of *Storyspace* and I'd basically finished "Afternoon." The first-ever international hypertext meeting in Chapel Hill came up in October of '87. John Smith was on the program committee and believed there were maybe 50 to 100 people seriously interested in hypertext. They set the meeting for 250 people, thinking maybe graduate students and hangers on would come. However, they had thousands of applications. The '87 meeting was when people came and realized how many systems there were. Apple probably showed up with their presumptuously named Hypercard to find out that there was a long tradition there and that people weren't going to take Hypercard in with open arms; that there were real questions. Jay and I were in the lobby, demo-ing *Storyspace*. I was giving away copies of the first edition of the "Afternoon," and we were on the margins, we were quite literally on the margins. The establishment was inside, and the narrative and humanities were marginal.

At that point it was a field very largely controlled by technical writing, by the needs of doing documentation for engineering, defense, and business settings. We were all, Intermedia, the Perseus Project and *Storyspace*, on sidetracks. But, nonetheless, it was a great meeting in the sense of that there was enormous excitement, there was press coverage and what have you. There was a sense of this bustle. Ted Nelson was there and gave a talk; Doug Englebart was there. People had a sense that we were on the edge of some sort of revolution, and they, in fact, probably over promised it. Surely, by 1987, we were involved in shaping and creating a new discourse of writing, pedagogy, theory and what have you. Now, much of that is retrospective; at that point, it was all just an adventure!

Michael Joyce is Visiting Associate Professor of English and the Library at Vassar College.

5

1992–1994:
LOOKING FORWARD

The global Internet . . . has suddenly become the most universal and indispensable network on the planet. . . . It's a wild frontier, befitting its origins amorphous, unruly, impolite and anarchic.

—James Gleich

Spring 1994: Jim Kinneavy tells a group of visitors to the [lab] that if someone as old as he is can learn computers, anyone can. Then he tells them that he "net surfs."

—Denise Weeks, C&W, 1994

THE CONTEXT:
THE FIELD OF COMPOSITION
STUDIES, 1992–1994

As a community of researchers and scholars, composition studies continued to flourish during the period 1992–1994. The Spring 1994 issue of *Rhetoric Review* was entirely devoted to a survey of graduate programs in Rhetoric and Composition, a survey that demonstrated steady (roughly 10% year) growth in the num-

PhD Programs in Rhetoric and Composition
Alabama, University of, Tuscaloosa
Arizona, University of
Arizona State University
Auburn University
Ball State University
Bowling Green State University
California, University of, San Diego
Carnegie Mellon University
Catholic University of America
Cincinnati, University of
Connecticut, University of
East Texas State University, Commerce
Florida State University
Hawaii, University of
Illinois, University of, Chicago
Illinois, University of, Urbana–Champaign
Illinois State University
Indiana University of Pennsylvania
Iowa State University
Kansas, University of
Louisiana State University
Louisville, University of
Maryland, University of, College Park

ber of graduate programs in the field. Indeed, during the 1979–1994 period covered by this history, the number of programs increased from 22 to 72, a growth of 227%. The graph that *Rhetoric Review* featured shows a relatively steady slope: As the total number of programs increased, so did the annual increment of increase. Thus between 1992 and 1993, the field added six new graduate programs—rapid growth in the world of English which was, by other measures, imploding. Other indicators also suggested the strength of the research community in our field: In 1992, MLA published the first volume in its new series, *Research and Scholarship in Composition*; in 1993 more than 4,000 proposals were submitted to CCCC—a 25% increase over 1992, itself a record year. The market for PhDs trained in rhetoric and composition continued to be strong, despite a dismal job market in English generally; and in December 1992 *RTE* established a new category in its annotated bibliography, "Researcher Education," to encompass the increased submissions that focused on the training of researchers. A final indicator of the strength of the research community was the serious consideration, at both the 1993 and 1994 CCCCs, of the topic "should we abandon Freshman English?" The *we* that was speaking was, of course, the research community, not those who taught first-year students.

The growth of the research community took place, to a great extent, at the expense of the community of teachers. For every well-paid, tenure-track research position with its light teaching load, there were multiple part-time or TA positions with low pay and high teaching loads. This was a zero-sum equation, or worse: Demographics and economics combined forces, and postsecondary education lost federal and state funding. Most institutions, especially public 4-year research universities, were forced both to cut programs and increase tuition. In this fiscal and political climate, the field put on hold any hopes it may have had of improving the working conditions of those who teach the majority of writing courses. Indeed, Robert Connors and Andrea Lunsford (1993), in a report of their research on teachers' responses to student writing, find in those responses "a world of teaching writing that was harder and sadder than they wanted it to be—a world very different from the theoretical world of composition studies most readers hoped to inhabit" (p. 214).

The field showed professional concern for this widening division between the tenured and tenure-track researchers and individuals who taught the bulk of writing classes—usually GTAs or part-time instructors. The symposium in the May 1992 issue of *CCC's* responded to the "Progress Report from the CCCC Committee on Professional Standards" and showed that the profession was both thinking and writing about this challenge. In 1993, NCTE's *Teaching English in The Two-Year College* and *College English* became available free with one membership—the members needed only to choose the one that best fit with their professional needs. In 1992 the editor of CCC moved to bring the articles formerly printed in its "Staffroom Interchange" section into the body of the journal, giving these pedagogically oriented pieces the same type size and page format as the articles that focused on theory or research.

None of these moves narrowed the gap between the working conditions of full-time, tenure-track faculty and the growing academic underclass, the part-time lecturers and teaching assistants who actually taught our writing classes. The "Statement of Principles and Standards for the Postsecondary Teaching of Writing," informally known as the "Wyoming Resolution," described what its authors saw in 1989 as "an enormous academic underclass": More

University of
Southern Illinois University at Carbondale
Southern Mississippi, University of
Southwestern Louisiana, University of
Syracuse University
Temple University
Tennessee, University of, Knoxville
Texas, University of, Arlington
Texas, University of, Austin
Texas A&M University
Texas Christian University
Texas Tech University
Texas Woman's University
Utah, University of
Washington, University of
Washington State University
Waterloo, University of (Canada)
Wayne State University
Wisconsin, University of, Milwaukee.

As explained in its "Progress Report," the CCCC Committee on Professional Standards has been thorough and responsible in seeking the views of the profession concerning the "Statement on Principles and Standards." This work has proved the "Statement" a significant document insofar as it reflects the mores of the CCCC membership. Yet it is as much an instrument of reform as a position paper. Thus the "Progress Report" protests the "second-class intellectual status" (337) accorded the teaching of writing, especially freshman English. The Committee reminds us that even English department faculty may hold freshman English in low esteem (338). However, in its attempt to correct one inaccurate perception, the Committee ignores another. Writing centers are seen as, at best, the site of third-class intellectual endeavor, not only by English faculty but even by some freshman English directors. Revision of the "statement" to address specifically and more accurately the needs, rights, and work of writing centers should be an important step toward improving their image and consequently raising their status. (Balester, 1992, p. 167)

It has now been over two years since the CCCC "Statement" was sent to over 10,000 people involved or interested in the teaching of writing at post-secondary institutions. By far the most common reaction to the document in these two years, judging from the many convention speeches, articles, and editorials that followed on its heels, has been to raise questions of action. What should we *do*, individually and collectively, to reform the profession? How can we improve class size during times of financial exigency and continued in-

than half the English faculty at 2-year colleges, and nearly one-third of the English faculty at 4-year colleges and universities, work on part-time and/or temporary appointments. Almost universally, they are teachers of writing ("Statement," 1989, p. 330). In 1994 the lead article in *Forum*, the newsletter of CCCC's Part-Time Faculty Forum, announced that 48% of the English teachers in California state colleges and universities were part-time or GTA, up from 35% in 1980 and 42% in 1990 (Flachmann, 1994). Yet our field during this time, despite its attention to critical pedagogy and its focus on race, class, and gender, seemed unable, or unwilling, to attend to its own class structure and the widening gap between its "rich" and its "poor." In most quarters, and computers and composition no exception, composition studies increasingly privileged research, reproducing the model it found in English Departments at research universities.

RESEARCH AND PROFESSIONAL PUBLICATION: THE SOCIAL PERSPECTIVE

In 1992 Anne Ruggles Gere, speaking as Program Chair of that year's CCCC and one who had, therefore, read the thousands of program proposals for that conference, invoked the metaphor of the quilt to describe the order she had found in this mass articulation of professional interests. This metaphor served an embodiment of our field's central concerns during this period: community, collaboration, cultural diversity, and the social construction of composition studies and what professionals in this field knew. In the CCCC program for the following year, Lillian Bridwell-Bowles built on the quilt-as-metaphor, placing on the Program's cover a picture of the assembling of the National Quilt and asserting by this act that our community was itself part of the larger community: "AIDS has touched the lives of our students and all the members of our profession." In her "Greetings from the 1993 Program Chair," Bridwell-Bowles described her vision of the ways in which knowledge would be created during the conference. "Throughout the conference, some of the most important work will be done as we meet informally, and we have provided additional places for Conversation Clusters near the food services" (p. 3). Although composition professionals had always known that "some of the most important work will be done as we meet informally," this knowledge had been, insofar as the CCCC program had been concerned, tacit. Now this knowledge moved into the foreground, explicit, and the conference structure, as well as its contents, enacted the profession's continuing focus on the social.

Publications during this period also demonstrated the field's interest in the ways in which composition studies, as a field, were socially constructed, and in particular in the ways in which race, gender, class, culture and cultural difference influenced the business of writing and teaching, constituting the discipline. Anthologies of essays published during this time announced their central concerns with titles such as *Social Issues in the English Classroom* (Hurlburt & Totten, 1992) and *Cultural Studies in the English Classroom* (Berlin & Vivion, 1992). The May 1992 CCC had as its focus "Political and Social Issues in Composition, " and the October 1992 issue had a double focus: "Feminism and Composition" and "Collaboration and Composition." The May 1992 *CCC* included Hairston's "Diversity, Ideology, and Teaching Writing," in which she argued that writing courses "should not

stitutional scorn for composition instruction? How *can* tenure codes be revised to reflect the importance of pedagogy in writing? Will it be possible in our lifetimes to do away with part-time instructors moonlighting for meager wages at five different local colleges? (Anson & Gaard, 1992, p. 171)

Greetings from the 1992 Program Chair
The annual convention of the Conference on College Composition and Communication, which in recent years has had an attendance of more than three thousand, is the largest professional meeting in our field. The program before you describes the workshops, meetings, special events, and concurrent sessions that comprise this, our 43rd annual meeting. It is my pleasure to welcome you to the convention and to express my hope that you will enjoy its intellectual riches as much as I did when I read proposals last summer. (Gere, 1992, p. 4)

The theme "Twentieth Century Problems, Twenty-First-Century Solutions: Issues, Answers, Actions" comes at a moment in U.S. history when we have just inaugurated a new President whose commitments to change are well known to us. ... This year we have a number of special speakers who will enrich our understanding of the issues that affect our profession. (Bridwell-Bowles, 1993, p. 3)

What I find most troublesome about Maxine's line of reasoning is that she doesn't trust her students' ability to handle the social and cultural differences that organize the realities of contemporary America. The implicit message is that they can share their differences, but they shouldn't have to engage in the rhetorical art of negotiation. For Maxine, students are too "unsophisticated" and "uninformed," and besides the teacher his "all the power" (188). This representation of students as potential dupes "ripe for intellectual intimidation" (188) can only have the effect of reproducing students as spectators, perpetually on the verge of being overwhelmed by the experts who have the credentials to speak. (Trimbur et al., 1993, p. 249)

It strikes me as a healthy sign for our profession to be having such a spirited discussion about what and how we should teach in writing courses, particularly in required first-year English courses. What an encouraging change from those days when English 101 was dismissed as a service course not important enough to argue about. The issue of what goes on in freshman English has always been primary for me; in fact, my first professional article, published more than 20 years ago, was titled "What's a Freshman Theme For?" It seems appropriate that "Diversity, Ideology, and Teach-

be for anything or about anything other than writing itself, and how one uses it to learn and think and communicate" (p. 179). In this article, Hairston maintained that the writing class had boundaries—that there was an "inside" and an "outside," and that the writing teacher chose to import, or not, the outside material into writing classes. Hairston's article, *CCC* editor Gebhardt (1993) wrote, "has provoked more Counterstatement submissions than any *CCC* article since the start of 1987" (p. 295). The responses to Hairston's article, all of which made in different ways the point that the classroom was "always already" part of its social, cultural, and political context, were published as a major section in the May 1993 issue of *CCC*. Their volume and depth suggest the centrality of the issue for this time; the article itself, in its passionate resistance to the new ideology, suggests the depth of the change that was occurring.

A final indicator of the power of the social perspective in this period is the increasing centrality of the "conversation" as metaphor in our publications. Herrington and Moran (1992), in *Writing, Teaching, and Learning in the Disciplines*, included an "Interchange," a polylogue among five teachers that concluded with a collaboratively written "chorus." In *CCC* during this period, the editor foregrounded the "symposium" as a genre and encouraged responsive writing in situations such as the response to Hairston's article mentioned earlier. Even *RTE* felt the need to cast its discourse in a social mode. In the October 1993 issue, its editor announced the journal's "first effort . . . to reflect the give and take of an academic conversation . . . an essay followed by critical commentaries, followed in turn by the author's response to the commentators." The editor noted that this format was not original: "It is simply new for *RTE*" (Stotsky, 1993, p. 221).

RESEARCH AND PROFESSIONAL PUBLICATION: NEW GENRES, NEW VOICES

Concern for the writer's personal voice had been a part of the field since its beginnings, yet interest in this area seemed, in the light of more recent theories of social construction, to be somewhat suspect. Indeed, the mainstream in the mid 1980s through the beginning of the 1990s (Bartholomae, 1985; Berlin, 1987a; Tuman, 1988) had characterized those who focused on the personal as romantics, teachers who fostered, for their own unacknowledged political ends, an allegedly apolitical pedagogy that made it certain that compositionists would reproduce in the next generation the inequities of the present. Yet, during this period, a concern for personal voice appears with a frequency that suggested writing teachers were experiencing a reaction to the field's privileging of social construction and the diminished sense of agency that can come with it. It may well have been, too, that the antifoundationalism of poststructuralist thought suggested only the single, human voice telling its own story—not "the" story, but a story nonetheless.

Personal voices were foregrounded in the February 1992 issue of *CCC*, which carries on its cover the heading "In Focus: Personal and Innovative Writing." Richard Gebhardt (1992) argued that he has included the personal essay in *CCC* since the beginning of his tenure, yet in this issue he almost seemed to say, with Samuel Richardson's Clarissa, "Let this expiate." The February 1992 issue of *CCC* included Cheryl Geisler's multivocal, multilayered "Exploring Academic Literacy: An Experiment in Composing"; McQuade's account of a visit with his dying mother; Terry Zawacki's "Recomposing as a Woman: An Essay in Different Voices," which begins "I learned to garden from my

ing Writing," which will most certainly be my last major professional article, focuses on the same topic. Today, however, the context for the discussion is more complex, given a changing student population and a changing world. The tone is also far more emotional. That's unfortunate—some good professional friendships have dissolved in the heat of the argument. (Hairston, 1993, p. 255)

Rhetoric Review: Burkean Parlor
Some of us are uncomfortable in parlors ... .We timidly enter such rooms, their ceilings seemingly higher than the roofs of our modest houses, feeling that we have entered an alien world. We're swept into conversations that seem remote from our workaday lives, conversations that enrich the opulent surroundings with an apparent wealth of experience that extends beyond (the truth be told) the range of our acknowledged desires and even of our dreams. (Review of "On Keeping Afloat in the Parlor," *Rhetoric Review*, 1992, p. 247)

My thesis is that the teacher-as-researcher concept contains the seeds of a new model for the reaching profession—a model described elsewhere by such observers as Paulo Freire, Ira Shor, and Stanley Aronowitz and Henry Giroux as the "transformative teacher." (Berlin, 1990, p. 3)

teacher teach thyself!

When one attempts to write outside the dominant discourse, one often has to begin by naming the new thing. I have used various terms for our experiments, including "alternative" and "feminist," but recently we have been using the term "diverse discourse." "[A]lternative discourse" does not allow us to reform thinking, to imagine the possibility that writing choices that are now marginal could someday be positioned alongside, or in place of, the dominant ones. "Feminist discourse" has been my sentimental favorite because feminist theory, gave me, personally, new ways of thinking and writing, but many students still felt excluded by this term. (Bridwell-Bowles, 1992, p. 350)

Composition Studies emerged as a scholarly research discipline during the 1970s as (a) empirical methods became available to investigate the problem of meaning in discourse and, concomitantly, (b) the work of an international writing research community became institutionalized in the form of new journals and graduate programs. Distinguishing their efforts from prior histories of the field,

mother"; Beverly Clark and Sonja Wiedenhaupt's "On Blocking and Unblocking Sonja: A Case Study in Two Voices"; and Betsy S. Hilbert's meditation, "It Was A Dark and Nasty Night . . . ." which begins, "Now I am alone with the first writing samples . . . ." (p. 75).

Because this issue of *CCC* is explicitly focused on personal writing, it is not a reliable sample. Yet a review of other issues of *CCC*, and of *RTE* as well, indicates in these professional publications an increasing use of first-person, autobiographical accounts and a general move towards the inclusion of new genres in the work of our field. A few luminous examples: In *RTE*, Solsken (1993), singing "The Paradigm Misfit Blues," used personal voice and autobiographical narrative to argue for the value of the bits of everyday life caught in the nets of the ethnographic, naturalistic research. In *CCC*, Peritz (1993) argued for "Making a Place for the Poetic in Academic Writing." And in *CCC*, Bridwell-Bowles (1992), in "Discourse and Diversity: Experimental Writing within the Academy," called for "new processes and forms" that will make it possible for us to "express ways of thinking that have been outside the dominant culture" (p. 349).

WRITING, AND REVISING, OUR HISTORY

In addition to the bipolar attention to the social and to the individual, during this period, composition studies exhibited a steady interest in writing its own history, a project of which this book is a part. This history writing has not, of course, involved the simple recovery of data; it has constituted the steady revision of the way in which composition professionals—and computers and composition specialists—perceive ourselves, and of the way in which we

want to be perceived. Implicit in this project has been the perspective of self-critique: the need to revise ourselves in the light of new circumstances and new information.

In editor Joseph Harris's first issue of *CCC*, three of the four lead articles contributed to this focus on history. Lucille M. Schultz (1994) looked at 19th century "first books" of composition and found evidence to suggest that the "landscape that had, from the perspective of a wide-angle lens, appeared uniform, even seamless, is, from the perspective of a telescopic lens, highly differentiated" (p. 10). In the same issue, Anne Ruggles Gere (1994) argued that composition studies needed to extend its history beyond the classroom to include the teaching/learning of writing that goes on outside the academy, and in particular, the activity of writing groups. Her essay was an extension and deepening of her earlier work (1987) on the history of writing groups in America. In the same issue, Karyn Hollis (1994) offered the story of the Bryn Mawr Summer School for Women Workers, a 1920s institution that, in its concern for literacy across class boundaries, was Hollis argued, "an important antecedent to the feminist and progressive pedagogies we strive to develop today" (p. 32). In the December 1992 issue of *CCC*, Don Stewart examined "Harvard's Influence in English Studies," and JoAnn Campbell recovered the history of English A at Radcliffe College, using this history to argue that composition studies needed to consider issues of intimacy in contemporary classrooms.

Thus interest in the history of composition studies was further signaled by the establishment within CCCC of the category of "Exemplar," whereby the community honored its founding forefathers/foremothers—and at the closing exercises of the annual conference "The Exemplar's Address," an occasion that called for historical narrative. The first exemplars were Richard Lloyd-Jones and Janet

the authors argue that the development of composition studies needs to be understood as part of a broader intellectual history affecting linguistics and literary studies, as well as composition. (Nystrand, Greene, & Wiemelt, 1993, p. 267)

Richard Lloyd-Jones, professor and long-time English Department Chair at the University of Iowa, is a Past Chair of the Conference on College Composition and Communication and a Past President of the National Council of Teachers of English. His many publications include *Research in Written Composition* (1963), co-authored with Richard Braddock and Lowell Shoer, and *The English Coalition Conference* (1989), written with Andrea Lunsford. In 1991, he was selected as the first

recipient of the CCCC's Exemplar Award . . . .
(Biographical Information on Lloyd-Jones, 1992, p. 486)

We're offering here a book full of stories and readings of stories that favor positions we've taken from the beginning. The stories are argumentative, not true or false. Are we representing functional literacy or misrepresenting it? Who gets to say? Is there more justice in the representations of its proponents than in ours? Is one story less self-serving than the other? We contest reality and our contestations are themselves contested. The alternative (which may only be conceivable rather than possible) is cultural stagnation. Readers can read our stories and agree or disagree, assisted by their subsequent judgments and actions in the renegotiation of educational life. (Knoblauch & Brannon, 1993, p. 175)

These classrooms are thus student centered without focusing exclusively on the narrow experience of the individual learner. As indicated earlier, all of us live within contexts that influ-

Emig. Lloyd-Jones' address, "Who We Were, Who We Should Become," was published in the December 1992 *CCC*, and was followed by a first-person, autobiographical account of Lloyd-Jones' teaching, "With Jix," written by Margaret Finders.

CLASSROOM PRACTICE

During this period, the field continued to refine and qualify the pedagogy that it had inherited. John Trimbur mapped this territory in his February 1994 *CCC* review of books by Pat Bizzell, Kurt Spellmeyer, Cy Knoblauch and Lil Brannon, a review titled "Taking the Social Turn: Teaching Writing Post-Process." In his review Trimbur wrote, "What is significant about these books—and to my mind indicative of the current moment in rhetoric and composition studies—is that they make their arguments not so much in terms of students' reading and writing processes but rather in terms of the cultural politics of literacy" (p. 109). In these three books, Trimbur read "a crisis within the process paradigm and a growing disillusion with its limits and pressures." As noted in earlier chapters, this "crisis" had been building for some time in the world of theory. These three books, and Trimbur's review, suggested that the move in the world of theory had begun to impact the classroom, at least insofar as the three authors had been themselves able to influence, through teacher education and program administration, the teaching that actually happened in writing classrooms.

Perhaps a better indicator of classroom practice during this period was Tom Newkirk's 1993 anthology, *Nuts and Bolts: A Practical Guide to Teaching College Composition*. The book provided a window into teachers' practice:

Written by practicing teachers about their teaching, it was anchored to classroom practice by course syllabi and class plans. In the introduction, titled "Locating Freshman English," Newkirk told the story of Freshman English at UNH and its move beyond a Writing Process curriculum. It was here at this university that Don Murray first "purified" freshman English of all academic content, making it a course in which writers taught writers. "Freshman English," Newkirk wrote, "from this time forward, might be technically in the English Department, but it was no longer of it. It looked elsewhere—to established writers—for insights about teaching and learning" (p. 4). Newkirk and the teachers in the UNH program found much that was valuable in the legacy that they inherited. The early process movement's assumption of students' latent fluency (Macrorie, Elbow, Murray)—that students can write if the conditions for writing are there— was "pedagogically healthy" (p. 9) and, as Newkirk noted, "I have seen it happen too often to dismiss it."

However, the authors in this book also felt the need to go beyond their heritage:

> The dozens of writing exercises described in this book are precisely focused; the conferences and evaluation systems are carefully structured to teach students to comment on their work; the chapters on the research paper and on writing about literature provide careful and thoughtful guidance for the student, who is often working in new territory. This is not "hands-off teaching" that merely frees the student to discover an inner self. It is hard and careful work. (p. 9)

Not only was the work "hard and careful"; it was different. Most of the authors brought

ence and limit us. Awareness of the possibilities of our experience is available only through understanding the ways these contexts operate upon us. Thus, whatever independence and uniqueness are available to the individual can be understood only by coming to terms with the conditions of experience that work against becoming independent and unique. (Berlin, Foreword to *Changing Classroom Practices*, 1994, p. ix)

Three Generations of PowerPC Macs: Bridges to a New Interface.
Yes, it's odd to start thinking about the second and third generation of a product before the first even arrives. But with PowerPC Macs it makes sense because the new processor is the foundation for interesting future technologies that promise to revitalize the Macintosh. (Mello, 1994, p. 21)

reading into the curriculum—not as prose models, or as literature, but as a means for teaching the process of reading. Both reading and writing were taught, in Sullivan's (1993) words, "to expand my students' ways of seeing as readers and writers—to make visible, to unsettle, and to augment their customary habits of thinking and expression so that they may become more active and reflective participants in the various cultures that comprise their world" (p. 19).

The Technological Context, 1992–1994

In the computer world, the late 1980s and early 1990s saw the refinement and dispersal of existing technologies. Microsoft's Windows operating system had brought the GUI interface to the immense DOS market; networks were now a standard part of the computing environment; Intel's 80486 processor and its endless incarnations became the de facto standard for high powered desktop computing; and the release of better and less-expensive components like sound cards and storage systems laid the foundation for multimedia computing. This was a period when the field of computer technology was consolidating its gains.

Apple Unveils First PowerPC Product:
As part of Apple's effort to maintain sales of existing Macs while raising confidence in the impending PowerPC line, the company announced a PowerPC processor upgrade board that will work in several current MAC models. Shown for the first time in January at *Macworld* Expo in San Francisco, the add-in board fits in the Mac's 040 Processor Direct Slot, contains a 66 MHz PowerPC 601 chip,

Next-Generation Processors

The development of graphic user interfaces, multimedia, and complex, large software applications drove a quest for ever-more-powerful microprocessors (Seymour, 1993). In 1992 Intel released its Pentium chip. (Intel moved from the 80__ numbering sequence with the Pentium, otherwise this would have been their 80586 chip.) This chip, which ran at 66 megahertz and in 32 bit mode, offered unprecedented computing power for the desktop. The Intel engineers had packed 3.1 million transistors on the new chip. To put that in perspective, in 1974 the state-of-the-art was the 8080 chip—a 2-megahertz, 8-bit chip with 6,000 transistors. Compared to its immediate predecessor, the 486, the Pentium doubled the speed of the fastest 486 chip and offered a 90% improvement in overall system performance. The first Pentium systems sold for around $5,000, and sales were brisk despite problems with flawed chips that resulted in user frustration and a massive buy-back program. By the end of 1994, consumers could purchase a Pentium system for under $2,000, as Intel felt the heat competition from two new chips: the PowerPC, developed by IBM, Apple, and Motorola, and the Alpha, developed by DEC.

The developers of the PowerPC and Alpha used RISC (Reduced Instruction Set Computing) technology instead of the CISC (Complex Instruction Set Computing) technology that provided the foundation for Intel's chips, including the Pentium. The fundamental difference between the two approaches was that CISC processors executed a simple instruction in between 5 and 50 clock cycles, while RISC processors execute an instruction in 1 clock cycle. As one might guess from the terminology, CISC chips required more complex information pathways (or "processing pipelines," as engineers like to call them), whereas RISC chips kept the pipelines simple and used increased clock speeds to improve performance. RISC chips in a microcomputer could theoretically outperform the Pentium. In 1993 theory became reality, as the IBM–Apple–Motorola partnership announced its PowerPC and DEC announced its Alpha.

At the writing of this book, the Alpha 21164 is the fastest general-purpose micro processing chip in existence (Ryan, 1994). It is the

and can work on the Quadra 610, 650, 700, 800, 900, and 950, as well as the Centris 610 and 650. Of those machines, only the Quadra 800, Centris 610, and Centris 650 are currently publicly scheduled by Apple for a logic-board upgrade. Apple said it expects the board to list for less than $700. (News, edited by T. Moran, in *Macworld*, March 1994, p. 34)

We Are the Wired: Some Views on the Fiberoptic Ties That Bind.
Someday, the visionaries tell us, we will be able to communicate with just about anybody by sending an electronic message; no mat-

ter where they are, the bundle of bits will find them. On the information superhighway, the literature of the world and the videos, too, will be just a point and a click away. So will anyone we want to hear from. (Johnson, 1993, p. E16)

first chip to execute over 1 billion instructions per second (to the extent that it could be clocked at such a level, it performs 1.2 BIPS). The chip performs 600 transactions per second compared to around 240 for a 66-megahertz Pentium. It has 9.3 million transistors (Intel hopes to hit the 10 million mark with the P6, predicted for 1995–1996), and runs at either 266 or 300 megahertz. In some ways (and there are seemingly countless ways to measure processing performance), the Alpha far outpaces the PowerPC. For example, 2 clock cycles on the Alpha take less time than 1 clock cycle on the 100 MHz. PowerPC 64. The race for fastest processor will undoubtedly continue on the micron and submicron level. Experts predict that GSI (gigascale integration more than 1 billion transistors on a chip) will be achieved in the 2010s with the development of new optical technologies, like x-ray, for microchip production.

What will all of this mean for the user, and particularly for the teacher and student? These next-generation processors should provide the processing power to do well what individuals now can do only adequately. Further, these new processors should support emerging technologies—multimedia and beyond—that demand vast amounts of processing. Pentiums, PowerPCs, and Alphas help make GUI performance snappy and support processing-intensive applications like 3-D design, drawing, animation, and rendering programs, as well as the proliferating multimedia titles that now crowd retail shelves. The new processors should supply the power required to run programs that include sound and video files, and should make possible desktop implementation of 3-D interfaces and virtual reality. Finally these new chips will also support the high level multitasking implicit in the convergence of computer, telephone, and television that we are now seeing in the marketplace.

THE INTERNET COMES OF AGE

During the period of 1992–1994, the Internet—that removed electronic domain of researchers, academics, and "bit-heads"—exploded into the public imagination. In fact, 1993 was often dubbed "The Year of the Internet." A combination of factors arose in that year to encourage such designations, including the election of Albert Gore to the office of Vice-President, the development of new and easier-to-use tools for navigating the Internet, a rapid increase in the number of networks connecting to the Internet, and the business world's discovery of the Internet as an aid in communication, planning, and marketing. During this period commercial online services like CompuServe and Prodigy rushed to offer their customers access to the Internet (and brought some 4 million more of the uninitiated onto the Nets, much to the chagrin of some long-term users). Although it was difficult to measure the actual number of users connected to the Net and the kinds of activities in which they were engaged (one connected computer could serve any number of users), 1994 estimates ranged between 30 and 40 million users, and some 1.5 million host computers (Kantor, 1994).

The experience of the Internet, during this period, was most often described through spatial metaphors: the Net was an information-containing space, a space through which the user navigated. Navigation in this space continued to be difficult, however. There were few charts, few stable markers, and the features of the space continued to undergo rapid change. The unorganized nature of the Net and the boundless and bewildering amounts and kinds of information found there could be daunting to navigators (a condition that gave rise to Net "surfing," or serendipitous browsing through the eclectic and unorganized environment).

Staking a Claim on the Virtual Frontier.
For the hardy bands of pioneers who staked out the first electronic communities in the early 1970s, the sprawling web of computer networks known as cyberspace had the anarchist, individualist feel of an electronic frontier. Now the Net, as it is called, is feeling the pressures of suburbanization, as efforts to commercialize it are creating the electronic equivalent of neon signs and endless avenues of strip malls. (Markoff, 1994a, p. E5)

For the community of scholars, "being connected" takes on a whole new meaning. With more than 2,000 discussion groups, the Internet provides the first truly worldwide seminar room. (DeLoughry, 1994b, p. A25)

NCSA Mosaic is a hypermedia system designed for information discovery and retrieval over the WorldWideWeb (WWW), which includes the Internet. It provides a unified interface to the various formats used on the Internet and enables powerful new methods for discovering, using, and sharing information. NCSA Mosaic uses a client/server model for information distribution; a *server* sits on a machine at an Internet site fulfilling queries sent by Mosaic *Clients*, which may be located anywhere on the WWW (i.e. your computer acts as a client when you run Mosaic). Units of information sent from servers to clients are simply termed *documents*. Documents may contain plain text, formatted text, inlined graphics, sound, and other multimedia data, and hyperlinks to other documents located anywhere on the WWW.

You can download NCSA Mosaic from ftp.ncsa.uiuc.edu. Within the "MOSAIC" directory there are "MAC" and "WINDOWS" directories for the respective Mosaic versions. NCSA Mosaic is available at other anonymous FTP sites as well. (NCSA Mosaic Tutorial, p. 1)

URLs:

http://www.umich.edu/~$df
wbutler/UC153Syl.html

http://gertrude.art.uiuc.edu/
wits/witshomepage.html

http://aitg.soc.uiuc.edu/cws/
cwshome.html

http://www.win.tue.nl:80/
teletext/nos/

http://mistral.enst.fr/

http://sailfish.peregrine.
com/WebWorld/welcome.
html

http://gertrude.art.uiuc.edu/

http://aitg.soc.uiuc.edu/
irgchome.html

http://ziris.syr.edu/themes.ht
ml

http://www.sloan.org/
Education/top.html

http://owl.trc.purdue.edu/

However, in the early 1990s, the tools available for navigators significantly improved. Added to established search tools like Archie and Veronica were new ones, the most well known being Gopher, developed at the university of Minnesota. Gopher brought an hierarchical structure to information residing on gopher servers on the Net. Using a menu structure, a person could logically follow a hierarchical pattern in a search for information.

The real breakthrough for those who would travel the nets was MOSAIC, the first of a new generation of Internet browsing tools that promised to make the arcane and often confusing landscape of the Internet much clearer and easier to navigate. Developed by the University of Illinois' National Center for Super Computing Applications (NCSA), MOSAIC brought the GUI interface to Net navigation. Its name, as a metaphor for online space, suggested separate pieces connected in a single, interrelated design, and recalled the metaphor of the quilt invoked by Gere in 1992 to describe CCCC, and by Bridwell-Bowles to describe her vision of composition studies. MOSAIC was a WorldWideWeb browser (the WWW is a metaindex of network servers on the Internet with data classified by service, subject, or individual server's directories) that allowed hypertext linking of documents across the Net. Although not wholly intuitive, MOSAIC, and its descendants, like NETSCAPE, were much easier to use than any other navigation or search tool then available, and, with its programming language HGML, it became easy for individuals or organizations to create Mosaic "Home Pages" on the Net. These home pages could connect to information on a person's or organization's server and could be designed to contain hypertext links to additional information on other servers (including non-MOSAIC servers like Gopher or ftp servers) in a way that was transparent to users. Sun Microsystems, for example, designed an award-winning home page that could be accessed with Mosaic. Once at this home page, users could jump from Sun's product catalogs to pricing information to technical updates to anything else Sun included. In addition, Sun provided links to a user-group discussion list residing on a server across the country. During the period from 1992–1994, home pages proliferated on the Net—designed by everyone from IBM and DEC to the Rolling Stones. With the right complementary software and hardware, Mosaic could deliver audio and video files as well as text and graphics.

Although programs like Mosaic helped users navigate WWW and pull together video, audio, and text files from around the globe, the backbone of the Internet, the physical structure of the networks that it linked continued to exhibit problems, primarily because these structures were not well-designed for supporting the wide bandwith requirements (that is, the amount of information that a medium like sound or video requires to pass through or along the wires) that multimedia demanded. Fiber optic cable provided tremendous bandwidth during this period, but it was expensive. The speed at which a large video file could travel from a WWW site to one's desktop was limited by the slowest link in the chain of networks that the file had to travel through—often, this was the twisted-pair cable from the user's desktop to the local server. When a substantial video file met the twisted-pair cable, the transfer often seemed to slow to a crawl.

Given these developments, 1992–1994 saw much public debate about how high-bandwidth connections would be made to classrooms, homes, and workplaces, as telephone, television, and cable companies jockey for position. As this struggle went on, fiber optic backbones were being installed on campuses and in communities, and ISDN (Integrated Services Digital Network) slowly became available to the gen-

http://nosferatu.cas.usf.edu/JAC/index.html

http://www.iquest.net/cgi-bin/cr/

http://www.hu.mtu.edu

Getting Started with Multimedia: What is it? Can you use it? What will it cost?

Multimedia is many things—literally and figuratively. Literally, multimedia is the integration of two or more communications media. It's the use of text and sounds, plus still and moving pictures, to convey ideas, sell products, educate, and/or entertain. It's built around the premise that anything words can do—words, sounds and pictures can do better. The more, the media.

Some see multimedia as the harbinger of an era when computers will routinely convey information with sound and animation, as well as text images, and when television will become more interactive. But others see it as the victory of sound bites and flashy visuals over the printed word. (Heid, 1991, p. 225)

eral public. As the information infrastructure continued to develop, some users pinned their hopes on ATM (Asynchronous Transfer Mode) technology: high bandwith, low-delay switching with lightning-fast transfer speeds for voice, video, and data signals. Others focused on wireless satellite connections (such as the IBM/Motorola Iridium Project, which planned a network of 66 satellites) and radio transmission. Although it was—and continues to be—impossible to predict the eventual shape of the Net or who will be its primary providers, most people came to expect that the National Information infrastructure would make it possible to access vast amounts of information, in all media, in homes, schools, and businesses.

The Newton MessagePad 110

Newton's ability to learn your handwriting improves every time you use it. It can recognize cursive and printed letters simultaneously, translate your writing to neat type if you like—even mix text and graphics to format your documents. Newton can send faxes to any location in the world, print on a wide variety of printers or "beam" messages to another Newton through the built-in infrared beam and sensor. Apple Computer, Inc. (Advertisement in *The Mac Zone*, 24B, 1994, p. 7)

Personal Digital Assistants: Dick Tracy Redux

Perhaps no innovation in the personal computing world was so radical, promised so much, fell so short of its goal, and was subject to so much ridicule as Apple's Newton MessagePad, the best known Personal Digital Assistant (PDA). Released in 1993, the Newton was a commercial failure, yet subsequent versions of the MessagePad showed significant improvements. Although the Newton was dismissed as an expensive toy for business people and early adapting techies, it and the other PDAs on the market offered a vision of highly portable, miniaturized, personal computing. The MessagePad, as well as competing products like the Amstrad PenPad, AT&T's EO 440, and the Tandy 2-PDA, were small, hand-held computers using pen computing, handwriting recognition, and innovative 32 bit, low-power, low-cost computing. With the addition of wireless communications capability and PCMCIA (Personal Computing Memory Card International Association) cards, which could hold extra memory, fax/modems, paging receivers, or network adapters, PDAs continued to develop as increasingly powerful communication devices.

Indeed, one of the benefits of PDAs for desktop and portable computing generally was the increased miniaturization of computer components. Laptop computers, common instruments of business users, continued to decrease in size and increase in power during the late 1980s and early 1990s, but they still suffered from limited battery life and limited portable peripherals. However, PCMCIA cards enabled a user to carry a fax/modem or network adapter in a shirt pocket. The introduction of a new technology, Flash Memory, although still expensive, offered low power consumption, reliability, and high speed, clocking at 120 nanoseconds for data retrieval compared to the 15 to 30 milliseconds of the standard hard drive. The demands of portable computing, whether laptop or PDA, continued during this period to drive technological solutions that came to offer great benefits to regular desktop computing.

The Newton MessagePad's portability and size were less compelling than its promise of handwriting recognition. Pen-based computing had been long heralded as a new interface but had not extended far beyond the hand-held units some express delivery companies used to fill out customer orders. With pen input, the MessagePad promised freedom from the keyboard (a necessity, given the unit's small size), but it did not deliver on this promise. The system often failed to recognize users' handwriting, converting input into endless and absurd permutations, a tendency that was painfully parodied in the comic strip *Doonesbury*. However, the MessagePad 110, the second version of the PDA, offered vastly-improved handwriting recognition and allowed direct exchange of information between the unit and a desktop system. PDAs eventually began to find use in

The Ready-for-the-Road Bundle: Apple's best color PowerBook and much more.

Apple's top-of-the-line color sub-notebook computer, the PowerBook Duo 280C, offers the speed of a 68LC040 processor, extensive memory and storage expansion. Its backlit, active matrix display offers thousands of vivid colors, for maximum impact.

Apple PowerBook Duo 280C 12/320 Bundle.... $ 3,929.95 (Advertisement in *Mac's Place*, Nov.–Dec. 1994, p.5)

professions where workers were in the field and needed access to large amounts of information. For example, MessagePads were used in Boston hospitals, where they gave physicians making their rounds instant access to pharmaceutical information. In the long run, PDAs like the MessagePad offered not-so-distant, early warning of the hand-held and even wrist-worn devices once imagined only in science fiction and in comic strips.

What's an Interface? What do interface designers do? Where in the process of product development do they do their work? What parts of a product concern them? Upon what principles and intuitions do they base design decisions?

We must begin, predictably, by defining what we mean by the human–computer interface. When the concept of the interface first began to emerge, it was commonly understood as the hardware and software through which a human and a computer could communicate. As it has evolved, the concept has come to include the cognitive and emotional aspects of the user's experience as well. (Laurel & Mountford, 1990, p. xi)

After GUI: Next Generation Interfaces

By 1992, command lines and text-driven interfaces had given way to the graphical user interface, yet the GUI interface still had considerable room for improvement. GUIs were still not necessarily intuitive. Indeed, interface designers often overwhelmed users with icons and button bars. As a result, continued improvement in GUI interface design was demanded by users. There were two significant changes in GUIs during this period. One was the customized interface that allowed users to choose what icons were displayed and to design, in a sense, the look and content of their interface. The second change appeared in the integration of context-sensitive help and menus. With Microsoft's "Wizards," Apple's "Guides," Lotus' "Assistants," and WordPerfect's "Coaches," the system made assumptions about what the user needed in terms of on-call guidance or the functions on which they were likely to call. In the latter case, the icons and menu choices that were not relevant may either be hidden or grayed out, making the interface cleaner and tuned to the activities of the user. In a competitive business where software developers had to out-feature their competitors, progress in interface design did not mean all new applications would offer improved interfaces, especially when the array of icons presented on the screen embodied the ostensible power of the program (a marketing strategy attributed to Microsoft—a company accused of "never met a feature it didn't like").

Even as GUIs continued to improve, interface designers were beginning to tap the potential of sound, video, and 3-D graphics to create "real world" interfaces. Real World Interfaces (RWI) attempted to create spaces that mimicked for users realistic environments. An example of an RWI was the way multimedia software presented as its interface a graphic image of a real audio CD player and its operating controls. Users then worked with a visual representation of a known control panel to operate their computer's CD drivers. Lotus ORGANIZER's interface mimicked a spiral-bound notepad, and Meca's MANAGING YOUR MONEY created the image of a home study or office. Objects in these interfaces were working icons that reflected their familiar function. Game developers had long pushed the limits of graphics and 3-D environments, with the result that the engagement factor of high-quality games like *Myst* influenced the interface design of application software. As organizations and users increasingly came to inhabit virtual spaces, they demanded interfaces that reflected real-world analogs to anchor and domesticate the sometimes unsettling nature of electronic meeting spaces.

Although the keyboard remained the fastest input device for large amounts of information, developers also were working hard on a wide range of alternative input devices, many of which are now on the market. Handwriting recognition systems, although less-than-perfect, began showing improvement. Speech input, although still presenting significant technical challenges, could be used for simple commands ("Computer, print document" or "Computer, zoom in"), and next generation processors were supplying speech technologies with the power they long needed. The venera-

A point that's often missed is that the shape of the interface also reflects who is doing what to whom. The doorknob extends toward the user and its qualities are biased toward the hand. The door will be opened; a human will open it—the human is the agent and the door is the patient of the action. In a high-security government office I visited the other day, there was no doorknob at all. I was screened by a hidden camera and the door opened for me when I passed muster. My sense of who was in control of the interaction was quite different from the way I feel when I enter a room in my house. In the office, the door—representing the institution to which it was a portal—was in control. (Laurel & Mountford, 1990, p. xiii)

Perhaps the most distinctive aspect of the Macintosh in 1984 was its use of the mouse as a primary input device. Like all controls, the mouse is better suited to some operations than others; further, as one component in an integrated system, its effectiveness will be largely determined by how well the design of the mouse interface is coordinated with other factors. (Blake, 1990, p. 289)

ble mouse was been joined by a host of new pointing devices including trackballs, electronic pens, touch screens, tongue balls (for disabled users), and track pads. Experiments continued with virtual reality environments in which individuals physically (through a VR glove, for example) manipulated objects within 3-D environments, the objects representing real-world systems or data. Although these systems were employed in different ways for different applications (writing, for example, continued to be a largely silent activity served by the keyboard), humans began to interact with computers in a range of ways that seemed likely to continue to expand in the future.

OBSERVING TRENDS

Driven both by the social epistemologies dominant in composition studies and by the new computing power available to users during the period of 1992–1994, computers and composition specialists were deeply interested in what writers and teachers could do with multimedia and CMC. The focus on hypertext that had characterized the field earlier in this period gave way to a focus on hypermedia, or, as it would come to be called, "multimedia," as most linked structures included sound and graphics as well as text. As the press and the public belatedly discovered the Internet, it became chic to be online. Many veterans of Bitnet and even of Arpanet found themselves being told by colleagues about the wonders of online, computer-mediated communication. In one of the many articles in the popular press, Markoff (1993) described the Internet as a "computer-generated neighborhood dotted with avenues, residences, and commercial centers"(p. E7)—a vast web of computer networks, which in 1993, according to the same article, reached 15 to 20 million users in 134 countries and was growing by 20% a month. Seven months later, *Lingua Franca* predicted that—at its current rate of growth—the Internet would have 160 million users by the year 2000 (Bennahum, 1994). Within the seemingly infinite spaces of the Internet—hardly, despite Markoff's use of the metaphor, a "neighborhood"—computers and compositionists found and created their own neighborhoods, constellations of friends and colleagues from whom they might borrow not a cup of sugar or a lawnmower, but a bit of information a reference, a teaching strategy, a reading list, some needed encouragement in mid-draft. With the development of WWW browsers, CMC and multimedia became increasingly one technology.

With the surge in Internet use, computers and compositionists increasingly saw themselves as an international community, turning more frequently than before to international issues and linking classes globally. During this period, *Computers and Composition* became an international journal, and the 1994 Computers and Writing conference featured Australian scholar Dale Spender as its keynote speaker. This widening of the field's scope was accompanied by a complementary exclusion: Only those who could afford it could use the Internet; only those who could afford to travel attended international conferences.

The field of multimedia was discovered by the popular press too, though without the same gee-whiz excitement that had characterized the discovery of the Internet. The *New York Times Book Review* featured hypertext/hypermedia in 1992 and 1993 (Coover, 1992, 1993)—choosing not to focus on "multimedia," because this was a print journal and a "book" review, written by a practicing writer and aspiring maker of literature. In the first article, the author, novelist Robert Coover, argued that "though [hypertext was] used at first primarily

Fred Kemp
Kathleen Kiefer
Diane Langston
Paul LeBlanc
Mark Lester
Carol Lipson
Stuart Moulthrop
Charles Moran
Joel Nydahl
Michael Palmquist
Barry Pegg
Michael Pemberton
Joy Kreeft Peyton
James Porter
Ruth Ray
Dawn Rodrigues
Raymond Rodrigues
Mike Sharples
John Slatin
Sarah Sloane
Catherine Smith
Ilana Snyder
Elizabeth Sommers
Patricia Sullivan
Bernard Susser
Thea Vander Geest
Rosalie Wells
(*Computers & Composition*, *11*, 1994)

Some CD-ROMs have been replaced by more-recent offerings, since improvements in the use of QuickTime, sound, hypertext, and database search technology have redefined CD-ROM excellence. As a result, many of the top discs of a year ago look a bit creaky by today's standards. CD-ROM technology has come a long way in a year, and there's lots to enjoy in this year's list. (Bickford, 1994, p. 73)

From Alice to Ocean
Claris Clear Choice; $69 list, $49 street
This beautiful documentary of a woman's odyssey across the Australian outback is shipped with many of Apple's CD-ROM drives and has been enjoyed as a superb interactive coffee-table disc. The gorgeous scenery, captured in photos and QuickTime movies, still looks great, and the text on the outback's ecology remains fascinating. Best of all, the CD-ROM now comes packaged with the equally beautiful coffee-table book it's based on. (Bickford, 1994, p. 79)

One thing that does seem clear is that in the lucrative academic and reference markets, new media are quickly overtaking traditional books, and for good reason. Consider the Encyclopedia Britannica. The complete set costs more than $1,500, weighs 118 pounds and takes up more

as a radically new teaching arena," now fiction writers have been drawn "into its intricate and infinitely expandable, infinitely alluring webs" (p. 23). Among the fiction writers Coover mentioned were writing teachers intimately tied to the computers and composition community: Michael Joyce, author of *Afternoon*, which Coover called "the landmark 1987 hypertext fiction" (1992, p. 24); Carolyn Guyer and Martha Petry's *Izme Pass*, which was bundled with the profession's print journal, *Writing on the Edge* (1991); Stuart Moulthrop's *Victory Garden*; and John McDaid's *Uncle Buddy's Phantom Funhouse*. Coover's second *Times* piece, "Hyperfiction: Novels for the Computer," was published in the August 29, 1993 book review section, which bore on its cover a brightly colored graphical representation of hypertext—a remarkable document, really, one that, in linear, conventional print, suggested the possible death, or modification, of conventional print text. In a sidebar, Coover noted that "hypertext is only the beginning," and that it will inevitably give way to hypermedia.

Possibly related to the surge in Internet use, to the development of multimedia, and to the poststructuralists' need for new modes of writing, was an emerging focus on new, nontraditional text genres. Noted earlier in this chapter are the "Interchange" in Herrington and Moran's MLA book on Writing Across the Curriculum, the emergence of the personal voice and narrative in scholarly journals, and Bridwell-Bowles (1992) call for "new processes and forms" (p. 349) in the October 1992 issue of *CCC*. It is tempting to see a cause–effect relationship between this move toward new genres and the profession's work on and with computers. On the Internet, MOOs, MUDS, and MUSHes were there to be joined and explored, all requiring new kinds of textual formation. These new genres also received attention in 1994 from the popular press. The *New York*

Times (Malone, 1994) described what it called "chat rooms" where business professionals from Microsoft and other software companies gathered online regularly to check out the competition, discuss marketing issues, and even interview guest speakers. An article in the June 1994 issue of *Lingua Franca* bore the title "Fly Me to the MOO: Adventures in Textual Reality" (Bennahum, 1994) and listed MOOs and their telnet addresses. Among those listed were the "Tuesday Night Cafe of the Netoric Project," a MOO for rhetoric and composition scholars founded by Tari Fanderclai and Greg Siering, both working on advanced degrees in rhetoric and composition, and Brown University's "Hypertext Hotel," which had been accessible from the 1994 C&W's electronic forum.

> than four feet of shelf space. A commensurate encyclopedia on CD-ROM—Microsoft's Encarta, for instance—costs $99.99, holds up to 650 megabytes of data, weighs under an ounce, and could fit in your purse. (Lyall, *The New York Times Book Review*, August 14, 1994, p. 3)

The Conferences

The number of computer-related presentations at professional conferences continued to be small and steady. In the program for its annual conference, NCTE included 5 sessions on computers in 1992 and 1993, and the CCCC program included 22 in 1992, 14 in 1993, and 21 in 1994. Although the 1992 CCCCs featured a few sessions on CAI and word processing, including "A Room of One's Own: Departmental and University Support for CAI in Composition" (Parris, 1992) and "Integrating Writing and Word Processing: Costs and Benefits" (Gibson, 1992), such sessions were rare in 1992 and had all but disappeared in 1993 and 1994. As in 1989–1991, computer-related sessions focused on multimedia and CMC, but the dominant perspective was that of cultural critique. At CCCC, typical sessions on multimedia were "Theoretical and Historical Perspectives on Hypertext" (1992); "The Rhetorics of Hypertext" (1994), and "Patriarchs and Perverts: Some Reproductive Logics of Hypertext" (1993). The

> Let's assume that an enterprising young scholar undertakes to construct a hypertext edition of a famous novel with a vexed textual history. It will include all textual possibilities plus suggestions as to their relationships. ... Who "wrote" such a "text"? Who gets the royalties? (Lanham, 1993, p. 20)

focus in these sessions on *hypertext*, as op-posed to *multimedia*, is characteristic of a field defined by writing and its connection to Eng-lish departments, where the study of texts is the norm and was echoed in the print publica-tions of this period (see Landow, later in this chapter). Typical CCCC sessions on CMC in-cluded "Gender and Writing Technologies" (1993); "Does Egalitarian Access Mean Equal Access?" (1993); and "Sexual and Racial Differ-ence in the Electronic Classroom (1993).

Driven by our early explorations of the WorldWideWeb, a new interest at these confer-ences was global, world-wide communication. The 1993 NCTE program included a session ti-tled "Linking Classrooms Internationally with Global Computer Networks," sponsored by NCTE's newly formed International Consor-tium; the 1992 CCCC conference program in-cluded papers titled "Writing for the World: Student Writing on International Computer Networks" (Perelman, 1992) and "Using Com-puters to Teach International Writing" (Halio, 1992). The 1994 CCCC program included such papers as "Global Networking: Creating Sites of Collaborative Inquiry" (DeWitt, 1994) and "Communicating on Global Computer Net-works" (December, 1994).

The Computers and Writing conferences dur-ing this period also included sessions that cen-tered on global interconnections. The 1993 program included presentations like "The In-ternational Poetry Guild" (Stanzler, 1993), "Eq-uity of Access to Computer Writing Technology in Australian Schools," (Snyder, 1993), and "In-ternational Collaboration: Email Across the Globe," a story of electronic connections be-tween college classes in Regensburg, Germany, and Kansas City, Missouri (Sutherland & Black, 1993). The 1994 Computers and Writing Conference went further in the same direction, incorporating global interconnection in its title: "The Global Web of Writing Technologies." This conference featured such presentations as "Hypertext: A Panacea for International and Intercultural Communications?" (Thrush, 1994), "Interactive Writing in the Global Community" (Bauman, 1994), and a session titled "International Perspectives."

Lillian Bridwell-Bowles had added face-to-face "conversation clusters" to the 1993 CCCCs Conference, foregrounding the social construction of knowledge in physical space. To the 1993 and 1994 Computers and Writing Conferences, the organizers added online conferences, foregrounding the social construction of knowledge in virtual space. These online conferences were designed to accompany or replace the on-site encounters that took place at the face-to-face conferences in Ann Arbor, Michigan, and Columbia, MO. The 1993 Ann Arbor Conference drew 367 participants to its on-site conference, and it drew almost half that number—145 participants—to its online conference. Thirty-four of these online participants came *only* to the online conference. Three hundred forty-five conference participants come to Columbia, Missouri in May 1994; 92 connected virtually. Dave Allen, when asked to describe how he came into the field of computers and writing, describes in this note how he joined the community in 1994:

I became involved electronically. A colleague passed on a mention of the [1994] conference from an electronic forum, with Eric Crump's e-mail address. I requested (January 1994?) information by email, got it by email. I registered by email (early, mid-May 1994—and followed up by FAX—could email be trusted? The electronic forum will be fascinating after the fact—time was limited for me before the 1994 conference, and I screwed up the log-on process but I'm looking forward to getting home and using it now. [I had] only a

Topics to be covered in the online conference:
— History and state-of-art of computer use in writing instruction
— Keystroke analysis as a method for studying writing processes
— Networked classrooms.
— Electronic conferencing
— Writing at work
— Writing online documentation
— Computer tools for writing professionals
— Computer-mediated feedback on texts . . . .

The online conference uses the Internet facilities for communication. The conferencing software is ELECTRONIC FORUM. This program was made available by the courtesy of Karen Schwalm and Chris Zagar, Glendale Community College, Glendale AR, USA, developers of ELECTRONIC FORUM. (7th European Conference on Writing and Computers, 1994, p. 198)

Begun in the spring of 1993, the Netoric Project is a series of real-time discussions, conferences, and workshops for those who use computers in teaching writing. The Netoric Project provides the computers and writing community with an ongoing forum for professional development and collaboration. Not only does the project regularly bring together geographically distant colleagues; it also promotes the value of networked communication many of us advance in our own classrooms. events are held in various rooms of the Netoric Complex on MediaMOO. Participants connect to MediaMOO, go to the scheduled room, and talk to each other in real time. To participate, all you need is the ability to telnet and the attached MediaMoo Guide for Netoric Guests. As well as special events, Netoric coordinates weekly informal discussions, held on Tuesdays at 8:00 p.m. Eastern time at Tuesday Cafe. Topics for Netoric events and discussions are announced on the MBU (MegaByte University, Computers and Writing) listserv and on information boards in the Netoric Headquarters and the Tuesday Cafe on MediaMoo. (The Netoric Project) (Vanderdei & Siering, 1994)

"MOO" stands for MUD, Object Oriented, and a MUD is a Multi-User Dimension—a site that allows users to connect through telnet or other clients. MUDs offer users a text-based virtual reality and the ability to communicate in real time. A good source of beginning information about MUDs is the FAQs from the various newsgroups on MUDs. Many of those FAQs are also stored at the ftp site ftp.math.okstate.edu in pub/nuds/misc/mud-faq and at rtfm.mit.edu in the news.answers archives. MediaMOO is a MOO based at M.I.T. and used by media researchers to share ideas

vague awareness of C&W prior to that first electronic note. (C&W, 1994)

At the 1994 Computer and Writing conference, participants greeted MOOs, MUDs, and MUSHes (multi-user shared hallucinations) with an enthusiasm that reminded other participants of the enthusiasm *they* had felt in the early 1980s when they first encountered the microcomputer and its word-processing capabilities. The directors of the 1994 conference attached MOOs to the online conference component, real-time online meeting places where conferees could chat and interact. MOOs, MUDs, and MUSHes are the most intensely social of all electronic media, as participants interact within text-based virtual sites such as The Techno-Rhetoricians' Bar and Grill, Schoolhouse Hallway, and the Coat Closet (Bennahum, 1994). Participants meet in real time to build virtual environments in which they interact—some might, without prejudice, call this play—and discuss professional issues ranging from how to use MOOs in first-year composition classes to how to get a job in academe. These new text environments were the subject of several papers at the 1994 conference—their first appearance as a topic in our field's professional conferences. In one of the six papers devoted to MOOs at the 1994 C&W, Bauman (1994) argued that interactive collaborative writing would increasingly be required of the "citizens of the world" and included MOOs among her list of online genres. Other representative titles included "Building Cyberspace Communities: Using Lists and MOOs to Foster Regional Communication and Debate" (Wambean & Harris, 1994), "Pedagogical and Professional Uses of MUDs: Lessons from the Virtual Trenches" (Fanderclai, Siering, & Costello, 1994), and "Experiments in Teaching the New Electronic Discourse: Multimedia, Hypertext, and the MOOs." (Lipson & Wagner, 1994)

Publishers: Books

The books that were important to computers and composition during this time emanated from different parts of the academy and varied in their perspectives. George Landow (1992), writing as a literary scholar, for example, brought literary criticism and multimedia together in his *Hypertext: The Convergence of Contemporary Critical Theory and Technology*. His book was remarkable for its almost exclusive consideration of hypertext as "written words," albeit electronic, rather than as the combination of words, sounds, and images. In its focus on text, and on canonical literary texts at that, Landow's book was a good example of the ways in which literature specialists had connected with computer technologies—continuing to study and focus on the texts they have been trained to teach.

Martin Lea's (1992) edited collection, *Contexts of Computer-Mediated Communication* coming from the field of social psychology, makes an important break with conventional thinking on CMC, the line of thought which grew out of Sara Kiesler and her colleagues' experimental studies at Carnegie Mellon. In Kiesler's model, CMC lacks paralinguistic cues—tone and register of voice, pace, facial expression, mode of dress cues that help shape discussants' responses to one another. This "reduced social cues context model" represented the CMC environment as one where high-status people had less influence than they would in person, because the text-only message appeared without the trappings of power that provided context in face-to-face communication. In arguing against these accepted views of CMC, Lea (1992) maintained that not all CMC contexts were the same—that participants' view of the electronic group or community in which they are situated shaped their communicative practices. In 1992, he wrote

and collaborate on projects. An important note about MediaMOO is that it is not one of the MUDs that permit teachers to bring in their students. For more information about MediaMOO's purpose and policies, connect to MediaMOO as a guest and enter <help purpose>. (The Netoric Project)

In S/Z, Roland Barthes describes an ideal textuality that precisely matches that which has come to be called computer hypertext—text composed of blocks of words (or images) linked electronically by multiple paths, chains, or trails in an open-ended, perpetually unfinished textuality described by the terms *link*, *node*, *network*, *web*, and *path*. (Landow, 1992, p. 3)

A cursory review of the literature might convince the reader quickly to assume that the social dimension is of very little relevance to CMC. Broadly speaking, the prevailing analyses—which we collectively term the "social cues perspective"—indicate that communicating via computers is bereft of social cues. This is quickly followed by the inference that CMC is devoid of social or normative context and (thus) forms a particularly inefficient medium for social influence. If all this were true there would presumably be little need for any detailed social psychological analysis of CMC at all. We consider this received wisdom to be profoundly flawed. (Spears & Lea, 1992, pp. 30–31)

I remember the first time I saw a transcript of an electronic written discussion. Paul Taylor, the principal author of the Interchange software, brought one to a graduate course I was teaching in fall 1987. Seemingly out of the blue, a text was laid before us that answered the implicit question raised by the postmodern theory we had been reading: What would a nonliterary text look like that is inherently multiaccentual and defies the conventions of clarity, unity, and coherence? I do not claim priority for this recognition because postmodern theory with its deconstructions of the points of the rhetorical triangle—writer, subject, and audience—has been frequently used for discussing electronic texts as postmodern forms of discourse. (Faigley, 1992, p.184)

Suddenly the conventional college writing classroom seems an odd place, a "virtual reality" of its own, frozen in time, remarkably similar to the turn-of-the-century urban school classrooms pictured in histories of American education. . . . This writing classroom is an expensive, impersonal structure serially inhabited by different classes, none of which leaves any trace in the room . . . .There are no books in the room, except for those that students and teachers bring with them. There is a teacher's desk at

that "rather than attempting to determine the different 'levels' of impacts or to quantify effects, [the book] demotes these concerns in favor of the reverse: an examination of the contextual influences of the processes and outcomes of computer-mediated communication" (p. 1).

Faigley's (1992) *Fragments of Rationality: Postmodernity and the Subject of Composition,* coming from the world of composition studies, placed CMC in the context of postmodernism and of first-year writing classes. Faigley's text was the first book in composition studies to include mainstream electronic classrooms in its field of vision and to argue that they were one of the few sites where the classroom conditions of teaching writing were radically changing. In reproducing and including transcripts from real-time networked discussions, Faigley foregrounded the alternate kinds of writing that are occurring in college classrooms, new text forms which to him represented a postmodern turn.

Several books from within the computers and composition community also presented changing visions of school-based writing and learning. In Hawisher and LeBlanc's (1992) *Re-Imagining Computers and Composition: Teaching and Research in the Virtual Age,* Moran pointed to the real possibility of a writing classroom that was not a classroom at all—or at least not one supported by four walls and brick and mortar. In this same volume Burns demonstrated that real-time "classrooms" could cut across geographical borders and connect classes in Austin, Texas, and Jackson, MI, with a teacher in Cupertino, CA (Burns, 1992); and P. Taylor, in "Social Epistemic Rhetoric and Chaotic Discourse," suggested how the actual writing that got done in class settings might be changing. Taylor argued that computer-mediated communication was evolving into a new genre, one that should be taught and prized in writing classes. At the end of his essay, he wrote:

> The world is changing, with or without us. Computers are transforming the nature of texts, and some forms (such as the expository essay) may not figure prominently in computer-based discourse of the (near) future. Certainly rhetoricians should use what we have learned to help shape the future. But we must also be prepared to reevaluate our old assumptions about how texts communicate. Otherwise, we will simply become the old guard that, according to Thomas Kuhn, will literally have to die off while the winds of change sweep past us. (p. 146)

The changed forms of text that Taylor pointed to also appeared in another book of this time period—Bruce, Peyton, and Batson's (1993) *Networked-Based Classrooms: Promises and Realities*. Growing out of Batson's ENFI Project, the essays in the book described and evaluated the use of Electronic Networks for Interaction in different ENFI consortium sites around the country. In his evaluation of the use of ENFI for the teaching of writing, Bartholomae (1993) concluded that real-time writing and communication fit well with a curriculum in which instructors "seemed particularly interested in raising questions about the academy and its ways of thinking and speaking and writing" and that, overall, networks seem to encourage a kind of "counterwriting" and support alternate ways of "imagining and valuing writing that [makes] a difference when students [write]" (p. 261).

Growing out of the computers-and-composition community was Selfe and Hilligoss' (1994) *Literacy and Computers: The Complications of Teaching and Learning with Technology*. Framed by the issues raised in Lunsford,

the head of the room, a symbol of authority that has in it only the fugitive piece of chalk and perhaps an old blue-book or two. Otherwise, there are no writing materials in this desk, which is a stage device, a prop, and not a workspace. The teacher works at another, "real" desk, at home or in a college office, where there are pencils, pens, staplers, paper, stamps, paper clips, a typewriter and/or a PC, an addressbook; and, somewhere the desk, there are bookshelves, a bulletin board with reminders and mementos on it, pictures, a telephone, a file cabinet. (Moran, 1992, pp. 7–8)

The linking of new technologies of new technologies to a vision of transformed pedagogy is a distinguishing feature in many proposed innovations in education. It is rare that the developer of an innovation would adopt the goal of simply facilitating current practices with a new technology. The reification of the developers' pedagogical theories is viewed as vital to achieving their pedagogical goals, and the argument is made that the expense of adopting new methods and tools is justified by the major improvements that will occur. (Bruce, 1993, p. 9)

Arguments for cultural and functional literacy plainly dominate the American imagination at the moment and for obvious reasons. They articulate the needs, hopes, anxieties, and frustrations of the conservative temper. They reveal in different ways the means of using an ideal of literacy to preserve and advance the world as it is, a world in which the interests of traditionally privileged groups dominate the interests of the traditionally less privileged. (Knoblauch, 1990, pp. 75-76)

Humans must move beyond information and skills to meaning and interpretation of learning to take place and to extend itself. So-called at-risk or slow learners frequently have learned in out-of-school experience a multitude of approaches that allow them to move away from the mere display of learning to the creation of learning. Schools too often demonstrate in their assignments that the meaning is that there is no meaning to be interpreted from self-experiences or comparisons between direct learning and the knowledge found in books. The clear message often seems to be that the meaning lies in the text and not in the active engagement of text and reader together. (Heath, 1990, p. 302)

When a new territory opens, the people who first explore it have different goals, activities, questions and rewards than those who follow to

Moglin, and Slevin's (1990) *The Right to Literacy*, the collection challenged conventional notions of schooling and questionsed current school-based literacy practices. In a section titled "Expanding the Definitions of Computer-Based Literacy," contributors focused on hypertextual reading and writing, suggesting that the kinds of readings given traditional texts in English Studies may be at odds with the new technologies. Moulthrop and Kaplan (1994) observed that "the more [they] experiment with hypertext in literature courses, the deeper [their] conviction grows that this new medium is fundamentally at odds with the aims and purposes of conventional literary education" (p. 236), which they took to be the control and constraint of the range of possible responses to a piece of literature. One of the arguments embedded in this collection was that new technologies could open up concepts of literacy to "debate and change" (Johnson-Eilola, 1994). Debate, if not change, was exactly what took place in the section of the book devoted to multimedia. Although several of the authors promoted hypermedia as a liberatory technology capable of radically changing the relationship between reading and writing and between readers and writers, Dobrin (1994) argued that hypertext was not a "a new text form," "not an evolutionary advance," nor "a new form of participatory literature" and noted that it had "no potential for fundamental change in how we write or read" (p. 308).

PROFESSIONAL JOURNALS

In reviewing the print journals of this period, readers can see three rather different forces operating: the impulse to review computers and composition studies and present it to a wider public; the impulse to forge ahead, welcoming and exploiting the new technologies; and the impulse to hold fast to the past, to what computers and compositionists already knew, to the familiar and the habitual. These three forces were at play in the issues of *College English* published during this period. The February 1992 issue of *CE* bore "Computers and English" on its cover and included three comprehensive review articles (Lanham, 1992; Moran, 1992a; Schwartz, 1992) of 10 books that had a direct relationship to technological change in English. Taken together, the reviews and their appearance in *College English* defined the field of computers and writing and presented it to the field of English generally. The October 1993 issue of *College English* included two additional articles, one suggesting that composition teacher incorporate electronic mail into composition pedagogy and theory (e.g., Hawisher & Moran, 1993) and another (e.g., Boyle, 1993) suggesting that teachers keep the new technology *out* of English classrooms. Boyle, Hawisher and Moran engaged in a heated exchange in *CE*'s "Comment and Response" section of November 1994, Boyle suggesting that Hawisher and Moran were techno-evangelists, and Hawisher & Moran suggesting that Boyle was himself an evangelist, but for a creed not theirs—that the writing classroom could not, and should not, be kept "free" of changes in modes of communication. The debate was framed in language that recalled Hairston's 1992 call for an apolitical writing classroom, and Trimbur et al.'s 1993 response that classrooms were "always already" political.

Other mainstream journal articles during this time demonstrated a continuing interest in both the new—CMC and multimedia—and the old—in the ways in which writers were interacting with wordprocessing. In the second category fall "The Effects of Revising with a Word Processor on Written Composition" (Joram, Woodruff, Bryson, & Lindsay, 1992), "The Ef-

map the area and those who plan to develop the new area. In the evolving use of computer technology, all three stages coexist and therefore none of these three collections serves as a codification of accepted wisdom, but they represent three types of guidebook with different purposes. Paul Delany and George P. Landow's collection, *Hypermedia and Literary Studies*, is narrowest in domain and most exploratory, trying to do some analytic mapping of the territory ... even while describing the newness of the place. Gail E. Hawisher and Cynthia L. Selfe's *Critical Perspectives on Computers and Composition Studies*, the earliest of the three books, includes the whole range of computer use ... in an attempt to survey what has been claimed, what has been established to date and what further questions are needed to develop and mine the riches of the territory. The subtitle of *Evolving Perspectives on Computers and Composition Studies* shows the combination of future orientation and philosophical sweep: "Questions for the 1990s." (Schwartz, 1992, p. 207)

As with the interrelation of spoken and written media, so between paper and screen-based text: we will see crossbreeding, with the uses and forms of one medium shape the uses and forms of the other, so that as the predominance of and our familiarity with screen-based text increases, the dimensions of variations discussed here will have a greater and greater shaping influence on paper text. But the real potential for full exploitation of these dimensions of variation lies in text on screens. It is the dynamic, fluid, graphic nature of computer-based text that will allow full play of these variables in shaping the texture of print on screens. (Bernhardt, 1993, p. 174)

[Hart and Daisley] report on their experiences negotiating within an alien culture while attending and presenting at a conference in Japan. They note that integrating computer technology into language skills classes is still new in Japan and also requires differences in approach because of cultural expectations, ways of thinking, and practices. Further, the cultural orientations of specific societies affects the

fects of Word Processing on Students' Writing Quality and Revision Strategies" (Owston, Murphy, & Wideman, 1992), and "The Role of Classroom Writing Practices and Pedagogy in Shaping Use of the Computer" (Greenleaf, 1994). Into the first category falls Hawisher and Moran's (1993) "E-mail and the Writing Instructor," Bernhardt's (1993) "The Shape of Text to Come: The Texture of Print on Screens" in *College Composition and Communication*, and Duin, Mason, and Lammers' (1994) "Responding to Ninth-Grade Students via Telecommunications: College Mentor Strategies and Development Over Time" in *Research in the Teaching of English*. The new technology was the subject of these articles mentioned; it was the *medium* of Nedra Reynolds et al.'s (1994) review of Faigley's *Fragments of Rationality*, presented as a written transcript of an electronic conversation. Although Reynolds and her class edited the transcript for publication, she noted that "while the postmodernist feel of the original discussion may have been muted in the process, this is still very much a conversation-in-progress that readers must join as and where they can, in keeping, we feel, with the spirit of the book" (p. 265).

Computers and Composition

The journal Computers and Composition continued to grow up during this period. It had changed its format slightly in November 1991, maintaining its smaller trim size but moving to a perfect binding, thereby becoming more book-like. In 1994, the journal moved to Ablex and changed its format radically, moving from 5.5 x 8.5 to a 10 x 7 trim size, substantially larger than *CCC* and other professional journals. The journal increased not only its physical size, but also its geographical scope. Driven by the community's extensive use of the Internet, the journal came to see itself as international, adding international members to its editorial board. In April of 1994, the journal published Hart and Daisley's "Computers and Composition in Japan: Notes on Real and Virtual Literacies," in which the authors described from their perspective what happens when American compositionists travel to another, very different culture. In November 1993 the journal published "Entries from A New E-Mail User's Notebook," a tale of how one teacher (and the former President of NCTE), motivated by her desire to connect with English professionals teachers in the former Soviet Union and eastern Europe, tackled the intricacies of email and was rewarded (Haley-James, 1993). Finally, in December of 1994 (Volume 11, number 3), *Computers and Composition* published its first Special International Issue, guest edited by Ilana Snyder (Monash University, Australia) and containing the work of scholars from England, Wales, Sweden, Australia, the Netherlands, and Finland.

Articles in *Computers and Composition* during this period reflected composition studies' interest in the social aspects of writing. "Sharing Authority: Collaborative Teaching in a Computer-Based Writing Course" (Balester, Halasek, & Peterson, 1992), for example, detailed three feminist teachers' attempts to bring their computer-supported writing classes together. The combined class, which for all intents and purposes became an online and face-to-face team-teaching effort, distributed responsibilities among all instructors. In evaluating the success of the class, the authors concluded that the networked classroom helped them make teaching—as well as writing—a richer, more social, collaborative act. Duin and Gorak's (1992) "Developing Texts for Computers and Composition: A Collaborative Process," described how

use which an individual society makes of technological tools. The authors conclude from their experience that the world electronic culture will ask that we consider that the technological tools we use and what they produce are "imbued with our cultural values and character." We must remember that it is our intentions that create change, not simply the use of new technological tools. (Hart & Daisley, 1994, p. 37)

May, '92, second entry
Egads! I just opened a letter from Cindy which included a printed copy of a response to the notice she posted about my looking for contacts in Estonia. It's from a teacher educator who is a composition specialist in Tartu. She responds that she will be glad to talk with me, and to put me in touch with English educators in her country. She inquires of Cindy whether I am set up to send and receive E-mail, and says telephone and FAX communication in and out of Estonia are more difficult than E-mail to accomplish.

June, '92
I called the computer center at GSU, and they reeled off this long list of things to buy, and steps to take, to get set up to work with E-mail. I am daunted, but desperate. I need to talk with that woman in Estonia. I'm off to the Micro Center store. (James, 1993, p. 7)

Hawisher and Selfe (1991) recently have argued that we must guard against utopian dreams, hold ourselves accountable, and turn over the stones in our networked classrooms to expose the pillbugs and fire-ants (here in Texas at least). In response, I am pointing out that although we should use networking technology as best we can to incubate and nurture even the most temporary equitable relationships, we must recognize the reifying impositions upon marginalized students that accompany the pursuit of egalitarianism; we should acknowledge the heady appeal of the term and the difficulty of defining it; we should confront the difficulties of quantifying a dynamic process by means of static textual traces. (Romano, 1993, p. 27)

Case was twenty-four. At twenty-two, he'd been a cowboy, a rustler, one of the best in the Sprawl. He'd been trained by the best, by McCoy Pualey and Bobby Quine, legends in the biz. He'd operated on an almost permanent adrenaline high, a byproduct of youth and

two authors used a variety of electronic and face-to-face strategies with students, reviewers, and publishers to write a college composition textbook. In "Writing Ourselves Online," (Carbone, et al., 1993), the seven authors explore collaboratively how each of their online voices corresponded to, or contrasted with, their off-line teaching behavior. Articles published in *Computers and Composition* during this period also reflected the profession's continuing interest in the political landscapes of electronic educational settings. Both Romano's (1993) "The Egalitarian Narrative: Whose Story? Which Yardstick?" and Regan's (1993) "Type Normal Like the Rest of Us: Writing, Power, and Homophobia in the Networked Composition Classroom" chronicled experiences in first-year composition classes and called into question the notion that networked classes were indeed the egalitarian social spaces promised in the research literature.

Going On Line

During this period, the field of computers and composition studies increasingly moved online, participating in a self-reinforcing cycle or feedback loop: As more computer-using teachers moved online, they increased, by their presence, the professional and personal value of the online world; as the value of this world increased, more of teachers moved online. Before 1992, teachers of English certainly had been an online presence. We think here of the pioneering online discussion groups begun in 1984 by Michael Spitzer, and MBU, begun in 1989 by Fred Kemp. We think, too of Ted Jennings' *EJournal*, begun in March, 1991, and promoted as "an all-electronic, Matrix distributed, peer-reviewed, academic periodical." By July 1993, *EJournal* had 3,059

Subscribers in 37 countries and was publishing articles touching on many aspects of academics' online lives. Included were Keep's (1993) "Knocking on Heaven's Door: Leibniz, Baudrillard, and Virtual Reality," and Rowland's (1994) "Electronic Journals Neither Free or Easy," among others. During 1992–1994, Jennings' *EJournal* was joined online by commercial information services that provided online access to such journals as the *Chronicle of Higher Education*. Among colleagues and in committees there was increasing talk of putting publications such as *CCCC Bibliography of Composition and Rhetoric* online, perhaps through NCTENet, a recent electronic service offered by the National Council of Teachers of English.

Some of the same people who worked to create the online space for the C&W conference also helped the CCCC develop "CCCC Online," an online complement to the physical conference to be held in Washington, DC in March 1995. Coordinated by members of the Committee on Computers in Composition, "CCCC Online" made available online convention information, including the texts of the convention preview and the convention program; abstracts of presentations; electronic mailing lists; and real-time online meetings, including a number of MOOs. In announcing "CCCC Online," the Committee of Computers in Composition described the advantages and limitations of both real and virtual conferences, portraying technology, once again, as a means of bringing marginalized groups into into more central positions, permitting those without status, salary, and travel funds to participate in the profession:

Professional conferences like CCC are examples of transportation technology put to communication purposes. Cars and planes

proficiency, jacked into a custom cyberspace deck that projected his disembodied consciousness into the consensual hallucination that was the matrix. (Gibson, 1984, p. 5)

CCCC95 Online is an effort to better serve those members of the organization who plan to attend the convention by offering access to information and conversations that typically are not broadly available. Moreover, CCCC Online is an attempt to provide some access to CCCC information and conversations to anyone on the Net who has some interest in composition, communications, and rhetoric studies, bringing the conversations and information of the convention to those who aren't likely to attend. (excerpted from CCCC95 Online Home Page: http://www.missouri.edu/~cccc95/online-intro.html)

Upon Elizabeth's agreement to set up a list between our classes, and in the spirit of the Judy Garland/Mickey Rooney attitude of, "let's put on a show," I sent a message to MBU asking if anybody else might want to join the fray. John Slatin at UT replied that he was teaching a graduate course concerning computers and writing and would like his students to be a part of this new virtual community. In the space of three days, with the spring semester already begun, with no shared knowledge of syllabi or course goals or any clear idea of what would happen on this list, the three of us had set up a significant technological component to our courses. (Kemp, email communication, July 27, 1994)

are wonderful things; they do deliver us to places where we can talk with our colleagues, which is good.

However, they are limited as modes of communication because their cost in money and time often prevents people from attending professional meetings such as CCCC.

The Internet, a global latticework of computer networks, offers opportunities to compensate for the limits of conventional conventions, and this year CCCC is going to take advantage of those opportunities to make convention information and discussions available to anyone with access to the Internet. CCCC Online will connect a broader spectrum of people to the conversations that will take place before, during, and after the convention, possibly reaching many students and teachers who are interested in rhetoric and composition studies, but may have little opportunity to participate. (CCCC Convention Preview, 1995)

In addition, graduate courses in computers and composition began to inhabit online spaces. In spring 1993, Elizabeth Sommers of San Francisco State, John Slatin of UT-Austin, and Fred Kemp of Texas Tech linked their three courses in Computers and Writing, calling this effort the "Interclass." The Interclass included its three instructors and members of the three graduate courses, of course, but drew as well on 54 "contributors" who added documents, chiefly works-in-progress, to the discourse of the class. Fred Kemp's account of this Interclass demonstrates that this experiment was not an unqualified success, yet the experiment gave computers and composition specialists valuable experience to draw on as they included more online components in their graduate instruction.

RECOGNIZING CHALLENGES

If the 1990s brought a growing professional sophistication to the field of computers and composition studies, they brought challenges as well. Among these challenges, three seemed especially prominent: the need for the expanding community to accommodate an increasingly diverse population of teachers and scholars; the need to see technology's potential as both conservator of existing values and structures and as agent of productive change in the American educational system, in writing programs, and in writing classrooms; and the need to understand, in a critical way, the global expansion of computer-supported communication.

Accommodating an Increasingly Diverse Population of Teachers

By 1992, the community that was computers and composition studies had become increasingly complex and mature. The community described in earlier chapters had been relatively small and homogeneous; the mature community included a wide range of participants with different needs and expectations and differing levels of experience and information. The tensions among these differing needs and levels—although normal, healthy, and associated with a community's growth and change—presented new challenges.

The organizers of the annual Computers and Writing Conference, for example—Helen Schwartz of Indiana University of Purdue University at Indianapolis in 1992; Bill Condon, Susanmarie Harrington, Emily Jessup, and Wayne Butler of the University of Michigan in 1993; and Eric Crump of the University of Missouri in 1994—felt these tensions keenly as they attempted to put together conference for-

As I have discovered in the local area writing classroom, once you allow students to send as well as receive, you can't get them back into the passive receiving mode again. They have become knowledge-makers, in whatever degree. And you don't have to be an expert in postmodern writing instruction to understand how giving students a legitimate voice stimulates motivation, engagement, and commitment. (Kemp, email communication, July 27, 1994)

If our profession is to succeed in preparing teachers to be effective educators in the virtual environments of the next decade, we will need to help them learn to use technology *and* to function actively as technology critics and reformers in the context of our educational systems. To these ends, we have to teach educators to function as lifetime learners within technological environments and to understand technology and technological change in terms of social, political, and educational implications. (Selfe, 1992, p. 25)

I write this as a brief angst-ridden homily to faculty members of English departments in high schools or colleges who may find themselves in the position we were in. The road is well mapped ... but for those of us shouldering heavy loads in colleges that pride themselves on being teaching institutions, a little well-meant cursory investigation and a few sincere phone calls are woefully inadequate. (Harralson, 1992, p. 71–72)

For those of us concerned with teaching college composition, the first decade of the personal computer revolution has been dominated by the wonders of word processing ... .With word processing, it becomes easy to revise a text as it is to leave it alone; indeed, most of the playful aspects of the computer only come into play when we begin manipulating text we have already entered. Although there are other advantages of word processing ... it is this first advantage of editing that has been at the center of the initial attraction to computers for most writers and teachers. Word processing, in this sense, triumphed completely, among my conservative col-

mats that would accommodate and attract the full community and its range of needs. All three groups of conference planners expressed the desire to increase conference involvement by public school teachers—those who were already working with technology as well as those who needed additional resources to do so. How, then, were public school educators to be attracted to the conference, which had the reputation, by this time, of catering primarily to a college audience? How, too, could the conference planners appeal to the entire range of possible participants' under the "public school" umbrella—future teachers new to computer use who needed appropriately challenging pre-service education grounded in practice and theory; new teachers who already felt more at home in multimedia environments informed by MTV than they did in the pages of Harbrace; practicing teachers who sought sound instructional materials and advice about technology aimed at appropriate grade levels; experienced teachers who had been working with computers for over a decade and who sought the latest information about cutting edge technologies; teachers in well-funded schools districts whose students were working with hypertext, wordprocessing, desktop publishing, and multimedia; teachers from poorly funded inner-city schools who had access to a single computer on a rolling cart for one afternoon a week; teachers who were the sole technology experts in their district; and teachers who were the last individuals in their buildings to use technology. The conference needed to speak to the full range of interests represented by the K–12 group, and to these groups as well: college and university teachers, teacher educators, hypertext authors, synchronous conferencing experts, multimedia specialists, lab directors, software authors, researchers, and community college educators.

The challenges involved in addressing such

a diverse audience made themselves felt in other forums as well. In *Computers and Composition*, the range of expertise addressed in articles was never more broad than during this period—from material that provided basic background in specific areas of computers and composition studies to pieces directed at individuals with extensive experience in complex applications of technology. In 1992, for example, *Computers and Composition* published Harralson's (1992) "We've Barely Started and We've Already Done It Wrong," for programs just beginning the project of establishing a computer-supported writing facility, and Tharon Howard's (1992) "WANS, Connectivity, and Computer Literacy: An Introduction and Glossary," an article aimed at novice users of wide-area networks. The next year, the journal published Myron Tuman's (1993) "Campus Word Processing: Seven Design Principles for a New Academic Writing Environment," an article that addressed sophisticated and interlocking concerns of curricula, technology, pedagogy, and administration and Pamela Takayoshi's (1994) "Building New Networks from the Old: Women's Experiences with Electronic Communication," a piece applying feminist theory to claims experienced users had made about email. Also reflecting the increasingly wide range of interests within the computers and composition community was a national teleconference entitled, "Seeing the Future by Knowing Our Past," organized by Rebecca Rickley at Ball State University in 1994, following on the heels of C&W94. Rickley, responding, in part, to her perception of the diverse audience in attendance at that conference, incorporated the voices of public school teachers and high school students, technical specialists and technology novices, researchers and graduate students in order to give some indication of the range of participants then comprising the field of computers and composition,

leagues who teach literature as well as among more radical teachers of composition, because of its effortless, transparent support for both the theory and practice of writing as process. (Tuman, 1993, p. 49)

Research on networked communications within composition studies argued that computers are potentially empowering tools for disenfranchised groups and marginalized students, particularly female students who have had few tools with which to carve out a space for themselves in the male world of the academy. Women can use computerized communications, the argument goes, to undermine traditional classroom discourse patterns where men are trained early to speak with authority while women learn to speak in questioning tones and to be supportive of (not argumentative with) the male voice. But are computerized communications tools that offer the possibility of dismantling these confining roles or are they, as Lorde (1981) says, "the master's tools?" Can we expect women to use computerized communication as a tool for empowering themselves and dismantling the "master's house," in this case traditional classroom

discourse patterns?
(Takayoshi, 1994, p. 21)

At a recent computers and writing workshop for secondary school teachers, a fourth-grade teacher explained that she would soon be getting an Apple IIe for her classroom. No one had asked her whether she wanted a computer or how it might fit into her teaching; she was not offered training, technical support, or release time, nor was she consulted on the software she would eventually be given for use with the machine. (LeBlanc, 1994, p. 22)

In March 1993, Fred Kemp and I talked at the 4Cs meeting in San Diego about crating an "institute" for computers and writing. Between the 4Cs and the Computers and Writing Conference at the University of Michigan in May, 1993, Fred and I managed to hammer out some ideas regarding the institute idea. We also invited a group of established c&w people to serve as a beginning board of directors. We intended to make the institute a combination of K–12 and college folks, and also a consortium of industry and academia. We also knew the institute should be a grass roots organization. (Batson, email communication, July 18, 1994)

and the needs and expertise that various individuals brought to the community.

The diversity of needs and experiences within the computers and composition community created tension in preservice teacher education programs across the country, as well. The fact that computer technology continued to be unevenly distributed in school districts and systems—usually along lines of race, class, and gender—meant that it was hard to predict what teachers would need to know about technology. Each program had to decide whether to prepare professionals to face technologically rich learning environments, and thus risk failing to provide them the skills they needed to make effective use of a single computer on a crash cart shared by four teachers, or whether to prepare teachers to face technologically impoverished environments, and thus risk failing to help them consider the implications of multimedia portfolios, access to the information superhighway, or hypertext document construction. The usual decision, of course, was a compromise that often served no group particularly well. This tension at the level of preservice teacher education placed increasing burdens on in-service programs that provided professional education responsive to local conditions. These in-service programs, given shrinking budgets and legislative constraints, were not always able to adapt, nor were administrators willing to make the necessary compromises for such situations to work (Graves & Haller, 1994).

One attempt to include and serve the widening range of groups associated with computers and composition studies was the founding of the Alliance for Computers and Writing—a consortium of scholars, teachers, organizations, and publishers committed to the productive use of computers in English and language arts classrooms. Members of the Alliance, conceived and founded by Trent Batson (Gallaudet

University) and Fred Kemp (Texas Tech University) met for the first time at the 9th Computers and Writing Conference in Ann Arbor, MI (1993) to discuss the ways in which such an umbrella organization could serve the needs of English teachers who used computers in instructional settings. An early contribution of the Alliance was to encourage the formation of regional groups: among the early groups, the California Alliance (the first to declare itself), the Mid-Atlantic Alliance, the Great Plains Alliance, and the Rocky Mountain Alliance.

Computers and the Challenge of Enacting Change

By the advent of the 1990s, it had become clear to computers and composition specialists that technology would not automatically increase the opportunities for the democratic participation of less privileged segments of our society. Charles Piller, in a 1992 article in *Mac-World*, for example, noted that minority populations and lower socioeconomic populations in secondary schools were America's fastest growing "technological underclass" (p. 218). Others offered evidence that what was true in secondary education was true in postsecondary education as well. Thomas DeLoughry (1994a), in a *Chronicle of Higher Education* article, wrote that "historically Black colleges, institutions serving American Indians, and those with large low-income populations" (p. A19) had a late start connecting to the information superhighway, because postsecondary institutions serving these marginalized populations could not afford the hardware, software, and infrastructure associated with that project. Even Vice President Gore, by 1993, had noted the gap between the "haves" and the "have nots" (Gore, 1993) in his speeches about the Information superhighway. According to the Clinton

At the initial meeting of the institute board in Ann Arbor, attended by Michael Joyce, John B. Smith, Cindy Selfe, Gail Hawisher, Trent Batson, Fred Kemp, Bill Condon, Carolyn Handa, Eric Crump, Diane Langston, Kim Richardson (Harper Collins Rep), Rob Epp (St. Martin's Rep), Marty Smith (Harcourt Brace Rep), Dmitri Korahais (GroupLogic Rep), Locke Carter (Daedalus Rep), John O'Connor, and William Wright, the board gave its approval to the institute concept, but with a change of name to Alliance, because it sounded "less heavy" and authoritative; less top-down and more grass-roots. (Batson, email communication, July 18, 1994)

What the Clinton Administration's view lacks most fundamentally—indeed what most conventional ideas about technology lack—is any notion of technological development as a dynamic social and cultural phenomenon. This is not an arcane topic. Every thorough-going history of the building of technological systems points to the same conclusion: Substantial technical innovations involve a reweaving of the fabric of society—a reshaping of some of the roles, rules, relationships, and institutions that make up our ways of living together. (Winner, 1993, p. B1)

The kinds of discursive spaces emerging in computer classrooms can represent contemporary versions of the public spaces—if they are designed and managed with an expanded vision of the radical democratic project in mind. It is not accidental that groups such as Minnesota Citizens On-Line have created an electronic forum that they call The Commons to foster democratic change. The work going on in our computer classrooms is essential in preparing students to understand and function in the new sites in which political action can and will occur. The commitment of English departments to supporting computer networks, electronic common spaces, is essential because we are among the few who understand to what extent we are constituted by, and can constitute others by, discursive practices. (Wahlstrom & Selfe, 1994, p. 44)

administration's estimates in 1992, only 14% of public schools had access to networks that could support broad-based email applications in even one classroom, and only 22% of schools had access to one modem. Given this situation, although groups like the Telecommunications Policy Roundtable (1994) called for "universal access," the Vice President noted that access for "*almost* everyone" (Gore, 1993, emphasis added) would be a more realistic goal.

The cost of technology, coupled with the declining public support—and funding—for education generally, limited the use of technology in most schools and programs. Departments of English—which had assumed a decade earlier that their initial capital investment in technology would be a one-time cost—were discovering and tracking the hidden costs of computer use: repair, maintenance, capital replacement, staff support, faculty time and energy. Such costs were high and difficult to justify in a time of shrinking budgets, as Wahlstrom and Selfe noted in a 1992 presentation to department heads at a meeting of the Association of Departments of English in Waterloo, Canada:

Certainly we now recognize departmental administrators supportive of computer-assisted writing facilities and computer-using humanists must confront a set of increasingly conflicting forces. For one, the university bureaucracy requires that scheduling and financial plans be made years in advance, but technological change and the faculty members who embrace it require more immediate solutions. Their work, often characterized by unexpected innovations, frequently generates non-budgeted equipment requests, new personnel expenses, as well as unanticipated problems with space and scheduling. Moreover, even though costs of computing have come down in terms of the amount of computing power one gets for the dollar, faculty who use computers are finding uses for more and more complex and expensive hardware and software, and are requiring more access to distant colleagues or sources of information only reached via local-area networks (LANs) and wide area networks (WANs).

These pressures, among many others, also require administrators to re-think the role computer-assisted writing facilities are now playing in their departments. This includes reassessing faculty members' involvement in such facilities, the facilities' support of departmental research agendas, and opposition from Luddites who feel money for computers is best spent *anywhere* else. Further, administrators who want to retain their computer-assisted writing facilities and support computer-using humanists must manage the cost of technology within universities experiencing significant retrenchments.

These issues, faced by heads struggling to maintain resources in the face of budget cuts, recessions, reallocations, and reductions, directly and indirectly affect the kinds of teaching and research that goes on in computer-supported facilities. At no time in the history of English departments and writing programs have departmental administrators had to make so many financially serious, politically sensitive, and educationally consequential decisions about technology, and, therefore, about the scholarly and teaching pursuits of faculty members within the department. (Wahlstrom & Selfe, 1994, p.36)

The forces that Selfe and Wahlstrom (1994) described can also be sensed in the words of Peter Montgomery who, when asked at the

I am a very new member of this community. I obtained my e-mail address only this semester, and this is my first conference. I am interested in incorporating hypermedia and internet access in my classes. This fall I will be asking my students in an honors first-year composition class to produce a hypermedia magazine. My university is giving me a part-time student assistant to accomplish this. (Carol Lea Clark at the 1994 C&W Conference)

1994 C&W to list significant events in his own historical connection with computers and writing, included these items:

- 1975—Creation of composition exercises on a PDPII using DECAL (Dec Authors' Language).
- 1984—Creation of computer classroom at Comosun College 16 XT's networked with Novell to serve 600 students/semester.
- 1994—Computer classroom cut from budget as English Department facility. (C&W, 1994)

Money, however, was not the only obstacle in the path of the substantive educational change. Also operative was the limited and traditionalist vision that many departments brought to the use of technology in composition programs and classrooms. As Hawisher (1988) and Klem and Moran (1992) had observed, many teachers continued to import current-traditional practices into the new landscape of computer-supported classrooms.

In part, Klem and Moran suggested, teachers did not develop new pedagogies because most were teaching assistants or part-time lecturers, themselves part of an academic underclass, overworked and underpaid, forced to spend additional, unpaid time learning to work with new technology in a new teaching environment. It is understandable—perhaps inevitable—that these teachers resorted to familiar teaching methods as a way of coping with the unfamiliar setting of computer-supported writing facilities. Tuman described one of the programmatic effects of this phenomena in an article that he wrote for *Computers and Composition* in 1993:

Despite pioneering a computer-based component of our first-year writing class that provided basic word-processing instruc-

All teachers and administrators concerned with language education must soon make difficult, concrete decisions regarding computers. It is in the process of contemplating these changes that educators rightly seek out sound advice . . . at workshops and in print—What impact will it have on my students' writing? Will it really encourage them to revise more? (Tuman, 1992, p. 265)

Workshop Information
It's a two-week workshop for English teachers wanting to incorporate computers

tion for almost 20,000 students over the last seven years, our use of computers actually did little to undermine the paradigm of the traditional writer, that solitary individual whom Linda Brodkey (1987) describes as "alone in a cold garret working into the small hours of the morning by the thin light of a candle." (p. 396)

That is not to say that we were blind to the larger shift in the profession from an emphasis on the individual and the writing process to an emphasis on the group and collaboration only that pedagogical changes reflecting this shift were happening in our classrooms largely independent of the computer-based instruction we were offering. We approached word processing, in other words, as a tool for allowing individual students to generate and later revise the texts that they worked on in classes that were increasingly given over to collaborative exchanges. (p. 50)

Nor did the numbers of teachers who needed initial introductions to technology-supported classrooms and teaching methods seem to be shrinking dramatically. Given the continuing lack of resources for preservice or in-service education in computer-supported teaching methods, the numbers of teachers new to technology seemed to remain relatively stable, and computers and composition specialists perceived the continuing demand for continuing education.

In 1985, Michigan Technological University offered the first of its two-week summer workshops for teachers who wanted to integrate computer technology into their writing classrooms and writing programs. Cynthia Selfe, who designed and directed these workshops, reasoned that the demand for such summer educational opportunities—especially in the remote upper peninsula of Michigan—would be

into their writing-intensive classrooms. The workshop will be held in a fully equipped computer lab designed especially for English teachers. The workshop will consist of ten, six-hour days. In addition to regularly scheduled sessions, the computer lab will be open and staffed during the evenings. All participants will receive one-on-one help learning and developing computer applications suited for their own classrooms and programs. The workshop is sponsored by the Division of Education and Public Services. (Workshop Brochure from MTU, June 13–24, 1988)

University of Illinois, Urbana, Summer Institute
Computers and Writing: The personal computer offers the chance to turn the high school English classroom into an efficient writing workshop in which the writer has direct contact with both instructor and

peer editors, and writing evaluation and revision may be done almost instantly. In this seminar, conducted in a fully networked computer classroom, participants will learn a simple but powerful word processing program and will then turn their attention to developing a syllabus for teaching computer rhetoric, and writing by revision, to high school seniors. We will capitalize on the ease with which the computer permits writers to move about in their work, deleting, shifting, or inserting words or large blocks of text while always seeing clean copy, in order to develop a more sophisticated understanding of how student writers edit their work, and to make the practice of revision an essential habit in their work. (Brochure for the Summer Institute at the University of Illinois, Urbana, June 20–July 18, 1986)

We have to learn to recognize—and teach students to recognize—the interface as an interested and partial map of our culture and as a linguistic contact zone that reveals power differentials. We need to teach students and ourselves to recognize computer interfaces as non-innocent physical borders (between the regular world and the virtual world), cultural borders (between the haves and the have-nots), and linguistic borders. These borders, we need to recognize as cultural formations "historically constructed and socially organized within rules

limited and would last for only a few years while a critical mass of teachers received an early introduction to computers. Entitled "Computers in Writing-Intensive Classrooms," this institute was open to teachers from all levels and attracted elementary, secondary, and college teachers. Contrary to initial expectations, however, the Institute continued to attract more than 20 teachers each year and by 1994, the 9th year of its offering, had worked with more than 200 educators. As workshops and summer courses like this one were held around the country at Gallaudet University, at Ball State University, at Texas Tech University, at the University of Massachusetts, and at dozens of other sites—it was clear that the need for such in-service or preservice introductions to the technology continued to manifest itself.

In short, substantive educational reform remained both complicated to envision and difficult to enact. Many teachers and school administrators remained undereducated about technology, and, hence, technology was often used to support traditional pedagogical approaches rather than innovative teaching methods. Adequate funds for technology remained unevenly distributed along existing axes of socioeconomic privilege and race. Although new technologies—like email, multimedia, and networking—were gaining attention in the marketplace, they were not always having the hoped-for impact they might have had in educational settings. By 1994—due, in part, to the influence of cultural studies, critical theory, Marxism, feminism, and other social theories—specialists in computers and composition were coming to understand more thoroughly the complex and overdetermined social formations and systems within which the process of education took place in this country and the attendant difficulties involved in making change within such systems.

The Challenge of Global Connection and Expansion

These important lessons continued to be learned as the computers and composition community watched use of the Internet increase. Email systems, for example, were initially perceived during this period as offering English teachers an innovative way to connect their students with individuals in other countries and expose them to the different perspectives of other cultures (e.g., Haley-James, 1993; Susser, 1993). Claims for the new medium echoed those of earlier technologies—the information superhighway that the Clinton Administration proposed to support—was to be a low-cost way of providng all citizens increased access to information, educational opportunity, and democratic involvement (Gore, 1991, 1993). Such claims echoed earlier statements about microcomputers made in the early 1980s (e.g., Gomez, 1991) and about online, synchronous discussion (e.g., Batson, 1988).

It soon became evident, however, that CMC technologies were constructed within the same social structures and with the same values that continued to shape other aspects of the culture and educational system of that time. Email, for example, was observed to support a privileging of the English language and, thus, to reproduce conditions that exerted a subtle but continuous colonial gesture toward the growing numbers of students in school systems who spoke English as a second, third, or fourth language, and toward computer-using students and teachers in other countries. As Petzold (1993) stated the case, large-scale, networked-based, email systems—linked computers using the common exchange standard called American Standard Code for Information Interchange (ASCII)—did not adequately support languages other than English. Petzold (1993) pointed out some of the implications of relying solely on ASCII:

and regulations that limit and enable particular identities, individual capacities, and social forms" (Giroux, 30). We also need to teach students and ourselves useful strategies of crossing—and demystifying—these borders. It is important to understand that we continually re-map and renegotiate borders in our lives. (Selfe & Selfe, 1994, p. 495)

If the promises of the Clinton campaign for science and technology now come to pass, America is headed for a new era in which the Government's focus on making armaments will shift to fostering a host of new civilian technologies and industries. No financial midget, the civil initiative would spend money twice as fast as the Pentagon's Star Wars anti-missile program, one of the biggest research efforts of all time. (Broad, 1992, p. B5)

I've been corresponding with an ESL teacher in Irkutsk. We are planning for her students to write mine, and mine to respond to hers. So far, we've each written about four messages, but I think we can get the student part together pretty soon. (B. Cooper, email correspondence, March 25, 1994)

I'm a Ph.D. student of the Interdisciplinary Program in Communication and Information Sciences at the University of Hawaii. Currently, I'm writing a dissertation on intercultural telecollaboration . . . .I'm planning a joint online class with Nanzan University in Japan next semester (Fall 1994). Each site is planning to have around 40 students and divide the total 80 students at both sides into groups of four (two at each site). Students are going to be assigned to write a paper collaboratively using tools on the Internet . . . .I came up with an idea of having a joint online class with Japanese universities [on APEX-L] . . . and [was] introduced [online] to Dr. Goto who was very supportive of my idea and agreed to have a joint online class next semester. (K. Aoki, email correspondence, March 26, 1994)

Denied tenure in 1986, [Jenny] Harrison] waged a seven-year battle against Berkeley, accusing it of sex discrimination. Since rejoining the department, she has been the subject of a heated electronic-mail exchange that she and others say borders on harassment.

Some professors in the department have attacked her appointment in e-mail messages they sent to mathematicians at Berkeley and around the country. One accused her of "years of lying and a massive propaganda campaign." Another wrote that she had obtained her appointment through "distortion and slander." (Magner, 1993, p. A16)

there's a big problem with ASCII and that problem is indicated by the first word of the acronym. ASCII is truly an American standard, but there's a whole wide world outside our borders where ASCII is simply inadequate. It isn't even good enough for countries that share our language, for where is the British pound sign in ASCII? . . . ASCII . . . is not only inadequate for the written languages of much of the world, but also for many people who live right in my own neighborhood.

We simply can't be so parochial as to foster a system as exclusive and limiting as ASCII. The personal computing revolution is quickly encompassing much of the world, and it's totally absurd that the dominant standard is based solely on English as it is spoken in the U.S. (p. 375)

Email also showed signs of continued alignment along the axes of gender privilege. Pamela Takayoshi (1994), for example, surveyed women on five electronic mailing lists and found that participants experienced inadequate institutional support when they tried to gain access to email systems, had difficulties in coping with masculinist models of teaching email systems within professional development situations, and encountered direct harassment once they got into email lists. In a related publication, Julian Dibbell (1993) wrote evocatively of a "rape in cyberspace," describing a *virtual* (hence, existing only within the memory of a computer), but nonetheless violent, sexual attack that occurred in LamdaMOO, a real-time conversational space on the Internet. And Hawisher and Sullivan (in press) continued the tradition of challenging the egalitarian claims for cyberspace by studying the online lives of 30 academic women in composition studies, using an electronic list, called women: waytoofast.

Contributing to the concern that colonialism and global capitalism were primary driving forces behind the new information superhighway was the increasing visibility of postmodern studies and the various critiques of such perspectives. At the 1994 CCCC, Cynthia Selfe argued:

The postmodern theory of Fredric Jameson (1991) can provide a context within which to understand . . . how the possibilities for collective action in a postmodern age are effectively limited by the multiplication of and disintegration of social identities that accompanies the global expansion of multinational capitalism . . . .

Jameson (1991) begins by unmasking the "self-congratulatory rhetoric" (p. 320) associated with pluralism, revealing the multiplication of microgroups based on non-class issues as a naturalized result of contemporary capitalism "in its third (or 'multinational') stage" (p. 319). Capitalism, as it expands globally, becomes "hungry and thirsty for . . . the endless production and proliferation of new groups and neoethnicities of all kinds" (p. 325). These groups function as "so many new markets for new products, so many new interpellations for the new advertising image itself" (p. 325). To rationalize this process, Jameson notes, an "ideology of groups" (p. 320) is constructed and framed in the rhetoric of pluralism. This ideology, in turn, serves two essentially reproductive purposes: to feed the appetite of global capitalism, and, at the same time, to hold out the false hope that our society has come to be based not on traditional class differences but on the increasingly democratic appreciation of various micropolitical groups. Through the process of naturalization that accompanies this ideology which effectively masks the authentic economic con-

It is safest to grasp the concept of the postmodern as an attempt to think the present historically in an age that has forgotten how to think historically in the first place. In that case, it either "expresses" some deeper irrepressible historical impulse (in however distorted a fashion) or effectively "represses" and diverts it, deep on the side of the ambiguity you happen to favor. Postmodernism, postmodern consciousness, may amount to not much more than theorizing its own condition of possibility, which consists primarily in the sheeer enumeration of changes and modifications. (Jameson, 1991, p. ix)

Postmodern theory decisively rejects the primacy of consciousness and instead has consciousness originating in language, thus arguing that the subject is an effect rather than a cause of discourse. Because the subject is the locus of overlapping and competing discourses, it is a temporary stitching together of a series of often contradictory subject positions. In other words, what a person does, thinks, says, and writes cannot be interpreted unambiguously because any human action does not rise out of a unified consciousness but rather from a momentary identity that is always multiple and in some respects incoherent. If consciousness is not fully present to ones own self, then it cannot be made transparent to another. (Faigley, 1993, p. 9)

ditions of classes and diffuses the potential of collective action the conditions under which global capitalism continues to expand are reproduced . . . .

If this postmodern vision of e-mail is disturbing, it is also a useful context for understanding several of the phenomena that currently characterize the growth of e-mail—the "prodigious enlargement" (Jameson, p. 354) of e-mail within the very territories claimed by the expansion of global capitalism; the explosion of self-established e-mail discussion groups, newsgroups, and bulletin boards focused on a multiplication of topics; the eagerness of groups to colonize cyberspace by claiming members in other countries; and the common practice of cross-posting messages to multiply the effects of communication. The postmodern perspective also serves to contextualize the emergence of the multiple in the compartmentalized realities of community nets, the electronic ventriloquism associated with Internet Relay Chats (IRC), and the multiplication of personalities in MOOs and MUDs. (Selfe, 1994)

A CONTEXT OF CONTINUED ENTHUSIASM

If the increasing diversity and complexity of teachers within the field, the continuing educational problems they faced, and the growing understanding of the forces that worked against educational change challenged the maturing field of computers and composition studies in the early 1990s, the underlying sense of optimism and enthusiasm that characterized the field remained surprisingly stable and vigorous. Certainly the continuing influx of new teachers, and teachers new to computers, contributed to the field's continuing energy and hopeful perspective.

In addition, for those seasoned veterans in the field, there were new technologies to become enthusiastic about—multimedia, email, telecommunications, MOOs, MUDs, and MUSHes. Discussions about possible uses of these technologies occupied the attention of the field in most of the professional forums available to computers and compositionists. In the opening keynote speech of the 1994 Computers and Writing Conference, for example, Amy Bruckmann of MIT tantalized participants with visions of the virtual worlds created in MOOs, MUDs, and MUSHes. Multimedia technologies also commanded considerable attention—both at the 1994 Computers and Writing and in other forums. In the MLA volume *Literacy and Computers* (1994), Lanny Dryden wrote about his participation in the Model Technologies in the Schools Project and the Macintosh Multimedia Institute. The aim of both programs was to "exploit the possibilities" (p. 288) of hypermedia and multimedia by identifying and undertaking projects that gave students "mastery over their own learning" (p. 287). Dryden's chapter ended with these words:

> We live in a postindustrial age, and hypermedia is the literacy of the twenty-first century . . . as educators we must learn to use the technology of our age, exploiting its full potential to make the past live for young people and to give them the means to discover and create their own futures." (p. 304)

Adding to the enthusiasm of new computer-using teachers and the continuing optimism of teachers discovering new technologies was the increasing professional influence of maturing computers and composition specialists who had entered the field in the early 1980s. In

MOO-fer-all
Sunday, 11:00 a.m. to 12:30 p.m. (May 22, 1994)
Instructional Computing Site, 5 South Memorial Union [University of Missouri, Columbia]
Michael Day and Rebecca Rickly (and any other veteran MOOers who are handy) will give an informal, hands-on demonstration of how to connect with, move around on, interact with other people in a textual virtual environment. (CWC, 1994 Addendum)

"Virtual Professional Community: Results from the MediaMOO Project"

MediaMOO is a text-based, networked, virtual reality environment designed to extend the type of casual collaboration which occurs at conferences to a daily activity.(1) Visitors to a conference share not just a set of interests, but also a place and a set of activities. Interaction is generated as much by the latter two as the former:

Person A: Can you tell me how to get to Ballroom A?
Person B: I'm headed that way now. It's up this way.
Person A: Thanks!
Person B: I see you're at Company X . . . .

A text-based virtual environment can provide both a shared place (the virtual world), and a shared set of activities (exploring and extending the virtual world).

Like at a coffee break at a conference, there is a social convention that it is appropriate to strike up a conversation with strangers simply based on their name tags. On MediaMOO, you can read descriptions of people's research interests as well as their names, and this can form a basis for striking up a substantive conversation. (Bruckman & Resnick, 1995)

What I dream about today is that we might *more often* make our classrooms places that connect with the world outside, the here and now; places that show students the power of writing to transform—writing that is not always about later, about jobs and careers, but writing that is about themselves as people, as individuals and as citizens of various communities. (Bridwell-Bowles, 1995, p. 51)

1993, Lillian Bridwell-Bowles, a pioneer of the computers and composition movement, served as the Program Chair the annual Conference on College Composition and Communication (CCCC) and the Associate Chair of the CCCC. In this post, she encouraged not only a focus on technology in the conference program, but also an increased use of technology within the CCC organization. As Bridwell-Bowles moved on to become Chair of the CCCC, other computers and composition specialists assumed similarly visible posts in national professional organizations. In 1993, Janie Hydrick, another early participant in the computers and composition community, assumed her duties as President Elect of the National Council of Teachers of English, and Cynthia Selfe completed her term as the Chair of the College Section for the NCTE. In 1994, Lester Faigley was elected Associate Chair of the CCCC and immediately identified technology as a focus of the 1995 CCCC program. At some institutions, computers and composition specialists had become directors of important campus writing or computing programs—among them, Texas Tech University (Fred Kemp), University of Massachusetts (Charles Moran), the University of Illinois, Urbana–Champaign (Gail Hawisher), Smith College (Hugh Burns), the University of Minnesota, Minneapolis (Lillian Bridwell-Bowles), and Governors State University (Deborah Holdstein). At other institutions, computers and composition specialists were serving as department heads or chairs—among them Michigan Technological University (Cynthia Selfe), the University of Minnesota, St. Paul (Billie Wahlstrom), and Springfield College (Paul LeBlanc). In such positions, these individuals were often able to encourage the integration of technology into the profession and English composition curricula, and to support the work of faculty who were specializing in the use and study of technology.

Finally, there were local, encouraging signs that teachers who used computers had brought about some changes—momentary, fragmentary, partial—in writing classrooms and writing programs. Experienced computer-using teachers seemed to be understanding more about the discursive landscapes they could create with new and emerging technologies, and they seemed to have become more adept at taking advantage of such landscapes to enact some of the classroom and programmatic changes. Among just a few of these signs were the popularity of WriteMUSH, the Internet-based "shared hallucination" for writing students across the country (Bennahum, 1994), and Diversity University; the advent of the experimental Online Writing Lab (OWL), pioneered by Patricia Ericcson at Dakota State University; the increasing offerings of online courses involving faculty and students from multiple universities, envisioned by colleagues such as Fred Kemp (Texas Tech University) in 1993 and Stephen Doheny-Farina (Clarkson University), Laura Gurak (University of Minnesota), and James Zappen (Rensselaer Polytechnic Institute) in 1994; and the vertical sequence of multimedia projects instituted by Ruth Huff, Karen Kay Leonard, Barbara Parker-Davis, and Joyce Vogt for literature instruction in Indianapolis middle and high school classrooms (presented at NCTE's 1994 Portfolio Conference in Indianapolis).

In these ways—with a steady influx of new and enthusiastic professionals in the field, with the excitement generated by new technologies, with the help of long-time professionals—the field of computers and composition studies was able to cope with the many challenges outlined earlier in this section, if not always to address them as successfully as might be hoped. The complicated and counterbalancing forces of change and tradition, enthusiasm and critical vision, growth and stasis

"Clearly we're going to lose certain things and gain others," said John Seeley Brown, the director of Xerox's Palo Alto Reserach Center. "We're moving toward a new literacy. The typewriter shaped our current view of literacy. Now we're finding new computer tools that honor visual/audio thinking as opposed to textual thinking." Television is for a passive audience. Digital video, with vast possibilities for manipulating images, exercises the mind. (Markoff, 1994b, p. D5)

also signaled a growing maturity for the community and the promise of continued vigor.

EMail Interview, Myron Tuman

> Date sent: Tue, 18 Oct 94 17:11:01 -0400
> From: "Paul LeBlanc" <leblancp@hmco.com>
> To: "Myron Tuman" <mtuman@english.as.ua.edu>
> Subject: RE: here i am

>
> Okay Myron,
>
> Let's start with some of the basics:
>
> 1. Your present position and duties.

I am professor of English at the University of Alabama, and Director of the English Computer Lab. One of my main duties is planning and organizing a yearly computer component taught to all students in the first semester of first-year composition here at UA (English 101). I also teach grad course in r&c as well as a range of undergrad courses, including first-year comp (taking my own medicine). I have continued to dabble in teaching literature as well, mostly various forms of 19th-century British, and will likely do more in this area, in part to work on new methods of integrating traditional literary study with computer-based collaboration.

> Your role with Norton.

It's probably not accurate to say that I have a "role" with Norton. I helped put together the original deal by which Norton published Textra in the college market and did the same sort of thing to get Connect started. In between, I continue to work with them on a range of matters all related to this single product (new editions, new documentation, etc.), and hence not unlike any author, I assume, involved with a major work in press. It is just that with software, things sort of stay "in press" more of the time.

> 2. How about a brief pre-history; that is, what you were doing before the

> period 1989 to 1992? We are especially interested in how you came to be involved
> with computers. By 1989 you were working with Norton, so please include a
> paragraph on that bit of time as well.

I got involved with computers in the early 1980s, like many academics, strictly to use word processing to help me complete my first book, _A Preface to Literacy_. I was—and still am—a terrible typist, the kind who bought Liquid Paper by the carton.

In any case, I was a new assistant professor at West Virginia University, when the Chair, Elaine Ginsburg, always with an eye for a bargain, bought one of the original Osborne computers (with the tiny 3x5 screen) when the company was going down (and out)—and then, thankfully, hid the thing in a basement closet. Only Pat Connor, for a long time now a Mac/Old English guru, and I dared use it—and we told no one!

My last year there, we got a room full of IBM PCs—Jrs, I believe, although not with the chicklet keyboards. What I do remember was getting all kinds of disk reading error messages our first day or two, and then finding out that the problem was that the monitors, too heavy for the computer cases, were weighting down on the floppy drives. Anyone with any sense would have started selling IBM SHORT that same day!

When I interviewed for the position here at UA (early 1985) I spoke with the Dean about getting a similar facility here, and when I arrived that fall I was given a small room in the basement of the library with 20 real IBM PCs and a 3Com network, which no one knew much about. My interest was basically in giving all students the ease of word processing in writing college essays. I was not terribly attracted then to arguments about the inner- or inherent value of computer-based writing. It was obvious to me that word processing was an incredibly more efficient means of managing texts compared to typing or handwriting and thus was going to replace typing regardless of anything else, much like talking pictures replaced silent ones and color TVs replaced black-and-white models.

Practically all my major thinking about computers originated that fall, especially the one driving force in everything I have done since: the commitment to involve ALL students, and thus to configure what we were going to do with computers around the basic assumption that it would have to be something EVERYONE could do. Here was a transformative new technology that made a basic, and at times onerous, task of all college students (typing) much easier, so I was determined to make it accessible to all students by making it part of the one university-required course: first-year composition. Considering I had only a single lab—and that we had record enrollments in the next few years, finally topping over 3000 first-year students—this was, in retrospect, recklessly bold and daring (or a little crazy).

The first consequence of this governing assumption was my decision to put a word processing program in every student's hand, with the idea that we would then give them some minimal training (in our small space) and send them on their way (to the great wide world) where they could find plenty of computers in which to use their new software.

This brought me into contact with ALL the cottage industry word processing developers of the mid-1980s (the places where the telephone receptionist is liable to yell, "Daddy, it's for you!"), including, of course, Scott Anderson of Ann Arbor Software. The story of our first telephone encounter has its own drama, since it turned out that Ann Arbor had just adopted a policy against sending out any examination copies of _Textra_ (the only developer on my list to do so). My explanation—that I was considering a university-wide adoption (the kind of thing book salespeople fly in editors from New York to secure)—had absolutely no effect—a pretty good sign then of the vast distance between software developers and textbook companies, and an indication in its own way of why the two desperately needed each other to get anything accomplished in the college market.

In any case, as an impecunious new assistant professor with no budget for this project I passed on using my Visa card and paying the $19.95 or whatever it was at the time. It was only a month or two later, after experimenting with another intriguing product (_Zenword_) that I dug into my wallet and ordered my own copy of _Textra_ (version 3.1, I believe).

The involvement with Norton grew directly out of my working with Scott, and the enthusiastic response we had here from students, faculty, and administrators to putting software and documentation (the latter at Scott's insistence) directly in students' hands. Basically, I told Scott that what we were doing was working here in Tuscaloosa, and thus should work at other school across the country, but that to do anything we needed someone out in the field calling on schools, etc. i.e., a college textbook company. I also realized, in experimenting with the user-defined help system with _Textra_ in May of 1987, that information and advice about writing, the kind traditionally found in handbooks, could be put within the program ("online")—thus was born the "online handbook," something that further justified the purchase of software since, like a traditional handbook, here was something that students would buy once (in first-year English) and then use throughout their college careers.

Meanwhile, in the fall of 1987, I drafted letters to college English editors at all the major publishing houses, in the spirit of Samuel Johnson and the brewery, promising them riches beyond their wildest dreams. I believe I talked about the next Harbrace Handbook, the next Norton Anthology of English Literature, etc.

At WW Norton, this letter was directed to the late John Benedict, a thoroughly learned man with not the slightest interest in technology of any sort. (I only meet him once and got the impression that never was a file cabinet beyond his reach.) In any case, he passed the letter on to Barry Wade, who just happened to be looking for something software-related to help Norton get into the first-year writing market, where at the time they had almost no presence.

That fall I met with Barry and Jim Jordan at SAMLA in Atlanta to start the process of putting together the deal. I was not involved in the next, all-important step—of getting Ann Arbor Software on board—but that too happened over the next month or so, and we were off and running, with Norton Textra Writer for the fall of 1987.

> 3. There are three focal points I'd like to have you start talking about for
> the period under consideration:
>
> A. The move from personal to interpersonal computing (maybe talk about where
> the revelation for Connect came from—the more details and specifics the
> better).

As I mentioned above, I had access to a network from the beginning but little support (and constant problems) and no network-aware software. As a result we used the network almost exclusively for printing.

At various stages I became aware of the fact that all this cabling running around the room could also be used for sharing files. But as anyone knows who first tries to do on his own, there is an immediate obstacle with files overwriting (a nice word for "erasing") each other—hence the need for complex, unwieldy file-naming conventions, something that I made tentative efforts at doing here (the first step in what I later learned Charles Moran did—and maybe still does—at U Mass in such a big way) but abandoned as hopeless. Again it goes back to my guiding belief in computing (in this case, word processing) as a tool for everyone, and hence my strict insistence on distinguishing kludges and workarounds that satisfy techies (indeed, that as in the case of MS-DOS itself that techies seem to delight in since it so separates them from everyone else) and the truly transparent nature of a well designed universal tool like a microwave oven or an autofocus 35mm camera.

File sharing was not going to work, at least not to my satisfaction, if we had to teach thousands of students a year the special UA function of each of the eleven spaces in a DOS filename.

There was another problem as well: When we were successful in downloading files—for example, directions—they would be on the screen telling students what to do to some other file (which obviously was not on the screen). The solution was obvious: to have students print out the directions—an obvious solution but one that created more confusion than distributing directions on paper in the first place: that is, we were back to teacher handouts, back to square one.

There were other interim solutions. I tried distributing directions and other materials through an online help system (Rescue from Polaris) but ran into another major obstacle: keystroke incompatibility, along with general confusion by students as to which program they were in. _Rescue_, activated by a hot key would pop up over _Textra_ and provide students with information, directions, etc. But students were never certain just what program they were in, and, getting out of _Rescue_ required, not Textra's universal [Esc] key, but (of all unlikely keys) [F10]. Hence my determination that whatever we used would be seamlessly integrated into word processing. There is only time in freshmen English to teach students the single universal tool they need to write in college (or, if two tools, two tools working as one to a novice user).

This problem of two programs did not end there, especially as we started to experiment with email and brainstorming programs. First there was the idea sharing program _Brainstorm_ (a shareware program from Mustang Software). We bought a 24-user license and experimented. Although the files were limited to barely a single paragraph, what did us in was in inability to move text smoothly back and forth between the program and word processing. The import–export features were far from transparent—in other words, something only a techie could love, and I believe they the text itself was invariably hard ascii, a nightmare for word processing.

We had a similar experience with using _Pegasus Mail_: the program itself was easy enough for students but there was no easy way to move text in and out of word processing. Indeed, in some ways both _Pegasus_ and _Brainstorm_ were much better than word processing, especially in freeing students from filenames and all the headaches of trying to share files. But I could not see a way to make their use with word processing (at least the DOS-based word processing we were using at the time) fully transparent.

Here too the solution should have been obvious: build the best file-sharing features of _P-Mail_ and _Brainstorm_ into word processing—and this is what we eventually did with a prototype for _Connect_ we put together here, starting the spring of 1991.

In the Instructor's Manual to _Connect_ I describe the single insight, driving down to the Computers & Writing Conference in Biloxi, that triggered the whole thing: the unremarkable observation that using the macro function within Textra 6.0 I could split the screen and scroll the top screen (via a macro) without ever leaving the bottom one. Here was the basic word processing environment we needed for true file–sharing: reading directions or student work in the top window, writing in the bottom.

Obviously, a lot happened between that one insight an the commercial release of _Connect_ last January, but the basic structure of the program was all in place—especially its basis in word processing and its effort to replicate traditional classroom teacher–student and student–student interaction.

> B. The stuff that was going on at the U. of Alabama.

The one thing I might add here is that networks were becoming ubiquitous, and hence students had fewer and fewer occasions to load the software themselves from disk, and thus, at least for campus use, less reason to purchase their own software. Indeed there was a year or two transition period between Norton Textra 2.1 and Connect when we were not a particularly good campus customer for W.W. Norton.

> C. Your experience in working with a publisher (as lots of C&W folk did and do:
> Wresch, Schwartz, Burns, you then and now, and me, now).

From the beginning we have had a great three-way relationship between myself, Ann Arbor Software, and WW Norton. With Norton one gets all the benefits, and a few of the liabilities, of a small, employee-managed company—including, most important of all, incredible loyalty to people and solid, unswerving commitment to whatever it undertakes. Norton is an old-fashioned company where the editors, not the accountants and financial vps, are in charge. Until his death in the spring of 1993, I might add, all my dealings at Norton were with a truly gifted and compassionate man, Barry Wade.

Much the same applies to Ann Arbor Software, a considerably smaller operation, but one with its own, incredibly high, standards.

Software development, as you know, is incredibly expensive and fraught with false alleys, from which even the biggest companies at times have trouble extricating themselves. Our success so far, I believe, is due less to the two great gods of software development—luck and deep pockets—than to solid, low-keyed but highly professional, meticulous way that both WW Norton and Ann Arbor Software approach everything they do.

> Date sent:　Sun, 23 Oct 94 22:31:01 -0400
> From:　　　"Paul LeBlanc" <leblancp@hmco.com>
> To:　　　　"Myron Tuman" <mtuman@english.as.ua.edu>
> Subject:　RE: my response
>
>
> Myron,
>
> What a great response to my questions. You've given me most of what I need
> already, but just a couple of follow ups, if you'll bear with me.
> First, you describe your struggles with networking and file sharing and so on.
> Who was helping you in all of this at UA? How did your colleagues view your
> work? Were you tenured by then? How did the techies at UA view your efforts?
> Many of the narratives are interesting for the way they capture quite often
> ambivalent or even hostile climates for the work people were doing.

I came to UA as an untenured associate professor and had my first book, _A Preface to Literacy_, accepted after I arrived, an act that essentially assured my tenure. In this regard I was under little professional pressure. Indeed, our department has a history of considerable professional tolerance in the area of r&c—perhaps more so than I would grant myself—in recognizing and rewarding the publication of textbooks and other pedagogical tools, in my case software. Indeed, while much of my visibility and notoriety on campus continues to derive from my practical work with software (including being honored as outstanding university professor in 1993), I continue to see my most important professional work in literacy theory—work that ironically often raises substantial questions about the value of computer-mediated writing.

There is one aspect of UA, however, that is particularly relevant to what I have been able to accomplish. As a large state university with a large grad program, all first-year comp sections are taught by temporary instructors of one sort or another, mostly GTAs and visiting instructors. Just as important, we train over half of these people each year. The result is that I have absolutely no institutional resistance from the people teaching the classes.

> Second, could you comment on how you've seen your work in the context of the C&W

> community? This book is about that emergence and growth of that field and I'd

> like your take on it and its relatedness to your work at UA.

I have always tended to define my academic work—in Victorian literature, in literacy theory, and now in C&W—as rigorously independent, almost iconoclastic (I guess just short of blindly oppositional). As I stated earlier, I was motivated from the start with regard to C&W by two deep commitments, each of which tended to move me in what seemed to be a largely different direction from that of the profession as a whole (at least how I perceived it at numerous C&W meetings and articles, etc.): one was the commitment to reach all students from the very beginning, and the other was the belief, based on my work in literacy theory, in the formal properties of texts (a belief that posits some fundamental, albeit not fashionable, differences between literate exchange and ordinary communication).

Taken together, these two commitments moved me away from casual, real-time exchange as the dominant model of the new classroom, and left me wedded to certain essential characteristics of traditional writing assignments, such as the sharing and revision of papers.

As to the influence of my work, it is largely, I assume, still in the future, and quite likely more from the pedagogic assumptions about asynchronous revision built into _Connect_ than from my theoretical work on literacy theory.

Myron Tuman (mtuman@english.as.ua.edu) Director, English Computer Lab, University of Alabama

AFTERWORD

"This field of computers and composition," we have said (among ourselves and to others) "is a young field, a nascent discipline, an emerging speciality. It has been around only a few short years, just barely more than a decade." "Teachers are just now beginning to learn what computers can do." "Members of this community are only starting to recognize the more complicated implications of technology use in classrooms; as a community, we have so little history to learn from." These are some of the words that motivated this book. They seemed true when we began in 1990; they seem less true now.

When we began this project, the task of documenting the history of computers and composition studies seemed relatively straightforward and nicely focused—a small field, with many familiar landmarks and inhabitants, less than 15 years old. As authors, we believed that gathering historical information would provide a relief from the analyses we usually engaged in— studies of current issues that changed their shape so rapidly they made us dizzy. History seemed somehow more stable and less tricky, better documented and less subjective, more accessible and less volatile than the kind of work computers and composition specialists generally engaged in.

However, we soon learned that history was also maddeningly elusive. The more artifacts we gathered as descriptive of a certain period in computers and composition studies, the less substantial seemed the results and the larger loomed the gap between what happened and

It is the mark of educated teachers of English composition to ask themselves constantly, "Why do we teach what we teach? What aspects of English composition are more important than others? Why do we think they are more important?" Many teachers of English composition could not answer these questions very well because (1) they have never asked them of themselves, and (2) even if they have asked them, they lack the historical knowledge necessary for significant answers. (Stewart, 1984, p. ix)

How writing was to be taught, and specifically how letter-writing was to be learned, relate closely to the functions of writing across the eighteenth and nineteenth centuries. Because the teaching of writing in schools before the mid-nineteenth century was largely confined to copying simple exercises of phrases and sentences and reciting grammar rules, the general opinion was that practical letter-writing could not be learned in school. Instead it was learned from manuals of letter-writing, self-discipline in reading, practicing writing, and corresponding with those who would criticize one's style and point out errors. (Heath, 1981, p. 32)

There has been very little systematic exploration of the history of the teaching of English, though there are a few very useful beginnings. Much of the material is relatively inaccessible, in doctoral dissertations and out-of-print reports. This has meant, inevitably, that each discussion has had to begin without any assumptions of prior knowledge. I hope this book will change that, reducing the need for each writer to recapitulate the universe. There is much to learn: I offer the book confident that it is accurate in its general tenor and emphasis and equally sure that it must be wrong in some of its detail. (Applebee, 1974, p. xi)

Composition studies is both the oldest and the newest of the humanities, and our gradual realization of this dual nature is probably the reason for the growing importance of historical study in composition. Traditionally melioristic and oriented toward a beckoning future, composition scholars are realizing that the future can most fruitfully be studied with a knowledge of more than a century's experience in teaching and studying writing. We may not always be able to claim that we see for because we stand on the shoulders of giants;

what our stories told about what happened. It became clear to us that neither artifacts nor the stories that surrounded them would ever represent the whole of the time period adequately. They would never form a fully textured fabric. History, in other words, could never be as rich and full as life.

This should not have surprised us. Hayden White (1978), James Berlin (1987a), and Howard Zinn (1970) have noted that historians should never undertake a project thinking that they can tell the whole story of history, or even believing that they can tell historical stories objectively. Rather, these scholars remind us, the study and the recreation of history is always incomplete, and there are always interests at stake (e.g., historians' interests, a community's interests, cultural interests, etc.) that help shape the partial nature of the particular histories that scholars collect. In this sense, the project of writing a history is as much a project of understanding the *here-and-now*, the *what-may-be-happening-and-why*, as it is of understanding the *then*. Zinn (1970) wrote:

To be "objective" in writing history, for example, is as pointless as trying to draw a map which shows everything—or even samples of everything—on a piece of terrain. No map can show all of the elements in that terrain, nor should it if it is to serve efficiently a present purpose, to take us toward some goal. Therefore, different maps are constructed, depending on the aim of the mapmaker. Each map, including what is essential to its purpose, excluding the irrelevent, can be accused of "partiality." But it is exactly in being partial that it is most true to its particular present job. A map fails us not when it is untrue to the abstract universal of total inclusiveness, but when it is untrue to the only realm in which truth has meaning—some present human need. (p. 10–11)

What we have relearned as we wrote, by looking through the historical lenses that we chose, is how political, social, and cultural articulations have influenced, and continue to influence, the ways in which computer technology is used within our educational system and within the classrooms of English and English composition teachers. However, even this knowledge is partial. The complexities of the stories, the histories, make it almost impossible to draw specific lessons, make specific predictions, or take particular action in one direction or another. The nature of what we have learned instead suggests that, informed by the stories of history and our own unfolding understanding of the world in which we operate, we are already making different kinds of decisions about technology, thinking in different and subtle ways about computers, seeing our field from different perspectives—moment by moment, day by day, on all sorts of levels—even as we write history, history is writing us.

What this means—in terms of the statements that opened this section—is that computers and composition, although it is a relatively young field, is, nonetheless, already informed by a lengthy and complex history; already located in rich and influential patterns of historical developments in education, composition studies, and the computer industry; already *old* in terms of cultural influences and relationships. In this sense, the project of rediscovering history is never a new undertaking, and, importantly, it is one that is never finished.

In light of this last realization, we close this book with two additional perspectives to be added to those we have offered in the preceding chapters. First, we offer a few thoughts that came to us as we gave this manuscript a final reading. These suggest some of the ways in

we do, however, stand on the shoulders of thousands of good-willed teachers and writers surprisingly like us, who faced in 1870 or 1930 problems amazingly similar to those we confront each time we enter the classroom. Listening carefully, those of us who have begun to try to hear their voices have found much there we can learn from. Impatient dismissal of the past was a hallmark of our field's early years, and as we mature as a discipline, we will need to draw more and more deeply on the experience of the teachers who came before us. (Connors, 1991, p. 49)

The fact that our age is alert to the possible consequences of a communications revolution featuring television and computers has made us all the more interested in understanding earlier transformations. The fashionable formulations of Marshall McLuhan have become the subject of serious research. Presses have poured forth books and articles whose central purpose is to determine how many people were literate in past societies, how they acquired their literacy, and what difference it made. (Kaestle, 1988, p. 95)

which the lessons of history have been filtered through our understanding of the present and are serving to construct our expectations for the future—ways in which history has written us, shaped our understanding of who we are, and composed our sense of where we may be going. In the last section, we offer a glimpse into the future, a synchronous, online conversation with a small group of the best and brightest new scholars of the computers and composition community—the voices of the future informed by history as we now live it.

The collection of oral evidence can make a number of important contributions to composition historiography. In general, I am proposing the use of oral data not as an alternative to documentary evidence but as a coordinate type of evidence, one that has a lengthy history but whose reliability now must be defended against an obsolete positivism. Although composition historians for the most part have rejected positivistic notions of historical "truth" in their explicit statements about historiography, we (for I am one of them) have allowed our histories to reinforce such notions implicitly. While I cannot prove that our failure to employ oral interviews has promoted positivism in our histories, I do suggest that our almost exclusive reliance on written documents as evidence has at least contributed to it—and that a use of oral interviews could help us to avoid it. (Nelms, 1992, p. 357)

PERSPECTIVES OF THE AUTHORS AFTER READING THIS MANUSCRIPT

About computers and composition specialists:

• Computers and composition specialists have seen themselves—alternately, and sometimes, simultaneously—as the chosen people and as a marginalized group. As a community of specialists, we have sometimes voiced the belief that our connection with computers makes us special: gives us insight, perspectives, expertise that others don't have. We have also said that what we do is not always appropriately valued by our parent group, "Composition Studies," and by its parent group, "English Studies." Perhaps both statements are true. In writing this book, the authors have sometimes felt energized by specialized knowledge and by the excitement of being on the cutting edge of a particular area of composition studies. We have also, sometimes, felt marginalized and moved to complain. A critical perspective on our situation, however, forces us to see that we, and many of the teacher/scholars we have focused on in this volume, occupy full-time, tenured and tenure-track faculty positions at respected institutions. In such positions we can hardly be considered marginalized. When we see our positions relative to those of part-time teachers and teaching assistants in the field of composition studies, we recognize that we occupy positions of privilege in today's field of postsecondary teaching.

- In one sense, computers and composition studies, as a subfield, has *followed* its parent field, composition studies. We've moved from computer support for process-based composing to computer support for feminist and critical pedagogy—as composition theory has changed its teaching values, so has computers and composition studies. Not only has the field reflected the prevailing theory, but individuals within the field have reflected this theory and have reviewed and often changed their stances on important issues connected with technology. Some consider it blowing with the prevailing intellectual winds; others consider it intellectual growth and change. We suspect it has elements of both—and more.

- In another sense, computers and composition, as a subfield, has also *led* its parent field of composition studies. Serving the function of Hermes, the messenger, individuals in this field have brought news of emerging technologies to colleagues and have sometimes changed the ways that other scholars think about teaching and presenting instructional material, altered the way that they think about literacy issues and issues in composition studies, and modified their understanding of theory and practice.

There are dangers in leading, just as there are in following. The first danger is that we may spend our lives trying to stay up with new technologies as they emerge, a task that may distract us from more important matters such as improving our teaching, working closely with students, and changing our educational

The advent of composition studies needs to be understood less as a local weather disturbance in departments of English and more as part of a fundamental climate change involving the evolution of general epistemologies animating thought about discourse. (Nystrand et al., 1993, p. 273)

Traditionally defined by others in terms of what it is not and, until recently, most often regulated by those not conversant in either its research methodologies or its pedagogical values, composition studies remains an academic borderland with a fractured history, an intellectual arena in which different traditions, languages, sets of practice, and political values compete daily for the attention and the loyalty (often expressed as continued enrollments) of hundreds, and often thousands, of undergraduates on every campus in this country. Despite recent efforts in the academy to ascribe to it a syncretic, suturing function, composition is still widely perceived as a wound between two domains, a laceration whose edges touch literary criticism and rhetoric—historically marginal to the intellectual interests of both and yet currently central to the institutional needs of each. (McQuade, 1992, p. 482)

Literacy seems to have as many definitions these days as there are people to define the word. At the MLA's landmark Right to Literacy Conference in 1988, much of the debate focused on distinctions between functional literacy, cultural literacy, critical literacy, and public literacy, to name but a few robust varieties (Luns-ford, Moglen, and Slevin). Why stretch the term still further to include some hybrid electronic species? One reason, amply argued in this book, is that computers are altering the way many of us read, write, and even think. It is not simply that the tools of literacy have changed; the nature of texts, of language, of literacy itself is undergoing crucial transformations. (Costanzo, 1994, p. 11)

What hasn't changed is the feeling of being on a frontier. The conference has always been run by people actively engaged in computers and writing in their classrooms and in their research. It has always emphasized cutting edge pedagogy and technology. Whatever our differences, we have all assumed that computers enrich our students' learning and our own professional lives, and we are enthusiastic about he future. What hasn't changed is the energy and optimism of this conference: we are always looking forward: every program from 1984 on is sprinkled with words like *Beyond, toward, future, new, innovation,* and *prospects.* We have also retained our joy in adventure: we speak of "the fringes of the frontier"

system for the better. The second danger is that our colleagues will become tired of hearing us sing the praises of yet another new technology that we now recognize can never result in fundamental improvements in the problems teachers face every day—racism; sexism; ageism; systemic bias against individuals for their sexual orientation, their disability, or their socioeconomic status.

• Our field has served, at least in part, the function of a support group for teachers of writing. To this extent, the field of computers and composition studies has been successful because of the people active within that community: people of energy and character who have been individually and collectively generative, who have drawn others into their work, who have drawn others' work into theirs, who have welcomed others into an intellectual collaboration. We recognize a possible danger, as the field ages, of its changing character in this sense—continuing, but becoming larger and more heavily bureaucratized, less welcoming and supportive to individual teachers.

About teachers and technology

• Computers have come into writing classrooms, in part, because teachers of writing wanted them there. To some extent—and even as we acknowledge the many cultural, social, and economic factors that influence computer use—teachers of writing have been active and effective in determining their own uses of computers. This observation reminds us that, for better and worse, teachers are agents who, as a regular part of their professional and personal lives, make informed decisions about the contexts within which they work and act on those decisions—even within those systems that seem the most overdetermined.

• People often see new technologies through the lens of their own hopes and dreams. Hence, what people say about technology reveals a great deal about their values and worlds. The prison administrator sees in high-tech the possibility of cheap incarceration; the academic administrator faced with declining budgets sees the possibility of cheap instructional delivery; the science teacher sees the possibility of simulated, and therefore not dangerous, lab experiments; the auto manufacturer sees an engine-management system that will permit the vehicle to meet antipollution standards; the writing teacher who feels the need to control her students sees the computer as a means to that end.

About history as a set of incomplete, partial, situated stories:

• The stories teachers tell of their own lives—personal and professional—during the years we have covered in this book, are in effect their "computer literacy autobiographies." These biographies may be most interesting because they have been collected during a cultural period when computers were new and strange to teachers of writing. The stories focus on a cultural phenomenon; their tellers notice and describe what it was that went on around computers, what we thought of them, how we understood them. As computers become increasingly ubiqitous, invisible to our eyes, naturalized within educational contexts, such stories may never again be quite so rich or complex. Individuals telling stories in the coming years may be so immersed in electronic technologies that they no longer see what is new and strange about these machines. This situation may represent a loss of perspective that is hard to recapture.

and "the shape of text to come," "sharing the fantasy," "breaking frames," and "riding the beast." And no doubt we'll keep on finding new "frontiers" to cross. (Gerrard, in press)

Ten years ago the promise of computer-assisted instruction in English appeared to lie in using word processing in order to get away from the limitations of formulaic drill and practice. So we pioneered with our clunky line editors on our cumbersome mainframes, and we soon were looking toward a third generation of CAI, envisioning even more promise within integrated software packages, those programs that could support writers throughout various stages of the writing process. That era produced style analyzers and revision prompting programs that drew attention to certain features of the writers' text. At the head of the pack of these computer-text analyzers was WRITER'S WORKBENCH. (Kaler, 1995, in press)

In the mechanical age now receding, many actions could be taken without too much concern. Slow movement insured that the reactions were delayed for considerable periods of time. Today the action and the re-action occur almost at the same time. We actually live mythically and integrally, as it were, but we continue to think in the old, fragmented space and time patterns of the pre-electric age. (McLuhan, 1964. p. 20)

Many educators have dreamed of making instruction both productive and enriching; wishing that children somehow could learn more and faster while teachers taught less. In any list of explanations for the errant passion for technology by educators (but not necessarily teachers), a solid candidate would be this dream of increasing productivity, that is, students acquiring more information with the same or even less teacher effort. This dream has persisted from the invention of the lecture centuries ago to the early decades of this century when reformers sought efficiency through film, radio, and television. The dream persists into the 1980s with promoters boosting desk-top computers for each student. In the insistent quest for increased productivity and efficiency, the lecture, film, radio, television, and microcomputer are first cousins. (Cuban, 1986, p. 3)

Women's intellectual creativity has been consistently dismissed through the years, their ideas assuming importance only when they are attributed to men. Because of this history and because we have no reason to assume that women's words will have a higher status on the Internet than they have had in conversations and publications, we have a special concern for women's electronic words. (Kramarae & Kramer, 1995, p. 35)

• The history we have told is as it is, in part, because we are teachers of composition, teachers of the act of composing in language—an activity not always considered a subject in the same way that American Literature, Organic Chemistry, or Calculus is. Teachers of history, chemistry, or literature might connect with computers in a very different way—perhaps understanding computers not so much as tools to build with but as instructional delivery systems. This realization also points to the fact that there are many other stories to be written, many other histories to be compiled, of the ways in which computers have come into related fields—K–12 education, journalism, publishing, the lives of professional writers.

About technology in schools and classrooms:

• With a few exceptions, schools and colleges are poorly equipped with new and emerging technologies; yet in the current zero-sum world of educational budgets, it is hard to justify spending funds on technology when we know that such a move might result in fewer teachers, larger classes, less money for professional development, and more difficult situations for students and teachers. Technology is not always the answer, not always the best choice.

• Technology (and access to technology) is not evenly distributed in schools, and it never has been—not in this country, not anywhere else. The differential distribution of technology (and access to technology) is clearly driven—among other factors—by race, gender, socioeconomic status, age, and cultural factors. It is time to do a better job.

OUR COLLEAGUES INTERACT ON A MOO

Locke waves

beckster waves

beckster says, "howdy. Just got a note from johndan . . . .at least he and eric will be here"

beckster says, "don't know about pam and mary, though—darn!"

Locke says, "good"

Locke says, "er.. about j and e"

beckster grins . . . .figured that

Locke says, "so what can I do to help? stay out of your way?"

Marsha's_Guest materializes out of thin air.

beckster says, "I wonder . . . ..if pam and mary DON't show up . . . ..if you should pitch in, too?"

Johndan materializes out of thin air.

beckster waves to johndan and . . . .??

Locke waves

Johndan waves

Marsha's_Guest says, "Hi, this is Pam, known as 'Marsha's Guest' (?)"

Johndan says, ""Hi Pam."

beckster says, "Great, pam! Glad you could make it"

eric materializes out of thin air.

Johndan waves multiply

Locke waves

beckster waves

eric waves at all the wavers

eric says, "love the ascii-art room desc beck. You do that?"

Johndan says, "woops. I don't do this much. Is all the waving normal?"

pam materializes out of thin air.

Johndan says, "You have identity, Pam""

Locke (Locke-Robster) floats over pam, casting handfuls of glittery stardust all over pam's face.

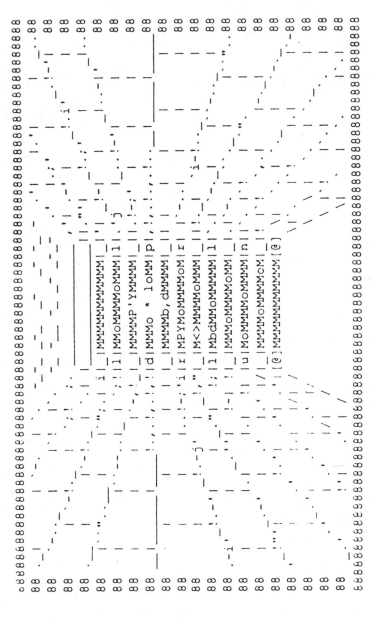

Obvious exits: east to Locke's Office and down to Barney's Place
Shiva (irritable) and Locke (Locke-Robster) are here.

beckster applauds the real pam

pam says, "I didn't realize it was so easy to have identity!"

Locke says, "'round here it is"

Johndan says, "The interface is easy. The hardware's expensive""

eric says, "school starts wednesday, but I have to do an all-day work-shop tomorrow for teachers about to stick their heads in the first computer classrooms at MU available to writing classes (previously math had a monopoly on all computer class-rooms)"

Johndan says, "Eric—I know how you feel. I got to spend a whop-ping hour in the lab. math was playing Monopoly probably (charging rent for Park Place, etc.)

beckster is glad the writing teachers have broken the monopoly!

mday materializes out of thin air.

beckster waves to mday

pamT says, "Is mday mary?"

mday hugs all

beckster says, "ok—many of us have been reading ACW and remi-niscing about how we all got into the field. Let's begin with that—how did you get involved in the C&W field?"

Johndan says, "Cindy Selfe made me. (I was a copy editor for C&C as an undergrad.)"

eric got entangled in mbu

pamT says, "talk about identity, Johndan. Woa."

Johndan says, "Both connotations seem to work, too."

mday was using Joe Williams' _Style_ book and got asked to com-puterize it. And I wanted to. Students were having trouble re-vising on paper instead of with a word processor.

beckster says, "I got into it when, in the midst of preparing to do my thesis on wordsworth, my WP director TOLD me to do my thesis on computers and writing . . . .so we conducted a pilot study at Ohio State, with the first ever writing classes who met in and used a computer lab"

eric says, "how'd that happen, mday? how'd the opportunity come along to computerize Style?"

Locke was doing a lot of programming and hanging around Fred Kemp at UT, then had a class with Hugh Burns, and then got hooked

mday says, "then the UC Berkeley Instructional Technology Program got wind of what I was doing and offered me a job."

You hear an electrical sizzling sound; pamT has disconnected.

eric says, "pooor pam!"

mday says, "Oh, we were required to use the _Style_ book. And Joe
  Williams wrote to Seymour Chatman, my advisor, asking if he
  could find someone to computerize the exercises in _Style_."
beckster says, "this was Frank O'Hare, strangely enough . . . ..I did
  an ERIC search, and found all sorts of stuff on word processing (from Cindy Selfe, Dawn Rodrigues, Lillian Bridwell,
  Colleen Daiute and other stuff like SEEN from helen schwartz,
  stuff by Hugh Burns, bill wresch . . . .there was a lot out there
  even then (1984–5)"
Johndan tells his daughter that he's working and to go watch tv. She
  barks at him.
beckster barks at johndan
Johndan says, "I'll pass on the message."
mday says, "My Berkeley job was to research the C & W field so that
  I could be a resource person for writing teachers at Berkeley.
  Of course that led me to Biloxi in 1991 and the whole C & W
  community. I loved the warm welcome I got, there and on
  MBU."
pamT has connected.
The housekeeper arrives to drop off Shiva, who is sound asleep.
pamT says, "The keyboard froze again. Any suggestions?"
beckster says, "Funny . . . .in my thesis, I remember stating there
  seemed to be two distinct threads: The word processors, and
  the CAI folks . . . ."
Locke [to pamT]: don't hit backspace, unless you can configure your
  terminal emulation
beckster nails pamt's foot to the floor
eric says, "sorry. had to go take care of a pee incident. Quincy decided to water the living room carpet. Sheesh"
mday got to subscribe to MBU, wcenter, WPA, purtopoi, newedu,
  IPCT, and a slew of Comserve lists as part of his job! I was a
  netmonitor (lizard).
Johndan says, "You mean you got paid to become part of the field"
beckster says, "locke got involved in computers first, then C&W—
  any of you do that?"
mday says, "Me?"
beckster says, "I was a writing teacher who was simply trying to: 1)
  be a better teacher, and 2) make my director happy . . . :)"
mday says, "paid as an RA, but also sent to conferences."
Johndan says, "I started out in computing (my minor as an undergrad). Then switched after doing C&C for a while."
mday says, "Beck, me too. That's why I really enjoyed doing it."

beckster says, "johndan, what did you say your first exp. w/ C&C was—with Cindy?"

Locke remembers the interview for his first teaching job out in Chico, CA, where they asked him if he saw any way for all the computer science he'd been taking to apply to the composition classroom. He said I don't really see how, unless we perfect Artificial Intelligence.

eric says, "I got into this stuff when nobody was looking. My bosses looked up one day and realized I was gone, sucked into the net, into C&W. It was too late by then"

beckster says, "and pamt . . . .did you do writing THEN computers? Or the other way around?"

Johndan says, "Yes. Cindy 'stole' me from another departmental journal, Reader, to do copyediting."

eric says, "only my feet were sticking out of the monitor . . . "

beckster smiles . . . Good for Cindy!!!

beckster says, "I can imagine it, eric . . . ..I often picture you in that position"

Locke says, "the two areas (computers and writing) were both interesting for me, but (like Reeses Pieces) they didn't come together until I'd been doing both separately for a while."

Johndan says, "That's it, Locke—early on, it was hard to see beyond word processing and better grammar checkers."

eric says, "I know what you mean, Locke, and when they come together it's suddenly hard to image they could possibly be separate"

mday has to go very shortly. Any other questions?

beckster says, "I was doing writing, and learned about C&W as I was TEACHING it and doing it (writing thesis on a WANG). "

mday agrees with ERic and Locke

Locke [to eric]: it was the explosion of connectivity that made it all possible, not really computing power. the LAN (for sharing printers and other resources) really did it, I think

Johndan says, "beckster—weren't those the machines that ran on coal?"

pamT says, "I took a class with Helen Schwartz on a very strong recommendation from a friend. At the time, I had never touched a computer."

beckster says, "OK, when you finally got the peanut butter and the chocolate together, did you see it as a fluke? As a field?

eric says, "I like to quote something Trent said on mbu once. so long ago I no longer know if it's even an accurate paraphrase, but basically: computers & networks are a fad like the automobile was a fad"

Johndan says, "I remember those nets—we used to do asynch conferences by passing a disk around the room."

beckster says, "I thought of it as a field from the beginning, simply because I could do an ERIC search on it!!"

Locke [to beckster]: I took a bite of the choco-peanut butter and liked it —I didn't start thinking of it as a field until I went to the Minnesota C&W

mday says, "One becoming increasingly acceptable, at least in composition circles . . . "

pamT says, "i guess I always thought of it as a field, since my first intro was a seminar in it, but i never saw myself getting involved in it. Now, five years later . . . "

beckster [to Locke]: true. When I heard of/went to Minnesota, I thought we were big time—and I'd recalled hearing several presentations on C&W at 4C's before then, too

mday says, "One even as we speak developing a beaurocracy with dues, a central power base (Trent), a newsletter, many regional satellites, a journal, a conference . . . "

Locke [to eric]: I agree. I think we embraced computers, connectivity, and constructionism because they were natural tools for what we wanted to do. It's impossible to imagine things being any other way, and we can't go back.

beckster [to mday]: does that make us "real?" what do y'all think?

eric says, "speaking of mainstream and all: one thing I wonder about is the extent to which the field can get all legitimate & whatnot AND keep pushing at boundaries. Trent asked on ACW-L (to paraphrase) whether the field would succumb to all the usual forces of power once it gets a little. does that mean conservatism to follow shortly?"

Johndan says, "But what made connectivity 'natural'?"

pamT says, "the community making us real makes me nervous. This is something I've been thinking about—the separatism between us and composition"

mday believes it does, but unfortunately being real means being able to exclude, in these times. It is a power thing.

beckster says, "yep, eric, I wonder if we'll lose some of that collaborative/explorer/community feel . . . .and suddenly be struck down with hierarchy"

Locke [to Johndan]: we were all completely bought in to the idea of peer-work, mostly

beckster nods to pamt—go on!

Locke [to Johndan]: and the computer-based connectivity was an easy extension of that model — no extra brain power involved to move into it

mday says, "yes, conservatism, bureaucracy, tradition, rules, both written and unwritten."

mday must go before he is drawn and quartered IRL.

mday waves

Locke waves

You hear an electrical sizzling sound; mday has disconnected.

beckster says, "I must say that in Minnesota, I was introduced to cindy selfe, who was welcoming, inviting, etc . . . ..but everyone kept talking about things like "MBU"—and I had no CLUE what that WAS, and no one took much time to explain. I think it's even worse now"

pamT says, "I mean, there are people writing in computers and composition and its specialized but along with that comes separate space which it doesn't seem to me many mainstream comp people enter"

Johndan says, "And this jargon will get worse, I think, as we push at the edges."

eric says, "but I'm hoping, beck, that we can *insist* upon innovation and collegiality as primary traits. I move that we write that into the constitution. anyone second?"

Locke met robert royer in Minnesota, and he was the biggest name I knew of. We hit it off great, since he's a computer-geek doing composition, too.

pamT says, "How do you insist on collegiality? "

Johndan says, "But isn't part of being a discourse community learning the discourse?"

Locke produces a red pen and threatens to veto any charter that doesn't include collegiality

Johndan says, "I think eric means insist on it in ourselves. Or, we could punch people who aren't collegial."

beckster says, "I wish it could stay that way, but I worry, too. I remember the C&W in Ann Arbor . . . .I was FURIOUS that this ACW we kept hearing was having meetings that only a select few—all the big names—could attend. I felt very left out, and wondered about the budding hierarchy"

pamT says, "I agree, Johndan, but that's also part of boundary building. Jargon works both ways—to establish borders which keep people in and also keep others out"

Johndan says, "Right, Pam. But do you see a movement to keep C&W from being overspecialized?"

eric says, "that's it, johndan. I mean, here in this virtual room are people who will (if we can manage it) have a say in how the field continues to develop. We insist on it!"

Locke sees the C&W "field" spinning apart pretty soon

Johndan says, "My god. We're supposed to be role models?"

beckster says, "BUT I have found much collegiality from those "on my level"—grad students/young professors starting out in the field. THat's what amazed me . . . .the support I found among folks I was competing with for JOBS! But only in this field"

eric says, "and if we have to punch people, well . . . virtual punches don't hurt too bad ;-)"

beckster insists on johndan being a role model

pamT says, "I fear, however, that collegiality is something that will characterize early interactions, but as a field grows, this is something that goes, because academia itself is so based in an agonistic, argumentative model"

beckster says, "did any of y'all have negative experiences either just starting out, or even more recently?"

Johndan says, "Right— saying something worth publishing academically often requires saying what someone else did wrong."

Locke [to beckster]: horrible politics at Texas, coming from the English Department

beckster [to pamT]: do you see a competitiveness here? Or the possibility of one developing?

The housekeeper arrives to cart mday off to bed.

eric says, "pam: I'm hoping we can influence the shape of the academy, too. I refuse to believe that it can't be helped"

eric ← willfully naive

beckster nods to locke . . . yet look what came of it! No thanks to them

beckster ← just naive

Locke ← naively willful

beckster says, "really, locke? do you think you'd have bonded so closely, done as much if you weren't in an adverse position?"

Johndan Beck—but doesn't that tend towards the position of trial by fire?

beckster says, "I hear rumblings of competitiveness, and that scares me . . . .but I still see a support system here among netcolleagues unlike any other"

Locke [to beckster]: hard to say. I think bureaucracy would have had the same effect as adversity, probably.

eric says, "good point, johndan: the conventional rhetorical stance in academic conversations is confrontational—but network en-

Paradox ⚡

vironments have the *potential* to dislodge that default stance, eh? "

Johndan says, "Yes, Eric. It's hard to sustain an attack here. But certainly not impossible . . . ."

eric thinks folks should learn to love paradoxes: the coexistence of ⚡ contention and collegiality, etc

beckster says, "yes, johndan. But the fact that C&W is a marginalized field makes us react by forming bonds, being colleagial. Eric, you've got a double whammy—WC AND C&W—do you see that happening?"

Johndan says, "Does anyone worry about the economics of information forcing us to compete to get networks? To get library access? Email? Do we already?"

eric says, "yeah, johndan. network environments *can* be used to extend print-based cultural conventions. but I put my hope on that one word: potential. there is the *chance* that the network opens a window of opportunity to shake things up in productive ways"

beckster [to Johndan]: perhaps. But aren't we driven by other things too? Like, we *enjoy* this?

Johndan says, "I see the potential too. I guess that's why we need to not only talk"

beckster says, "and, uh, yeah, what eric said. It's productive . . . .for us and for our students. But I can see it being a status thing, too, which is a bit frightening"

Johndan says, "Enjoy? Of course. But what about everyone else?"

eric says, "sure, johndan (re: competing for resources), but geez, it seems like we all would benefit from widely distributed resources. that's a position we can choose to take, anyway"

Johndan says, "But eric—as information becomes more commodified, not everyone will want to have it public."

pamT says, "although they are widely distributed, they are available to those with computers, remember."

beckster says, "a big rift between haves and have nots?"

beckster nods to pamt. probably need to modify our thinking/the question

Locke says, "either a rift, or something controlled by the info-providers like telephone service, so that everyone has access to 99 channels of e-shopping, etc. "

beckster says, "you know, just the fact that we're dealing with/thinking about issues like that makes us different, at least from the folks I read for my thesis."

eric says, "I was intrigued by paul's comment about the obsolescence of C&W, too. yes & no, I'd guess. C&W *as we know it* will fade away fairly soon, but I think R&T (rhetoric & technology) has a longer life ahead of it. Much broader & more nimble, I think (or hope)"

Johndan says, "Eric—I like that, 'R&T'."

Locke thinks that what we really have that's unique is the constructionism approach right now. And that's not really the direction the information InfoBahn is going, it seems.

pamT says, "Don't you see the rift between R&T as you put it and R alone to be a problem, eric?"

Locke agrees with Eric

beckster says, "boy, eric, you've been to different schools than I have. I think it'll be a long time before c&w will be obsolete . . . .simply because writing programs get the trickle down, and many are just now getting labs"

eric says, "I never know what to think about that, johndan. commodification also spreads technologies. or *can* anyway. look at tv. at telephone. well, they aren't directly comparable technologies, maybe, but it's possible that the commercialization of the net will not be the nightmare of exclusivity we fear"

beckster likes R&T, too

Locke sees rhetoricians applying their skills to all sorts of 'texts' — the computer revolution is what makes that flexibility possible, I think.

pamT says, "What I guess I'm thinking about is the resistance I still sense from a lot of comp people—for example, the Miami conference this last year was on directions of for comp in the 21st century or something like that—and no computer papers."

Johndan says, "But Tv is still one-way; will 500-channel tv be multidirectional?"

Locke [to Johndan]: unlikely

Johndan says, "Like Locke, I see the infobahn as potentially a very big shopping mall."

beckster [to pamT]: but papers on how rhetoric will change?

Locke [to Johndan]: unlikely, at least to the degree that we're using technology this very instant. I think we'll be encouraged to vote for our favorite soap opera ending, etc.

eric says, "I know pam. you're right. so's beckster. there's still a lot of resistance out there. I get real impatient with it, but know that it's natural as can be and folks just won't be rushed . . . "

beckster says, "and we need to intertwine learning/ rhetoric/ technology in our studies, practice, theory"

Johndan says, "Most of do that, don't we?"

Locke thinks that what is really going to be the test for rhetoricians is whether we can deal with the larger bandwidth technology affords in 5–10 years, effectively bringing to an end this renaissance of writing on the net as it's replaced with visual and audio texts

beckster says, "do we? I wonder, johndan. Take this MOO . . . .I see it as something powerful. Yet so far, I've used it only as an extension of the traditional classroom—a larger InterChange. I think we need to re-think things a bit more before we've intertwined rhet and technology"

Johndan says, "I guess I think of InterChange as a combination of R & T."·

Locke [to eric]: yes. I think our "community" is doing the right thing in looking forward to non-linear texts, and documents that include movies and sound in addition to text. We can take up the task, or let speech communication, or art, or someone else.

eric says, "the question may be: will rhetoricians *deal* with the bandwidth explosion or mutate and *inhabit* it?"

pamT says, "Maybe we intertwine technology and rhetoric in smaller ways, though. If we expect big changes, don't we give tech too much power?"

Johndan says, "What's important is that we're doing all of this self-reflectively. And trying to teach our students to do the same."

Locke [to eric]: good question. I'd prefer to mold it

Johndan says, "Yes—I see MOOs as going beyond InterChange."

pamT says, "How, Johndan? How for students?"

beckster [to Locke]: I agree . . . .but I also worry that as we look forward, what happens to the teachers who aren't up with "the latest"

Johndan says, "Grade them on it. (joke)."

Johndan says, "Well, asking students to critique InterChange sessions is a form of helping them learn to look rhetorically at technology, no?"

Locke [to beckster]: I don't know. the university will either get up to speed or fall by the wayside on this one. I can't see hiring someone in 10 years who couldn't integrate these elements

beckster says, "I guess we need to trace our steps, or something—I'm not sure how we can explain what it is we're doing and why we're doing it to those not immersed in the techno-rhetorical culture"

Johndan says, "Or MOOs, or USENET groups, or whatever"

beckster [to Locke]: ah, but you're not doing the hiring . . . .:)

eric says, "this is always hard to articulate (unless you're Sandy Stone or Donna Haraway) but I think we're slightly off the mark if we think about technology has having power over us, or us as having to control technology. As if tech and us were separate entities or forces. When really, we are it/ It are us. Technology is a fundamental characteristic of the human animal. Stuff like that"

pamT says, "Im not sure I see a lot of difference in students' use of MOO and InterChange (or mine, for that matter)—maybe because I don't use this alot (2 words, I know)."

Johndan says, "Technologies are articulations."

Locke [to eric]: I think that's basically right, mostly because we're into the constructionism that language provides, and not so much the object-oriented database that the MIT project (papert, etc) is studying

eric says, "beck: good question about the teachers and students who are "behind," but I think this community is trying like hell to help address that situation. That's a big reason for the ACW to exist, I think"

beckster says, "pamt, I think of Amy Bruckman's talk at C&W—the whole idea of this being a model for an epistemology: a *constructivist* epistemology that values BOTH the individual AND the community (and subcommunity). ONe that's constantly changing and BEING changed. InterChange is more like an e-chat"

pamT says, "The problem with being behind in this area is that often the bottom line is economic—you can want to be a part of the field, but if you can't get access to classrooms with computers, you are outside it."

eric says, "yes, johndan. I like that. "

beckster [to eric]: yes, I think some members of our community are trying to address that . . . .but I see an increasing rift—almost an annoyance—with folks who aren't up to speed

Johndan says, "This is where technology becomes difficult—if information is articulated as commodity, we'll (academic/ compositionists) will *always* be at the bottom."

Locke [to pamT]: they'll be handing us the computers in 10 years. I think what's more difficult is the kind and quality of technology we'll have in our classrooms at that point.

beckster [to Johndan]: and within our field, those w/ access and knowledge will be on the top o' the heap

pamT says, "exactly, Locke. And at this point, too."

eric says, "goooooood point, pam. but people within and without those under-technologized schools can only lobby and write proposals and whine and wheedle. That's what I do, anyway. change comes pretty unevenly. got to help it along all we can "

Locke [to pamT]: yes. we could all have Channel One in our class-rooms

beckster thinks we need more whiners and wheedlers like eric

Johndan says, "But are the computers we're getting going to be ten years out of date? With limited connectivity or m/media ac-cess?"

beckster [to Johndan]: undoubtedly!

pamT says, "lobbying and proposal writing take a lot of time and ef-fort, and once again, I think that time is often an unrecognized privilege. Compare research institution teaching loads with community college teaching loads. And community colleges are most likely the ones which don't have great tech.

eric says, "Johndan: we'll be at the bottom IF hierarchy is inevitably the dominant social structure. But what if lateral structures really and fully assert? What if we really take the shape of a web and there ain't no bottom? seems unlikely, but it's not impossible"

Johndan says, "I agree, Eric. I'm being pessimistic because I think it's not likely. But we can hope (and work)."

eric says, "we may need to start thinking differently about technol-ogy and pedagogical change. for example (lemme find a quote to lay on ya) . . . "

beckster says, "all kidding aside, it DOES make me feel pretty good to see folks like Eric, and greg, and others—mostly grad stu-dents—who are still not just trying to forge ahead themselves, but who are working for access for others"

Locke [to eric]: I think our task is to articulate the kinds of things we need to be doing with technology so as to make it clear that old word processors (or in 10 years, old internet connec-tions) won't cut it.

eric says, "this is Lewis Perelman referring to Peter Drucker who is commenting on why japanese businesses are often more nim-ble than US businesses . . . "The key to the more productive pace of R&D, as Drucker sees it, is that leading Japanese com-panies now have a deadline in place for *abandoning* a brand-new product the first day it is marketed."

beckster says, "I wonder if the grad students can *afford* to do that because they're not fighting for tenure? Yet there are folks like cindy and gail and fred and trent, too. "

beckster says, "wow, eric. *We're* obsolete!"

Johndan says, "True—and new faculty have the older faculty to help them as well."

eric says, "right on, Locke. We (we! compositionists, even) need to start looking a little farther ahead, maybe thinking in terms of being more assertive and innovative. why not be leaders, for chrissakes?"

Locke says, "Hear Hear!"

beckster says, "Lead on, Eric!"

eric says, "tenure is one thing I hope never to fight for. "

beckster thinks at this rate, eric has little to worry about

pamT says, "Tenure is an issue computers and composition specialists need to consider, I think. So much of what we do is not measurable by those standards."

Locke agrees with pam

beckster says, "pam has a good point. Is that changing?"

Johndan says, "Before I left New Mexico Tech, I got them to add moderating an email conference as worth points in the merit pay system."

beckster applauds johndan!

Locke cheers Johndan

pamT says, "good for you, Johndan. Was that a battle?"

Johndan says, "That's not the same as tenure, but it's a start."

eric says, "right, pam. Heck, so much of what any teacher does is not measurable by those standards. "

beckster says, "and Fred was able to use the Daedalus software as a publication in his tenure review"

Johndan says, "Not really. I think they understood it when I explained it. (Surprisingly.)"

Locke [to eric]: based on e-mail bytes, you can be the first to get tenure without even a tenure-track job!

eric says, "good show, johndan!"

Johndan says, "There was a lot of discussion, though, about paper-journal vs electronic journal publications."

beckster [to Johndan]: what was the outcome of that?

Johndan says, "Does Fred have the sense that it helped?"

eric says, "yee-hah, johndan. That's a conversation I wish I'd been at. tell

 us about it"

beckster [to Johndan]: I'm sure it did. I interviewed there, and they told me they needed a book. And Fred doesn't have one . . .

Johndan says, "The basic problem was they understood the internet enough to know that anyone could publish; hence, they thought all internet pubs were mainly vanity press things."

beckster [to Johndan]: that is, a book or "equivalent publications"
. . . .

eric says, "beck: I'll bet you've written the equivalent of a book out there on IRC & various MU*s"

beckster [to eric]: and you've written *volumes*. But none of it's been refereed . . . .

Johndan [to eric]: and therefore not real?

eric says, "see what you mean, though. nobody (or *almost* nobody) is screening the stuff on the net, insuring its *quality*. "

beckster [to eric]: is that a bad thing?

pamT says, "you know, we're talking about the time involved in these "tech" activities, and I wonder how you all came to be so involved in R&T because that initial time investment (excuse the capitalism creeping in) is overwhelming to some newbi"

Johndan says, "At my dissertation defense, a faculty member wanted to know how she would know, in a hypertext, if someone who added a node knew what they were doing, or if they were "just some student" . . . ."

Locke had lots of time on his hands — just grad school

eric says, "that's part of the point of Rhetnet: to start trying to create some net-appropriate means of valuing what's out on the net, on its own terms"

pamT says, "So even if someone wants to get involved, has the tech, they may not have the time, you know?"

beckster thinks pam has a valid point. How long will it take a "newbie" to "catch up?"

eric says, "just some student? ARGH!"

Johndan says, "Maybe not long. Isn't it easier to use Mosaic than telnet? or Unix??"

beckster [to pamT]: yet Greg Siering learned everything in a year . . . and sure went beyond me in a lot of realms!

Locke [to beckster]: well, folks like Slatin are incorporating an awareness of the internet into basic rhetoric and composition classrooms, so one would hope that new grad students get a good dose

eric says, "the time thing seems to be based on the assumption that talking on the net is *extra*, that it's not work, but other-than-work, or is at least not a primary task. "

pamT says, "Locke—I think that'll help, cause I'm thinking of a friend who doesn't have time to invest because she's working on her diss in another area and she keeps saying this is the first thing she wants to find out more about when she's done."

Johndan The grad training was true at MTU. Do other places work with grad students (as a rule, not an exception) to get them looking critically/rhetorically at technology?

beckster says, "I think john's on the right track. This is a *situation* with its own rhetorical constraints . . . ."

Locke says, "maybe there needs to be some kind of Wyoming resolution about grad students and technology"

beckster [to Johndan]: most do it on their own . . . then teach the teachers! ;)

Johndan says, "How 'bout the "DaedalusMOO resolution?"

eric says, "probably wouldn't hurt, locke. shall we draft it? "

beckster nods—you first, johndan! Where have we been, where are we, and where are we going?

Locke gets out the pencil and yellow legal pad

pamT says, "at Louisville they have not done much, Johndan, but what is encouraging is the number of students who seem very eager to learn more. As the desire to learn about it increases, the field changes, no?"

Johndan says, "Start with the fact that literacy *is* a technology."

Locke says, "yes"

eric says, "yes"

beckster nods

Johndan beams, a role model.

eric says, "inseparable"

Locke says, "you can cite writing space as support for writing as technology
(and literacy more generally)"

Johndan says, "not only WS, but Eisenstein, McLuhan, Haraway . . . "

beckster says, "and that their are multiple literacies"

Locke says, "indeed"

Johndan says, "And that computers are both malleable and prevalent"

Locke says, "and if we teach literacy, then it's a given that technology must be present"

eric says, "You getting this down, locke? "

Locke says, "in fact, it's a fallacy to exclude it"

beckster says, "and that the rhetoric of these literacies is flexible, too"

eric says, "and it's a given that technology must be *accounted for*"

Johndan says, "period."

Locke [to beckster]: yes. And our responsibilities as techno-rhetoricians are at least twofold: to promote techno-rhetoro-literacy in society, and to shape the technology that we use through

our understanding of literacy (rather than, for instance, marketing or advertising, etc)"

Johndan says, "Exactly."

eric says, "and grad students should be given BIG raises for their
technorhetorical work. "

beckster thinks we often neglect the second part

beckster [to eric]: hear, hear!

eric says, "yes, locke. nicely put"

Locke says, "the first principle is pedagogy, the second scholarship
and theory"

beckster says, "but the two are intertwined, one informing the
other"

Johndan says, "with the assertion that pedagogy cannot be without
theory, but that people frequently act like it is."

beckster grins

pamT says, "in computers and composition, I think the two are even
more intertwined than ever. Theory is pedagogy and vice versa."

beckster says, "yes. And people still see them as separate—perhaps
even more so

Locke agrees with Pam, and the C&W community has made that
marriage happen

beckster says, "and it's our responsibility to see that they remain
blissfully happy"

Johndan says, "We may be at a nexus point, where our pedagogy
still *can* act to rearticulate the technology. (Think about trying to reconstruct a pencil.)"

eric says, "have to give a girl a bath. brb"

pamT says, "Composition is a field based in pedagogy more radically
than most others in the academy and computers and composition particularly, since we focus on technology as pedagogical intervention."

Johndan waves. Tell her my daughter barks to her.

Locke [to pamT]: yes

Locke waves to the dog-girl

beckster says, "I agree, johndan, which *requires* that we understand new technology as more than an extension of the past"

Johndan says, ""Yes, Beck—slippage in the chains of signification
can allow new possibilities."

beckster says, "thanks, y'all. I'll let you know if/when we'll need to
do another one of these. But this has been wonderful"

pamT says, " I like to think of technology as rupture—it is more
than an extension of the past, it interrupts the way we've
thought of literacy, writing, writing instruction."

beckster says, "could be that paul will ask you to go further in an e-mail message, or ask us to focus as a group. But this gives him lots of fodder"

Johndan says, "Focus? We don't *do* focus."

Johndan says, "But tell Paul (and the rest of you) thanks for this opportunity to talk (and wave)."

beckster nods to pam

Locke waves

Locke feels ruptured

beckster nods to johndan, and waves him under the table

pamT says, "this has been great!"

beckster nods

beckster grins . . . we COULD do this all the time, ya know . . . .:)

Locke is running out of battery power, so waves to everyone

Johndan says, "Bye everyone.""

eric waves at locke

beckster says, "I'll be in touch virtually. See y'all!"

Locke waves

You hear an electrical sizzling sound; Johndan has disconnected.

eric says, "so long, johndan"

pamT says, "good luck to everyone with their fall semesters (in new places and old)> Johndan—tell the gang up there i said hi! Good night!"

eric says, "you too, pam. hope the allergies clear up soon"

You hear an electrical sizzling sound; pamT has disconnected.

beckster says, "thanks, pam . . . .you, too!"

eric says, "guess I better duck out, too. gotta get ready for that workshop. got web pages to write. etc!"

Locke says, "just like the good old days, eh?"

beckster hugs eric

Locke waves

beckster says, "great to see you again, pard"

eric says, "this was just like ole times, eh? great!"

beckster sighs

eric grins & bails out

MOOers in this session are Eric Crump (University of Missouri, Columbia); Michael Day (South Dakota School of Mines); Locke Carter (University of Texas, Austin); Johndan Johnson-Eilola (Purdue University); Becky Rickly (University of Michigan, Ann Arbor); Pamela Takayoshi (University of Louisville).

REFERENCES

Adams, R. (1983). Letter to Readers. *The Writing Instructor*, 2(4), i.

Advertisement. (1994). *The MAC Zone*. Bellevue, WA.

Advertisement (Nov.–Dec. 1994) *MAC's Place*. Kalispell, MT. p. 5.

Anandam, K. (1980, March). *RSVP: Feedback programs for individualized analysis of writing*. Paper presented at the Convention of the Conference on College Composition and Communication, Washington, DC.

Anderson, N. (1985). Writing-process software and the individual writer. *NCTE–ACE Newsletter*, 1(2), 11–12.

Anson, C., & Gaard, G. (1992). Acting on the "Statement": The all-campus model of reform. *College Composition and Communication*, 43, 171–175.

Applebee, A. N. (1974). *Tradition and reform in the teaching of English*. Urbana, IL: NCTE.

Appleby, B. C. (1983). A review of *The Word Processing Book* by Peter A. McWilliams. *College Composition and Communication*, 34, 221–222.

Appleby, B. C., & Bernhardt, S. (1987). Review essay. *College Composition and Communication*, 38, 478–483.

Arms, V. (1983). Creating and recreating. *College Composition and Communication*, 34, 355–358.

Arms, V., Schwartz, H., & Balestri, D. (1986). University of Pittsburgh conference on computers and writing program. Pittsburgh Learning Research & Development Center.

Atwell, N. (1987). *In the middle: Writing, reading and learning with adolescents*. Portsmouth, NH: Boynton/Cook-Heinemann.

Bakhtin, M. M. (1986). *Speech and other late essays* (V. W. McGee, Trans.). Austin, TX: University of Texas Press.

Balester, V. (1992). Revising the "Statement": On the work of writing centers. *College Composition and Communication*, 43, 167–171.

Balester, V., Halasek, K., & Peterson, N. (1992). Sharing authority: Collaborative teaching in a computer-based writing course. *Computers and Composition*, 9(1), 25–40.

Ball, C. C., Dice, L., & Bartholomae, D. (1990). Telling secrets: Student readers and disciplinary authorities. In R. Beach & S. Hynds (Eds.), *Developing discourse practices in adolescence and adulthood* (pp. 337–358). Norwood, NJ: Ablex.

Barclay, D. (1990, March). *Mail, female, ENFI, and e-mail: How computerized conversations strengthen community through diversity*. Paper presented at the Convention of the Conference on College Composition and Communication, Chicago, IL.

Barker, T. T. (1985). The English department microlab: An endangered species. *Research in Word Processing Newsletter, 3,* 2–5.

Barker, T. T. (1985, Fall). Microlab Facts. *The English Microlab Registry, 2*(1), 2.

Barker, T. T. (1986). *The English Microlab Registry, 2*(2).

Barker, T. T., & Kemp, F. O. (1990). Network theory: A postmodern pedagogy for the writing classroom. In C. Handa (Ed.), *Computers and community: Teaching Composition in the twenty-first century* (pp. 1–27). Portsmouth, NH: Boynton/Cook-Heinemann.

Bartholomae, D. (1985). Inventing the University. In M. Rose (Ed.), *When a writer can't write: Studies in writer's block and other composing problems* (pp. 134–165). New York: Guilford Press.

Bartholomae, D. (1993). "I'm talking about Allen Bloom": Writing on the network. In B. Bruce, J. Kreeft Peyton & T. Batson (pp. 237–262). *Network-Based Classrooms*. New York: Cambridge University Press.

Bartholomae, D., & Petrosky, A. (1986). *Facts, artifacts, and counterfacts: Theory and method for a reading and writing course.* Portsmouth, NH: Boynton/Cook-Heinemann.

Batson, T. (1986). *EnfiLOG.* Washington, DC: Gallaudet College.

Batson, T. W. (1988, February/March). The ENFI project: A networked classroom approach to writing instruction. *Academic Computing,* 32–33; 55–56.

Bauman, M. (1994, May). *Interactive writing in the global community.* Paper presented at the Tenth Computers and Writing Conference, Columbia, MO.

Bazerman, C. (1988). *Shaping written knowledge: The genre and activity of the experimental article in science.* Madison: The University of Wisconsin Press.

Bean, J. C. (1983a). A review of *Computers in Composition Instruction. College Composition and Communication, 34,* 368–369.

Bean, J. C. (1983b). Computerized word-processing as an aid to revision. *College Composition and Communication, 34,* 146–148.

Belanoff, P. (1990). The generalized other and me: Working women's language and the academy. *Pre/Text, 11,* 61–73.

Bender, E. (1987). The master plan. *PC World, 5*(8), 174–185.

Bennahum, D. (June, 1994). Fly me to the moo: Adventures in textual reality. *Lingua Franca, 1,* 22–36.

Berlin, J. A. (1984). *Writing instruction in nineteenth-century American colleges.* Carbondale: Southern Illinois University Press.

Berlin, J. A. (1987a). *Rhetoric and reality: Writing instruction in American colleges, 1900–1985.* Carbondale: Southern Illinois University Press.

Berlin, J. (1987b). Revisionary history: The dialectical method. *Pre/Text 8,* 47–61.

Berlin, J. (1990a). The teacher as researcher: Democracy, dialogue, and power. In D. A. Daiker &. M. Morenberg (Eds.), *The writing teacher as researcher: Essays in the theory and practice of class-based research* (pp. 3–14). Portsmouth, NH: Boynton/Cook-Heinemann.

Berlin, J. A. (1990b). Writing instruction in school and college English, 1890–1985. In J. J. Murphy (Ed.), *A short history of writing instruction: From ancient Greece to twentieth century America* (pp. 183–220). Davis, CA: Hermagoras Press.

Berlin, J. (1994). Foreword. In D. B. Downing (Ed.), *Changing classroom practices: Resources for literary and cultural studies* (pp. vii–xii). Urbana, IL: NCTE.

Berlin, J. A., & Vivion, M. J. (Eds.). (1992). *Cultural studies in the English classroom.* Portsmouth, NH: Boynton/Cook.

Bernhardt, S. A. (1993). The shape of text to come: The texture of print on screens. *College Composition and Communication, 44,* 151–175.

Bernhardt, S. A., Wojahn, P. G., & Edwards, P. R. (1990). Teaching college composition with computers. *Written Communication, 7,* 342–374.

Bickford, C. (1994). The 50 best CD-ROMs. *MacUser, 10*(10), 73–81.

Bitzer, D. (1960). Plato [Computer program]. Urbana: University of Illinois.

Bizzell, P. (1982). Cognition, convention, and certainty: What we need to know about writing. *Pre/Text, 31,* 213–243.

Bizzell, P., & Herzberg, B. (Eds.). (1984). *The Bedford bibliography for teachers of writing.* Boston: Bedford Books.

Bizzell, P., & Herzberg, B. (1990). The rhetorical tradition: Readings from classical times to the present. Boston: Bedford Books.

Blake, T. (1990). Adventures with hybrid systems: Integrating the Macintosh interface with external devices. In B. Laurel (Ed.), *The art of human–computer interface design* (pp. 289–297). Reading, MA: Addison-Wesley.

Bloom, A. (1987). *The closing of the American mind: How higher education has failed democracy and impoverished the souls of today's students.* New York: Simon and Schuster.

Blumenthal, J. C. (1972). *English 3200: A Programmed Course in Grammar and Usage.* New York: Harcourt Brace Jovanovich.

Bogel, F. V. (1986). Cornell University freshman seminar program. In P. Connolly &. T. Vilardi (Eds.), *New methods in college writing programs* (pp. 29–35). New York: MLA.

Bolter, J. D. (1984). *Turing's man: Western culture in the computer age.* Chapel Hill: The University of North Carolina Press.

Bolter, J. D. (1991). *Writing space: The computer, hypertext, and the history of writing.* Hillsdale, NJ: Erlbaum.

Bolter, J. D., Joyce, M., & Smith, J. (1991). StorySpace [Computer program]. Cambridge, MA: Eastgate Systems.

Bork, A. (1980). Alfred Bork. In R. P. Taylor (Ed.), *The computer in the school: Tutor, tool, tutee* (pp. 13–82). New York: Teachers College Press.

Bourque, J. H. (1983). Understanding and evaluating: The humanist as composition specialist. *College English, 45,* 67–73.

Boyle, F. T. (1993). IBM, Talking Heads, and our Classrooms. *College English*, *55*(6), 618–643.

Braddock, R., Lloyd-Jones, R. & Schoer, L. (1963). *Research on written composition*. Urbana, IL: NCTE.

Braverman, H. (1974). *Labor and monopoly capital: The degradation of work in the twentieth century*. New York: Monthly Review Press.

Breininger, L. J., & Portch, S. (1983). A visit to Professor Cram: Attractive computer learning. *College Composition and Communication*, *34*, 358–361.

Brenner, G. (1982, March). *Programming and writing*. Paper presented at the Convention of the Conference on College Composition and Communication, San Francisco, CA.

Bridwell, L. (1983, March). *Computers and composing: Implications for instruction for studying experienced writers*. Paper presented at the Convention of the Conference of College Composition and Communication, Detroit, MI.

Bridwell, L. S., Nancarrow, P.R., & Ross, D. (1984). The writing process and the writing machine: Current research on word processors relevant to the teaching of composition. In R. Beach &. L. S. Bridwell (Eds.), *New directions in composition research* (pp. 381–398). New York: Guilford.

Bridwell, L., & Ross, D. (1982). Access [Computer Program]. Minneapolis, MN: University of Minnesota.

Bridwell, L., & Ross, D. (1984a). Announcement. *Computers and Composition*, *1*(3), 10.

Bridwell, L. S., & Ross, D. (1984b). Integrating computers into a writing curriculum; or, buying, begging, and building. In W. Wresch (Ed.), *The computer in composition instruction: A writer's tool* (pp. 107–119). Urbana, IL: NCTE.

Bridwell, L., Sirc, G., Brooke, R. (1985). Revising and computing: Case studies of student writers. In S. W. Freedman (Ed.), *The acquisition of written language*: Response and revision (pp. 172–94). Norwood, NJ: Ablex.

Bridwell-Bowles, L. (1992). Discourse and diversity: Experimental writing within the academy. *College Composition and Communication*, *43*(3), 349–368.

Bridwell-Bowles, L. (1993). Greetings from the 1993 program chair. *Twentieth-century problems, twenty-first century solutions: Issues, answers, actions* [Program of the 44th Annual Meeting of the Conference on College Composition and Communication]. Urbana, IL: NCTE.

Bridwell-Bowles, L. (1995). Freedom, form, function: Varieties of academic discourse [revised version of the 1994 CCCC Chair's address]. *College Composition and Communication*, *46*(1), 46–61.

Bridwell-Bowles, L., Johnson, P., & Brehe, S. (1987). Composing and computers: Case studies of experienced writers. In A. Matsuhashi (Ed.), *Writing in real time: Modeling production processes* (pp. 81–107). Norwood, NJ: Ablex.

Britton, J. (1970). *Language and Learning*. Coral Gables, FL: University of Miami Press.

Britton, J. (1975). Preface. In J. Britton, T. Burgess, N. Martin, A. McLeod, & H. Rosen (Eds.), *The development of writing abilities* (11–18) (pp. xi–xiii). London: Macmillan Education.

Britton, J. (1983). Language and learning across the curriculum. In P. Stock (Ed.), *Forum: Essays on theory and practice in the teaching of writing* (pp. 221–224). Upper Montclair, NJ: Boynton/Cook.

Broad, W. J. (1992, November 10). Clinton to promote high tech technology, with Gore in charge. *The New York Times*, pp. B5–B6.

Brodkey, L. (1989). On the subjects of class and gender in "The Literacy Letters." *College English, 52*(2), 125–141.

Brown, J. (1980). *Programmed Vocabulary*. Englewood Cliffs: Prentice Hall.

Brown, E., Knorr, E., & Bermant, C. (1987). IBM Personal System. *PC World, 5*(8), 220–223.

Brown, S. C., Meyer, P. R., & Enos, T. (Eds.). Doctoral programs in rhetoric and composition. [Special issue] *Rhetoric Review, 12*(2).

Bruce, B. C. (1993). Innovation and social change. In B. C. Bruce, J. K. Peyton & T. Batson (Eds.), *Network-based classrooms: Promises and realities* (pp. 9–32). New York: Cambridge University Press.

Bruce, B., Peyton, J. K., & Batson, T., (Eds.). (1993). *Network-based classrooms: Promises and realities*. New York: Cambridge University Press.

Bruckman, A., & Resnick, M. (1995). *Virtual professional community: Results from the MediaMOO Project*. Excerpted from MOOInfo [On-line]. Available on: http://www.missouri.edu/~cccc95/online-intro.html

Bruffee, K. (1972). *A short course in writing*. Cambridge, MA: Winthrop.

Bruffee, K. (1984). Collaborative learning and the conversation of mankind. *College English, 46*, 635–652.

Bunderson, V. (1971). TICCIT [Computer program]. Austin: University of Texas.

Bureau, W. E. (1989). Computers: Catalysts for change at Springfield High School. In C. L. Selfe, D. Rodrigues, & W. R. Oates (Eds.), *Computers in English and the language arts: The challenge of teacher education* (pp. 97–110). Urbana, IL: NCTE.

Burns, H., & Culp, G. (1980, August). Stimulating invention in English composition through computer-assisted instruction. *Educational Technology, 20*, 5–10.

Burns, H. (1977a). Burke [Computer program]. Austin: University of Texas.

Burns, H. (1977b). Tagi [Computer program]. Austin: University of Texas.

Burns, H. (1977c). Topoi [Computer program]. Austin: University of Texas.

Burns, H. (1979). *Stimulating rhetorical invention in English composition through computer-assisted instruction*. Doctoral dissertation, University of Texas, Austin.

Burns, H. (1979). Stimulating invention in English composition through computer-assisted instruction. ERIC document ED193693.

Burns, H. (1981, March). Stimulating thinking with computer technology. *Proceedings of the task force on the implications of educational technology*. Denver, CO: Colorado Commission on Higher Education.

Burns, H. (1982). *A writer's tool: Computing as a mode of invention.* (ERIC Document Reproduction Service No. ED 193 693)

Burns, H. (1983, March). *Computer literacy and the composition teachers.* Paper presented at the Convention of the Conference on College Composition and Communication, Detroit, MI.

Burns, H. (1984). Recollections of first-generation computer-assisted prewriting. In W. Wresch (Ed.), *The computer in composition instruction* (pp. 34–46). Urbana, IL: NCTE.

Burns, H. (1987). Computers and composition. In Gary Tate. (Ed.), *Teaching composition: 12 bibliographical essays* (2nd ed.) (pp. 378–400). Fort Worth, TX: Texas Christian University Press.

Burns, H. (1992). Teaching composition in tomorrow's multimedia, multi-networked classrooms. In G. E. Hawisher & P. LeBlanc (Eds.), *Re-imagining computers and composition: Research and teaching in the virtual age* (pp. 115–130). Portsmouth, NH: Boynton/Cook.

Bush, Vannevar. (1945, July). As we may think. *Atlantic Monthly, 176,* 101–108.

Bush, V. (1991). As we may think. In J. M. Nyce & P. Kahn (Eds.), *From memex to hypertext: Vannevar Bush and the mind's machine* (p. 85–107). Boston, MA: Academic Press.

Butler, W., Carter, L., Kemp, F., & Taylor, P. (1988). Daedalus Instructional System [Computer program]. Austin, TX: The Daedalus Group.

Caldwell, R. *Guidelines for review and evaluation of English language arts software.* Urbana, IL: NCTE.

Campbell, J. (1992). Controlling voices: The legacy of English A at Radcliffe College, 1883–1917. *College Composition and Communication, 43,* 472–485.

Campbell, J. L., & Zimmerman, L. (1981). *Programming the Apple.* Waco, TX: Mesa Research.

Carbone, N., Daisley, M., Federenko, E., McComas, D., Moran, C., Ostermiller, D., & Vanden Akker, S. (1993). Writing ourselves online. *Computers and Composition, 10*(3), 29–48.

Case, D. P. (1985). Processing professorial words: Personal computers and the writing habits of university professors. *College Composition and Communication, 36,* 317–20.

Catano, J. V. (1985, October). Computer-based writing: Navigating the fluid text. *College Composition and Communication, 36,* 309–316.

Cayton, M. (1990). What happens when things go wrong: Women and writing blocks. *Journal of Advanced Composition, 10,* 321–337.

CCCC Program. (1984). *Workshop: Word Processing in the Classroom.* Urbana: NCTE.

Chambers, J. A. (1988). The effects of academic software on learning and motivation. In J. W. Sprecher (Ed.), *Facilitating academic software development* (pp. 19–45). McKinney, TX: Academic Computing Publications.

Clark, B. L., & Wiedenhaupt, S. (1992) On blocking and unblocking Sonja:

A case study in two voices. *College Composition and Communications, 43,* 55–74.

Clark, G. (1990). *Dialogue, dialectic, and conversation: A social perspective on the function of writing.* Carbondale: Southern Illinois University Press.

Classroom Computer News Directory of Educational Computing Resources. (1983). Commodore Computer. Watertown, MA: Intentional Educations Inc.

Cleary, L. M. (1991). *From the other side of the desk: Students speak out about writing.* Portsmouth, NH: Boynton/Cook-Heineman.

Cohen, M. (1981). Homer [Computer program]. New York: Scribners.

Collier, R. M. (1982). *The influence of computer-based text editors on the revision strategies of inexperienced writers.* ERIC Document Reproduction Service No. ED 266 719.

Collier, R. M. (1983). The word processor and revision strategies. *College Composition and Communication, 36,* 149–155.

Collins, J. (1985). A writing teacher's guide to computerese. In J. L. Collins & E. A. Sommers (Eds.), *Writing on-line: Using computers in the teaching of writing* (pp. 11–18). Upper Montclair, NJ: Boynton/Cook.

Collins, J. L. (1989). Computerized text analysis and the teaching of writing. In G. E. Hawisher & C. L. Selfe (Eds.), *Critical perspectives on computers and composition instruction* (pp. 30–43). New York: Teachers College Press.

Collins. J. L., & Sommers, E. L. (Eds). (1985). *Writing on-line: Using computers in the teaching of writing.* Upper Montclair, NJ: Boynton/Cook.

Collymore, J. C., Fox, M. L., Frase, L. T., Gingrich, P. S., Neenan, S. A., & MacDonald, N. M. (1982). Writer's Workbench [Computer program]. Greensboro, NC: AT&T Technology System Software Sales.

Communications, computers, and networks: How to work, play and thrive in cyberspace. (1991, September). *Scientific American.* [Special issue.]

Computers and writing conferences. (1989). *College Composition and Communication, 40*(3), 327.

Conference program. (1984). *Computers and writing: Research and applications, April 12–April 14.* (1984). Minneapolis: The University of Minnesota.

Connolly, P., & Vilardi, T. (Eds.). (1986). *New methods in college writing programs.* New York: MLA.

Connors, R. J. (1986). Textbooks and the evolution of the discipline. *College Composition and Communication, 37*(2), 178–94.

Connors, R. J. (1991). *Writing the history of our discipline.* In E. Lindemann & G. Tate (Eds.), *An introduction to composition studies* (pp. 49–71). New York: Oxford University Press.

Connors, R. J., & Lunsford, A. A. (1993). Teachers' rhetorical comments on student papers. *College Composition and Communication, 44,* 200–223.

Cook, L. (1985). Who is ACE. *ACE Newsletter, 1*(2), 1.

Cooper, M. M. (1986). The ecology of writing. *College English, 48,* 364–375.

Cooper, M. M., & Selfe, C. L. (1990). Computer conferences and learning: Authority, resistance, and internally persuasive discourse. *College English, 52,* 847–869.

Coover, R. (1992, June 21). The end of books. *New York Times Book Review, 1,* 23–25.

Coover, R. (1993, August 29). Hyperfiction: Novels for the computer. *New York Times Book Review, 1,* 8–9.

Corbett, E. P. J. (1987). Approaches to the study of style. In G. Tate (Ed.), *Teaching composition: 12 bibliographical essays* (pp. 83–130). Fort Worth: Texas Christian University Press.

Costanzo, W. (1987). The English teacher as programmer. *Computers and Composition, 4*(3), 65–76.

Costanzo, W. (1994). Reading, writing, and thinking in an age of electronic literacy. In C. L. Selfe & S. Hilligoss (Eds.), *Literacy and computers: The complications of teaching and learning with technology* (pp. 11–21). New York: MLA.

Covey, P., Geisler, C., Kaufer, D., & Neuwirth, C. (1986). Comment [Computer program]. Pittsburgh, PA: Carnegie-Mellon University.

Cowley, M. (Ed.). (1977). *Writers at work: The Paris Review Interviews.* First Series. Harmondsworth: Penguin Books.

Crew, L. (1990, May). *Discourse analysis of GayNet.* Paper presented at the Sixth Conference on Computers and Writing, Austin, TX.

Cuban, L. (1986). *Teachers and machines: The classroom use of technology since 1920.* New York: Teachers College Press.

Diagon, A. (1966). Computer grading and English composition. *English Journal, 55,* 46–52.

Daiute, C. (1983). The computer as stylus and audience. *College Composition and Communication, 34,* 134–145.

Daiute, C. (1985). *Writing and computers.* Reading, MA: Addison–Wesley.

Daiute, C. (1985–1986). Computers and writing: Course description. *Harvard Graduate School of Education Course Catalogue.*

Daiute, C. (1986). Physical and cognitive factors in revising: Insights from studies with computers. *Research in the Teaching of English, 20,* 141–159.

December, J. (1994, March). *Communicating on global computer networks.* Paper presented at the Annual Convention of the Conference on College Composition and Communication, Nashville, TN.

Delaney, P., & Gilbert, J. K. (1991). HyperCard stacks for Fielding's *Joseph Andrews*: Issues of design and context. In P. Delaney & G. Landow (Eds.), *Hypermedia and Literary Studies* (pp. 287–297). Cambridge: MIT Press.

Delaney, P. & Landow, G. P. (Eds.) (1991). *Hypermedia and literary studies.* Cambridge: MIT Press.

Deleuze, G., & Guattari, F. (1987). *A Thousand plateaus: Capitalism and schizophrenia.* (B. Massumi, Trans.). Minneapolis: University of Minnesota Press. (Original work published in 1980)

DeLoughry, T. J. (1993, July 7). Software designed to offer internet users easy access to documents and graphics. *The Chronicle of Higher Education*, A23.

DeLoughry, T. J. (1994a, February 23). Unconnected. *Chronicle of Higher Education*, A19–20.

DeLoughry, T. J. (1994b, November 2). For the community of scholars, "being connected" takes on a whole new meaning. *The Chronicle of Higher Education*, pp. A25–A27.

DeWitt, S. L. (1994, March). *Global networking: Creating sites of collaborative inquiry.* Paper presented at the Annual Convention of the Conference on College Composition and Communication, Nashville, TN.

Dibble, J. (1993, December 21). A rape in cyberspace or how an evil clown, a Haitian trickster spirit, two wizards, and a cast of dozens turned a database into a society. *Village Voice*, 36–41.

Dickinson, D. (1986). Cooperation, collaboration, and a computer: integrating a computer into a first–second grade writing program. *Research in the Teaching of English*, 20, 357–378.

DiMatteo, A. (1991). Communication, writing, learning: An anti-instrumentalist view of network writing. *Computers and Composition*, 8, 5–20.

Dinan, J. S., Gagnon, R., & Taylor, J. (1986). Integrating computers into the writing classroom: Some guidelines. *Computers and Composition*, 3, 33–39.

DiPardo, A., & DiPardo, M. (1990). Towards the metapersonal essay: Exploring the potential of hypertext in the composition class. *Computers and Composition*, 7(3), 7–22.

Dobrin, D. N. (1990). A limitation on the use of computers in composition. In D. H. Holdstein & C. L. Selfe (Eds.), *Computers and writing: Theory, research, practice.* New York: MLA.

Dobrin, D. (1994). Hype and hypertext. In C. L. Selfe & S. Hilligoss (Eds.), *Literacy and computers: The complications of teaching and learning with technology* (pp. 305–318). New York: MLA.

Doctoral programs in rhetoric and composition. (1994). *Rhetoric Review*, 12(2), 240–389.

Douglas, J. Y. (1989). Wandering through the labyrinth: Encountering interactive fiction. *Computers and Composition*, 6, 93–104.

Dryden, L. M. (1994). Literature, student-centered classrooms, and hypermedia environments. In C. L. Selfe & S. Hilligoss (Eds.), *Literacy and computers: The complications of teaching and learning with technology* (pp. 282–304). New York: MLA.

Duin A. H., & Gorak, K. S. (1992). Developing texts for computers and composition: A collaborative process. *Computers and Composition*, 9, 17–40.

Duin, A. H., Mason, L., & Lammers, E. (1994). Responding to ninth-grade students via telecommunications: College mentor strategies and development over time. *Research in the Teaching of English*, 28, 117–153.

Duling, R. (1985) *Word processors and student writing: A study of their im-*

pact on revision, fluency, and quality of writing. Unpublished doctoral Dissertation, Michigan State University.

Durst, R. K., & Marshall, J. (1986a, May). Annotated bibliography of research in the teaching of English. *Research in the Teaching of English, 20,* 198–215.

Durst, R. K., & Marshall, J. (1986b, December). Annotated bibliography of research in the teaching of English. *Research in the Teaching of English, 20,* 410–29.

Durst, R. K., & Marshall, J. (1987a, May). Annotated bibliography of research in the teaching of English. *Research in the Teaching of English, 21,* 202–223.

Durst, R. K., & Marshall, J. (1987b, December). Annotated bibliography of research in the teaching of English. *Research in the Teaching of English, 21,* 422–445.

Durst, R. K., & Marshall, J. (1988a, May). Annotated bibliography of research in the teaching of English. *Research in the Teaching of English, 22,* 213–227.

Durst, R. K., & Marshall, J. (1988b, December). Annotated bibliography of research in the teaching of English. *Research in the Teaching of English, 22,* 434–452.

Eagleton, T. (1991). *An introduction to ideology.* London: Verso.

Earthman, A. E. (1992). Creating the virtual work: Readers' processes in understanding literary texts. *Research in the Teaching of English, 26,* 351–384.

Eastgate Systems, Inc. PO Box 1307, Cambridge, MA 02238 (617) 924-9044

Ede. L. (1992, October 11). *The writing process: Reflections and speculations.* Paper delivered at the University of New Hampshire Conference, Durham, NH.

Edwards, B. (1987). *Processing words: Writing and revising on a microcomputer.* Englewood Cliffs: Prentice-Hall.

Edwards, P. N. (1990). The army of the microworld: Computers and the politics of gender identity. *Signs, 16,* 102–127.

Eichhorn, J., Farris, S., Hayes, K., Hernández, A., Jarratt, S. C., Powers-Stubbs, K., & Schiachitano, M. M. (1992). A symposium on feminist experiences in the composition classroom. *College Composition and Communication, 43,* 297–322.

Eklund, J. (1993). Personal Computers. In A. Ralston & E. D. Reilly (Eds.), *Encyclopedia of computer science* (pp. 460–461). New York: Van Nostrad Reinholt.

Elbow, P. (1973). *Writing without teachers.* New York: Oxford University Press.

Elbow, P. (1981). *Writing with power: Techniques for mastering the writing process.* New York: Oxford University Press.

Elbow, P. (1987). Closing my eyes as I speak: An argument for ignoring audience. *College English, 49*(1), 50–69.

Elbow, P. (1990). *What is English?* New York: MLA.

Elbow, P. (1991) Reflections on academic discourse: How it relates to freshmen and colleagues. *College English, 53,* 135–155.

Elder, J., Schwartz, J., Bowen, B., & Goswami, D. (1989). *Word processing in a community of writers.* New York: Garland.

Eldred, J. (1989). Computers, composition, and the social view. In G. E. Hawisher & C. L. Selfe (Eds.), *Critical perspectives on computers and composition studies: Questions for the 1990s* (pp. 201–218). New York: Teachers College Press.

Eldred, J. (1990, March). *Debugging computer pedagogy: Electronic networks and the illusion of equality.* Paper presented at the Convention of the Conference on College Composition and Communication, Chicago, IL.

Emig, J. (1971). *The composing processes of twelfth graders.* Urbana, IL: NCTE.

Emig, J. (1977). Writing as a mode of learning. *College Composition and Communication, 28,* 122–127.

Emig, J. (1980, November). *Language and Learning.* Workshop at a Meeting of the National Council of Teachers of English, Cincinnati, OH.

Emig, J. (1983). Non-magical thinking: Presenting writing developmentally in schools. In D. Goswami & M. Butler (Eds.), *The web of meaning: Essays on writing, teaching, learning, and thinking* (pp. 132–144). Upper Montclair: Boynton/Cook.

Engstrom, J., & Whittaker, J. (1963). Improving students' spelling through automated teaching. *Psychological Reports, 12,* 125–126.

Erickson, F. (1984). School literacy, reasoning, and civility: An anthropologist's perspective. *Review of Educational Research, 54,* 525–546.

Faigley, L. (1985). Nonacademic writing: The social perspective. In L. Odell & D. Goswami, (Eds.), *Writing in nonacademic settings* (pp. 231–248). New York: Guilford Press.

Faigley, L. (1986). Competing theories of process: A critique and a proposal. *College English, 48*(6), 527–540.

Faigley, L. (1990a). Subverting the electronic workbook: Teaching writing using networked computers. In D. A. Daiker &. M. Morenberg (Eds.), *The writing teacher as researcher: Essays in the theory and practice of class-based research* (pp. 290–311). Portsmouth, NH: Boynton/Cook-Heinemann.

Faigley, L. (1990b, May). *The postmodern condition of the networked classroom.* Paper presented at the Sixth Conference on Computers and Writing, Austin, TX.

Faigley, L. (1992). *Fragments of rationality: Postmodernity and the subject of composition.* Pittsburgh: University of Pittsburgh Press.

Faigley, L., & Miller, T. P. (1982). What we learn from writing on the job. *College English, 44,* 557–569.

Falk, C. J. (1985). English skills tutorials for sentence combining practice. *Computers and Composition, 2*(3), 2–4.

Fallon, M. A. C. (1993) Apple Computer Corporation, In A. Ralston, & E. D.

Reilly (Eds.), Encyclopedia of Computer Science (3rd ed.), (pp. 70–73). New York: Van Nostrand Reinhold.

Fanderclai, T., Siering, G., Costello, N. (1994, May). *Pedagogical and professional uses of muds: Lessons from the virtual trenches.* Paper presented at the Tenth Computers and Writing Conference, Columbia, MO.

Feenberg, A. (1991). *Critical theory of technology.* New York: Oxford University Press.

Finders, M. (1992). With jix. *College Composition and Communication, 43*(4) 497–507.

Flachmann, K. (1994, Spring). Terms and conditions of employment in the California State University. *Forum, 5,* 1–6.

Flesch, R. R. (1955). *Why Johnny can't read—and what you can do about it.* New York: Harper & Row.

Flinn, J. Z. (1987). Case studies of revision aided by keystroke recording and replaying software. *Computers and Composition, 5*(1), 31–50.

Flinn, J. Z. (1986). The role of instruction in revision with computers: Forming a construct for good writing. (ERIC Document Reproduction Service No. ED 274 963)

Flinn, J. Z., & Madigan, C. (1989). The gateway writing project: Staff development and computers in St. Louis. In C. L. Selfe, D. Rodrigues, & W. R. Oates (Eds.), *Computers in English and the language arts: The challenge of teacher education* (pp. 55–68). Urbana, IL: NCTE.

Flores, M. J. (1990). Computer conferencing: Composing a feminist community of writers. In C. Handa (Ed.), *Computers and community: Teaching composition in the twenty-first century* (pp. 106–117). Portsmouth, NH: Boynton/Cook.

Flower, L,, Wallace, D. L., Norris, L., & Burnett, R. E. (Eds.). (1994). *Making thinking visible: Writing, collaborative planning, and classroom inquiry.* Urbana, IL: NCTE.

Flower, L. & Hayes, J. R. (1981). A cognitive process theory of writing. *College Composition and Communication, 32,* 365–387.

Flower, L., Stein, V., Ackerman, J., Kantz, M. J., McCormick, K., & Peck, W. C. (1990). *Reading to write: Exploring a cognitive and social process.* New York: Oxford University Press.

Flynn, E. A. (1988). Composing as a woman. *College Composition and Communication, 39,* 423–435.

Fogarty, D. (1959). *Roots for a new rhetoric.* New York: Columbia University Press.

Fortune, R. (1989). Visual and verbal thinking: Drawing and word-processing software in writing instruction. In G. E. Hawisher & C. L. Selfe (Eds.), *Critical perspectives on computers and composition studies* (pp. 145–161). New York: Teachers College Press.

Fortune, R. (1990, March). *HyperCard in the classroom: Literature, writing, and manuscript studies.* Paper presented at the Convention of the Conference on College Composition and Communication, Chicago, IL.

Foucault, M. (1979). *Discipline and punish: The birth of the prison* (Alan Sheridan, Trans.). New York: Random House. (Original work published in 1975)

Fox, T. (1990). Basic writing as cultural conflict. *Journal of Education, 172*(1) 65–83.

Freire, P. (1990). *Pedagogy of the oppressed* (Myra Bergman Ramos, Trans). New York: The Continuum Publishing Co.

Freisinger, R. (1982). Cross-disciplinary writing programs: Beginnings. In T. Fulwiler & A. Young (Eds.) *Language connections: Writing and reading across the curriculum.* Urbana, IL: NCTE.

Friedman, M., Von Blum, R., Cohen, M., Gerrard, L., & Rand, E. (1982). Wandah (later HBJ Writer) [Computer program]. San Diego, CA: Harcourt Brace Jovanovich.

Fuchs, I. H. (1983). BITNET—Because it's time. *Perspectives in Computing, 3*(1), 16–27.

Fulkerson, R. (1990). Composition theory in the eighties: Axiological consensus and paradigmatic diversity. *College Composition and Communication, 41,* 409–429.

Gebhardt, R. (1983, Spring). Notes to would-be word processors. *Focus: Teaching English Language Arts, 9*(3), 62–71.

Gebhardt, R. (1992a). Diversity in a mainline journal. *College Composition and Communication, 43,* 7–10.

Gebhardt, R. (1992b). Theme issue feedback and fallout. *College Composition and Communication, 43,* 295–296.

Geertz, C. (1973). *Interpretation of cultures.* New York: Basic Books.

Geisler, C. (1992) Exploring academic literacy: An experiment in composing. *College Composition and Communications, 43,* 39–54.

George, L. (1989, May). *Female authority in the computerized classroom.* Paper presented at the Fifth Computers and Writing Conference, Minneapolis, MN.

Gere, A. R. (1987). *Writing groups: History, theory, and implications.* Carbondale: Southern Illinois University Press.

Gere, A. R. (1992). Greetings from the 1992 Program Chair. In *1992 CCCC, March 19–21: Contexts, communities, and constraints: Sites of composing and communicating* (pp. 4–6).

Gere, A. R. (1994). Kitchen tables and rented rooms: The extracurriculum of composition. *College Composition and Communication, 45,* 75–92.

Gerrard, L. (Ed.). (1987a). *Writing at the century's end: Essays on computer-assisted composition.* New York: Random House.

Gerrard, L. (1987b). *Writing with HBJ Writer.* San Diego: Harcourt Brace Jovanovich.

Gerrard, L. (1989). Computers and basic writers: A Critical view. In G. E. Hawisher & C. L. Selfe (Eds.), *Critical perspectives on computers and composition studies* (pp. 94–108). New York: Teachers College Press.

Gerrard, L. (1991). Computers and compositionists: A view from the floating bottom. *Computers and Composition, 8*(2), 5–15.

Gerrard, L. (in press). The evolution of the computers and writing conference. *Computers and Composition.*

Gibbs, A. (1979). *Assessing children's language: Guidelines for teachers.* London: Ward Lock International.

Gibson, W. (1984). *Neuromancer.* New York: Ace Books.

Gibson, W. A. (1975). Letter to the editor in response to *Why Johnny Can't Write.*

Gibson, W. A. (1992, March). *Integrated writing and word processing at UMD: Costs and benefits.* Paper presented at the Convention of the Conference on College Composition and Communication, Cincinnati, OH.

Gleich, J. (Oct. 24, 1993) *New York Times.* p. 16E.

Gomez, M. L. (1990). The national writing project: Staff development in the teaching of composition. In G. E. Hawisher &. A. O. Soter (Eds.), *On literacy and its teaching* (pp. 68–83). Albany: State University of New York Press.

Gomez, M. L. (1991). The equitable teaching of composition. In G. E. Hawisher & C. L. Selfe (Eds.), *Evolving perspectives on computers and composition studies: Questions for the 1990s* (pp. 318–335). Urbana, IL & Houghton, MI: NCTE & Computers and Composition Press.

Gore, A. (1991, September). Infrastructure for the global village. *Scientific American,* 150–153.

Gore, A. (1993, December 21). Remarks to the National Press Club. Washington, DC.

Gorilla Software (1986). *Building skills. 48,* 3.

Gorrell, R. M., Bizzell, P., & Herzberg, B. (1984). *The Bedford bibliography for teachers of writing.* Boston: St. Martin's Press.

Gould, J. D. (1981). Composing letters with a computer-based text editors. *Human Factors, 23,* 593–606.

Goulde, M. (1991, October 14). Surveying groupware's competitive landscape: Lotus' Notes heads the field, but other products also neet users' needs. *PC Week,* p. 5.

Graves, D. H. (1983). *Writing: Teachers and children at work.* Exeter, NH: Heinemann Educational Books.

Graves, G., & Haller, C. (1994). The effect of secondary school structures and traditions on computer-supported literacy. In C. L. Selfe & S. Hilligoss (Eds.), *Literacy and computers: The complications of teaching and learning with technology* (pp. 144–156). New York: MLA.

Greenleaf, C. (1994). The role of classroom writing practices and pedagogy in shaping use of the computer. *Written Communication, 11,* 85–130.

Gregg, L. W., & Steinberg, E. R. (Eds.). (1980). *Cognitive processes in writing.* Hillside, NJ: Erlbaum.

Guyer, C., & Petry, M. (1991) Izme Pass. [Computer program]. Boston: Eastgate Systems.

Guyer, C., Seward, A., & Green, A. (1994). Collaboration and conversation: Three voices. *Computers and Composition, 11,* 3–20.

Haas, C. (1989a). How the writing medium shapes the writing process: Effects of word processing on planning. *Research in the Teaching of English, 23,* 181–207.

Haas, C. (1989b). Seeing it on the screen isn't really seeing it: Computer writers' reading problems. In G. E. Hawisher & C. L. Selfe (Eds.), *Crit-*

ical perspectives on computers and composition studies (pp. 16–29).
New York: Teachers College Press.

Haas, C., & Hayes, J. R. (1986). What did I just say? Reading problems in writing with the machine. *Research in the Teaching of English, 20,* 22–35.

Hairston, M. (1982). The winds of change: Thomas Kuhn and the revolution in the teaching of writing. *College Composition and Communication, 33,* 76–88.

Hairston, M. (1985, March). *Breaking our bonds and affirming our connections.* Conference chair's address at the Meeting of the Convention on College Compositon and Communication, Minneapolis, MN.

Hairston, M. (1992). Diversity, ideology, and teaching writing. *College Composition and Communication, 43,* 179–193.

Hairston, M. (1993). Reply to Trimbur, Wood, Strickland, Thelin, Rouster, and Mester. *College Composition and Communication, 44,* 255–256.

Haley-James, S. (1993). Entries from a new e-mail user's notebook. *Computers and Composition, 10,* 5–10.

Halio, M. P. (1990). Student writing: Can the machine maim the message. *Academic Computing, 4*(4), 12–15.

Halio, M. P. (1992, March). *Using computers to teach international writing.* Paper presented at the Convention of the Conference on College Composition and Communication, Cincinnati, OH.

Hamilton-Wieler, S. (1988). Empty echoes of Dartmouth: Dissonance between the rhetoric and the reality. *The Writing Instructor, 8,* 29–41.

Handa, C. (Ed.). (1990a). *Computers and community: Teaching composition in the twenty-first century.* Portsmouth, NH: Boynton/Cook.

Handa, C. (1990b). Politics, ideology, and the strange, slow death of the isolated composer or why we need community in the writing classroom. In C. Handa (Ed.), *Computers and community: Teaching composition in the twenty-first century* (pp. 160–184). Portsmouth, NH: Boynton/Cook.

Haney-Peritz, J. (1993) Making a place for the poetic in academic writing. *College Composition and Communication, 44,* 380–385.

Hansen, C., & Wilcox, L. (1984). An authoring system for use by teachers of composition. *Computers and Composition, 1,* 3–4.

Haraway, D. (1990). A manifesto for cyborgs: Science, technology, and socialist feminism. In L. J. Nicholson (Ed.), *Feminism/postmodernism* (pp.190–233). London: Routledge, Chapman & Hall.

Hardison, O. B., Jr. (1989). *Disappearing through the skylight: Culture and technology in the twentieth century.* New York: Penguin.

Harpold, T. (1990, May). *The grotesque corpus: Hypertext as carnival.* Paper presented at the Sixth Conference on Computers and Writing, Austin, TX.

Harralson, D. (1992). We've barely started—and we've already done it wrong: How not to start a computer-assisted writing classroom. *Computers and Composition, 9*(3), 71–78.

Harris, J. (1985). Student writers and word processing: A preliminary evaluation. *College Composition and Communication, 36,* 323–330.

Harris, M. (1982). *Tutoring writing: A sourcebook for writing labs.* Glenview, IL: Scott, Foresman.

Harris, M., & Cheek, M. (1983). Computers across the curriculum: Using Writer's Workbench for supplementary instruction. *Computers and Composition, 1*(2), 3–5.

Hart, B., & Daisley, M. (1994). Computers and composition in Japan: Notes on real and virtual literacies. *Computers and Composition, 11,* 37–48.

Hartzog, C. P. (1986). *Composition and the academy: A study of writing program administration.* New York: MLA.

Haselkorn, M. (1983, March). *The computer in the English Department.* Paper presented at the Conference on College Composition and Communication, Detroit, MI.

Haugeland, J. (1986, May). *Natural language: Understanding and being somebody.* Paper presented at the Computers & Writing Conference, Pittsburgh, PA.

Hawisher, G. E. (1984a). *Computers and writing—Research and applications: An evaluation of the conference, 12 April 1984–14 April 1984.* Urbana: University of Illinois.

Hawisher, G. E. (1984b). *Computers and writing—Research and applications: An evaluation of the conference.* Unpublished manuscript.

Hawisher, G. E. (1986). Studies in word processing. *Computers and Composition, 4,* 6–31.

Hawisher, G. E. (1987). The effects of word processing on the revision strategies of college freshmen. *Research in the Teaching of English, 21,* 145–159.

Hawisher, G. E. (1988). Research update: Writing and word processing. *Computers and Composition, 5,* 7–27.

Hawisher, G. E. (1989a). Research and recommendations for computers and composition. In G. E. Hawisher & C. L. Selfe (Eds.), *Critical perspectives on computers and composition instruction* (pp. 44–69). New York: Teachers College Press.

Hawisher, G. E. (1989b, November). *Toward effective pedagogy: Uses of software in the English classroom.* Paper presented at the Convention of the National Council of Teachers of English, Baltimore, MD.

Hawisher, G. E. (1990). Reading and writing connections: Composition pedagogy and word processing. In D. Holdstein &. C. L. Selfe (Eds.), *Computers and writing: Theory, research, practice* (pp. 71–83). New York: MLA.

Hawisher, G. E. (1992). Electronic meetings of the minds: Research, electronic conferences, and composition studies. In G. E. Hawisher & P. LeBlanc (Eds.), *Re-imagining computers and composition: Research and teaching in the virtual age.* (pp. 81–101). Portsmouth, NH: Boynton/Cook.

Hawisher, G. E., & LeBlanc, P. (1992). *Re-imagining computers and composition: Research and teaching in the virtual age.* Portsmouth, NH: Boynton/Cook.

Hawisher, G. E., & Moran, C. (1993). E-Mail and the Writing Instructor. *College English, 55,* 627–43.

Hawisher, G. E., & Selfe, C.L. (Eds.). (1989). *Critical perspectives on computers and composition instruction.* New York: Teachers College Press.

Hawisher, G. E., & Selfe, C. L. (1990). Letter from the editors. *Computers and Composition,* 7[Special Issue], 5–12.

Hawisher, G. E., & Selfe, C.L. (Eds.). (1991a). *Evolving perspectives on computers and composition studies: Questions for the 1990s.* Urbana, IL and Houghton, MI: NCTE & Computers and Composition Press.

Hawisher, G. E., & Selfe, C. L. (1991b). The rhetoric of technology and the electronic writing class. *College Composition and Communication, 42,* 55–65.

Hawisher, G. E., & Selfe, C. L. (1991c). Reply. *College Composition & Communication, 42*(4), 502.

Hawisher, G. E., & Selfe, C. L. (1992). *CCCC Bibliography of Composition and Rhetoric.* Carbondale, IL: Southern Illinois University Press.

Hawisher, G. E., &·Selfe, C. L. (1994). Tradition and change in computer-supported writing environments: A call for action. In P. Kahaney, J. Janangelo, & L. A. M. Perry (Eds.), *Theoretical and critical perspectives on teacher change* (pp. 155–186). Norwood, NJ: Ablex.

Hawisher, G. E., & Sullivan, P. (in press). Women on the networks: Searching for e-spaces of their own. In S. Jarratt & L. Worsham *Feminism and Composition.* New York: MLA.

Hawkins, T. (1984b). Introduction. In G. A. Olson (Ed.), *Writing centers: Theory and administration (pp. xi–xiv). Urbana, IL: NCTE.*

Heath, S. B. (1981). Toward an ethnohistory of writing in American education. In M. F. Whiteman (Ed.), *Writing: The nature, development, and teaching of written communication, volume 1: Variation in writing: Functional and linguistic–cultural differences* (pp. 25–45). Hillsdale, NJ: Erlbaum.

Heath, S. B. (1983). *Ways with words: Language, life, and work in communities and classrooms.* New York: Cambridge University Press.

Heath, S. B. (1990). The fourth vision: Literate language at work. In A. A. Lunsford, H. Moglen, & J. Slevin (Eds.), *The right to literacy* (pp. 289–306). New York: MLA.

Heid, J. (1991, May). Getting started with multimedia: What is it? Can you use it? What will it cost? *Macworld,* 225–232.

Heidorn, G. E., Jensen, K., Miller, L. A., Byrd, R. J. & Chodorow, M. S. (1982). The Epistle text critiquing system. *IBM Systems Journal, 21,* 305–326.

Heidorn, G., Jensen, K., Richardson, S., & Braden-Harter, L. (1982). Epistle [Computer program]. Yorktown Heights, NY: IBM.

Heim, M. (1987). *Electric language: A philosophical study of word processing.* New Haven: Yale University Press.

Herrington, A., & Moran, C. (1992). *Writing, teaching, and learning in the disciplines.* New York: MLA.

Herrington, A. J. (1989). The first twenty years of *Research in the Teaching of English* and the growth of a research community in composition studies. *Research in the Teaching of English, 23,* 117–138.

Herrmann, A. W. (1987). An ethnographic study of a high school writing class using computers: Marginal, technically proficient, and productive learners. In L. Gerrard (Ed.), *Writing at the century's end: Essays on computer-assisted composition* (pp. 79–91). New York: Random House.

Hesse, D. (1986). *A brief introduction to WordStar.* Unpublished manuscript, Illinois State University.

Hilbert, B. S. (1992). It was a dark and nasty night . . . It was a hard beginning. *College Composition and Communication, 43,* 75–80.

Hill, J. (1981). CCC Program. Urbana: NCTE.

Hiller, J. (1968). Opinionation vagueness, and specificity distinctiveness: Essay traits measured by computer. *American Educational Research Journal, 6,* 271–286.

Hillocks, G. (1986). *Research on written composition.* Urbana, IL: NCTE/ERIC.

Hiltz, S. R. (1986). The "virtual classroom": Using computer-mediated communication for university teaching. *Journal of Communication, 36*(2), 95–104.

Hiltz, S. R., & Turoff, M. (1978) *The network nation: Human communication via computer.* Reading, MA: Addison-Wesley.

Hirsch, E. D., Jr. (1987). *Cultural literacy: What every Amrican needs to know.* Boston: Houghton-Mifflin.

Hocking, J., & Visniesky, C. (1983). Choosing a microcomputer system: A guide for English instructors. *College Composition and Communication, 34,* 218–220.

Hocks, M. (1993, May). *Technotropes of liberation: Reading hypertext in the age of theory.* Paper presented at the Ninth Conference on Computers and Writing, Ann Arbor, MI.

Holdstein, D. (1983). The Writewell Series. *Computers and Composition, 1*(1), 7.

Holdstein, D. (1987). The politics of CAI and word processing: Some issues for faculty and administrators. In L. Gerrard (Ed.), *Writing at century's end: Essays on computer-assisted composition* (pp. 122–130). New York: Random House.

Holdstein, D. (1989). Training college teachers for computers and writing. In G. Hawisher & C. Selfe (Eds.), *Critical perspectives on computers and composition instruction* (pp. 126–139). New York: Teachers College Press.

Holdstein, D., & Selfe, C. L. (1990). *Computers and writing: Theory, research, practice.* New York: MLA.

Hollis, K. (1994). Liberating voices: Autobiographical writing at the Bryn Mawr Summer School for Women Workers, 1921–1938. *College Composition and Communication, 45,* 31–60.

Hooven, S. (1989). Captain Jacobson and the Apple jocks: Computers and English teachers at Glendora High School. In C. L. Selfe, D. Rodrigues, & W. R. Oates (Eds.), *Computers in English and the language arts: The challenge of teacher education* (pp. 83–96). Urbana, IL: NCTE.

Horner, W. B. (1992). *Nineteenth century Scottish rhetoric: The American connection.* Carbondale: Southern Illinois University Press.

Houlette, F. (1991) Write environment: Using AI strategies to model a writer's knowledge of process. *Journal of Artificial Intelligence in Education, 2,* 19–37.

Howard, T. (1992). WANS, connectivity, and computer literacy: An introduction and glossary. *Computers and Composition, 9*(3), 41–58.

Hull, G. (1987). Computer detection of errors in natural language texts: Some research on pattern matching. *Computers and the Humanities, 21,* 103–118.

Hull, G., & Rose, M. (1989). Rethinking remediation: Toward a social-cognitive understanding of problematic reading and writing. *Written Communication, 8,* 139–154.

Hull, G., Rose, M., Fraser, K., & Castellano, M. (1991). Remediation as social construct: Perspectives from an analysis of classroom discourse. *College Composition and Communication, 42,* 299–329.

Hult, C., & Harris, J. (1987). *A writer's introduction to word processing.* Belmont, CA: Wadsworth Publishing.

Hurlbert, C. M., & Totten, S. (1992). *Social isses in the English classroom.* Urbana, IL: NCTE.

James, S. H. (1993). Entries from a new e-mail user's notebook. *Computers and Composition, 10*(3), 5–10.

Jameson, F. (1991). *Postmodernism or the cultural logic of late capitalism.* Durham, NC: Duke University Press.

Janangelo, J. (1991). Technopower and technoppression: Some abuses of power and control in computer-assisted writing environments. *Computers and Composition, 9*(1), 47–64.

Jarratt, S. C. (1991). Feminism and composition: The case for conflict. In P. Harkin & J. Schilb (Eds.), *Contending with words: Composition and rhetoric in a postmodern age* (pp. 105–123). New York: MLA.

Jennings, E. M. (1987). Paperless writing: Boundary conditions and their implications. In L. Gerrard (Ed.), *Writing at the century's end: Essays on computer-assisted composition.* (pp. 11–20). New York: Random House.

Jensen, G., & DiTiberio, J. (1989). *Personality and the teaching of composition.* Norwood, NJ: Ablex.

Jessup, E. (1991). Feminism and computers in composition instruction. In G. E. Hawisher & C. L. Selfe (Eds.), *Evolving persepctives on computers and composition studies: Questions for the 1990s* (pp. 336–355). Urbana, IL & Houghton, MI: NCTE and Computers & Composition Press.

Jobst, J. (1983). Computer-assisted grading of essays and reports. *Computers and Composition, 1*(2), 5.

Johnson, J. (1993, October 24). We are wired: Some views on the fiberoptic ties that bind. *The New York Times,* p. E16.

Johnson-Eilola, J. (1990, March). *Shifting perspectives: Evaluating hypertext for composition instruction.* Paper presented at the Convention of the Conference on College Composition and Communication, Chicago, IL.

Johnson-Eilola, J. (1992). Review essay: *Writing space & Storyspace. Computers and Composition, 9*(2), 95–129.

Johnson-Eilola, J. (1993). *Nostalgic angels: Rearticulating hypertext writing.* Unpublished doctoral dissertation, Michigan Technological University, Houghton.

Johnson-Eilola, J. (1994). Reading and writing in hypertext: Vertigo and euphoria. In C. L. Selfe & S. Hilligoss (Eds.), *Literacy and computers: The complications of teaching and learning with technology* (pp. 195–219). New York: MLA.

Johnston, J., & Kozma, R. B. (1988, November). The 1988 Educom/Ncriptal Competition. *Academic Computing,* 30–35.

Johnston, J., & Kozma, R. B., Vinik, E., & Hart, K. A. (October, 1989). Quality, Diversity, and New Media: The 1989 Educom/NCRIPTAL awards. *Academic Computing,* 22–25, 46–51.

Jolliffe, D. (1988). *Writing in academic disciplines.* Norwood, NJ: Ablex.

Jones, R. A. (1988, November). Building a hypermedia laboratory. *Academic Computing,* 24–29, 43–44.

Joram, E., Woodruff, E., Bryson, M., & Lindsay, P. H. (1992). The effects of revising with a word processor on written composition. *Research in the Teaching of English, 26,* 167–193.

Joyce, M. (1988) Siren shapes: Exploratory and constructive hypertexts. *Academic Computing, 3*(4), 10–14, 37–42.

Joyce, M. (1992). New teaching: Toward a pedagogy for a new cosmology. *Computers and Composition, 9,* 7–16.

Joyce, M. (1994). Hypertext/Hypermedia. *Encyclopedia of English Studies and Language Arts,* 599–600.

Kaestle, C. F. (1988). The history of literacy and the history of readers. In E. R. Kintgen, B. M. Kroll, & M. Rose (Eds.), *Perspectives on literacy* (pp. 95–126). Carbondale: Southern Illinois University Press.

Kaler, E. R. (in press). Autopsy: The life and death of Writer's Workbench. *Computers and Composition.*

Kantor, A. (1994, November/December). Aliens among us. *Internet World,* pp. 82–84.

Kaplan, N., & Moulthrop, S. (1991). Something to imagine: Literature, composition, and interactive fiction. *Computers and Composition, 9,* 7–23.

Kaplan, N. (1991). Ideology, technology, and the future of writing instruction. In G. E. Hawisher & C. L. Selfe (Eds.), *Evolving persepctives on computers and composition studies: Questions for the 1990s.* (pp. 11–42). Urbana, IL & Houghton, MI: NCTE and Computers & Composition Press.

Kaplan, N., Davis, S., & Martin, J. (1987). Prose. [Computer program]. McGraw–Hill

Kay, A. C. (1991). Computers, networks and education. *Scientific American, 267*(3), 138–148.

Kaye, A. (1989). Computer-mediated communication and distance education. In R. Mason & A. Kaye (Eds.), *Mindweave: Communication, computers and distance education* (pp. 3–21). New York: Pergamon Press.

Keane, D., & Gaither, G. (1988). The effects of academic software on learning and motivation. In J. W. Sprecher (Ed.), *Facilitating academic software development* (pp. 47–69). McKinney, TX: Academic Computing Publications.

Keep, C. J. (1993). Knocking on heaven's door: Leibniz, Baudrillard and Virtual Reality. *EJournal, 3.2*, 48–339. Available E-mail: ejrnl

Kelman, P. (Ed.). (1983). *Classroom computer news directory on educational computing resources*. Watertown, MA: Intentional Educations.

Kemp, W. (1985). Software review: Microsoft word. *3*, 15–20.

Kemp, F. (1988). Mindwriter [Computer program]. Austin, TX: The Daedalus Group Inc.

Kernan, A. (1990). *The death of literature*. New Haven, CT: Yale University Press.

Kerr, E. B. Electronic leadership: A guide to moderating online conferences. IEEE Transactions on Professional communication, *College Composition and Communication, 29*, 12–18.

Kiefer, K., & Selfe, C. (1986). Letter from the editors. *Computers and Composition*, 4(1), 4–5.

Kiefer, K., & Selfe, C. L. (1985). Letter from the editors. *Computers and Composition, 3*, 4–6.

Kiefer, K. & Smith, C. (1983). Textual analysis with computers: Tests of Bell Laboratories' computer software. *Research in the Teaching of English, 17*, 201–214.

Kiesler, S., Siegel, J., & McGuire, T. W. (1984). Social psychological aspects of computer-mediated communication. *American Psychologist, 39*, 1123–1134.

Kinata, C. (1989). *Working with Word*. Redmond, WA: Microsoft Press.

Kinkead, J. (1986). Matching software and curriculum: A description of four text-analysis programs. *Computers and Composition, 3*, 33–55.

Kinkead, J. (1987). Computer conversations: Email and writing instruction. *College Composition and Communication, 38*, 337–41.

Kinneavy, J. (1987). Writing across the curriculum. In G. Tate (Ed.), *Teaching Composition: 12 Bibliographical Essays* (pp. 353–377). Fort Worth: Texas Christian University Press.

Kirsch, G., & Sullivan, P. A. (1992). *Methods and methodology in composition research*. Carbondale: Southern Illinois University Press.

Klem, E., & Moran, C. (1992). Teachers in a strange LANd: Learning to teach in a networked writing classroom. *Computers and Composition, 9*(3), 5–22

Knoblauch, C. H. (1990). Literacy and the politics of education. In A. A. Lunsford, H. Moglen & J. Slevin (Eds.), *The right to literacy* (pp. 74–87). New York: MLA.

Knoblauch, C. H., & Brannon, L. (1993). *Critical teaching and the idea of literacy*. Portsmouth, NH: Boynton/Cook.

Kotler, L., & Anandam, K. (1983). A partnership of teacher and computer in teaching writing. *College Composition and Communication, 34*, 361–367

Kraemer, D. J., Jr. (1992). Gender and the autobiographical essay: A critical extension of the research. *College Composition and Communication, 43*, 323–339

Kramarae, C. (1988a). Preface. In C. Kramarae (Ed.), *Technology and women's voices: Keeping in touch* (pp. ix–xi). New York: Routledge.

Kramarae, C. (1988b). *Technology and women's voices: Keeping in touch.* New York: Routledge & Kegan Paul.

Kramarae, C., & Kramer, J. (1995, February). Net gains, net losses. *Women's Review of Books,* 33–35.

Kremers, M. (1990). Sharing authority on a synchronous network: The case for riding the beast. *Computers and Composition,* 7[Special Issue], 33–44.

Kuhn, T. S. (1970). *The structure of scientific revolutions.* Chicago: University of Chicago Press.

Kurzweil, R. (1990). The age of intelligent machines. Cambridge, MA: MIT Press.

Laclau, E., & Mouffe, C. (1985). *Hegemony and socialist strategy: Towards a radical democratic politics* (W. Moore & P. Cammack, Trans.). London: Verso.

Lanham, R. (1993). The Electronic word: Democracy, technology, and the arts. Chicago: U. of Chicago Press.

Landow, G. (1992). *Hypertext: The convergence of contemporary critical theory and technology.* Baltimore: Johns Hopkins University Press.

Landow, G. P., & Delany, P. (1991). Hypertext, hypermedia and literary studies: The state of the art. In P. Delany & G. P. Landow (Eds.), *Hypermedia and literary studies* (pp. 3–50). Cambridge, MA: MIT Press.

Langan, J. (1985). Software announcement. *Computers and Composition, 3*(1), 78.

Langer, J. A., & Applebee, A. N. (1987). *How writing shapes thinking: A study of teaching and learning.* Urbana, IL: NCTE.

Langer, J. A., & Applebee, A. N. (1991). Musings. *Research in the Teaching of English, 25,* 388–389.

Langston, D., & Batson, T. (1990). The social shifts invited by working collaboratively on computer networks: The ENFI project. In C. Handa (Ed.), *Computers and community: Teaching composition in the twenty-first century* (pp. 140–59). Portsmouth, NH: Boynton/Cook.

Lanham, R. A. (1984). *Revising prose.* New York: Macmillan.

Lanham, R. A. (1990). The extraordinary convergence: Democracy, technology, theory, and the university curriculum. *The South Atlantic Quarterly, 89*(1), 27–50.

Lanham, R. A. (1992). From book to screen: Four recent studies. *College English, 54,* 199–206.

Larson, R. (1987). Selected bibliography of scholarship on composition and rhetoric, 1986. *College Composition and Communication, 38,* 319–336.

Larson, R. (1988). Selected bibliography of scholarship on composition and rhetoric, 1987. *College Composition and Communication, 39,* 316–336.

Lauer, J. M., & Asher, J. W. (1988). *Composition research: Empirical designs.* New York: Oxford University Press.

Laurel, B., & Mountford, J. (1990). Introduction. In B. Laurel (Ed.), *The art of human–computer interface design* (pp. xi–xvi). Reading, MA: Addison-Wesley.

Lawlor, R. (1980). *One child's learning: Introducing writing with a computer.* (ERIC Document Reproduction Service No. ED 208 415)

Lea, M. (1992). *Contexts of computer-mediated communication.* New York: Harvester/Wheatsheaf.

LeBlanc, P. (1990). Competing ideologies in software design for computer-aided composition. *Computers and Composition, 7,* 7–19.

LeBlanc, P. (1993). *Writing teachers writing software: Creating our place in the electronic age.* Urbana, IL: NCTE.

LeBlanc, P. J. (1994). The politics of literacy and technology in secondary school classrooms. In C. L. Selfe &. S. Hilligoss (Eds.), *Literacy and computers: The complications of teaching and learning with technology* (pp. 22–36). New York: MLA.

LeFevre, K. B. (1987). *Invention as a social act.* Carbondale: Southern Illinois University Press.

Letter from the Editors. (1985). *Computers and Composition, 3*(1), pp. 4–6.

Lindemann, E., & Tate, G. (1991). *Introduction to composition studies.* New York: Oxford University Press.

Lindemann, E. (1987). *Longman bibliography of composition and rhetoric.* New York: Longman.

Lipson, C., & Wagner, D. (1994) *Experiments in teaching the new electronic discourse: Multimedia, hypertext, and the moos.* Paper presented at the Tenth Computers and Writing Conference, Columbia, MO.

Lloyd-Jones, R. (1992). Who we were, who we should become. *College Composition and Communication, 43,* 486–496.

Lloyd-Jones, R., & Lunsford, A. A. (Eds.). (1989). *The English coalition conference: Democracy through language.* Urbana, IL: NCTE.

Loveman, G. W. (1990, September). An assessment of the productivity impact of information technologies. Paper delivered at "Management in the 1990s," a conference held at the Sloan School of Management, MIT, Cambridge, MA.

Lucking, R. (1985). Marking papers and record keepers for Apple users. *Computers and Composition, 2*(2), 6.

Luhn, R. (1988). Still waiting for *Windows/386. PC World, 6*(4), 116–123.

Lunsford, A., Moglin, H., & Slevin, J. (1990). *The right to literacy.* New York: MLA.

Lunsford, A., & Ede, L. (1990). *Singular texts/plural authors: Perspectives on collaborative writing.* Carbondale: Southern Illinois University Press.

Lutz, J. (1987). A study of professional and experienced writers revising and editing at the computer and with pen and paper. *Research in the Teaching of English, 21,* 398–421.

Lyall, S. (1994, August 14). Are these books, or what? CD-ROM and the literary industry. *The New York Times Book Review*, pp. 3, 20-21.

Lynn, S. (1987). Reading the writing process: Toward a theory of current pedagogies. *College English*, 49, 902-910.

Mabrito, M. (1989). *Writing apprehension and computer-mediated peer-response groups: a case study of four high- and four low-apprehensive writers communicating face-to-face versus electronic mail.* Unpublished doctroal dissertatin, Illinois State dissertation, Illinois State University, Normal.

Macintosh advertisement. (Dec., 1986). *College Composition and Communication*, 37(4), front matter.

Macintosh advertisment. (1987). *The Technological Horizons in Education Journal*, 14(6), 24iv.

Macrorie, K. (1970). *Uptaught*. Rochelle Park, NJ: Hayden.

Madden, F. (1987). Desperately seeking literary response. *Computers and Composition*, 4(3), 17-34.

Madigan, C., & Sanders, S. P. (1988). Team planning a computerized technical writing course. *Computers and Composition*, 5(2), 39-50.

Magner, D. K. (1993, October 20). Debate over woman's tenure continues at Berkeley. *The Chronicle of Higher Education*, p. A16.

Maik, L. L., & Maik, T. A. (1987). Perceptions of word processing in composition classes: First-year and upper-level students compared. *Computers and Composition*, 4(3), 7-16.

Mailloux, S. (1982). *Interpretive conventions: The reader in the study of American fiction*. Ithaca, NY: Cornell University Press.

Malone, M. S. (1994, May 29). The conference rooms at the cyberspace inn. *New York Times*, F21.

Mandell, S. (1979). *Computers and information processing*. New York: West Publishing.

Manuscript submissions welcome. (1985). *Research in Word Processing Newsletter*, 3(9), 21.

Marcus, S. (1981). CompuPoem [Computer program]. Culver City, CA: Social Studies School Service.

Marcus, S. (1983). Real-time gadgets with feedback: Special effects in computer-assisted instruction. *The Writing Instructor*, 2(4), 156-164.

Marcus, S. (1989, November). *A HyperCard project for English teachers*. Paper presented at the Convention of the National Council of Teachers of English, Baltimore, MD.

Marcus, S., & Blau, S. (1983, April). Not seeing is relieving: Invisible writing with computers. *Educational Technology*, 12-15.

Markoff, J. (1993, October 24). Keeping things safe and orderly in the neighborhoods of cyberspace. *The New York Times*, p. E7.

Markoff, J. (1994a, January 2). Staking a claim on the virtual frontier. *The New York Times*, p. E5.

Markoff, J. (1994b, March 13). The rise and swift fall of cyber literacy. *The New York Times*, pp. D1, D5.

Marling, W. (1984). Grading essays on a microcomputer. *College English, 46,* 797–810.

Marling, W., & Marling, C. (1982a). Grader [Computer program]. Cleveland, OH: Case Western Reserve University.

Marling, W. & Marling, C. (1982b). Writer [Computer program]. Cleveland, OH: Case Western Reserve University.

Marshall, J. (1992, October 11). *Of what does skill in writing really consist? The political life of the writing process.* Paper presented at the University of New Hampshire Conference, The Writing Process: Retrospect and Prospect, Durham, NH.

Martin, N. (1983a). Contexts for writing. In P. L. Stock (Ed.), *FForum: Essays on theory and practice in the teaching of writing* (pp. 101–103). Upper Montclair, NJ: Boynton/Cook.

Martin, N. (1983b). *Mostly about writing: Selected essays.* Upper Montclair, NJ: Boynton/Cook.

Mason, R., & Kaye, A. (1989). *Mindweave: Communication, computers, and distance education.* New York: Pergamon Press.

McAllister, J. & Louth, R. (1988). The effect of word processing on the quality of basic writers' revisions. *Research in the Teaching of English, 22,* 417–427.

McCann, T. M. (1984). Sentence combining for the microcomputer. *Computers and Composition, 1*(3), 1–2.

McDaid, J. (1990b, March). *The shape of texts to come: Response and the ecology of hypertext.* Paper presented at the Convention of the Conference on College Composition and Communication, Chicago, IL.

McDaid, J. (1990a, May). *Hypermedia composition and consciousness.* Paper presented at the Sixth Conference on Computers and Writing, Austin, TX. "interactive fictions" + "Sim realities" &

McDaid, J. (1991). Toward an ecology of hypermedia. In G. E. Hawisher & C. L. Selfe (Eds.), *Evolving perspectives on computers and composition studies: Questions for the 1990s* (pp. 203–223). Urbana, IL: NCTE.

McDaid, J. (1993). Uncle Buddy's Phantom Funhouse. [Computer program]. Boston: Eastgate Systems.

McDaniel, E. (1985). Software for text analysis and writing instruction. *Research in Word Processing Newsletter, 3,* 7–12.

McDaniel, E. (1986). A comparative study of the first-generation invention software. *Computers and Composition, 3,* 7–21.

McDaniel, E. (1990). Assessing the professional role of the English department "computer person." In D. H. Holdstein & C. L. Selfe (Eds.), *Computers and writing: Theory, research, practice* (pp. 31–39). New York: MLA.

McDaniel, E., & Bailey, G. (1984). Research in human-computer communication. *Computers and Composition. 1*(3), 10–11.

McHugh, N. S. (1986). Greetings from the program chair. In *What we will be: Anniversary Convention, National Council of Teachers of English: November 21–26.* San Antonio, TX: NCTE.

McLuhan, M. (1964). *Understanding media: The extensions of man*. New York: New American Library.

McQuade, D. (1990, March). *Greetings from the 1990 program chair*. Convention Program of the Conference on College Composition and Communication, Chicago, IL.

McQuade (1992a) Living in—and on—the margins. *College Composition and Communication, 43*, 11–22.

McQuade, D. (1992b). Composition and literary studies. In S. Greenblatt & G. Gunn (Eds.), *Redrawing the boundaries: The transformation of English and American literary studies* (pp. 482–519). New York: MLA.

McWilliams, P. A. (1982). *The word processing book: A short course in computer literacy*. Los Angeles, CA: Prelude Press.

Mello, A. (1994, March). Three generations of PowerPC Macs: Bridges to a new interface. *Macworld*, 21–22.

Metzenberg, H., & Thompson, D. (1990). Editorial Advisor [Computer program]. San Francisco: Petroglyph Software.

Moffett, J. (1968). *Teaching the universe of discourse*. Boston: Houghton Mifflin.

Montague, M. (1990). *Computers, cognition, and writing instruction*. Albany: State University of New York Press.

Moraii, T. ed. (March, 1994). News. *Macworld*, 34.

Moran, C. (1983). Word processing and the teaching of writing. *English Journal, 72*, 113–115.

Moran, C. (1991). We write, but do we read. *Computers and Composition, 8*(3), 51–61.

Moran, C. (1992a). Computers and English: What do we make of each other? *College English, 54*, 193–198.

Moran, C. (1992b). Computers and the writing classroom: A look to the future. In G. E. Hawisher & P. LeBlanc (Eds.), *Re-imagining computers and composition* (pp. 7–23). Portsmouth, NH: Boynton/Cook-Heinemann.

Morgan, B. A. (1985). Bibliography update. *Research in word processing newsletter, 3*, 13–15.

Morgan, B. A., & Schwartz, J. M. (1985, December). *Research in Word Processing Newsletter*. Rapid City: South Dakota School of Mines and Technology.

Morrison, C. J., & Berndt, E. R. (1991). *Assessing the productivity of information technology equipment in U.S. manufacturing industries*. (Working Paper No. 3582). National Bureau of Economic Research: Cambridge, MA.

Morrison, C. J. (1991). *Investment in capital assets and economic performance: The U.S. chemicals and primary metals industries in transition*. (Working Paper No. 3828). National Bureau of Economic Research: Cambridge, MA.

Moulthrop, S. (1990a, March). *A rhetoric of response to hypertext*. Paper presented at the Convention of the Conference on College Composition and Communication, Chicago, IL.

Moulthrop, S. (1990b, March). *What kind of idea is hypertext?* Paper presented at the Sixth Conference on Computers and Writing, Austin, TX.

Moulthrop, S. (1991a). The politics of hypertext. In G. E. Hawisher & C. L. Selfe (Eds.), *Evolving perspectives on computers and composition studies: Questions for the 1990s* (pp. 253–271). Urbana, IL and Houghton, MI: NCTE & Computers and Composition Press.

Moulthrop, S. (1991b). Victory Garden. [Computer program]. Boston: Eastgate Systems.

Moulthrop, S., & Kaplan, N. (1994). They became what they beheld: The futility of resistance in the space of electronic writing. In C. L. Selfe & S. Hilligoss (Eds.), *Literacy and Computers* (pp. 220–237). New York: MLA.

Murray, D. M. (1968). *A writer teaches writing.* Boston: Houghton Mifflin.

Murray, D. M. (1972). Teach writing as process not product. *The Leaflet, 71*(3), 11–14.

Murray, D. M. (1979). The listening eye: Reflections on the writing conference. *College English, 41*(1), 13–18.

Murray, D. M. (1980). Writing as process: How writing finds its own meaning. In T. R. Donovan & B. W. McClelland (Eds.), *Eight approaches to teaching composition* (pp. 3–20). Urbana, IL: NCTE.

Murray, D. M. (1984). *A writer teaches writing.* (2nd ed.). Boston: Houghton Mifflin.

National Center for Education Statistics, Office of Educational Research and Improvement, & U. S. Department of Education. (1993). *Digest of education statistics.* Washington, DC: U.S. Government Printing Office.

NCSA Mosaic Tutorial, (1994). Handout from National Center for Supercomputing Applications (NCSA), 1–3.

NCTE Directory. (1986). Urbana, IL: NCTE.

NCTE guidelines for review and evaluation of English language arts software (Prepared by the Committee on Instructional Technology, National Council of Teachers of English). (1992). *Computers and Composition, 10*(1), pp. 37–44.

NCTE honors Heath for research on links between language differences, school failure. (1986). *Research in the Teaching of English, 20*(2), 197.

Nelms, G. (1992). The case for oral evidence in composition historiography. *Written Communication, 9*(3), 356–84.

Nelms, G. (1994, March). *An experientialist historiography for composition studies: Advancing a human objectivity in the writing of history.* Paper presented at the Convention for the Conference on College Composition and Communication, Nashville, TN.

Neuwirth, C. (1983, March). *From process to product: Integrating computer-assisted instruciton and word processing.* Paper presented at the Convention of the Conference in College Composition and Communication, Detroit, MI.

Neuwirth, C., Kaufer, D. S., & Geisler, C. (1984). What is Epistle? *Computers and Composition, 1*(4), 1–2.

Newkirk, T. (1993). *Nuts and bolts.* Portsmouth, NH: Boynton/Cook-Heinemann.

Nielsen, J. (1990). *Hypertext and hypermedia.* New York: Academic Press.

Noble, D. D. (1989). Mental materiel: The militarization of learning and intelligence in U.S. education. In L. Levidow & K. Robins (Eds.), *Cyborg worlds: The military information society* (pp. 13–41). London: Free Association Books.

Nold, E. W. (1975). Fear and trembling: The humanist approaches the computer. *College Composition and Communication, 26,* 269–273.

North, S. M. (1987). *The making of knowledge in composition: Portrait of an emerging field.* Upper Montclair, NJ: Boynton/Cook.

Nydahl, J. (1990). Teaching word processors to be CAI programs. *College English, 52,* 904–915.

Nystrand, M., Greene, S., & Wiemelt, J. (1993). Where did compostion studies come from? An intellectual history. *Written Communication, 10*(3), 267–333.

Odell, L. (1985). Beyond the text. In L. Odell & D. Goswami, (Eds.), *Writing in nonacademic settings* (pp. 249–280). New York: Guilford Press.

Odell, L. & Doheny-Farina, S. (1985). Ethnographic research on writing: Assumptions and methodolgy. In L. Odell & D. Goswami (Eds.), *Writing in nonacademic settings* (pp. 503–535). New York: Guilford Press.

Odell, L., & Goswami, D. (Eds.). (1985). *Writing in nonacademic settings.* New York: Guilford Press.

Ohmann, R. (1976). *English in America: A radical view of the profession.* New York: Oxford University Press.

Ohmann, R. (1985). Literacy, technology, and monopoly capitalism. *College English, 47,* 675–689.

Olson, C. P. (1987). Who computes? In D. Livingstone (Ed.), *Critical pedagogy and cultural power* (pp. 179–204). South Hadley, MA: Bergin & Garvey.

Our Profession: Achieving Perspectives for the 80s. (1981). Program of the Convention for the Conference on College Composition and Communication. Urbana, IL: NCTE

Owston, R. D., Murphy, S., & Wideman, H. H. (1992). The effects of word processing on students' writing quality and revision strategies. *Research in the Teaching of English, 26,* 249–276.

Page, E. & Paulus, D. (1968). The analysis of essays by computer. (ERIC Document Reproduction Service No. ED 028 633)

Papert, S. (1980). *Mindstorms: Children, computers, and powerful ideas.* New York: Basic Books.

Papert, S. (1987). Computer criticism vs. technocentric thinking. *Educational Researcher, 16,* 22–30.

Parris, P., (1985). Prewriting invention without special software. *Computers and Composition, 2*(2), 1–2.

Parris, P. B. (1992, March). *A room of one's own: Departmental and university support for CAI in composition.* Paper presented at the Annual Convention of the Conference on College Composition and Communication, Cincinnati, OH.

Perelman, L. (1992, March). *Writing for the world: Student writing on international computer networks.* Paper presented at the Annual Convention of the Conference on College Composition and Communication, Cincinnati, OH.

Peritz, J. H. (1993). Making a place for the poetic in academic writing. *College Composition and Communication, 44,* 380–85.

Petersen, B. T., Selfe, C. L., & Wahlstrom, B. J. (1984). Computer-assisted instruction and the writing process: Questions for research and evaluation. *College Composition and Communication, 35,* 98–101.

Peterson, N. (1989, May) *Sounds of silence: Listening for difference in the computer-networked collaborative writing classroom.* Paper presented at the Fifth Computers and Writing Conference, Minneapolis, MN.

Petzold, C. (1993, October 26). Move over, ASCII! Unicode is here! *PC Magazine, 12,* 374–76.

Phelps, L. W. (1991). Practical wisdom and the geography of knowledge in composition. *College English, 53,* 863–885.

Piller, C. (1992). Separate realities: The creation of the technological underclass in America's public schools. *MacWorld,* p. 218–230.

Pirsig, R. M. (1974). *Zen and the art of motorcycle maintenance.* New York: Bantam Books.

Plimpton, G., & Brooks, V. W. (Eds.). (1977). *Writers at work: The Paris Review Interviews.* Second Series. Harmondsworth: Penguin Books.

Plimpton, G., & Kazin, A. (Eds.). (1977). *Writers at work: The Paris Review Interviews.* Third Series. Harmondsworth: Penguin Books.

Plimpton, G., & Sheed, W. (Eds.). (1977). *Writers at work: The Paris Review Interviews.* Fourth Series. Harmondsworth: Penguin Books.

Plimpton, G. (Ed.). (1981). *Writers at work: The Paris Review Interviews.* Fifth Series. Harmondsworth: Penguin Books.

Pogue, D., & Schorr, J. (1994). *Macworld Mac and Power Mac secrets* (2nd ed.). San Mateo, CA: IDG Books.

Pool, I. d. S. (1990). *Technologies without boundaries: On telecommunications in a global age.* Cambridge, MA: Harvard University Press.

Poole, L., McNiff, M., & Cook. S. (1981). *Apple II user's guide.* Berkeley, CA: Osborne/McGraw-Hill.

Poteet, H. G. (1968). *The Computer and the teacher of English.* Camden, NJ: New Jersey Association of Teachers of English.

Poper, Sir K.R. (1966). *The open society and its enemies.* Princeton, NJ: Princeton University Press.

Poster, M. (1990). *The mode of information: Poststructuralism and social context.* Chicago, IL: University of Chicago Press.

Press, L. (1993). IBM PC and PC compatibles. In A. Ralston & E. D. Reilly (Eds.), *Encyclopedia of computer science* (pp. 644–648). New York: Van Nostrand Reinhold.

Protherough, R., & Atkinson, J. (1992). How English teachers see English teaching. *Research in the Teaching of English, 26,* 385–407.

Purves, A. C., & Purves, W. C. (1986). Viewpoints: Cultures, text models, and the activity of writing. *Research in the Teaching of English, 20*(2), 174–195.

Ralston, A., & Reilly, E. D. (Eds.) *Encyclopedia of computer science.* (3rd ed.). New York: Van Nostrad Reinholt

Regan, A. (1993). "Type normal like the rest of us": Writing, power, and homophobia in the networked composition classroom. *Computers and Composition, 10,* 11–24.

Reid, S., & Findlay, G. (1986). Writer's Workbench analysis of holistically scored essays. *Computers and Composition, 3*(2), 6–32.

Reither, J. (1986). Writing and knowing: Toward redefining the writing process. *College English, 48,* 650–28.

Report of the Commission on the Future of the Profession. (1982, Spring). *Publications of the Modern Language Association, 97,* 940–56.

Reynolds, N., Benson, A., Cardinale, M., Castline, H., Felix, C., Hudson, J., Kennedy, K., Moffitt, K., O'Grady, H., Regan, J., Saez, B., Satran, M., Stuart, T., & Faigley, L. (1994). Fragments in response: An electronic discussion of Lester Faigley's *Fragments of Rationality. College Composition and Communication, 45,* 264–273.

Rickly, R. (1990, May). *The electronic voice: Empowering women in the writing classroom.* Paper presented at the Sixth Conference on Computers and Writing, Austin, TX.

Roberts, E. (Ed.). (1993). *Computers and society.* New York: Van Nostrand Reinholt.

Rodrigues, D. (1985). Computers and basic writers. *College Composition and Communication, 36,* 336–339.

Rodrigues, D., & Rodrigues, R. (1983). Creative Problem Solving [Computer program]. Fort Collins, CO: Colorado State University.

Rodrigues, D., & Rodriques, R. (1989) How word processing is changing our teaching: New approaches, new challenges. *Computers and Composition, 7*(1), 13–26.

Rodrigues, D. W., & Rodrigues, R. J. (1986). *Teaching writing with a word processor, grades 7–13.* Urbana, IL: NCTE.

Rodrigues, R. (1983, March). *CAI invention and revision strategies.* Paper presented at the Convention of the Conference on College Composition and Communication, Detroit, MI.

Rodrigues, R. J., & Rodrigues, D. W. (1984). Computer–based invention: Its place and potential. *College Composition and Communication, 35,* 78–87.

Rogowski, S. J., & Reilly, E. D. (1993). Entrepreneurs. In A. Ralston & E. D. Reilly (Eds.), *Encyclopedia of computer science* (pp. 517–526). New York: Van Nostrad Reinholt.

Rohman, D. G. (1965). Pre-writing: The stage of discovery in the writing process. *College Composition and Communication, 16,* 106–112.

Romano, S. (1993). The egalitarianism narrative: Whose story? Whose yardstick? *Computers and Composition, 10*(3), 5–28.

Rose, M. (1989). *Lives on the boundary: The struggles and achievements of America's underprepared*. New York: Free Press.

Ross, D. (1985). Realities of computer analysis of compositions. In J. L. Collins & E. A. Sommers, *Writing on-line: Using computers in the teaching of writing* (pp. 105–114). Upper Montclair, NJ: Boynton/Cook.

Ross, D. (1986). *Some cautions from machine translations and AI on the limits of computer-aided analysis of texts*. Paper presented at the Computers &Writing Conference, Pittsburgh, PA.

Royland, F. (1994). Information and literacy studies. *EJournal 4.2* (11) 417–451. Available E-mail: ejrnl

Russell, D. R. (1991). *Writing in the academic disciplines, 1870–1990*. Carbondale: Southern Illinois University Press.

Ryan, B. (1994). Alpha rides high. *Byte, 19*(10), 197–198).

Sadler, L. V. (1987). The computers-and-effective-writing movement: Computer-assisted composition. *ADE Bulletin, 87,* 28–33.

Scharer, P. L. (1992). Teachers in transition: An exploration of changes in teachers and classrooms during implementation of literature-based reading instruction. *Research in the Teaching of English, 26,* 408–443.

Schlobin, R. C. (1984). Word choice: General guidelines for purchasing a microcomputer with a word-processing program. Excerpted in *Computers and Composition, 2,* 7–10.

Scholes, R. (1985). *Textual power: Literary theory and the teaching of English*. New Haven: Yale University Press.

Schriner, D. K., & Rice, W. C. (1991). Response to Gail E. Hawisher and Cynthia L. Selfe, "The rhetoric of technology and the electronic writing class," *CCC*, 42 (February 1991), 55–65. *College Composition and Communication, 42*(4), 501–503.

Schultz, L. (1994). Elaborating our history: A look at mid-nineteenth century first books of composition. *College Composition and Communication, 45,* 10–30.

Schwartz, H. (1982). Monsters and mentors: Computer applications for humanistic education. *College English, 44,* 141–152.

Schwartz, H. (1983, March). *Computers as a resource for research papers*. Paper presented at the Convention of the Conference on College Composition and Communication, Detroit, MI.

Schwartz, H. (1985a). *Interactive writing: Composing with a word processor*. New York: Holt, Rinehart & Winston.

Schwartz, H. (1985b). The confessions of Professor Strangelove; Or, an apology for literacy. *Computers and Composition, 2,* 6–16.

Schwartz, H. (1986). Seen [Computer program]. Iowa City, IA: CONDUIT.

Schwartz, H. (1989) Literacy theory in the classroom: Computers in literature and writing. *Computers and Composition, 7*(1), 49–64.

Schwartz, H. (1992). Computer perspectives: Mapping new territories. *College English, 54,* 207–212.

Schwartz, H. J. (1984a). Seen: A tutorial and user network for hypothesis testing. In W. Wresch (Eds.), *The computer in composition instrtuction: A writer's tool* (pp. 47–62). Urbana, IL: NCTE.

Schwartz, H. J. (1984b). Teaching writing with computer aids. *College English, 46,* 239–247.

Schwartz, H., & Bridwell, L. S. (1984). A selected bibliography on computers in composition. *College Composition and Communication, 35,* 71–77.

Schwartz, H. J., & Bridwell-Bowles, L. S. A selected bibliography on computers in composition: An update. College Composition and Communication. *38*(4), 453–457.

Schwartz, J. (1990, March) Using an electronic network to play the scales of discourse. *English Journal, 79,* 16–24.

Schwartz, M. (1982). Prewrite [Computer program]. Roslyn Heights, NY: Learning Well.

Schwartz, H. (1987). Organize [Computer program]. Belmont, CA: Wadsworth.

Selfe, C. L., & Hilligoss, S. (1994). *Literacy and computers: The complications of teaching and learning with technology.* New York: MLA.

Selfe, C. L., & Meyer, P. R. (1991). Testing claims for on-line conferences. *Written Communication, 8,* 163–192.

Selfe, C. L., & Wahlstrom, B. J. (1983a). The benevolent beast: Computer-assisted instruction for the teaching of writing. *The Writing Instructor,* 2(4), 183–92.

Selfe, C. L., & Wahlstrom, B. J. (1983b). Wordsworth II [Computer program]. Houghton, MI: Michigan Technological University.

Selfe, C. L., & Wahlstrom, B. J. (1985). Fighting the computer revolution: A field report from the walking wounded. *Computers and Composition, 2,* 63–68.

Selfe, C. L., & Wahlstrom, B. J. (1988). Computers and writing: Casting a broader net with theory and research. *Computers and the Humanities, 22,* 57–66.

Selfe, C. L. (1983, March). *CAI and the process of composing.* Paper presented at the Convention for the Conference on College Composition and Communication, Detroit, MI.

Selfe, C. L. (1986). *Computer-assisted instruction: Create your own.* Urbana, IL: NCTE.

Selfe, C. L. (1988a, November). *The tie that binds: Building community and fostering dialogic exchange through computer-based conferences.* Paper presented at the annual meeting of the National Council of Teachers of English, St. Louis, MO.

Selfe, C. L. (1988b, Fall). Computers in English Departments: The rhetoric of technopower. *ADE Bulletin, 90,* 63–67.

Selfe, C. L. (1988c, March). *Computers and politics: A feminist reading of techno/power in English departments.* Paper presented at the Convention for the Conference on College Composition and Communication, St. Louis, MO.

Selfe, C. L. (1989a). *Creating a computer-supported writing faciltity: A blueprint for action*. Houghton, MI: Computers and Composition Press.

Selfe, C. L. (1989b, November). *English teachers and computers in the classroom: Technology as a catalyst for social, political, and educational reform*. Paper presented at the Convention of the National Council of Teachers of English, Baltimore, MD.

Selfe, C. L. (1989c). Redefining literacy: The multi-layered grammars of computers. In G. E. Hawisher & C. L. Selfe (Eds), *Critical Perspectives on Computers and Composition Instruction* (pp. 3–15). New York: Teachers College Press.

Selfe, C. L. (1990a, March). *Technology and the changing nature of literacy education: Political implications of computer use*. Paper presented at the Convention of the Conference on College Composition and Communication, Chicago, IL.

Selfe, C. L. (1990b). English teachers and the humanization of computers: Networking communities of readers and writers. In G. E. Hawisher & A. O. Soter (Eds.), *On literacy and its teaching: Issues in English education* (pp. 190–205). Albany, NY: State University of New York Press.

Selfe, C. L. (1990c). Technology in the English classroom: Computers through the lens of feminist theory. In C. Handa (Ed.), *Computers and community: Teaching composition in the twenty-first century* (pp. 118–139). Portsmouth, NH: Boynton/Cook-Heinemann.

Selfe, C. L. (1992). Preparing English teachers for the virtual age: The case for technology critics. In G. E. Hawisher & P. LeBlanc (Eds.), *Re-imagining cmputers and composition: Teaching and research in the virtual age* (pp. 24–42). Portsmouth, NH: Boynton-Cook/Heinemann.

Selfe, C. L. (1994). *Theorizing e-mail for the practice, instruction, and study of literacy*. Paper presented at the Convention for the Conference on College Composition and Communication, Nashville, TN.

Selfe, C. L., & Kiefer, K. E. (1983). Letter from the editors. *Computers and Composition, 1*, 1.

Selfe, C. L., Rodrigues, D., & Oates, W. R. (1989). *Computers in English and the language arts: The challenge of teacher education*. Urbana, IL: NCTE.

Selfe, C. L., & Selfe, R. J., Jr. (1994). The politics of the interface: Power and its exercise in electronic contact zones. *College Composition and Communication, 45*(4), 480–505.

Seventh European conference on writing and computers, October 19–21: Abstracts. (1994). Utrecht, The Netherlands: Utrecht University, University of Twente, & University of Amsterdam.

Seymour, J. (1989, September 12). An interface you won't outgrow. *PC Magazine*, p. 97.

Seymour, J. (1993, December 21). The best ideas of 1993. *PC Magazine*, p. 101.

Shanahan, T., & Kamil, M. L. (1988) Academic libraries and research in the teaching of English. Unpublished monograph.

Shaughnessy, M. P. (1977). *Errors and expectations: A guide for the teacher of basic writing.* New York: Oxford University Press.

Shor, I. (1980). *Critical teaching and everyday life.* Chicago: University of Chicago Press.

Shor, I. (Ed.). (1987). *Freire for the classroom: A sourcebook for liberatory teaching.* Portsmouth, NH: Heinemann, Boynton/Cook.

Shute, V. (1986). *Intelligence in a computer tutor.* Paper presented at the Computers & Writing Conference, Pittsburgh, PA.

Simpson, L. (1988, January 3). Poetry and word processing: One or the other, but not both. *The New York Times Book Review,* p. 12.

Slatin, J. M. (1990). Reading hypertext: Order and coherence in a new medium. *College English, 52,* 870–883.

Sloan, G. (1979). The subversive effects of an oral culture on student writing. *College Composition and Communication, 30,* 156–164.

Sloane, S. (1991). *Interactive fiction, virtual realities, and the reading-writing relationship.* Unpublished doctoral dissertation, The Ohio State University, Ames.

Smith, C. F. (1991). Reconceiving hypertext. In G. E. Hawisher &. C. L. Selfe (Eds.), *Evolving perspectives on computers and composition studies: Questions for the 1990s* (pp. 224–252). Urbana, IL: NCTE.

Smith, C. R., Gingrich, P., Kiefer, K., (1982). *Writer's workbench: Computers and writing instruction.* Unpublished manuscript, Colorado State University.

Smith, R. (1974). The composition requirement today: A report on a nationwide survey of four-year colleges and universities. *College Composition and Communication, 25,* 138–148.

Snyder, I. (1993, May). *Equity of access to computer writing technology in Australian schools.* Paper presented at the Ninth Computers and Writing Conference, Ann Arbor, MI.

Snyder, I. (Guest Ed.). (1994). *Computers and Composition* [Special Issue] *11,* 2.

Solsken, J. (1993) The paradigm misfit blues. *Research in the Teaching of English, 27*(3), 316–325.

Sommers, E. A. (1983). A writing teacher experiments with word processing. *Computers and Composition, 1,* 1–3.

Sommers, E. A. (1985). Integrating composing and computing. In J. L. Collins & E. A. Sommers (Eds.), *Writing on-line: Using computers in the teaching of writing* (pp. 3–10). Upper Montclair, NJ: Boynton/Cook.

Sommers, N. (1992). Between the drafts. *College Composition and Communication, 43,* 23–31.

Southwell, M. G. (1983). Computer-assisted instruction in composition at York College/CUNY: Composition for basic writing students. *The Writing Instructor, 2,* 165–172.

Southwell, M. G. (1984). The COMP-LAB writing modules: Computer-assisted grammar instruction. In W. Wresch (Ed.), *The computer in composition instrtuction: A writer's tool* (pp. 91–104). Urbana, IL: NCTE.

Spears, R., & Lea, M. (1992). Social influence and the influence of the "social" in computer-mediated communication. In M. Lea (Ed.), *Contexts of computer-mediated communication* (pp. 30–65). New York: Harvester/Wheatsheaf.

Spender, D. (1994, May). *On ladies and laptops.* Paper presented at the Tenth Computers and Writing Conference, Columbia, MO.

Spitzer, M. (1985) Selecting word processing software. In J. L. Collins & E. A. Sommers, (Eds.), *Writing on-line: Using computers in the teaching of writing* (pp. 29–36). Upper Montclair, NJ: Boynton/Cook.

Spitzer, M. (1986). Writing style in computer conferences, *IEEE Transactions on Professional Communication, 29*(1), 19–22.

Spitzer, M. (1989). Computer conferencing: An emerging technology. In G. E. Hawisher & C. L. Selfe (Eds.), *Critical perspectives on computers and composition instruction* (pp. 187–200). New York: Teachers College Press.

Sproull, L. & Kiesler, S. (1991). *Connections: New ways of working in the networked organization.* Cambridge: MIT Press.

Stanzler, J. (1993, May). The *International Poetry Guild.* Paper presented at the Ninth Computers and Writing Conference, Ann Arbor, MI.

Statement of Principles and Standards for the Postsecondary Teaching of Writing. (1989). *College Composition and Communication, 40*(3), 329–336.

Stevenson, D. W. (1983). Two-point-five cheers: The computers are coming. *Focus: Teaching English Language Arts, 9*(3), 37–43.

Stewart, D. (1982). In *CCCC Program Introduction* (p. 3). Urbana: NCTE.

Stewart, D. (1992). Harvard's influence in English studies: Perceptions from three universities in the early twentieth century. *College Composition and Communication, 43,* 455–71.

Stewart, D. C. (1984). Foreword. In J. A. Berlin, *Writing instruction in nineteenth-century American colleges* (pp. ix–x). Carbondale: Southern Illinois University Press.

Stillman, P. R. (1985). A writer (and teacher of writing) confronts word processing. In J. L. Collins & E. A. Sommers (Eds.), *Writing on-line: Using computers in the teaching of writing.* (pp. 19–28). Upper Montclair, NJ: Boynton/Cook.

Stock, P. L. (1983). *Forum: Essays on theory and practice in the teaching of writing.* Upper Montclair, NJ: Boynton/Cook

Stotsky, S. (1993). From the editor. *Research in the Teaching of English, 27*(3), 221.

Stracke, R. (1988). The effects of a full-service computer room on student writing. *Computers and Composition, 5*(2), 51–56.

Strickland, J. (1985). Prewriting and computing. In J. L. Collins & E. A. Sommers (Eds.), *Writing Online* (pp. 67–74). Upper Montclair, NJ: Boynton/Cook.

Strickland, J. (1982). Free [Computer program]. Slippery Rock, PA: Slippery Rock Uiversity.

Strickland, J. (1987). Computers, invention, and the power to change student writing. *Computers and Composition, 4*(2), 7–26.

Students' right to their own language. *College Composition and Communication, 25*(3), 1–32.

Sudol, R. (1987). *Textfiles: A rhetoric for word processing.* San Diego: Harcourt Brace Jovanovich.

Sudol, R. A. (1985). Applied word processing: Notes on authority, responsibility, and revision in a workshop model. *College Composition and Communication, 36,* 331–335.

Sullivan, P. (1989). Human-computer interaction perspectives on word-processing issues. *Computers and Composition, 6,* 11–34.

Sullivan, P. A. (1992). Feminism and methodology in composition studies. In G. Kirsch & P. A. Sullivan (Eds.), *Methods and methodology in composition research* (pp. 37–61). Carbondale: Southern Illinois University Press.

Sullivan, P., & Dautermann, (Eds.). (in press). *Electronic Literacies in the Workplace: Technologies of Writing.* Urbana: NCTE.

Suppes, P. (1980). The teacher and computer-assisted instruction. In R. Taylor (Ed.), *The computer in the school: Tutor, tool, tutee* (pp. 231–235). New York: Teachers College.

Susser, B. (1993). Networks and project work: Alternative pedagogies for writing with computers. *Computers and Composition, 10*(3), 63–89.

Sutherland, J., & Black, P. (1993, May). *International collaboration: E-mail across the globe.* Paper presented at the Ninth Computers and Writing Conference, Ann Arbor, MI.

Table of contents. (1985). *Computers and Composition, 2*(4), 1.

Takayoshi, P. (1994). Building new networks from the old: Women's experiences with electronic communications. *Computers and Composition, 11*(1), 21–35.

Tate, G. (Ed.). (1987). *Teaching composition: Twelve bibliograhical essays.* (2nd ed.). Fort Worth: Texas Christian University Press.

Taylor, D. (1994, November/December). Usenet: Past, present, future. *Internet World,* pp. 27–30.

Taylor, H. J., Kramarae, C., & Ebben, M. (Eds.). (1993). *Women, information technology, scholarship.* Urbana, IL: Center for Advanced Study.

Taylor, P. (1988). Interchange [Computer program]. Austin, TX: The Daedalus Group

Taylor, P. (1992). Social epistemic rhetoric and chaotic discourse. In G. E. Hawisher & P. LeBlanc (Eds.), *Re-imagining computers and composition: Research and teaching in the virtual age* (pp. 131–148). Portsmouth, NH: Boynton/Cook.

Taylor, R. (Ed.). (1980). *The computer in the school: Tutor, tool, tutee.* New York: Teachers College.

Tchudi, S. (1983). The write idea: Computer-assisted invention. *Focus: Teaching English Language Arts, 9,* 10–16.

The process of writing: From rough draft to refinement. (1984). Workshop presented at the annual meeting of the National Council of Teachers of English, Detroit, MI.

Thiesmeyer, J., & Thiesmeyer, E. (1986). Editor [Computer program]. New York: MLA.

Thompson, D. (1988). Interactive networking: Creating bridges between speech, writing, and composition. *Computers and Composition, 5,* 17–27.

Thrush, E. (1994, May). *Hypertext: A panacea for international and intercultural communications.* Paper presented at the Tenth Computers and Writing Conference, Columbia, MO.

Thurston, C. (1994). Computer-assisted instruction. In *Encyclopedia of English studies and language Arts of the National Council of Teachers of English* (pp. 250–252). New York: NCTE.

To our customers. (1986). *Conduit: Catalog of educational software,* i.

Tompkins, J. (1985). *Sensational designs: The cultural work of American fiction, 1790–1860.* New York: Oxford University Press.

Tornow, J. (1993). *Discussing literature in high school English classes using a local area computer network.* Unpublished doctoral dissertation, The University of Texas, Austin.

Trimbur, J. (1994). Taking the social turn: Teaching writing post-process. [Book Review]. *College Composition and Communication. 45,* 108–117.

Trimbur, J., Wood, R. G., Strickland, R., Thelin, W. H., Rouster, W. J., Mester, T. & Hairston, M. (1993). Responses to Maxine Hairston, "Diversity, ideology, and teaching writing." *College Composition and Communication, 44,* 248–255.

Tuman, M. (1988). Class, codes, and composition: Basil Bernstein and the critique of pedagogy. *College Composition and Communication, 39,* 42–51.

Tuman, M. (1993). Campus word processing: Seven design principles for a new academic writing environment. *Computers and Composition, 10*(3), 49–62.

Tuman, M. C. (Ed.). (1992). *Literacy online: The promise (and peril) of reading and writing with computers.* Pittsburgh: University of Pittsburgh Press.

Turkle, S., & Papert, S. (1990). Epistemological pluralism: Styles and voices within the computer culture. *Signs: Journal of women in culture and society, 16*(11), 128–157.

Turner, J. A. (1987, February 4). Drive to require students to buy computers slows. *Chronicle of Higher Education,* pp. 1, 28.

Turoff, M. (1970). CMC [Computer program]. Newark: New Jersey Institute of Technology.

Turoff, M., (1993) Computer conferencing. In A. Ralston, & E. D. Reilly, (Eds.) *Encyclopedia of computer science.* (3rd ed., pp. 280–281). New York: Van Nostrand Reinhold.

Directory. (1985). *UCLA conference on computers and writing: New directions in teaching and research, May 4–5.* (1985). Los Angeles: UCLA.

Ulmer, G. (1989). *Teletheory: Grammatology in the age of video.* New York: Routledge.

Update. (1987). *PC World, 5*(12), 141–144.

Vanderclai, T. & Siering, G. (1994). *The Netoric Cafe*. Handout distributed at the 10th Computers and Writing Conference, Columbia, MO, 20–23 May.

Varnum, R. (1994, March). *The need for a cultural history of composition: Reflections on an Amherst study*. Paper presented at the Convention for the Conference on College Composition and Communication, Nashville, TN.

Virilio, P. (1987). *Speed and politics: An essay on dromology*. (Mark Polizzotti, Trans.). New York: Semiotext(e). (Original work published 1977)

Vitanza, V. J. (1991). Three countertheses: Or, a critical in(ter)vention into composition theories and pedagogies. In P. Harkin & J. Schilb (Eds.), *Contending with words: Composition and rhetoric in a postmodern age* (pp. 139–172). New York: MLA.

Volkswriter. [Advertisement]. (1984). *Softalk*, 2, 38.

Vose, G. M. (1987, October 15). Special issue: Inside the IBM PCs—The technical implications of the PS/2. *Byte*, *12*(12), 33.

Wadsworth Software. (1987). A new writing tool from Wadsworth *College English*, *49.7*, 2.

Wahlstrom, B. J. (1992, June), A view from the bridge: English departments piloting among the shoals of computer use. Paper presented at the 1992 ADE Conference in Waterloo, Canada.

Wahlstrom, B. J., & Selfe, C. L. (1994). A view from the bridge: English departments piloting among the shoals of computer use. *ADE Bulletin*, *109*, 35–45.

Waldrep, T. (1988). Edit! [Computer program]. New York: McGraw-Hill.

Wambeam, C., & Harris, L. (1994, May). *Building cyberspace communities: Using lists and moos to foster regional communication and debate*. Paper presented at the Tenth Computers and Writing Conference, Columbia, MO.

Wampler, B. (1981). Grammatik [Computer Program]. Oren, UT: Wordperfect Corporation.

Weiss, A. (1994, November/December). Gabfest: Internet relay chat. *Internet World*, pp. 59–62.

Weiss, T. (1988). Word processing in business and technical writing classroom. *Computers and Composition*, *6*(2), 57–70.

Weizenbaum, J. (1986, Oct/Nov). Not without us: A challenge to computer professionals to use their power to bring the present insanity to a halt. *Fellowship*, 8–10.

Welch, K. E. (1987). Ideology and freshman textbook production: The place of theory in writing pedagogy. *College Composition and Communication*, *33*, 269–282.

Wheeler, T. C. (1979). *The great American writing block: Causes and cures of the new illiteracy*. New York: Penguin.

White, H. (1978). *Tropics of discourse: Essays in cultural criticism*. Balitmore, MD: Johns Hopkins University Press.

Why Johnny can't write. (1975, Dec. 9). *Newsweek*, p. 58–65.

Wilcox, T. W. (1973). *The anatomy of college English*. San Francisco: Jossey-Bass.

Wilensky, R. (1986, May). *Teaching research writing in a word-processing composition class.* Paper presented at the Computers & Writing Conference, Pittsburgh, PA.

Winner, L. (1986). *The whale and the reactor: A search for limits in an age of high technology.* Chicago: The University of Chicago Press.

Winner, L. (1993, August 4). How technology reweaves the fabric of society. *The Chronicle of Higher Education,* pp. B1–B3.

Wittie, L. D., & Radics, A. (1993). Microprocessors and microcomputers. In A. Ralston & E. D. Reilly (Eds.), *The encyclopedia of computer science.* (p. 878). New York: Van Nostrand Reinhold.

Wood, D. (1992). The power of maps. New York: Guilford Press.

Woods, W. F. (1981). Composition textbooks and pedagogical theory, 1960–1980. *College English, 43,* 393–409.

Word Proof [Review]. (1984). *Softalk, 2,* 58.

Word processing. (1983). *Computer: Buyer's Guide and Handbook, 12,* 137.

Words at the flick of a key. (1983, March 14). *Time,* p. 61.

WordStar [Review]. (1983). *Computer: Buyer's Guide and Handbook, 12,* 140.

Wresch, W. (1982). Writer's Helper [Computer program]. Iowa City, IA: CONDUIT.

Wresch, W. (1983). Computers and composition instruction: An update. *College English, 45,* 794–799.

Wresch, W. (1984a). *The computer in composition instruction: A writer's tool.* Urbana, IL: NCTE.

Wresch, W. (1984b). Questions, answers, and automated writing. In W. Wresch (Ed.), *The computer in composition instruction: A writer's tool* (p. 143–153). Urbana, IL: NCTE.

Wright, B. (1994). Computer-mediated communication. *Encyclopedia of English studies and language arts, 260–263.*

Yager, T. (1992). The multimedia PC. Byte, 17(2), p. 217.

Yerkey, A. N. (1976). *The retrieval of rhetorical topoi: A computer-assisted system for the inentin of lines of argument and associated data.* Unpublished doctoral dissertation, Kent State University, Kent, Ohio.

Young, A., & Fulwiler, T. (1986). Introduction. In A. Young &. T. Fulwiler (Eds.), *Writing across the disciplines* (pp. 1–3). Portsmouth, NH: Heinemann.

Young, R. E. (1976). Invention: A topographical survey. In G. Tate (Ed.), *Teaching composition: 10 bibliographic essays* (pp. 1–43). Fort Worth: Texas Christian University Press.

Young, R. E. (1978). Paradigms and problems: Needed research in rhetorical invention. In C. R. Cooper & L. Odell (Eds.), *Research on composing: Points of departure* (pp. 29–47). Urbana, IL: NCTE.

Young, R. E., Becker, A. L., Pike, K. L. (1970). *Rhetoric: Discovery and change.* New York: Harcourt.

Zawacki, T. (1992) Recomposing as a woman—An essay in different voices. *College Composition and Communication, 43,* 32–38.

Zimmer, J. (1985). The continuing challenge: Computers and writing. *Computers and Composition, 2*(3), 4–6.

Zinn, H. (1970). *The Politics of history*. Boston: Beacon.

Zinn, K. L. (1993). Computer-assisted instruction. In A. Ralston & E. D. Reilly, (Eds.). *The encyclopedia of computer science* (pp. 260–262). New York: Van Nostrand Reinhold.

Zinsser, William. (1983). *Writing with a word processor*. New York: Harper & Row.

Zuboff, S. (1988). *In the age of the smart machine: The future of work and power*. New York: Basic Books.

AUTHOR INDEX

SUBJECT INDEX